W9-CER-368

tillie walden

spinning

:01
first second
New York

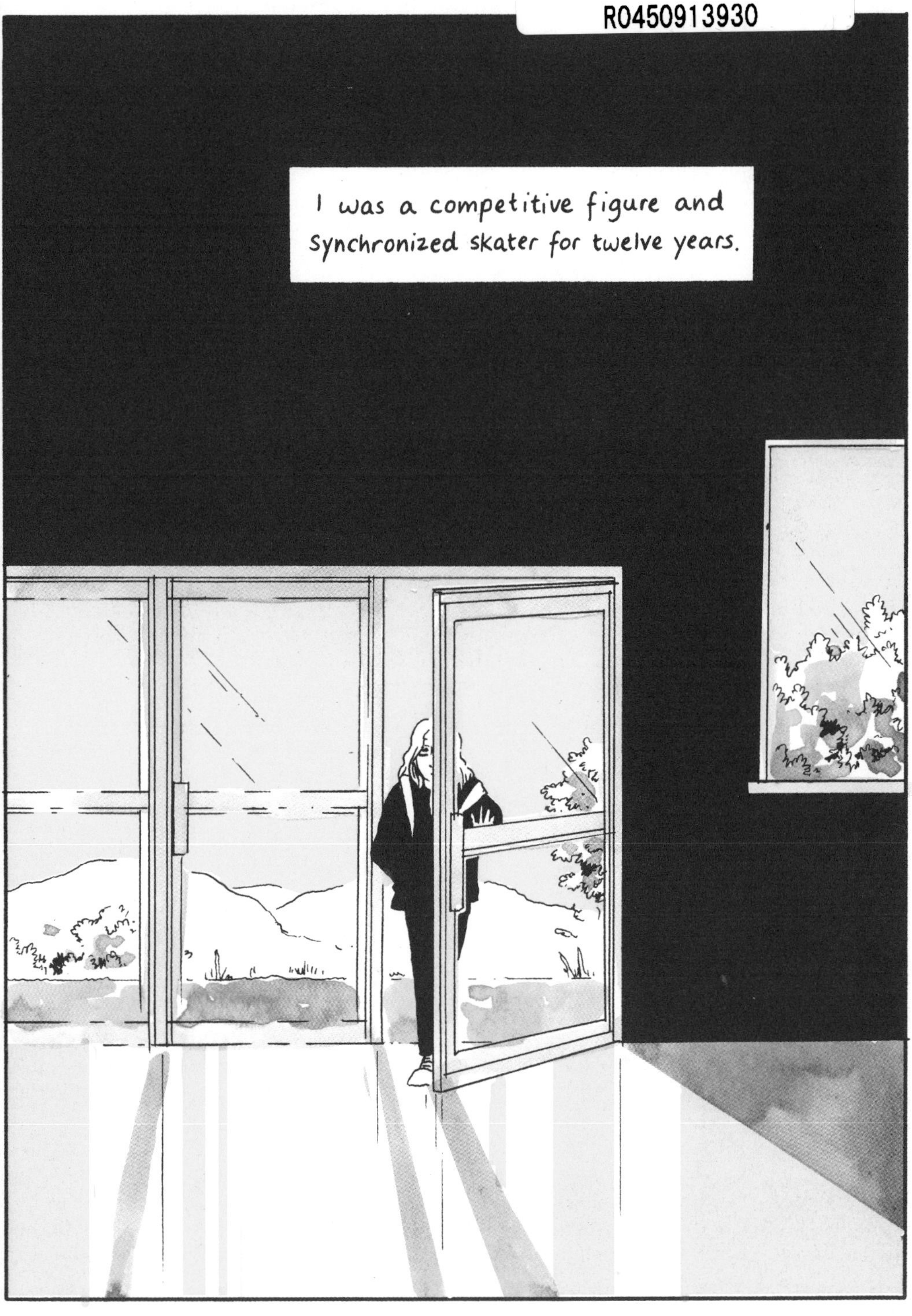
I was a competitive figure and synchronized skater for twelve years.

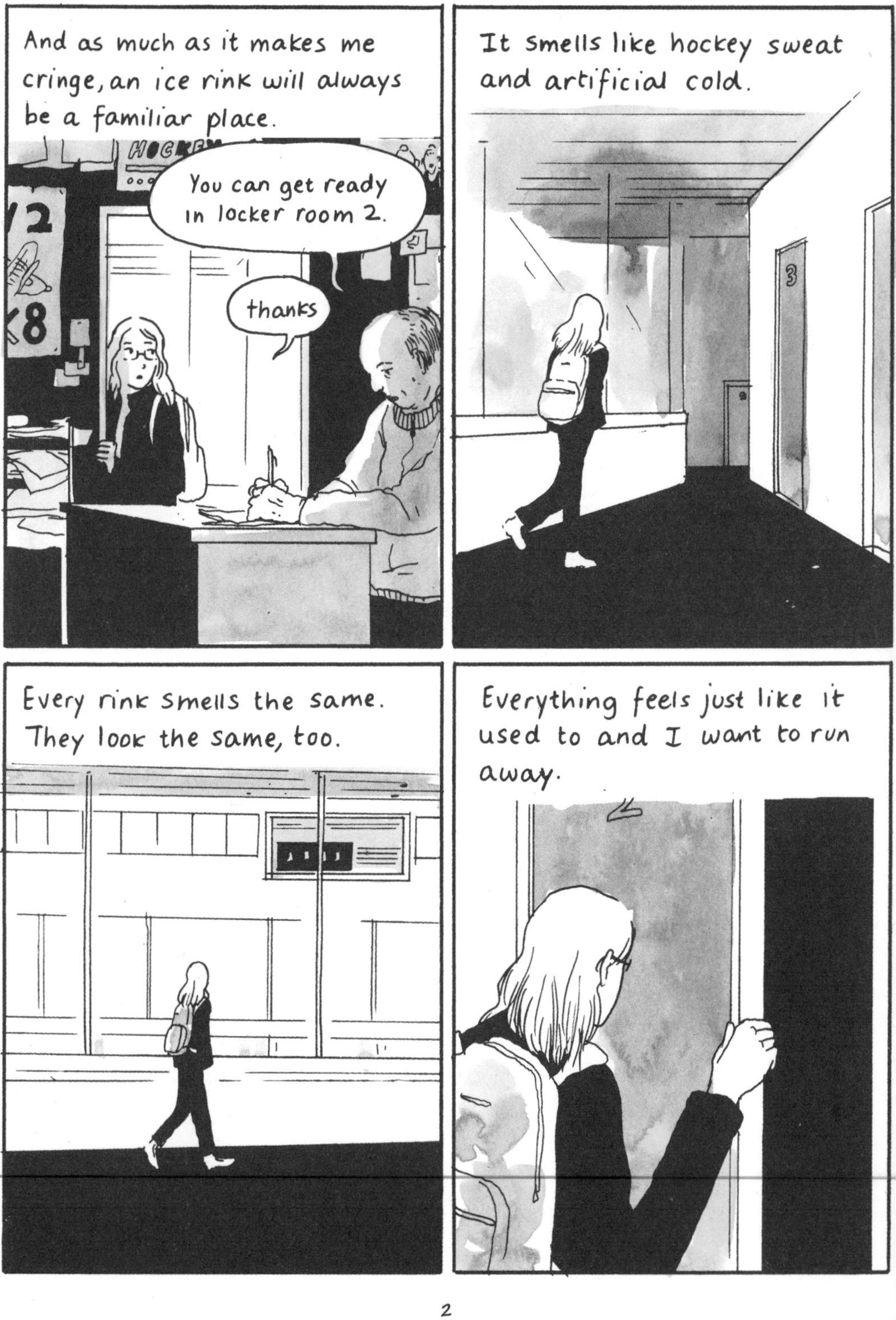
And as much as it makes me cringe, an ice rink will always be a familiar place.
You can get ready in locker room 2.
thanks
It smells like hockey sweat and artificial cold.
Every rink smells the same. They look the same, too.
Everything feels just like it used to and I want to run away.

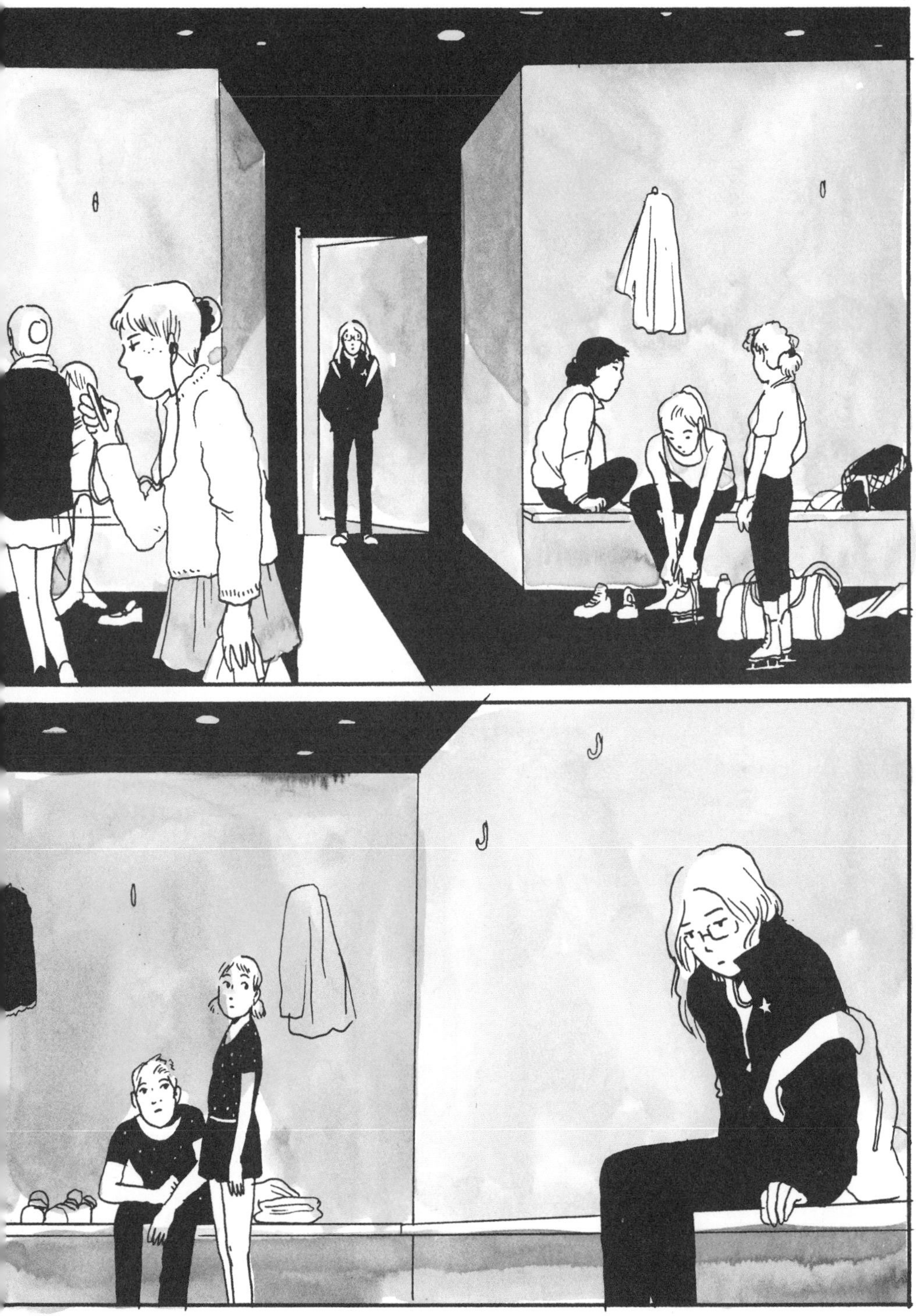

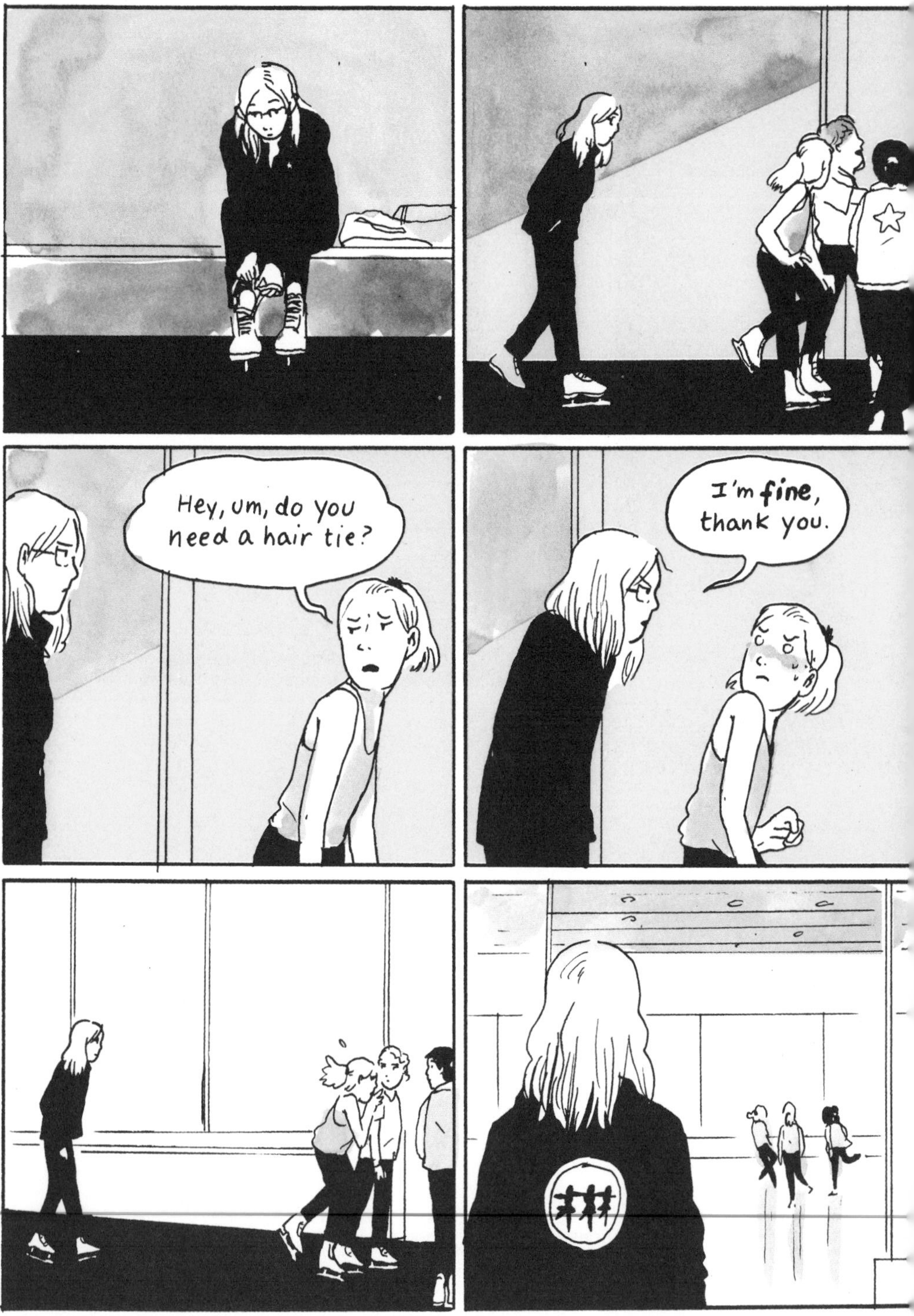
Hey, um, do you need a hair tie?
I'm **fine**, thank you.

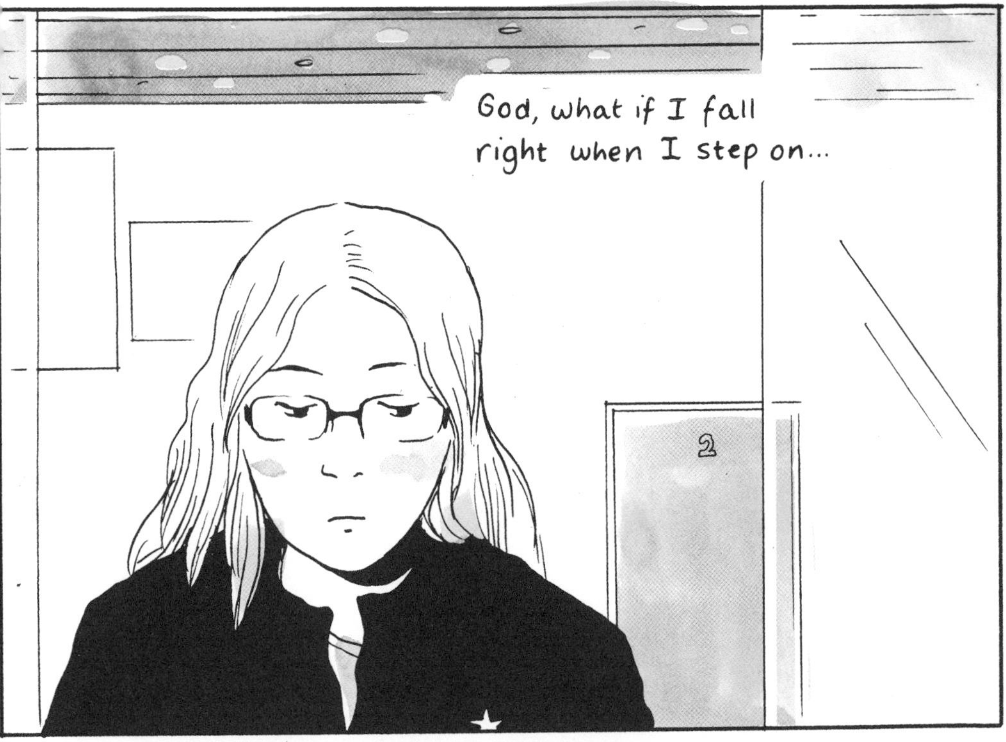
God, what if I fall right when I step on...
2
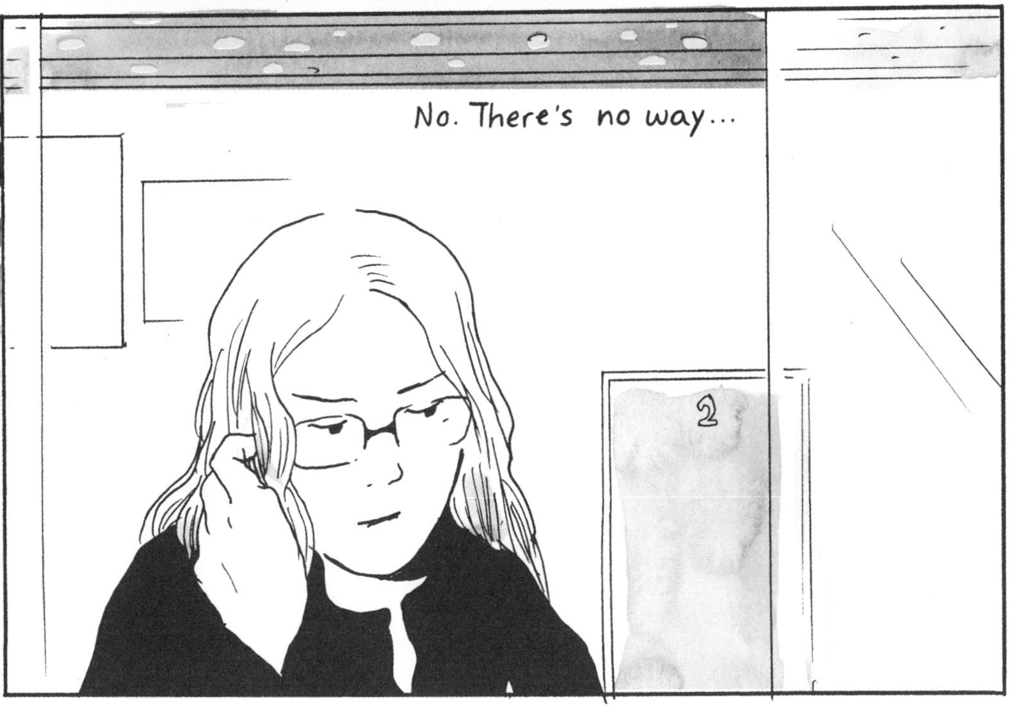
No. There's no way...
2

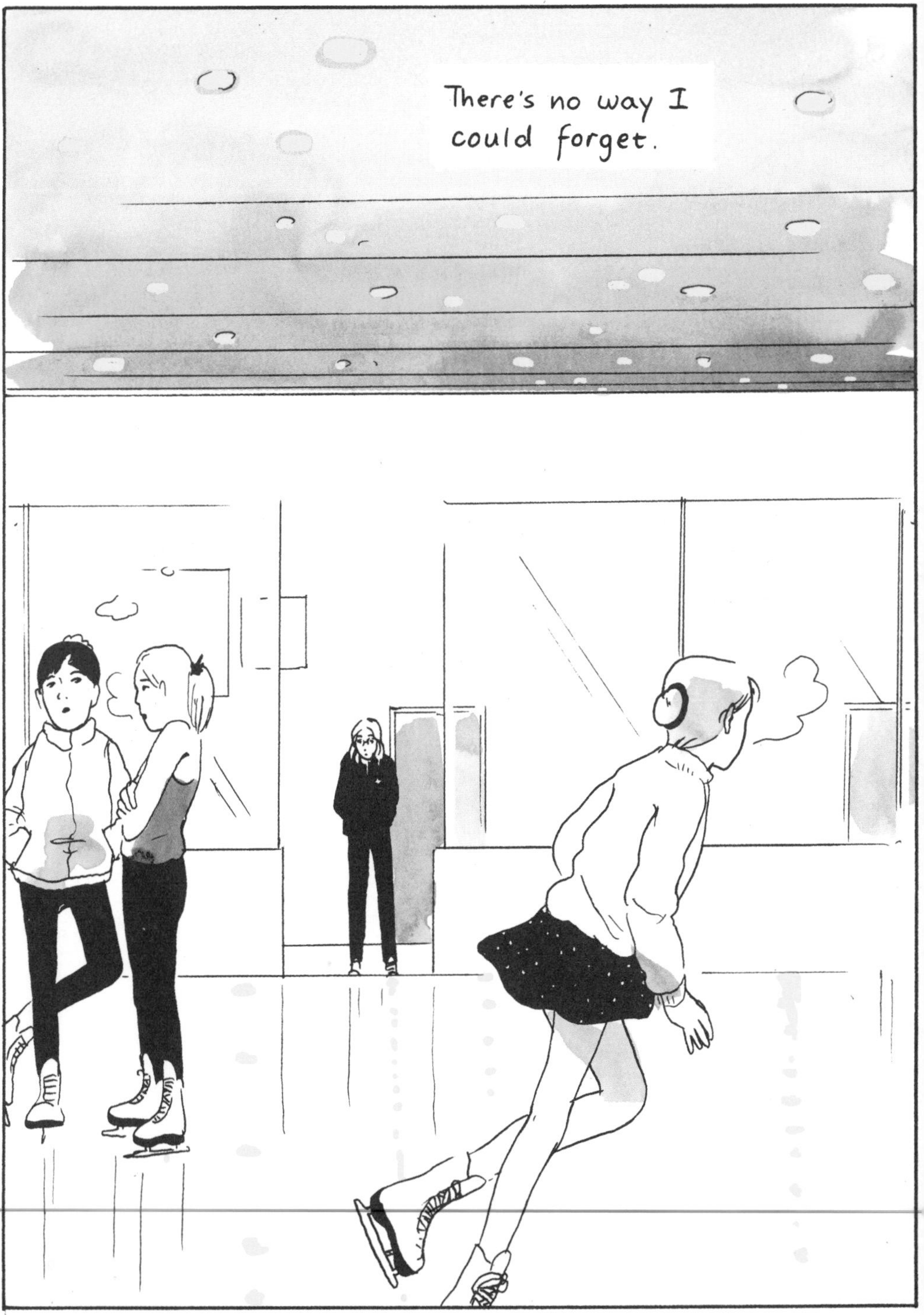
There's no way I could forget.

1

WALTZ JUMP

One of the first jumps I ever
learned. I still remember the
feeling of my leg swinging
through and the motion throwing
me into the air.

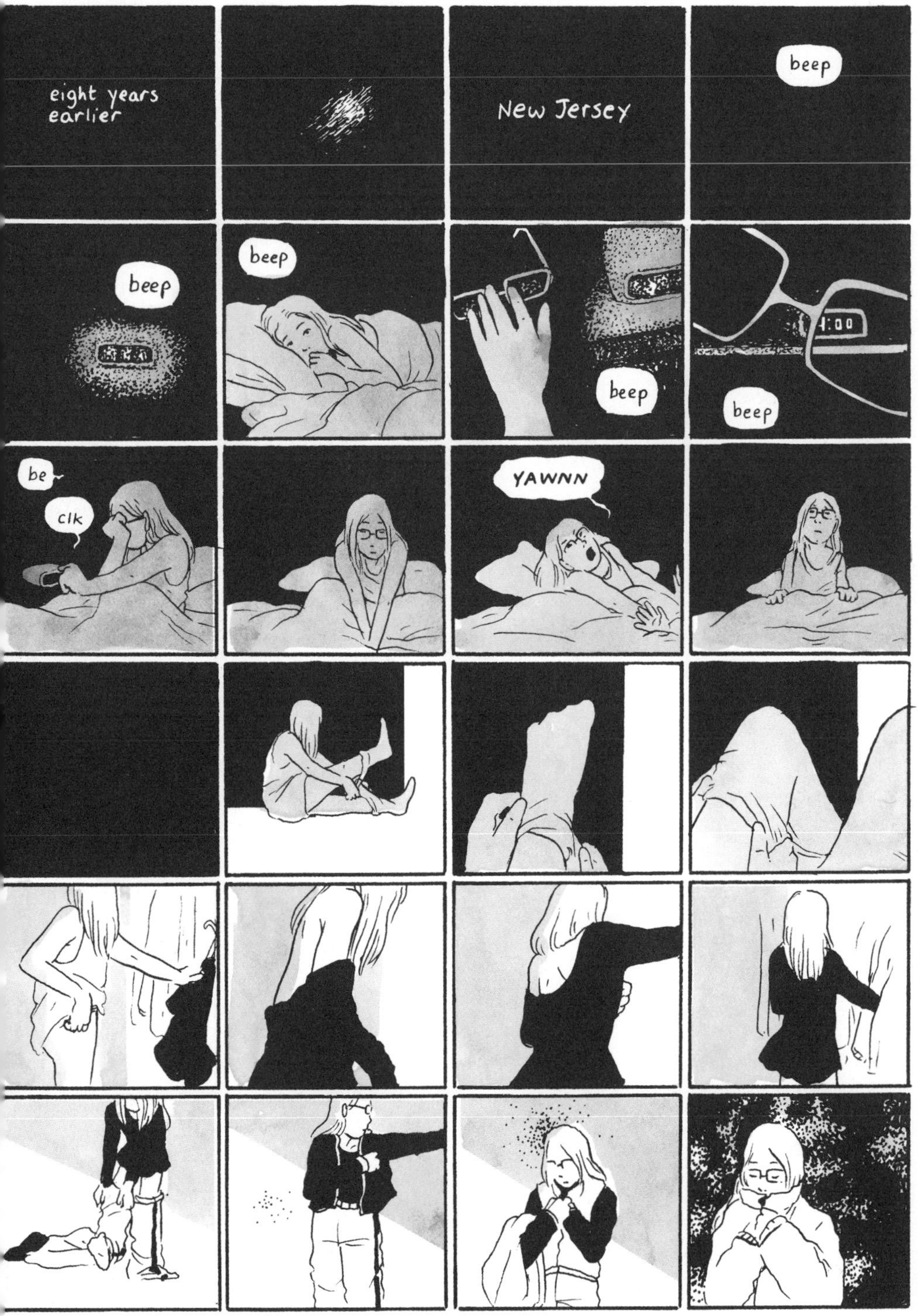
eight years
earlier
New Jersey
beep
beep
beep
beep
beep
1:00
beep
be
clk
YAWNN

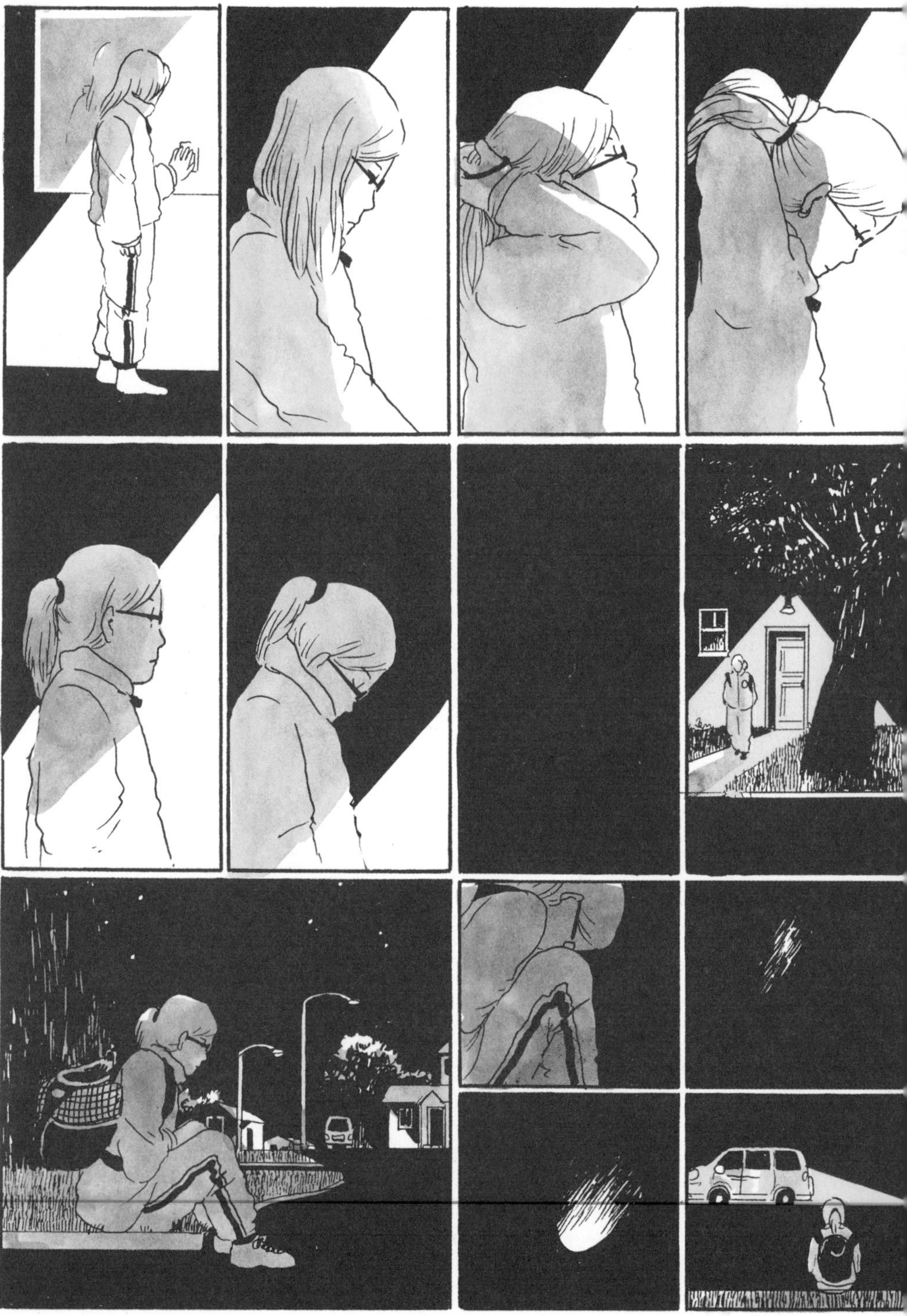

Hey, Molly.
mmm
There's a muffin for you, Tillie.
thank you

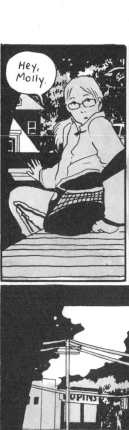

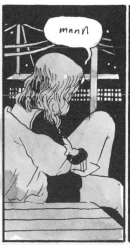

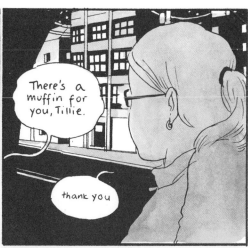

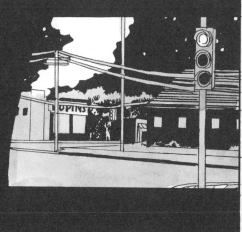

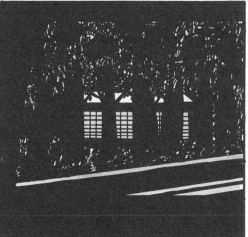

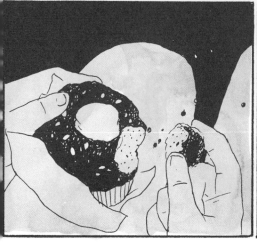

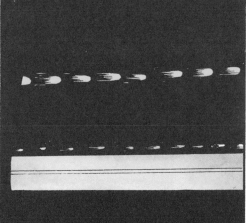

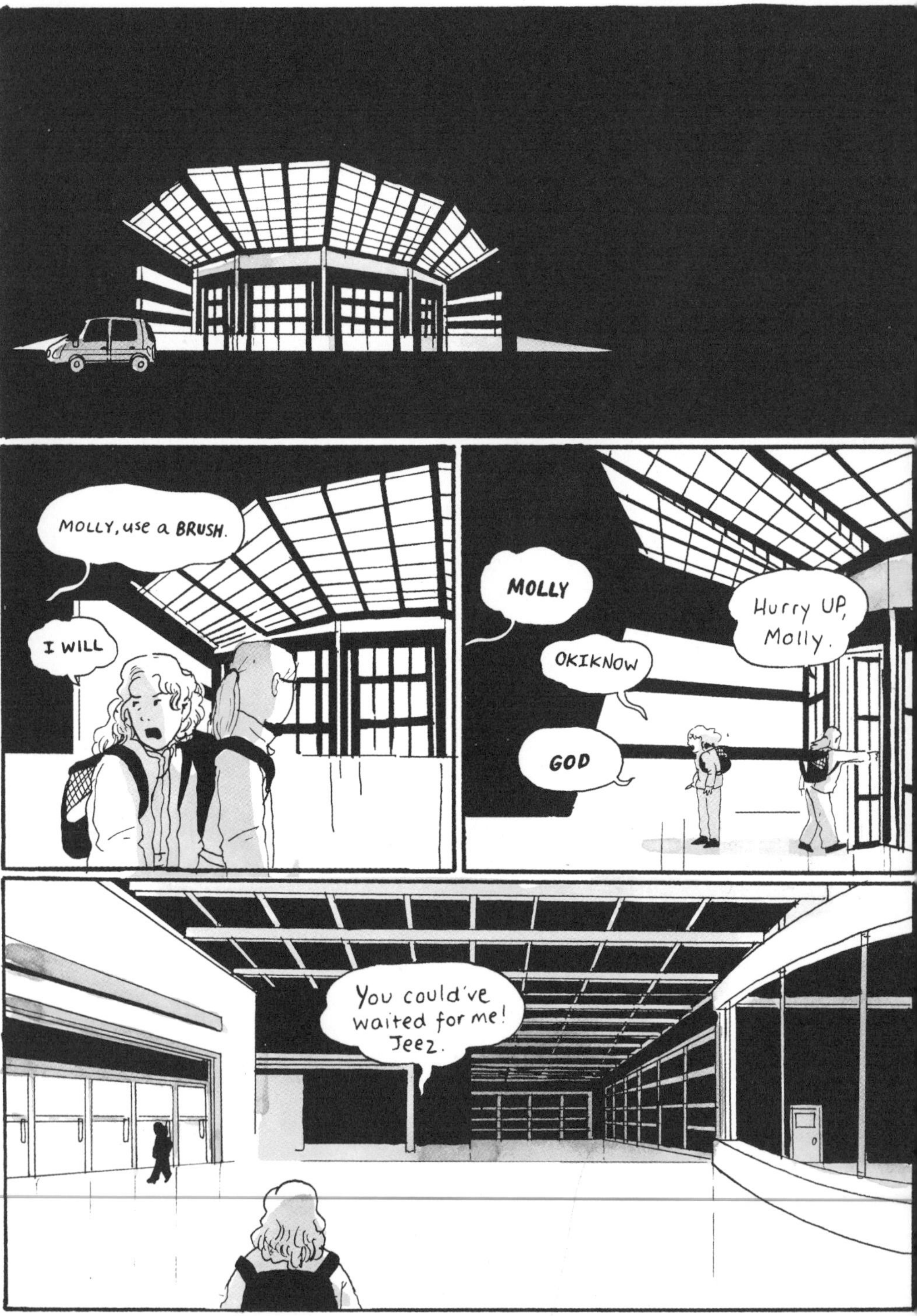
MOLLY, use a BRUSH.
I WILL
MOLLY
OKIKNOW
GOD
Hurry UP, Molly.
You could've waited for me! Jeez.

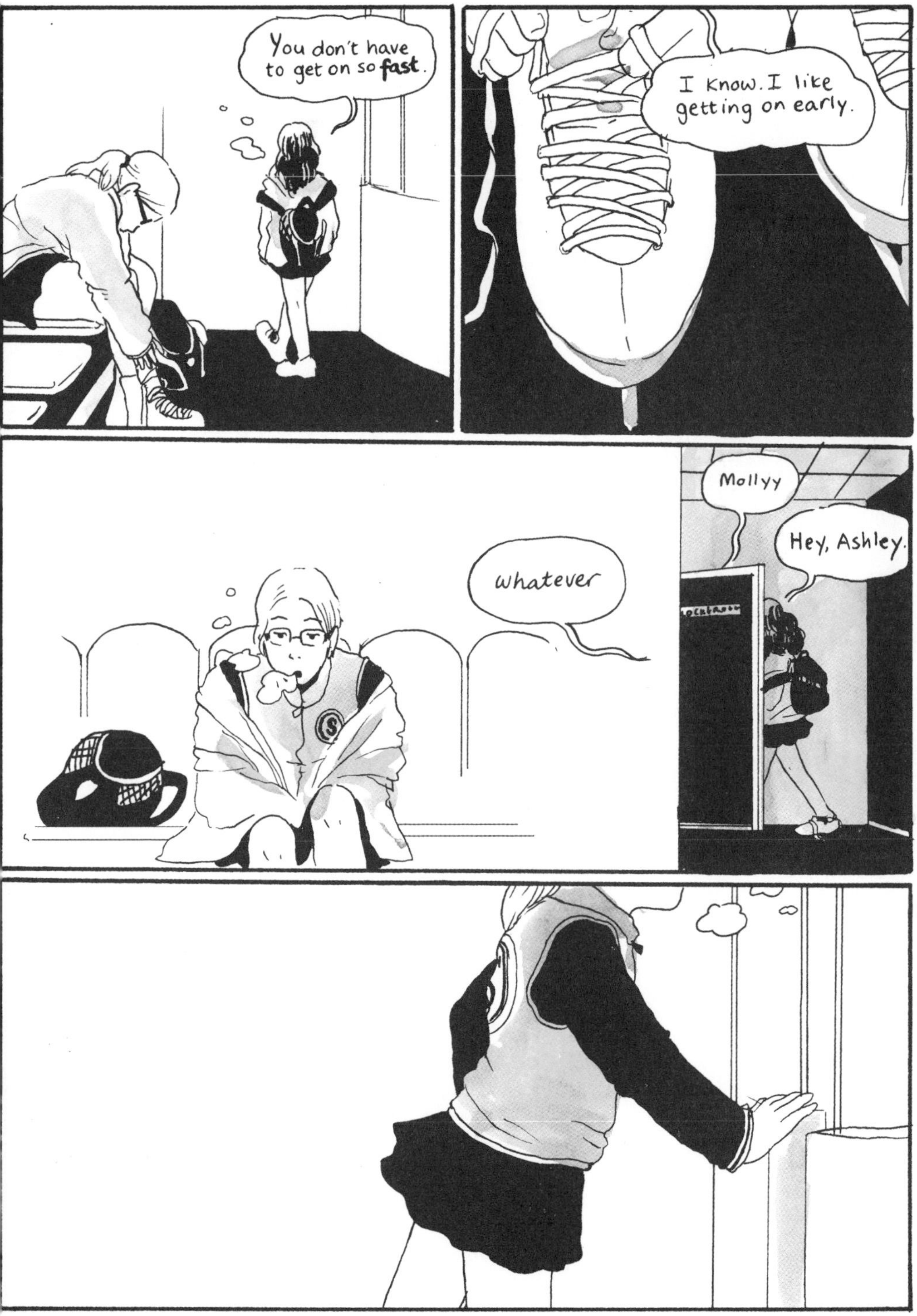
You don't have to get on so fast.
I know. I like getting on early.
whatever
Mollyy
Hey, Ashley.

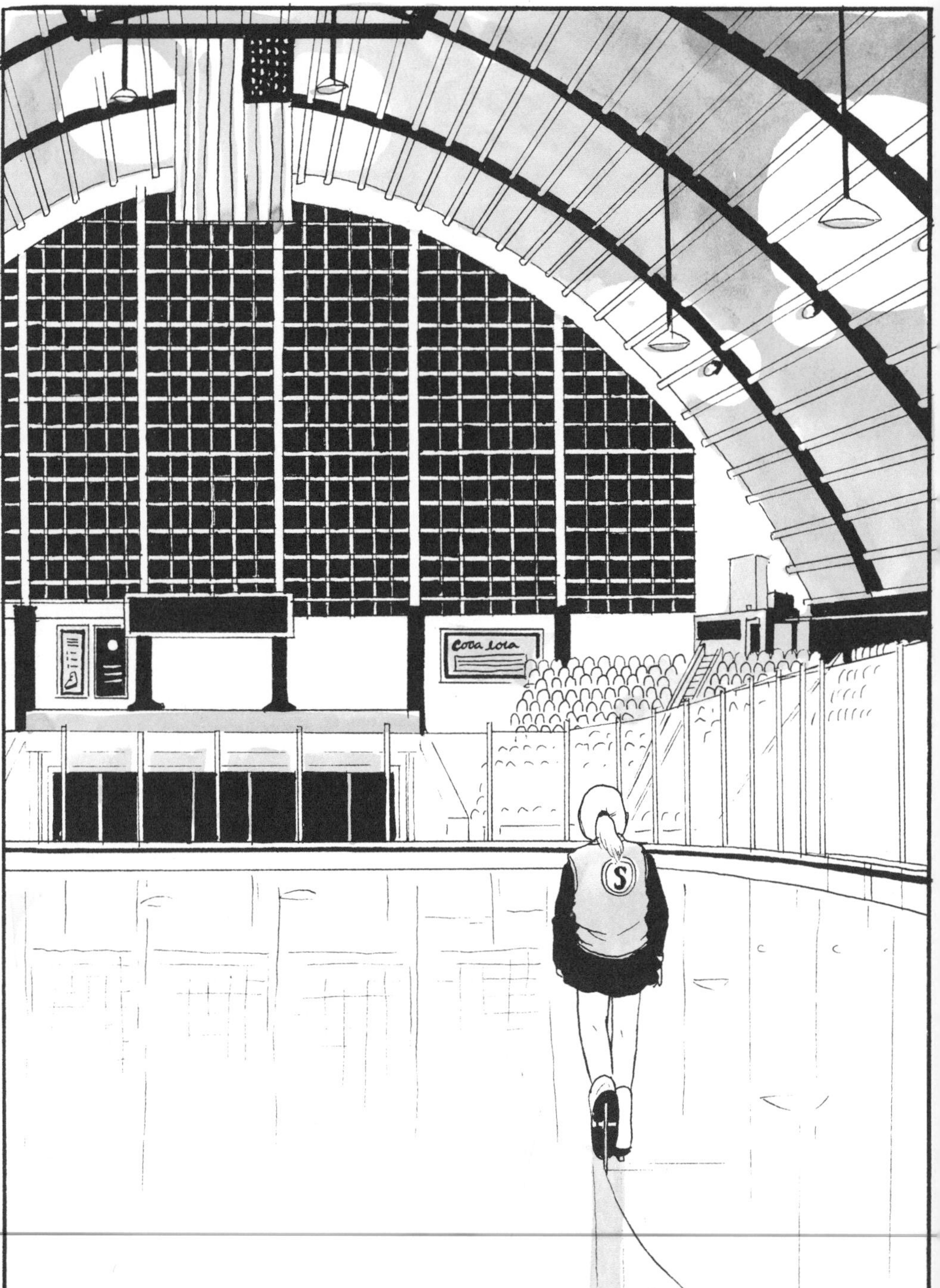

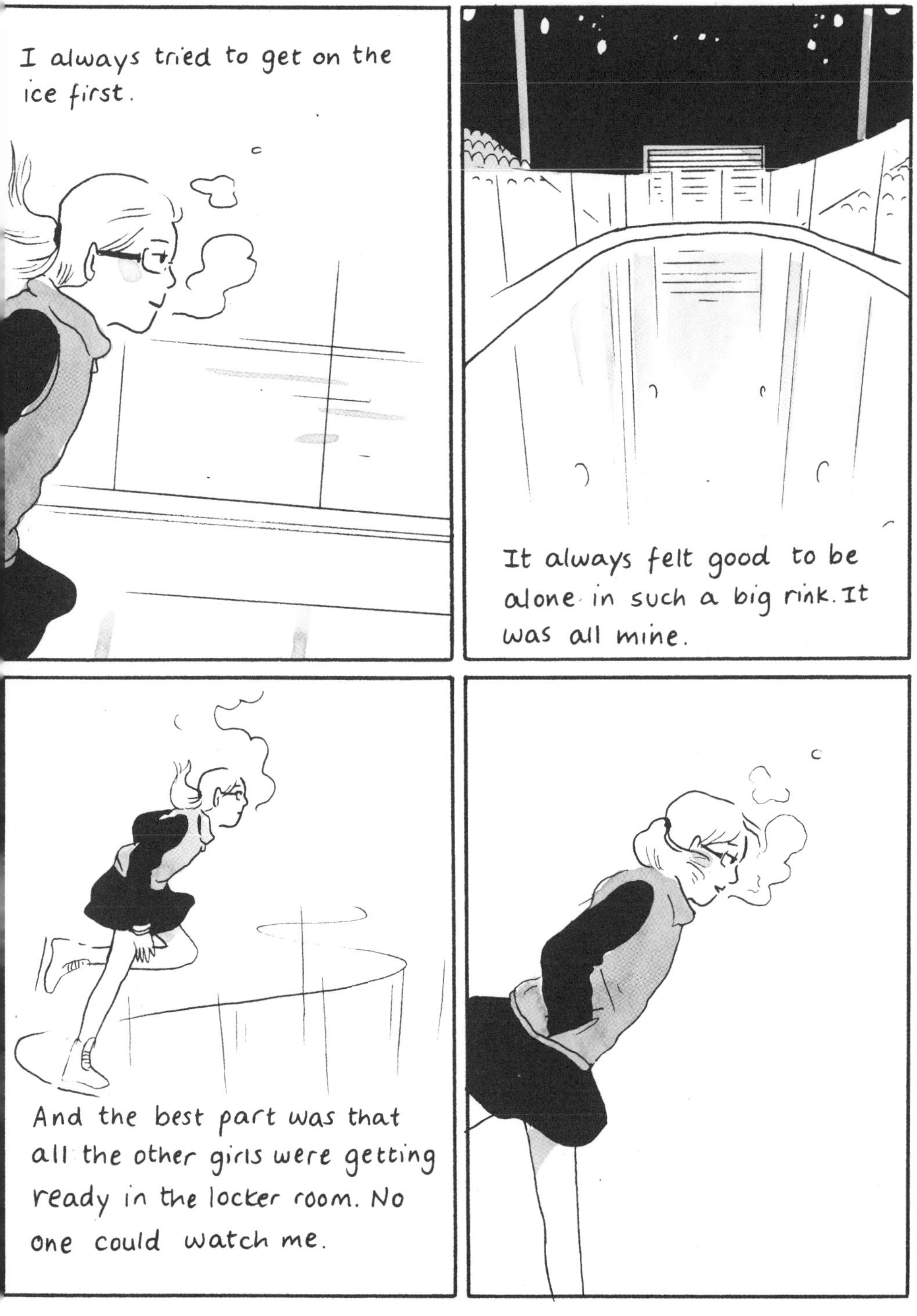
I always tried to get on the ice first.
It always felt good to be alone in such a big rink. It was all mine.
And the best part was that all the other girls were getting ready in the locker room. No one could watch me.

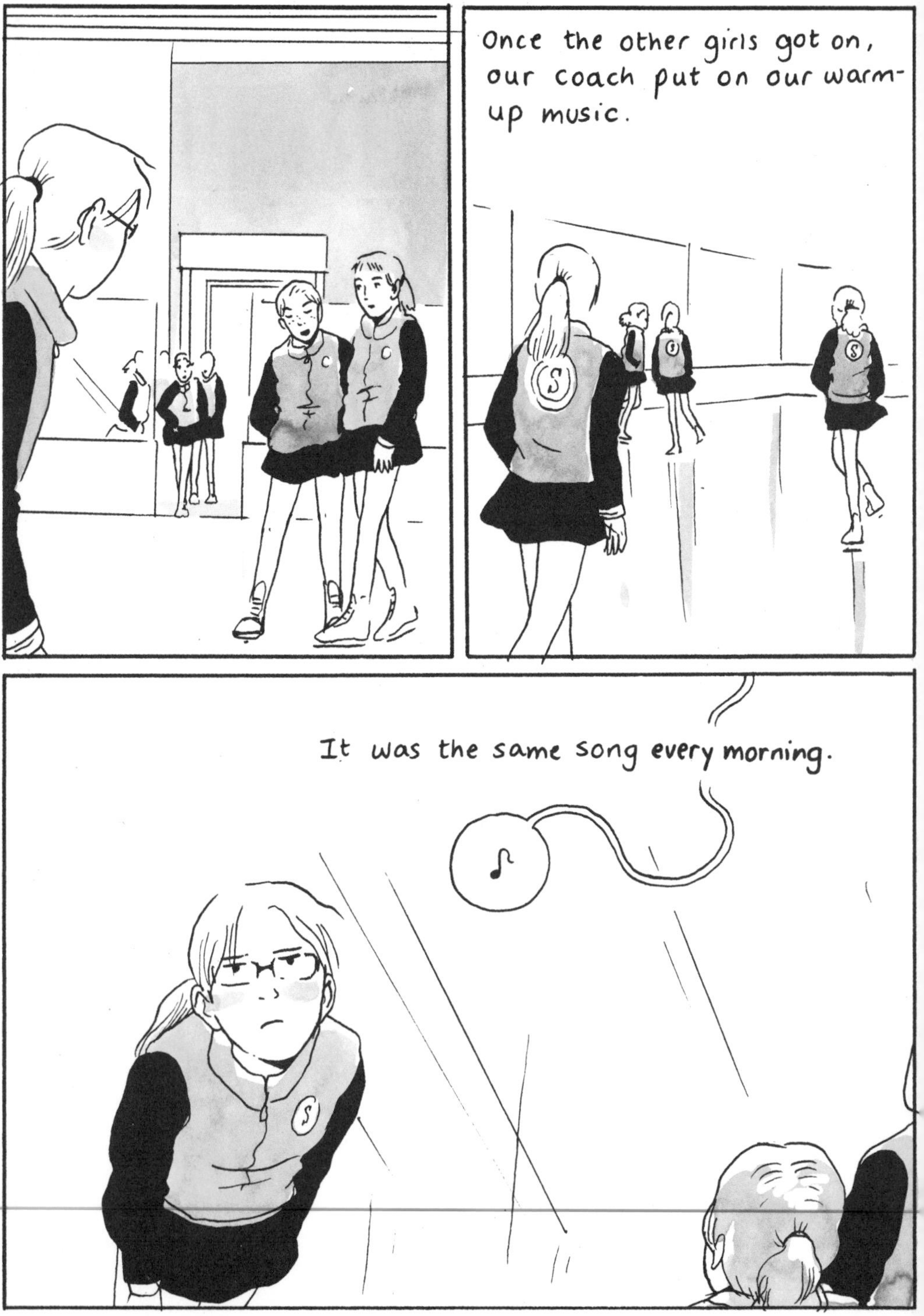
Once the other girls got on, our coach put on our warm-up music.
It was the same song every morning.

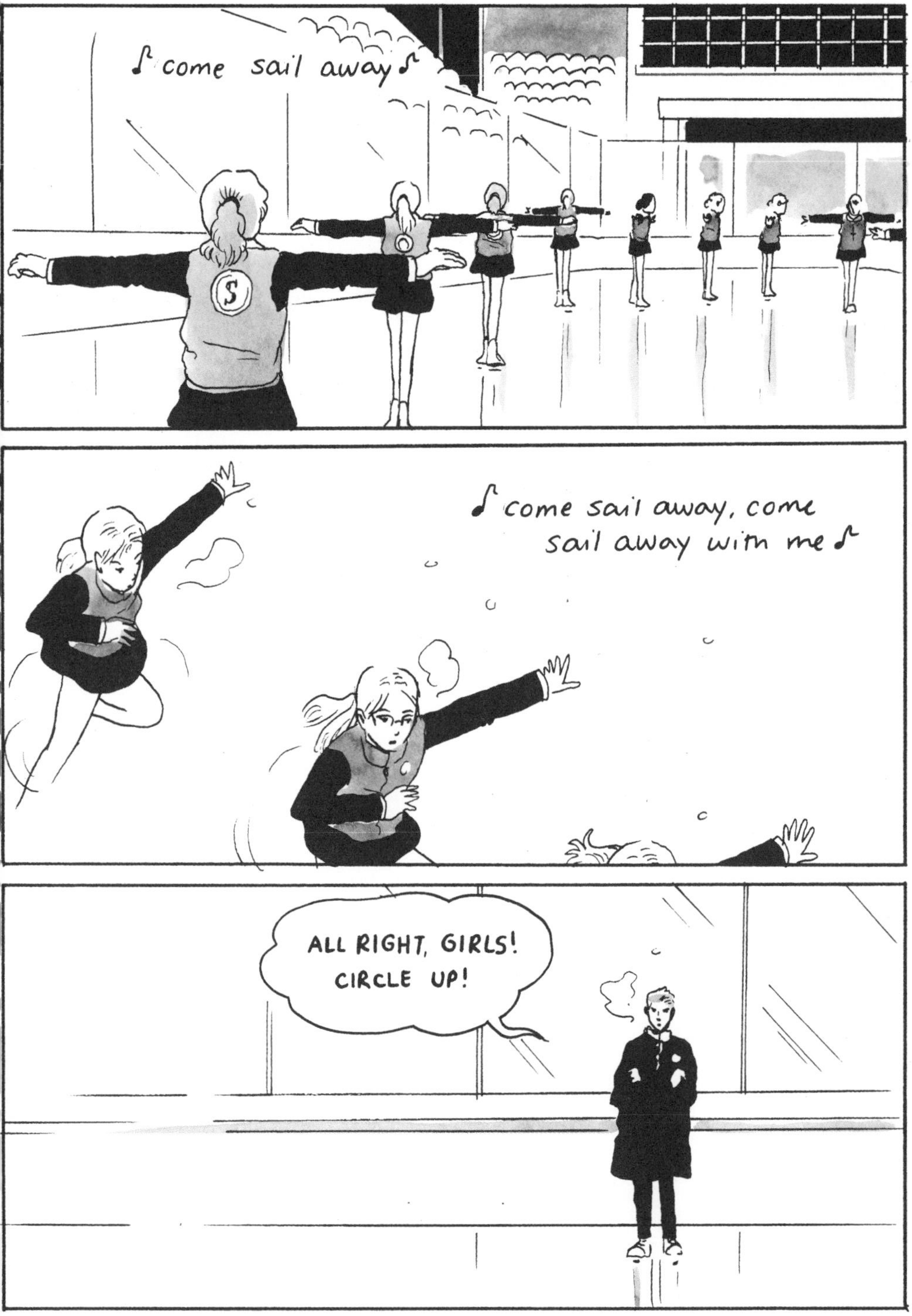
come sail away
come sail away, come sail away with me
ALL RIGHT, GIRLS! CIRCLE UP!

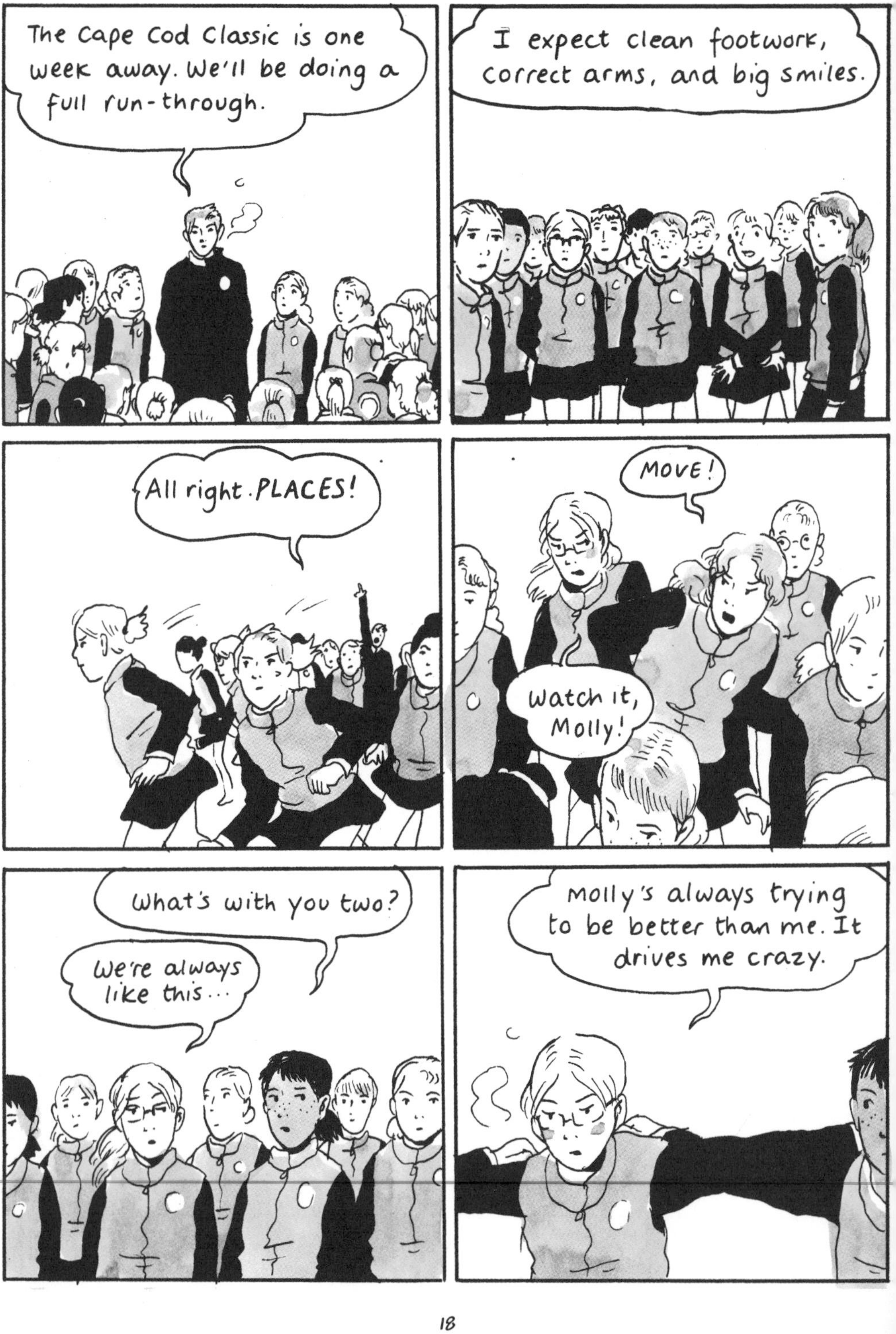
The Cape Cod Classic is one week away. We'll be doing a full run-through.
I expect clean footwork, correct arms, and big smiles.
All right. PLACES!
MOVE!
Watch it, Molly!
What's with you two?
We're always like this...
Molly's always trying to be better than me. It drives me crazy.

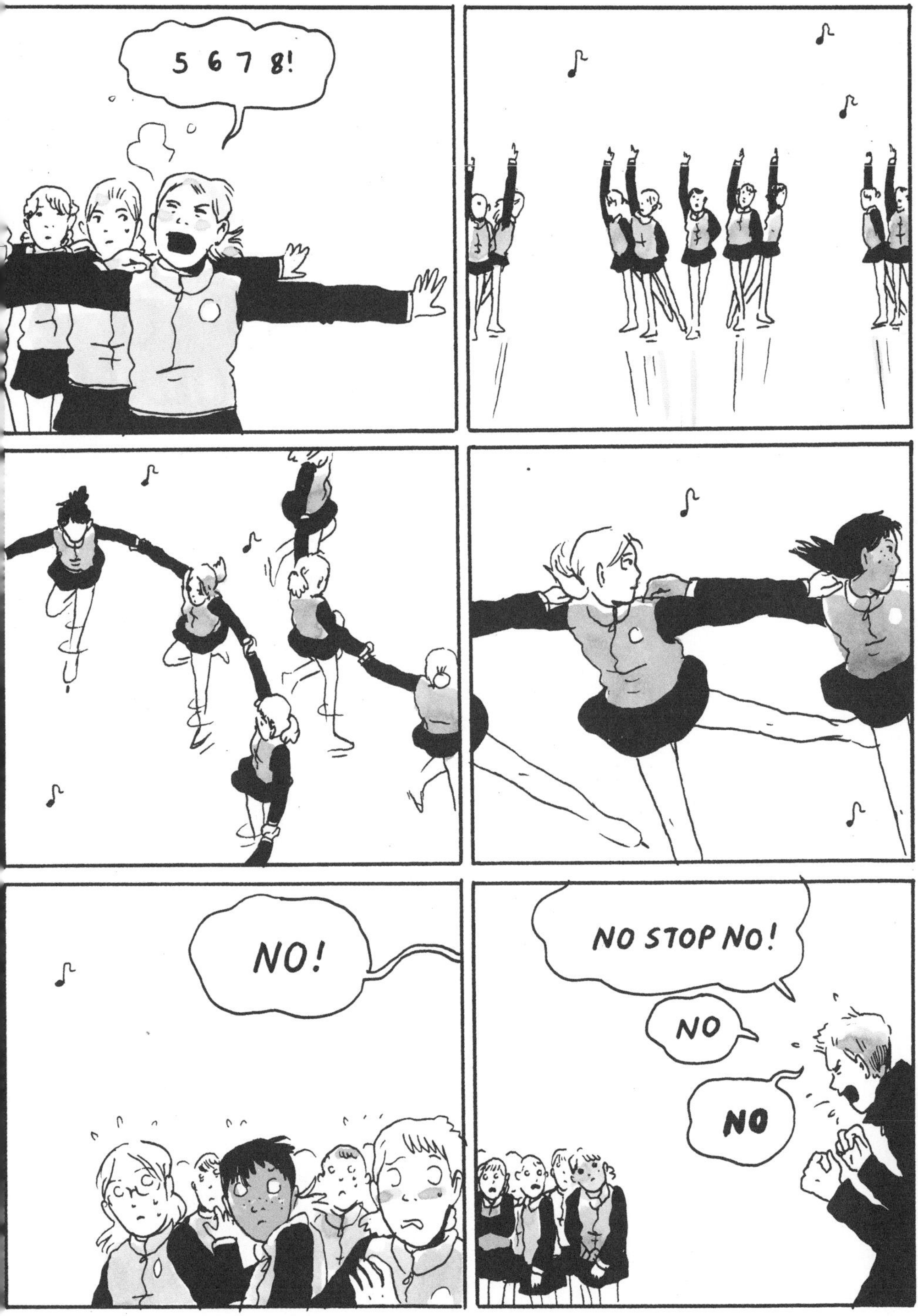
5 6 7 8!
NO!
NO STOP NO!
NO
NO

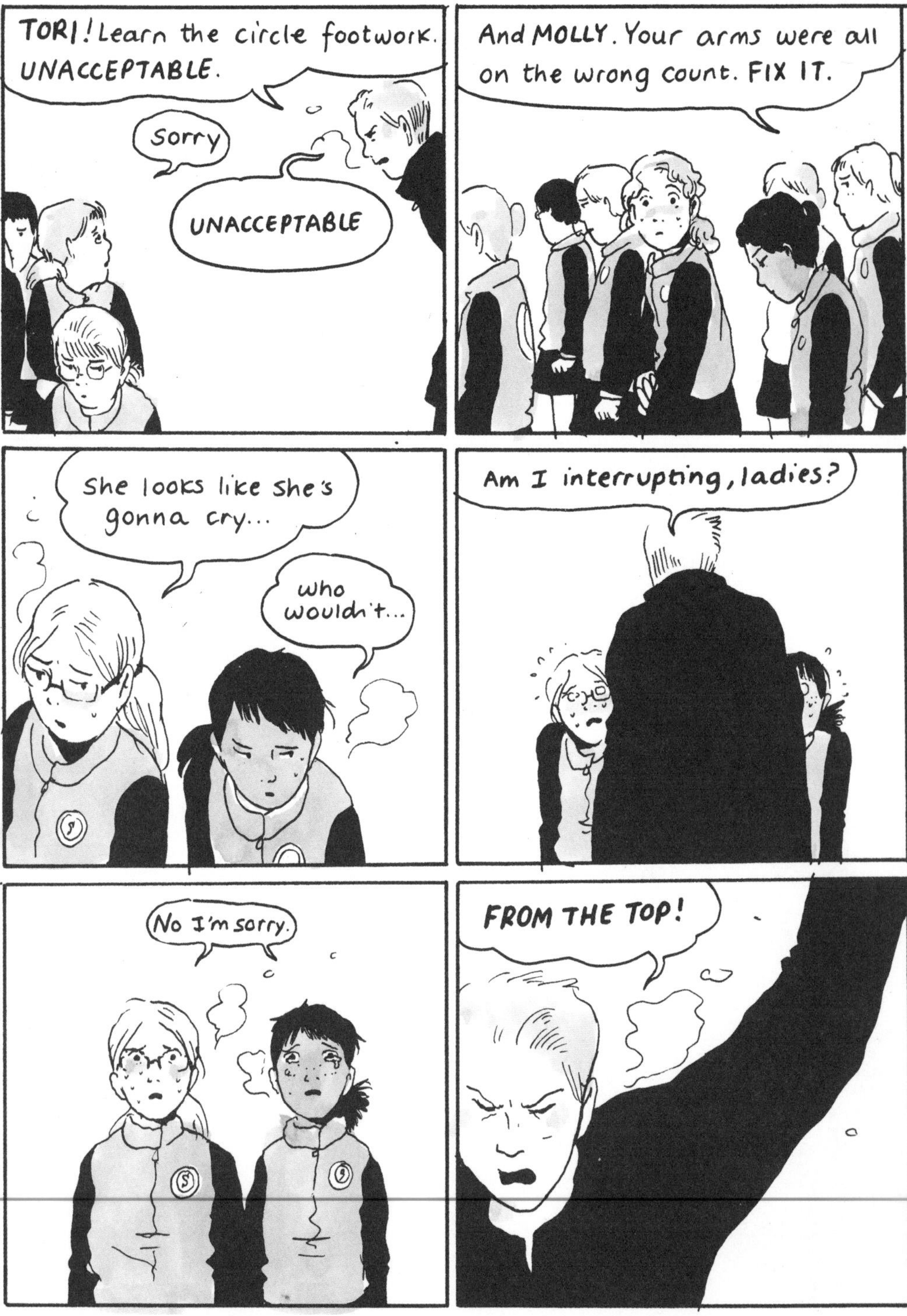
TORI! Learn the circle footwork. UNACCEPTABLE.
Sorry
UNACCEPTABLE
And MOLLY. Your arms were all on the wrong count. FIX IT.
She looks like she's gonna cry...
who wouldn't...
Am I interrupting, ladies?
No I'm sorry.
FROM THE TOP!

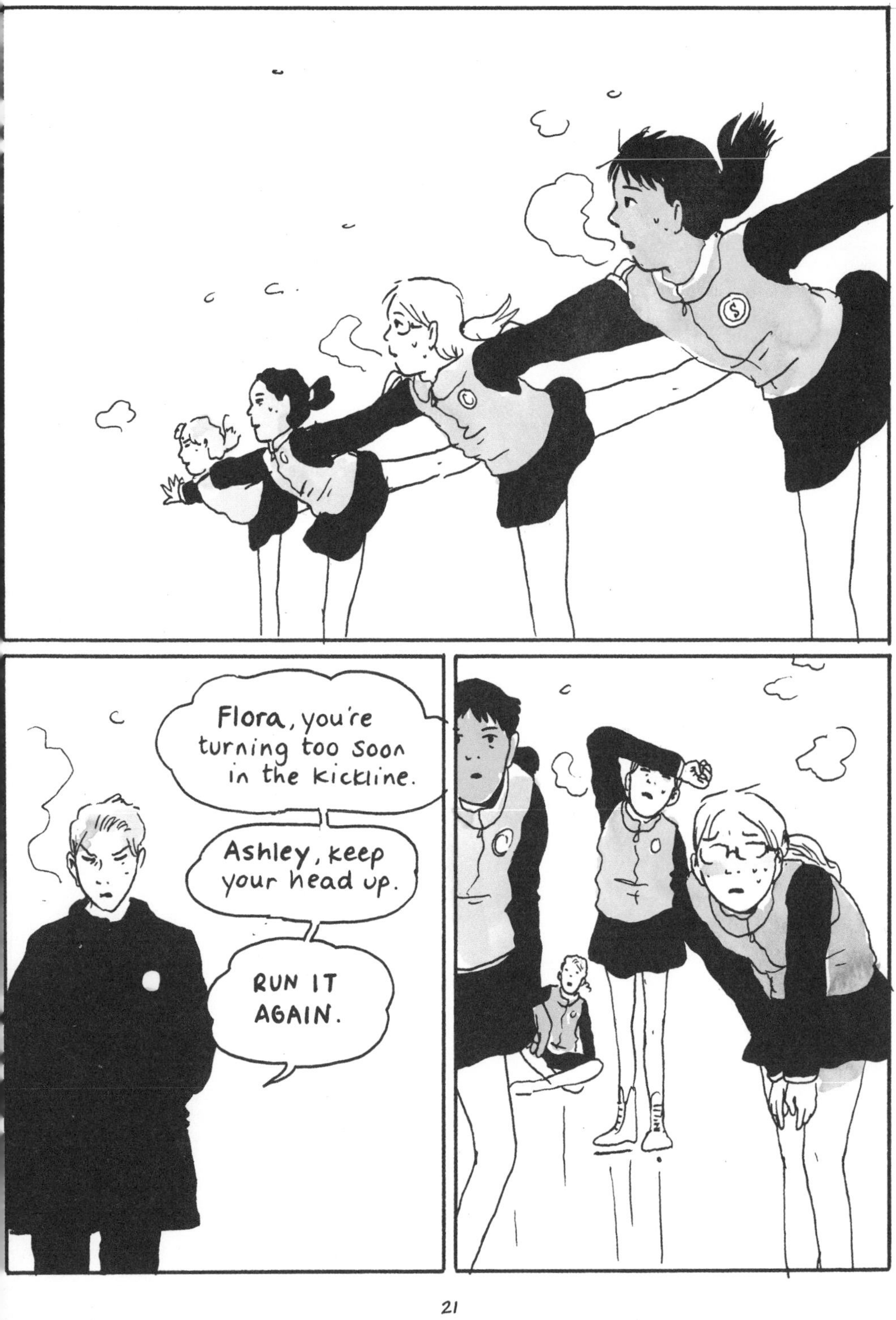
Flora, you're turning too soon in the kickline.
Ashley, keep your head up.
RUN IT AGAIN.

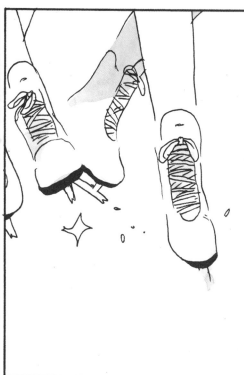

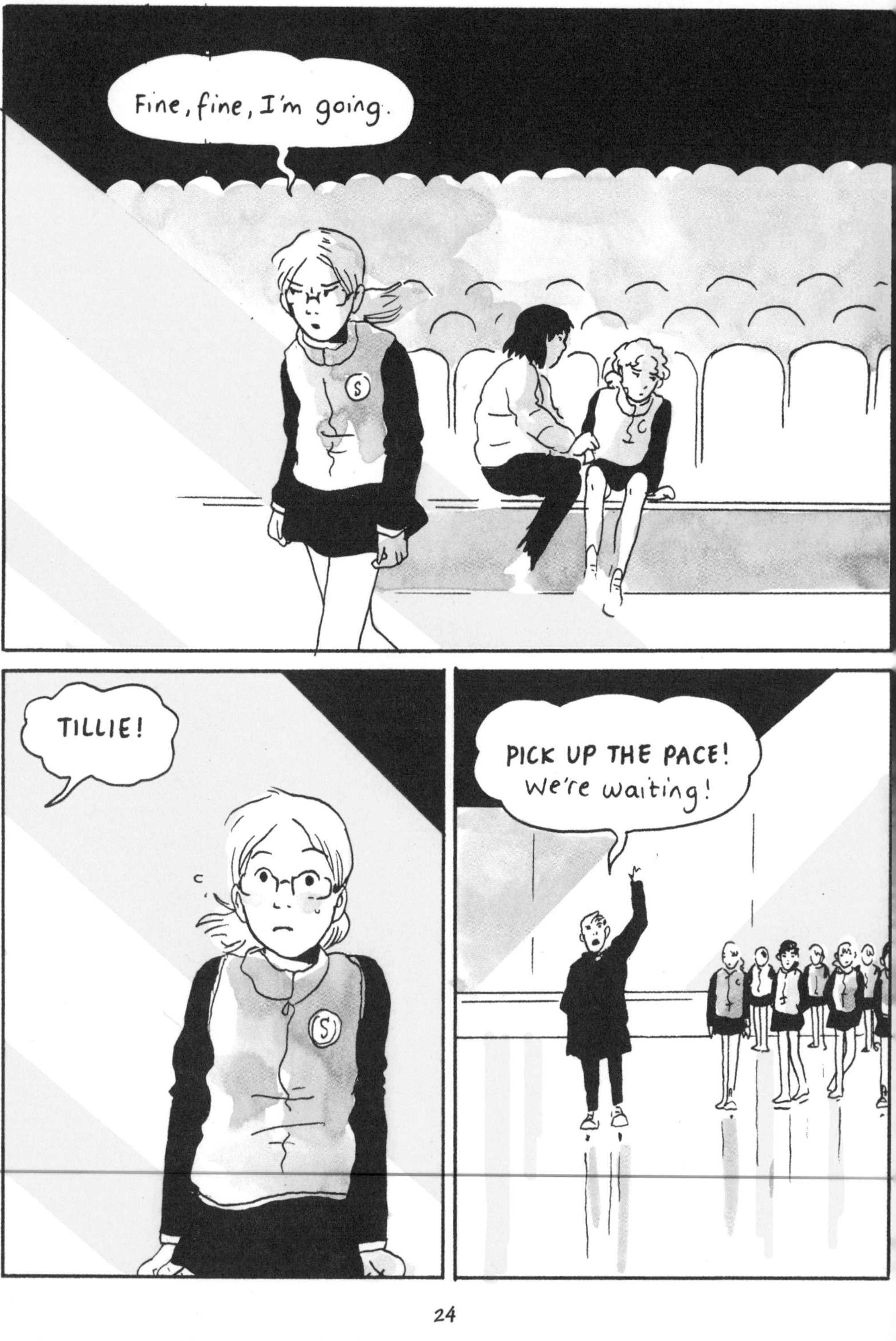
Fine, fine, I'm going.
TILLIE!
PICK UP THE PACE!
We're waiting!

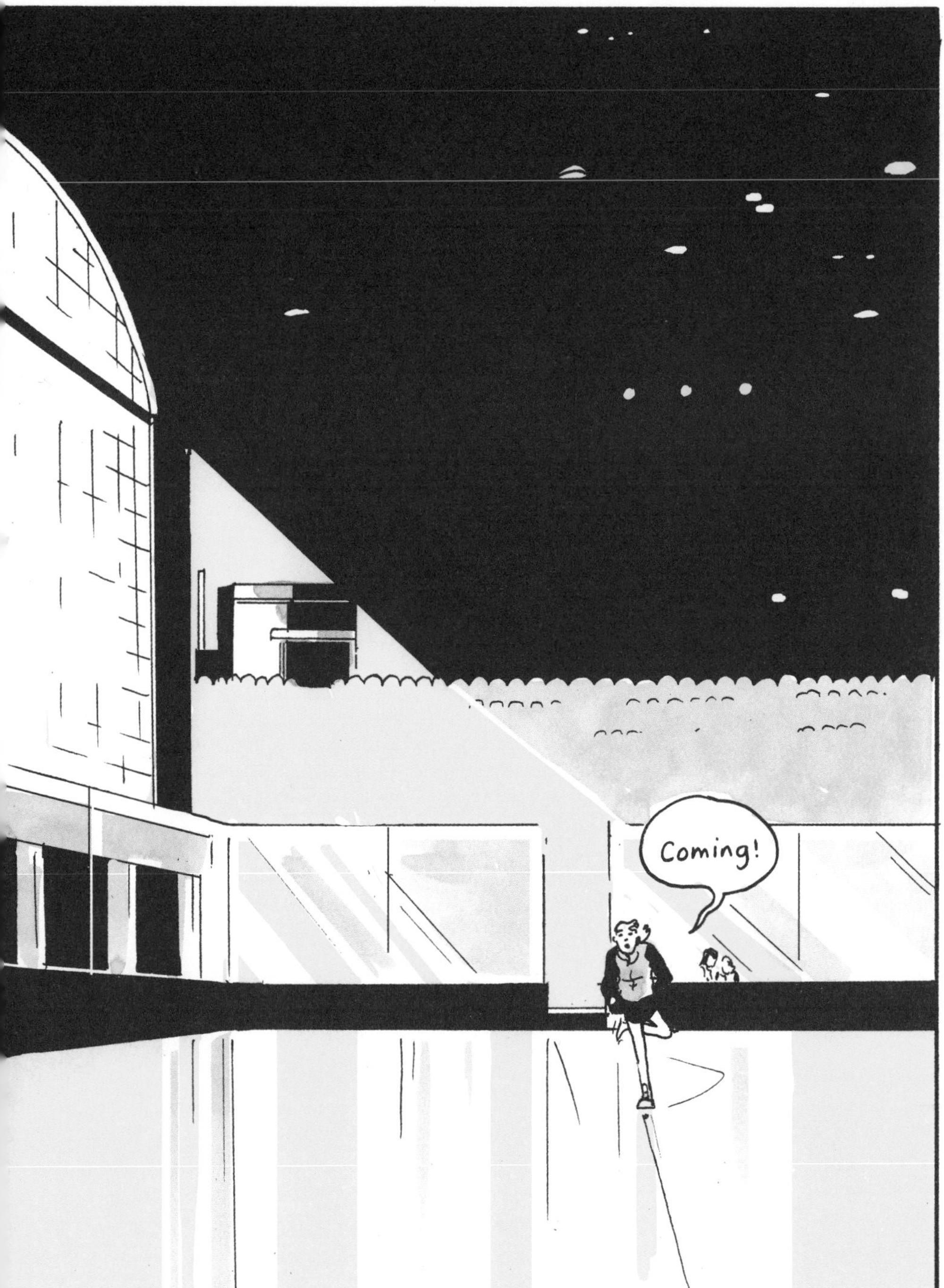
Coming!

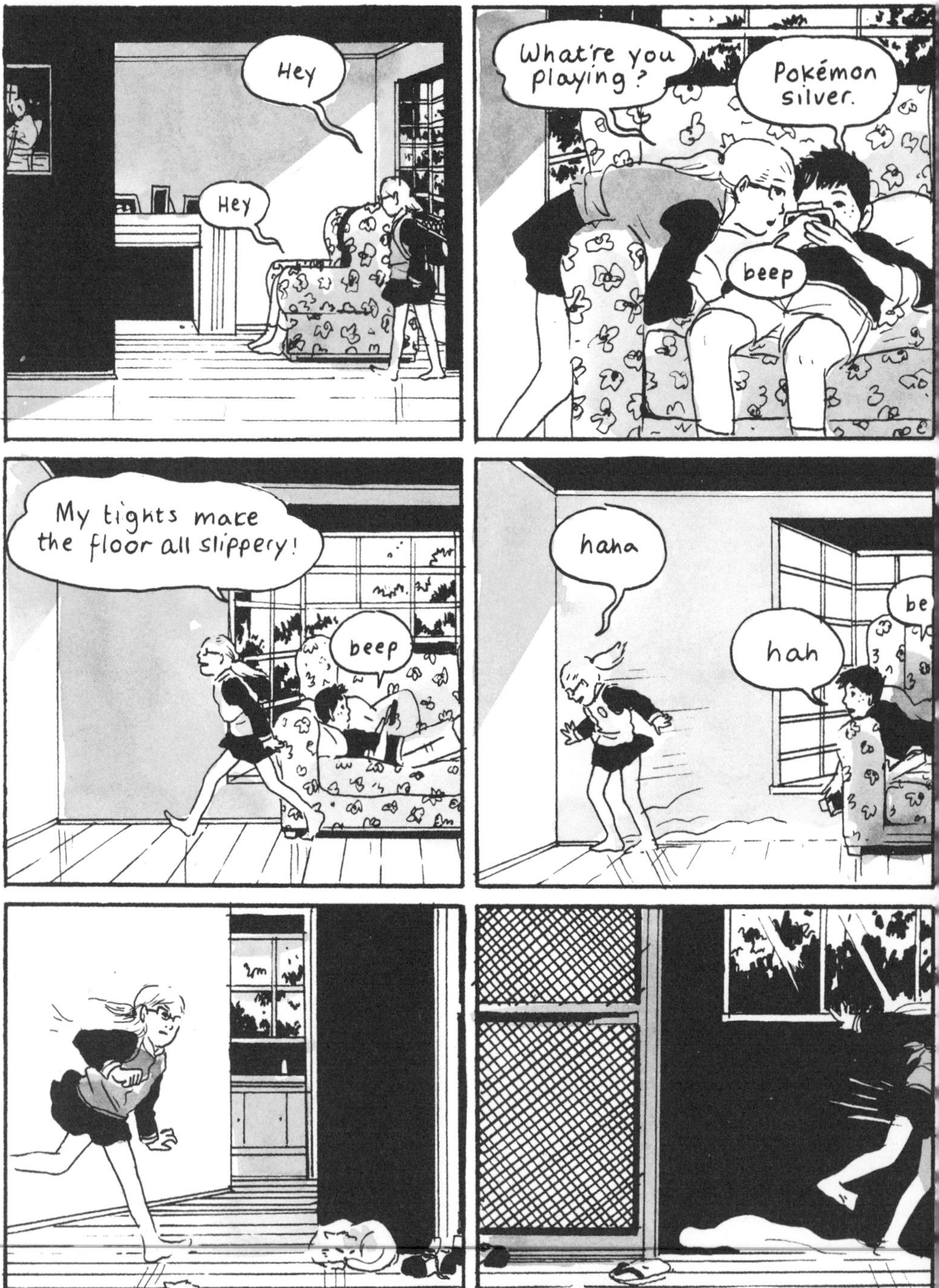
Hey
Hey
What're you playing?
Pokémon silver.
beep
My tights make the floor all slippery!
beep
haha
hah
be

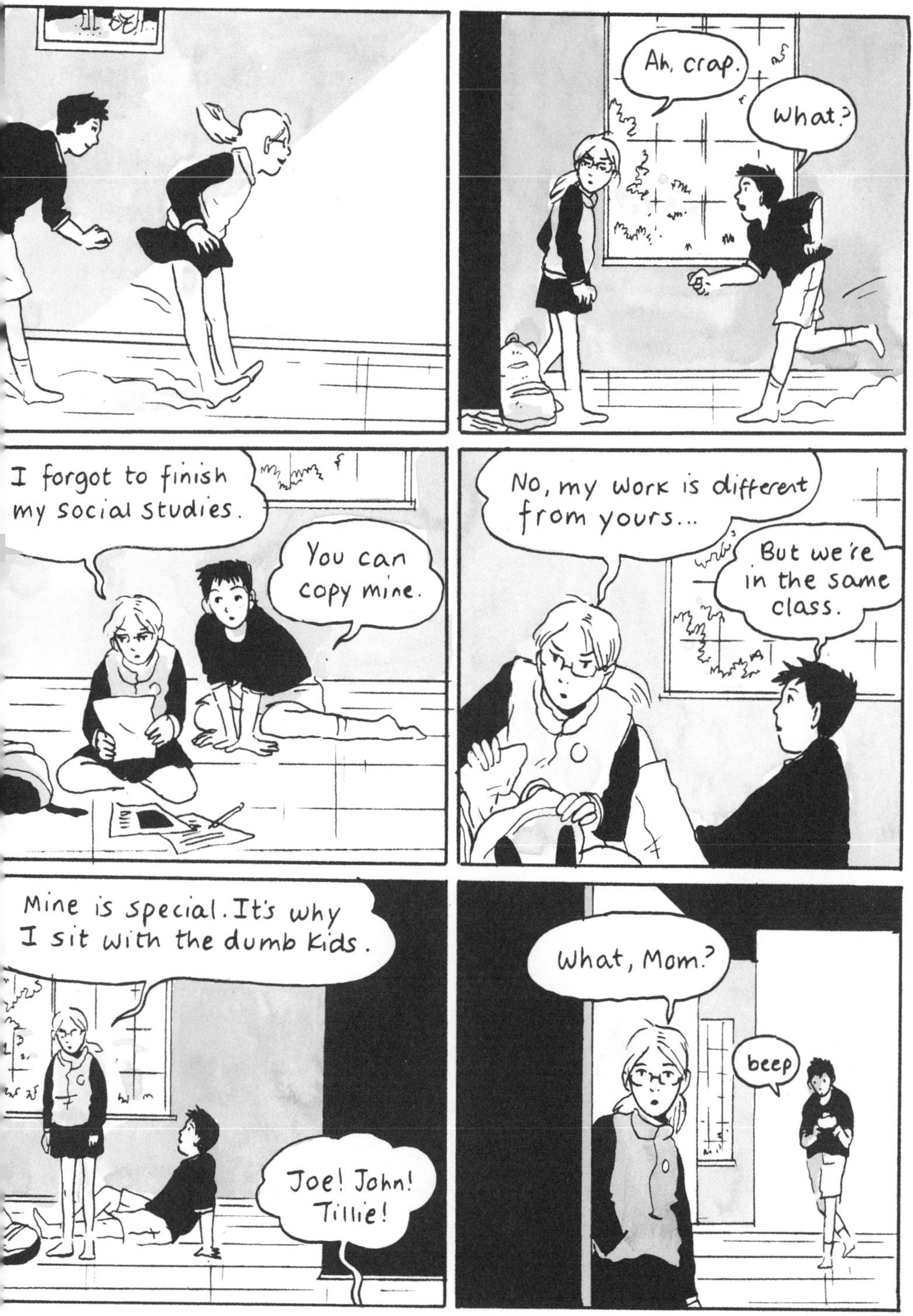
Ah, crap.
What?
I forgot to finish my social studies.
You can copy mine.
No, my work is different from yours...
But we're in the same class.
Mine is special. It's why I sit with the dumb kids.
Joe! John! Tillie!
What, Mom?
beep

28

2

SCRATCH SPIN

I always hated scratch spins.

I would get going too fast and could never figure out how to slow down.

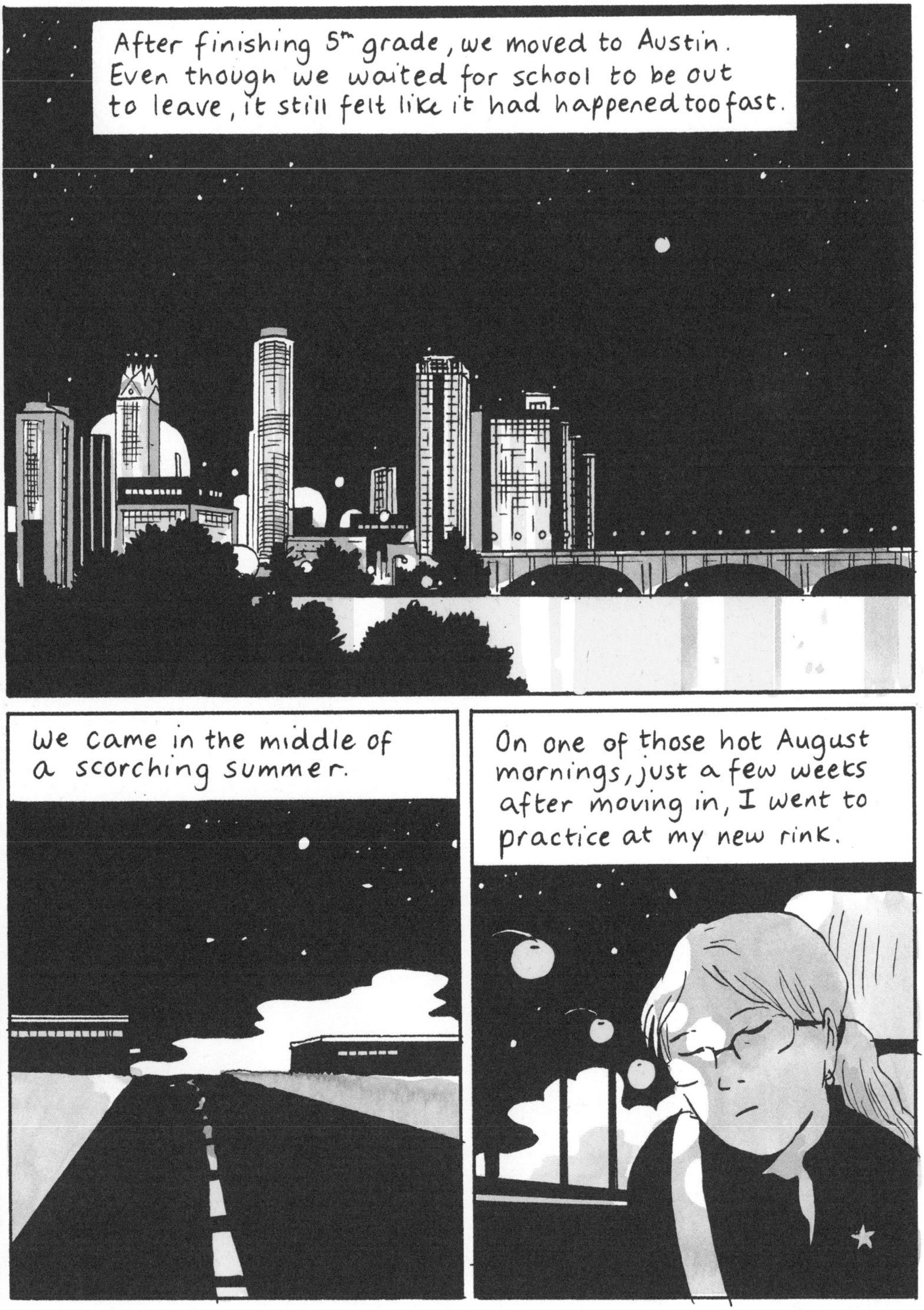
After finishing 5th grade, we moved to Austin. Even though we waited for school to be out to leave, it still felt like it had happened too fast.
We came in the middle of a scorching summer.
On one of those hot August mornings, just a few weeks after moving in, I went to practice at my new rink.

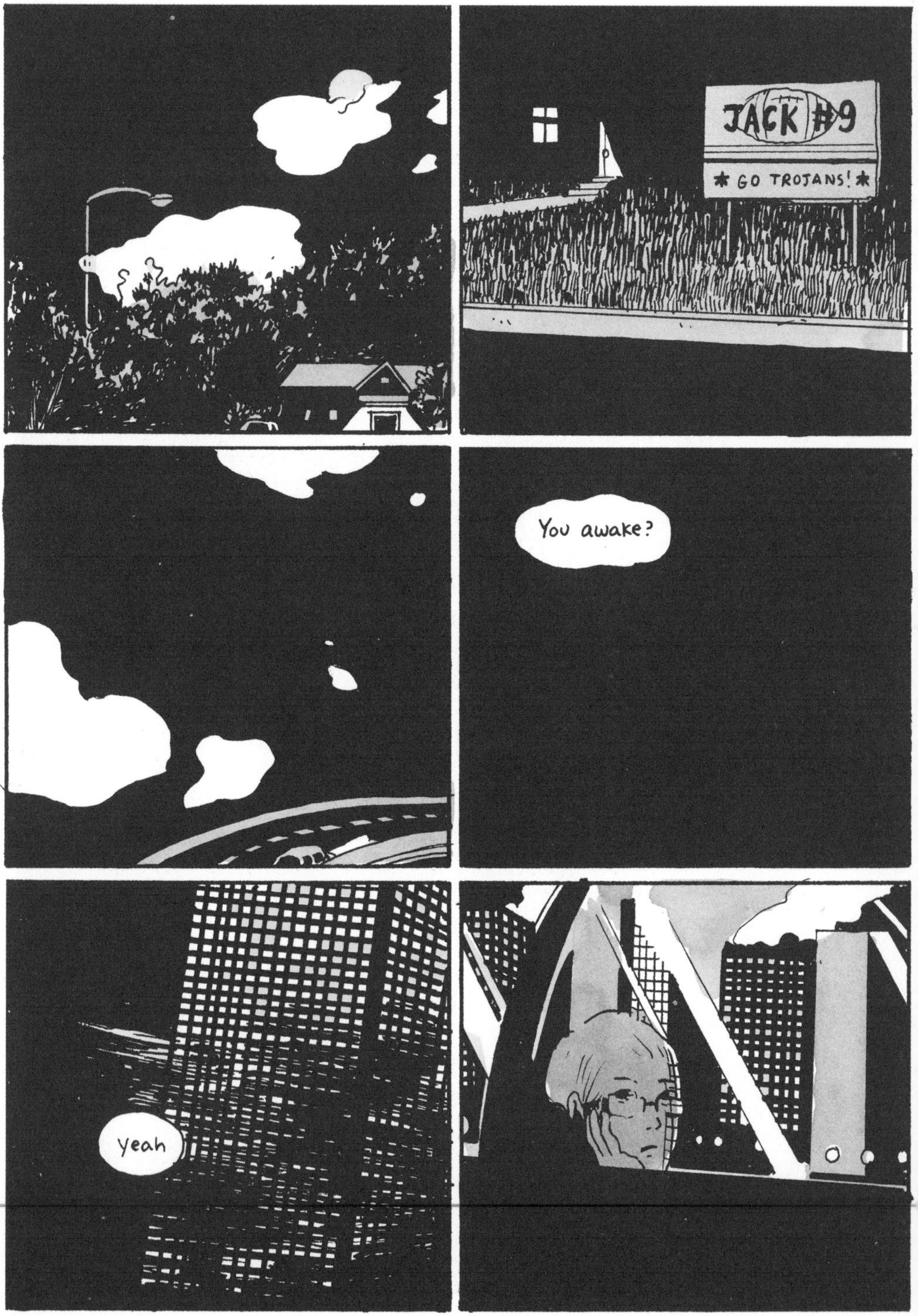
JACK #9
GO TROJANS!
You awake?
yeah

33

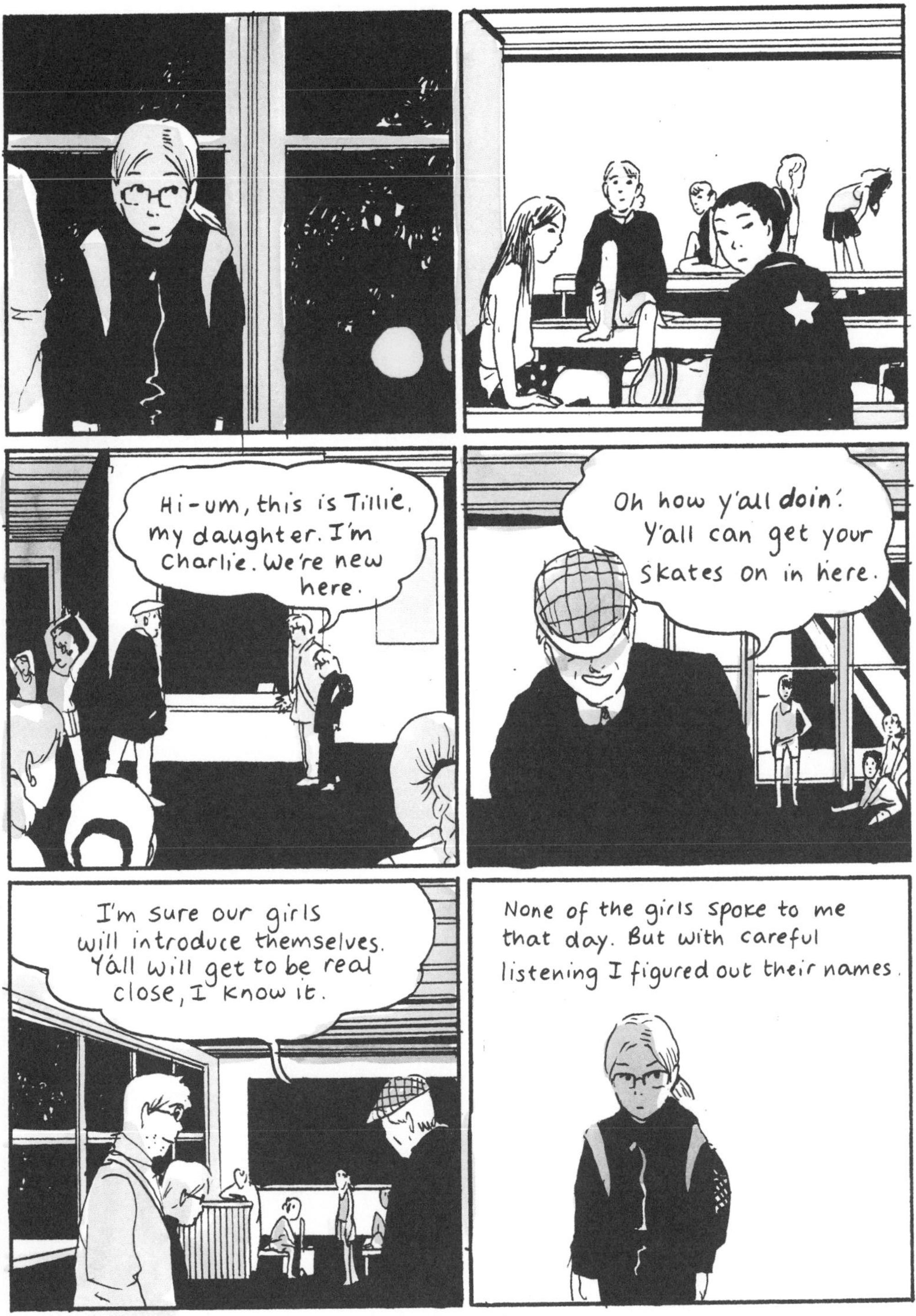
Hi-um, this is Tillie, my daughter. I'm Charlie. We're new here.
Oh how y'all doin'. Y'all can get your skates on in here.
I'm sure our girls will introduce themselves. Y'all will get to be real close, I know it.
None of the girls spoke to me that day. But with careful listening I figured out their names.

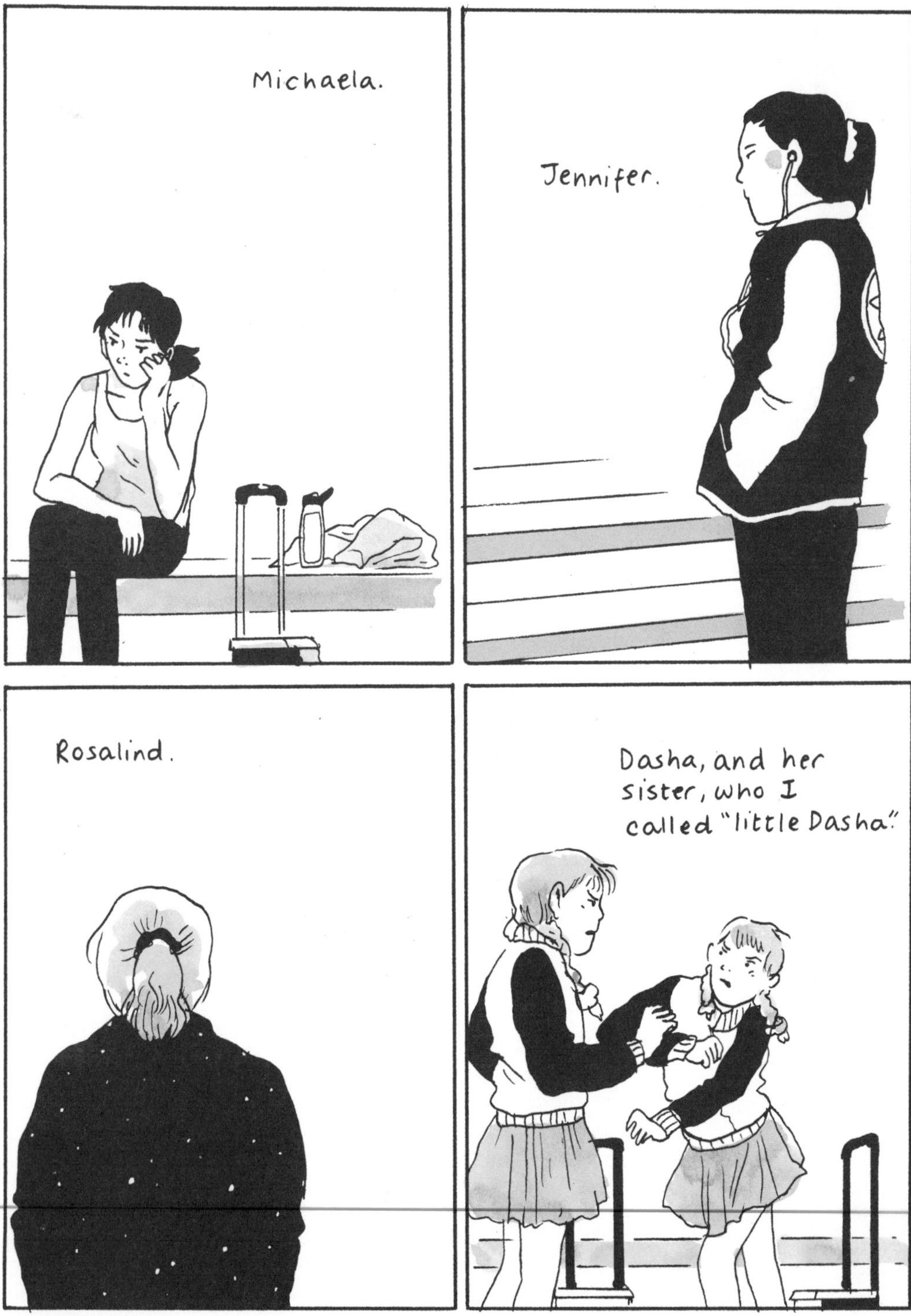
Michaela.
Jennifer.
Rosalind.
Dasha, and her sister, who I called "little Dasha."

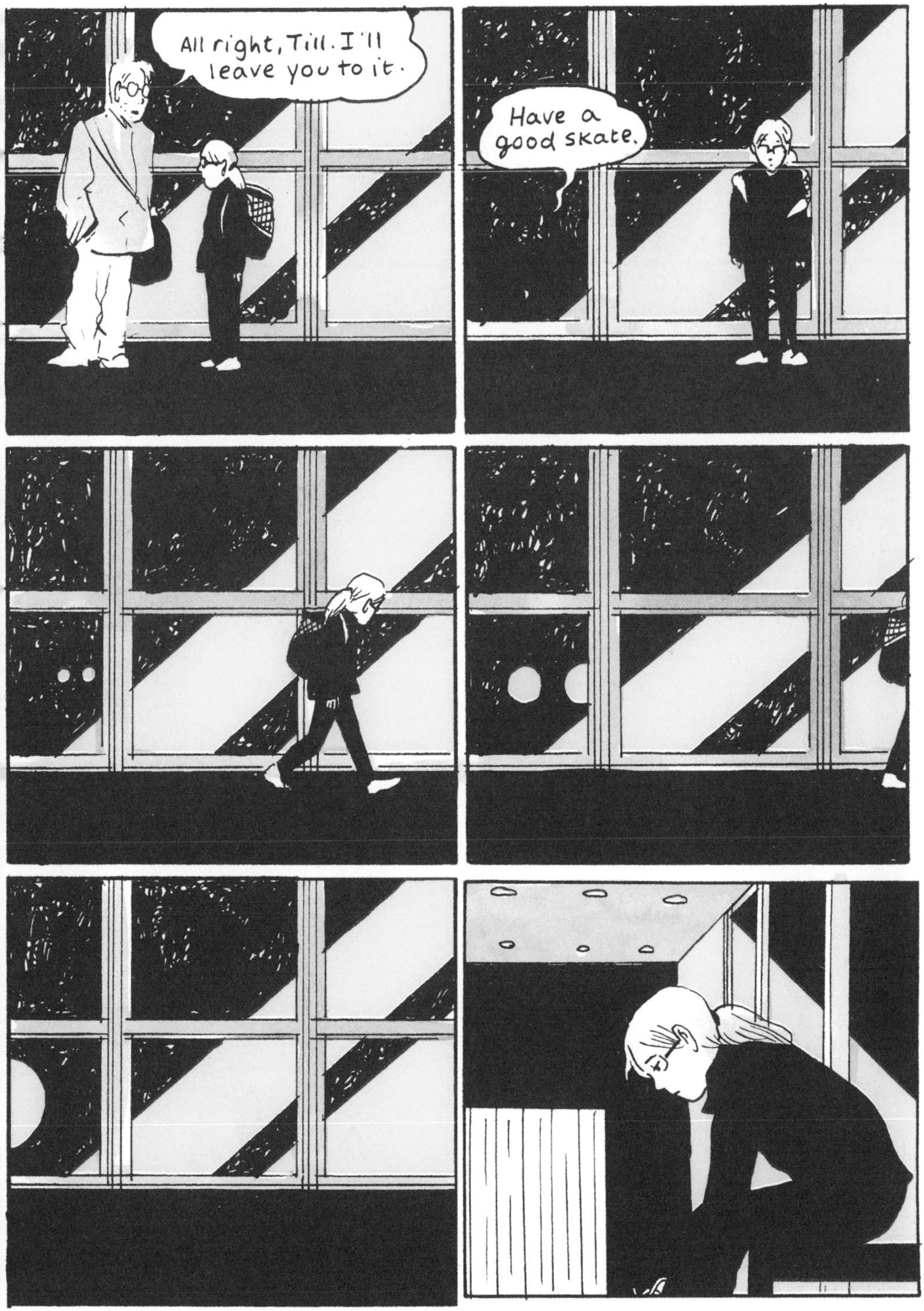
All right, Till. I'll leave you to it.
Have a good skate.

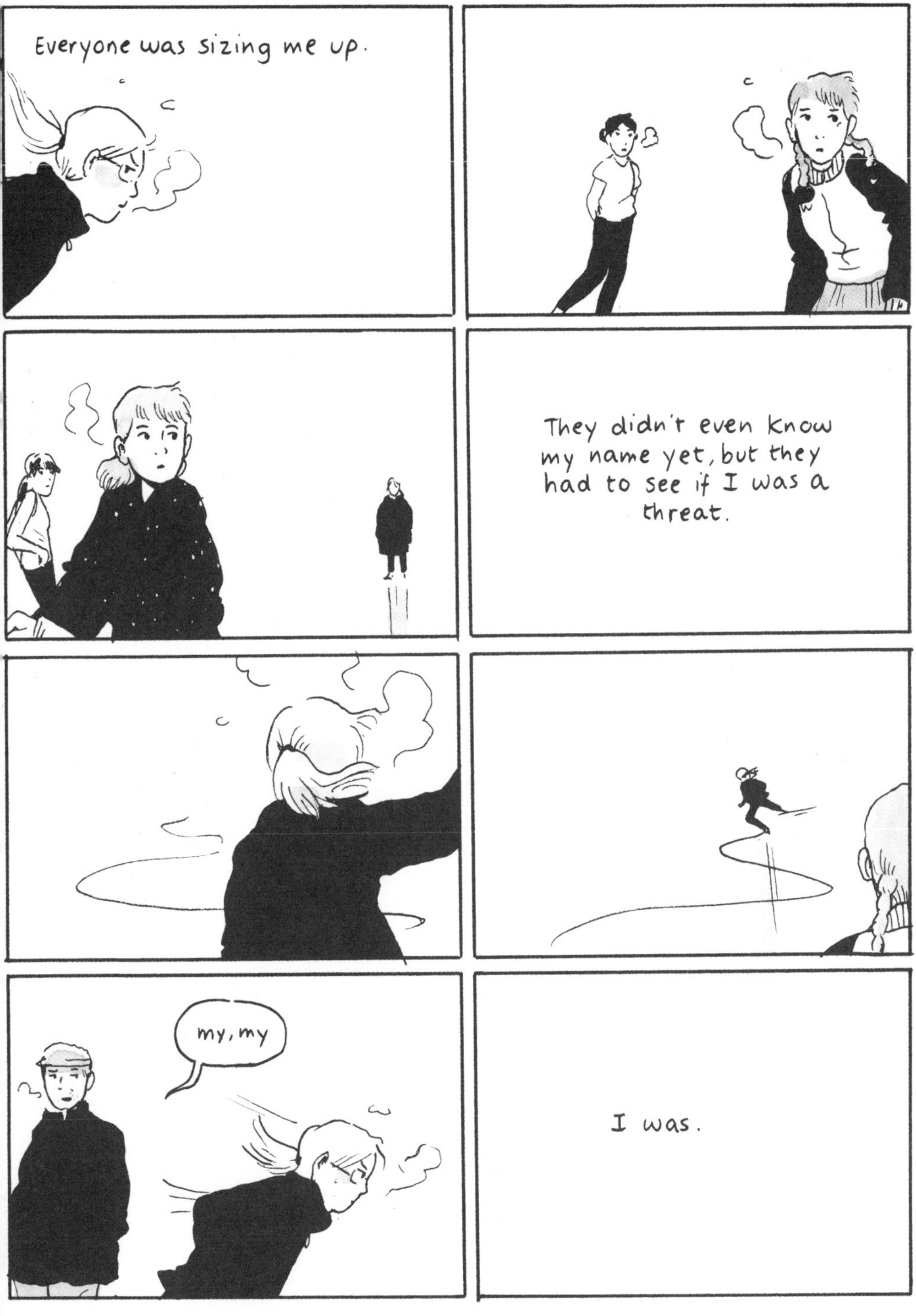
Everyone was sizing me up.
They didn't even know my name yet, but they had to see if I was a threat.
my, my
I was.

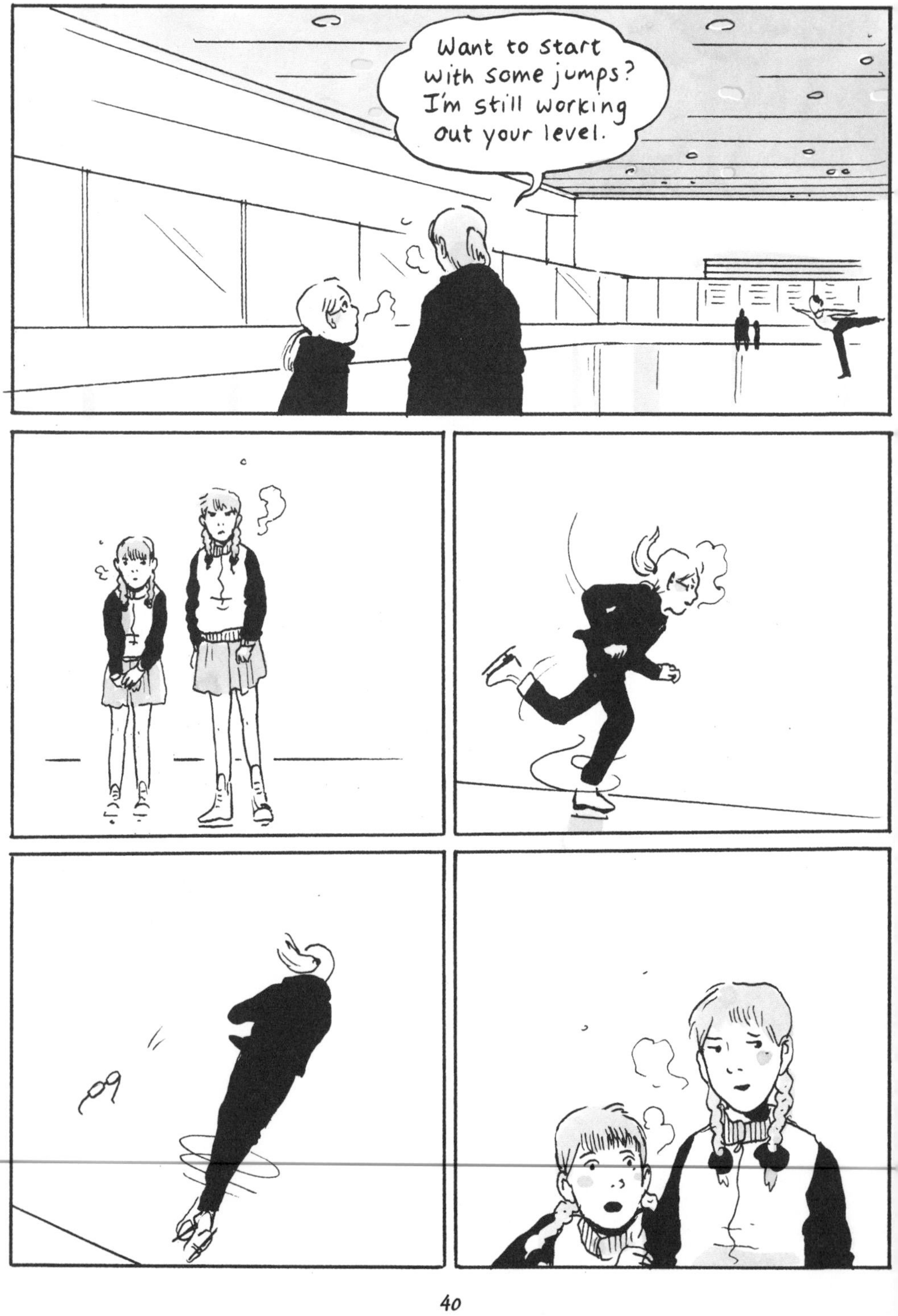
Want to start with some jumps? I'm still working out your level.

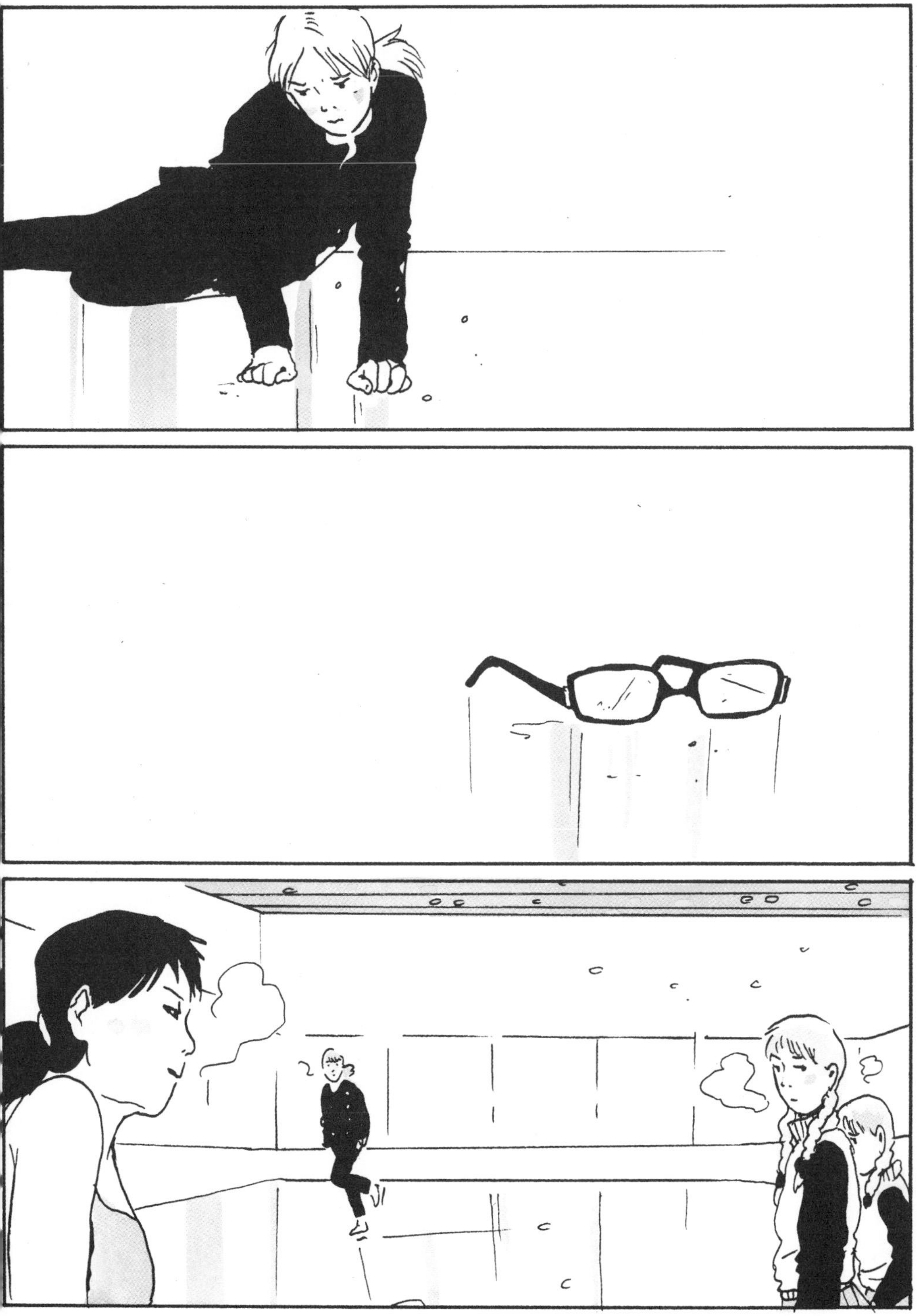

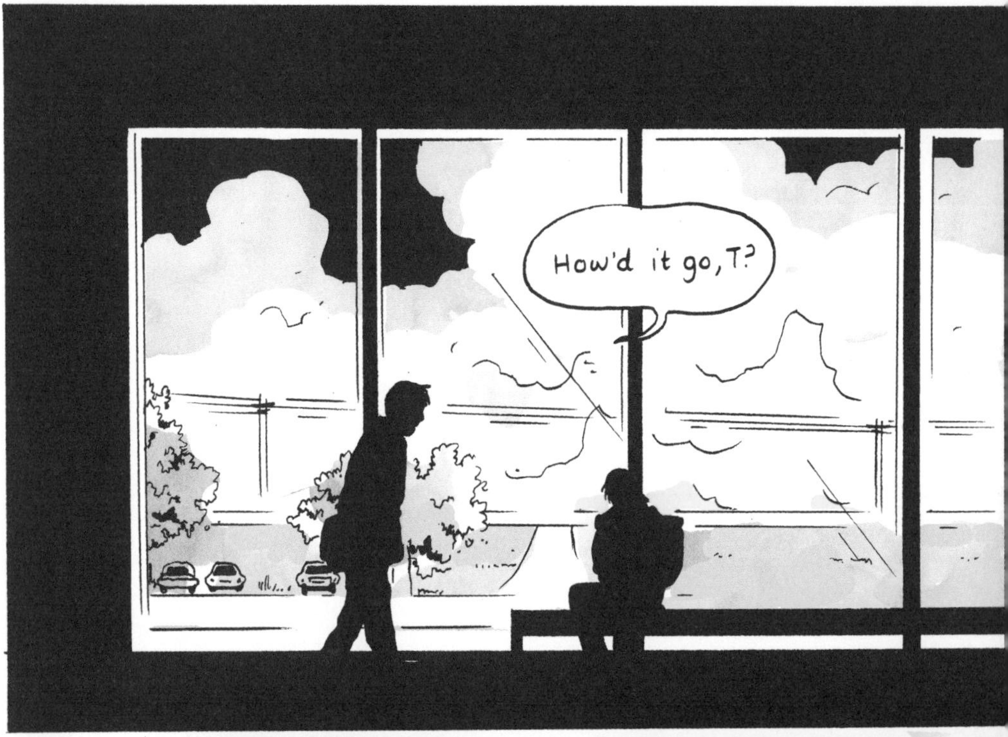
How'd it go, T?
Fine. Let's go.

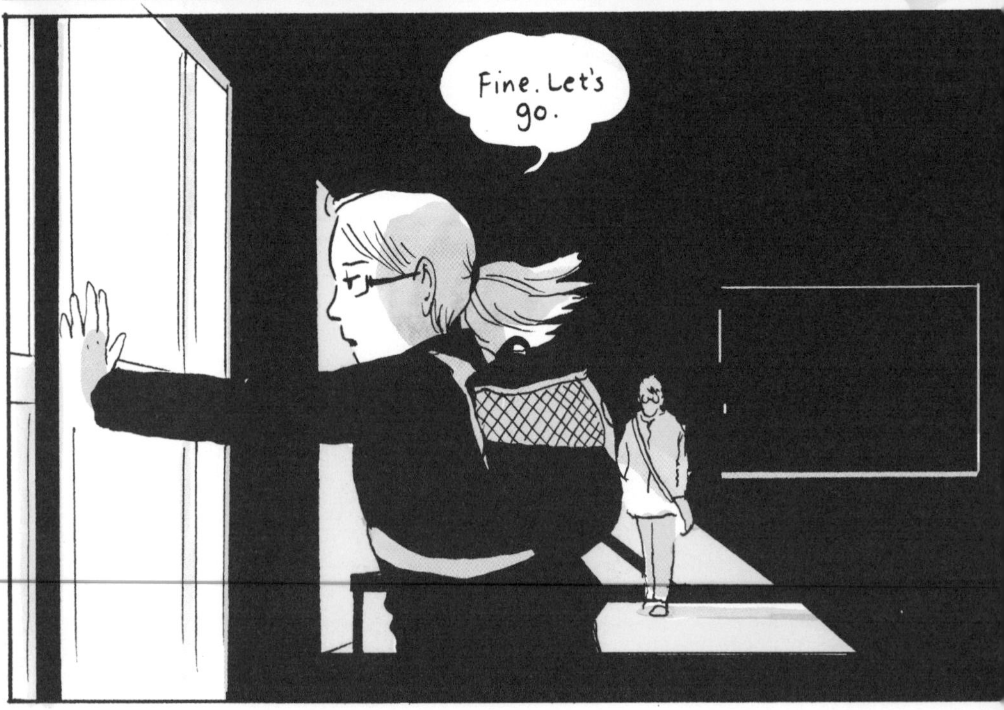

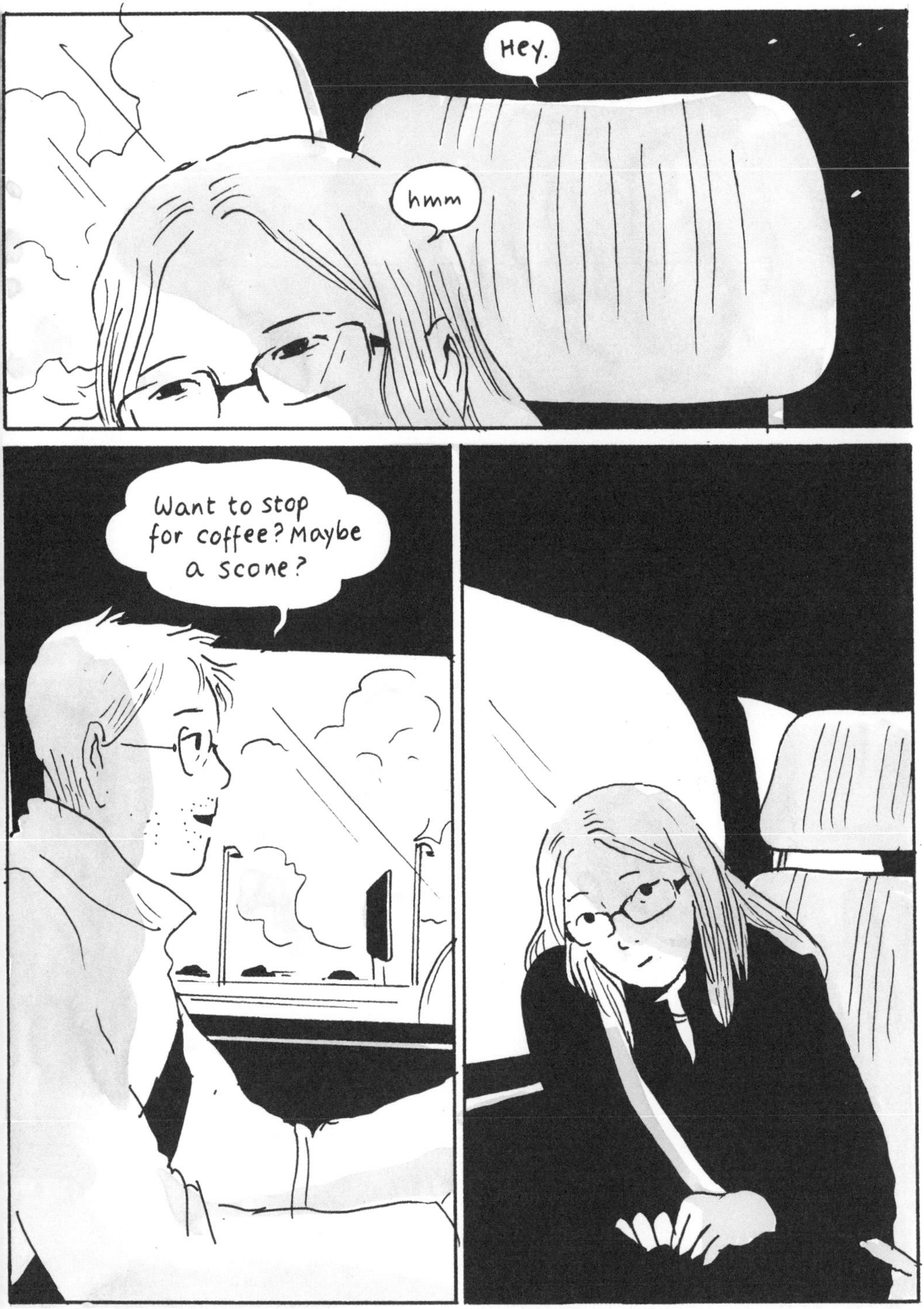
Hey.
hmm
Want to stop for coffee? Maybe a scone?

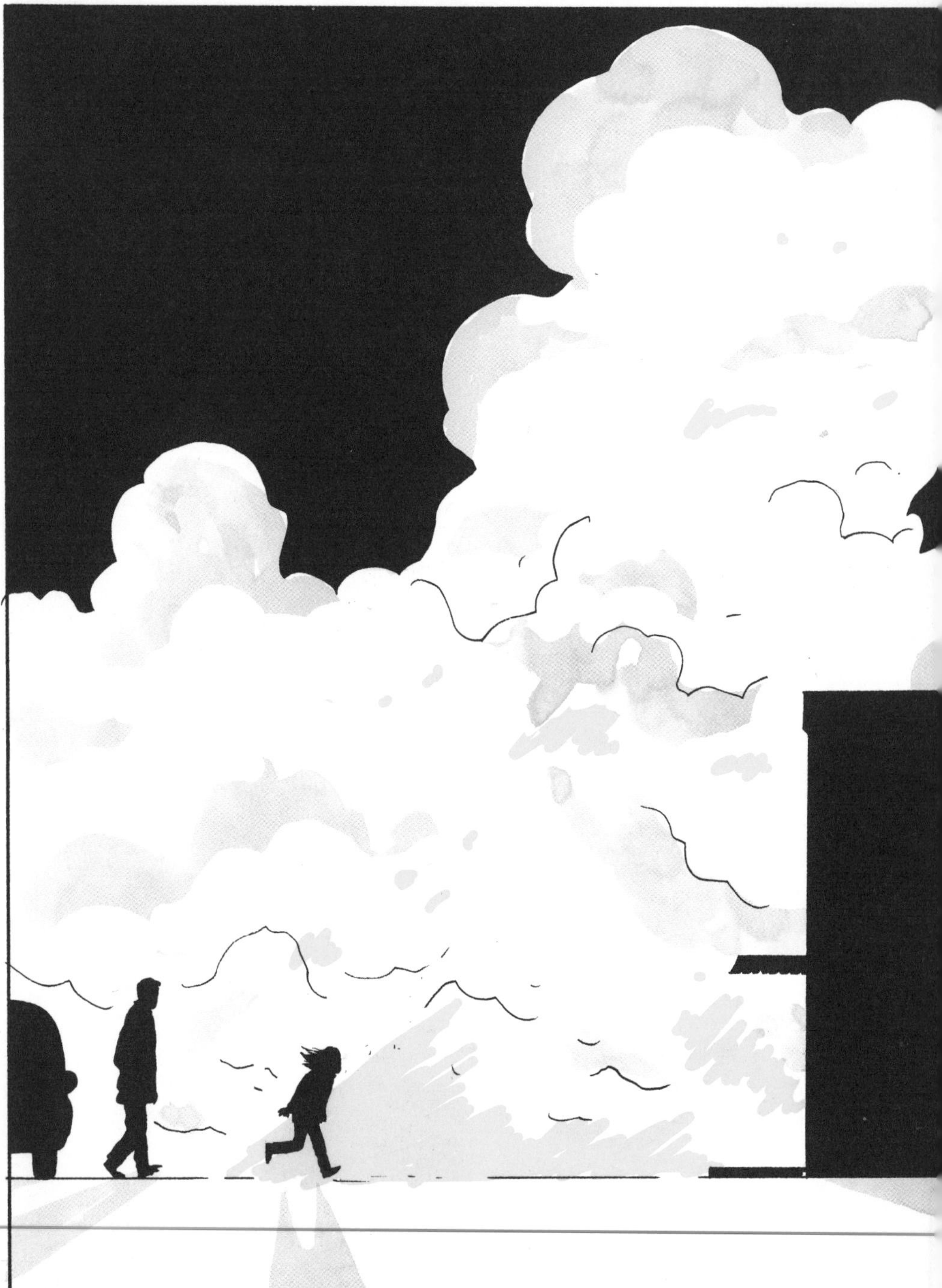

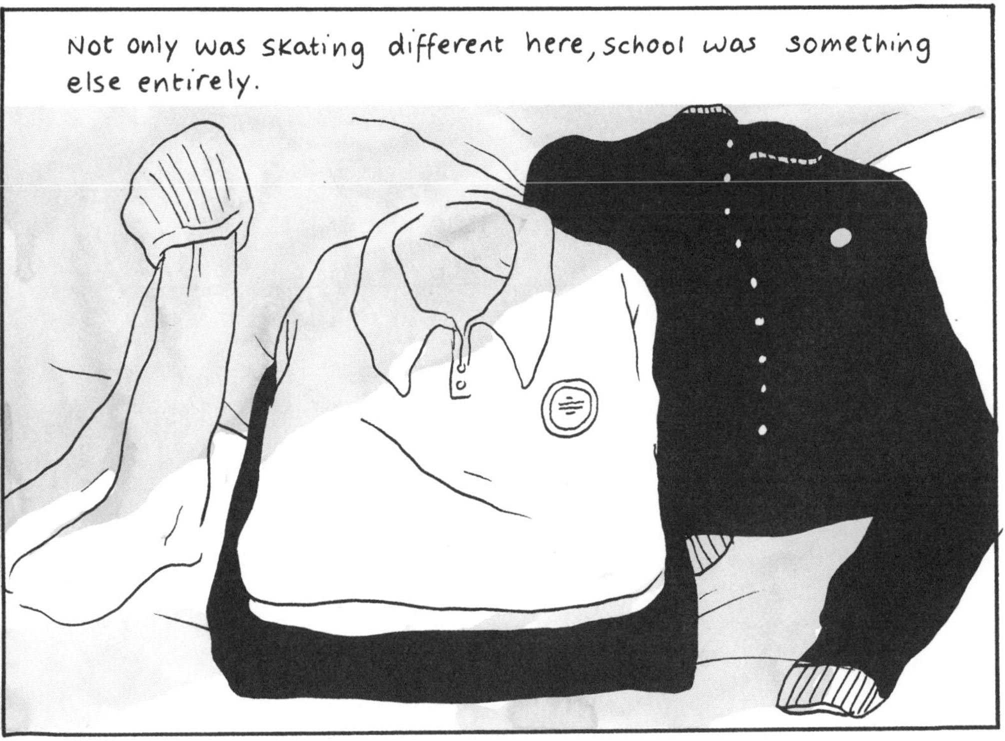
Not only was skating different here, school was something else entirely.

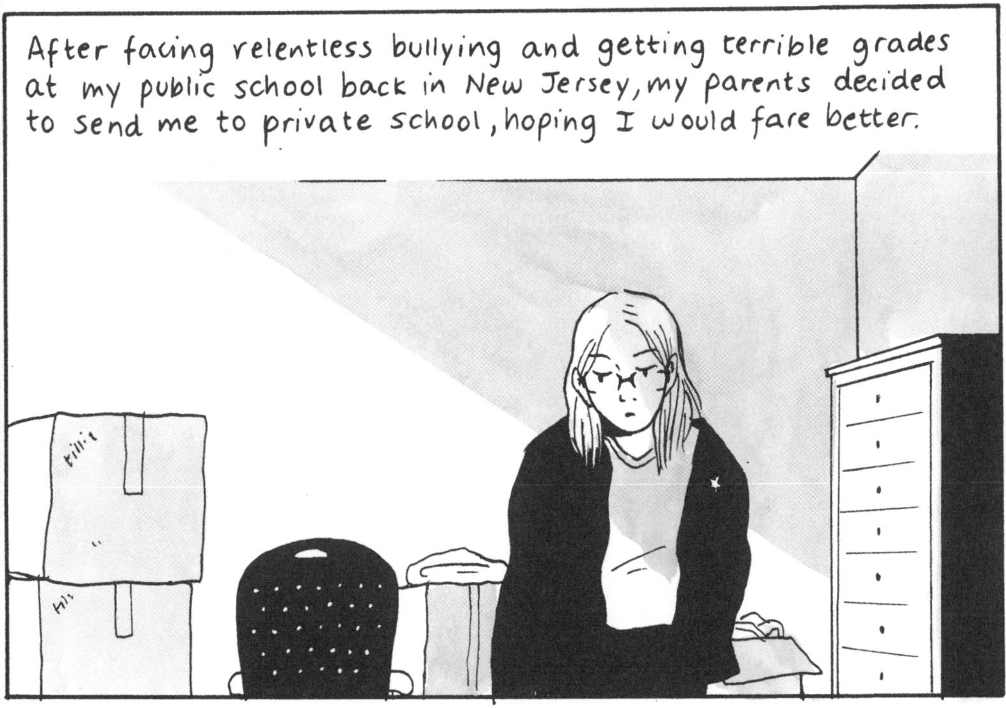
After facing relentless bullying and getting terrible grades at my public school back in New Jersey, my parents decided to send me to private school, hoping I would fare better.

What class?

What?

Oh - 6th grade math, I think.

Follow me.

49

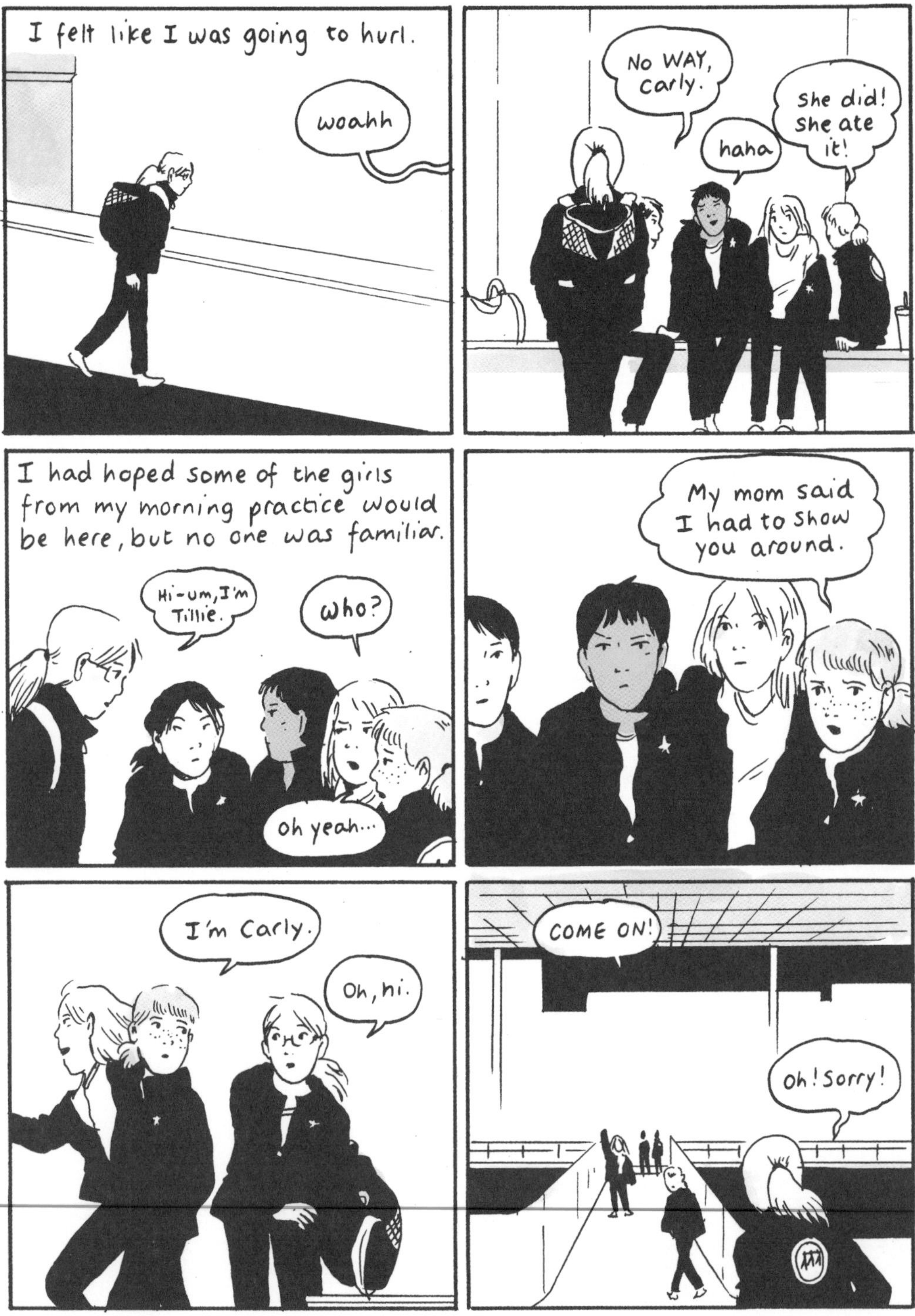
I felt like I was going to hurl.
woahh
No WAY, Carly.
haha
She did! She ate it!
I had hoped some of the girls from my morning practice would be here, but no one was familiar.
Hi-um, I'm Tillie.
who?
oh yeah...
My mom said I had to show you around.
I'm Carly.
Oh, hi.
COME ON!
Oh! Sorry!

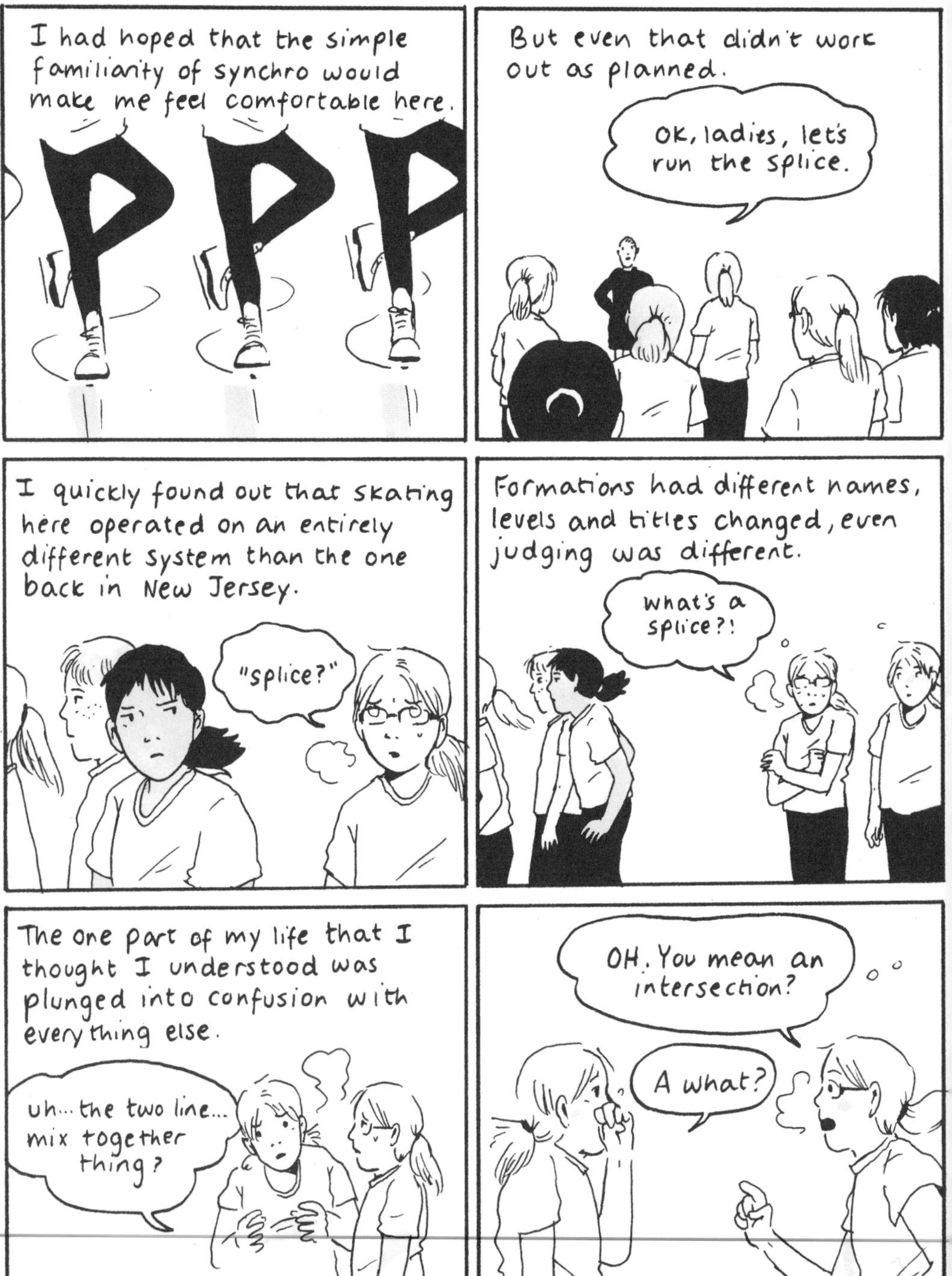
I had hoped that the simple familiarity of synchro would make me feel comfortable here.
But even that didn't work out as planned.
OK, ladies, let's run the splice.
I quickly found out that skating here operated on an entirely different system than the one back in New Jersey.
"splice?"
Formations had different names, levels and titles changed, even judging was different.
what's a splice?!
The one part of my life that I thought I understood was plunged into confusion with everything else.
uh... the two line... mix together thing?
OH. You mean an intersection?
A what?

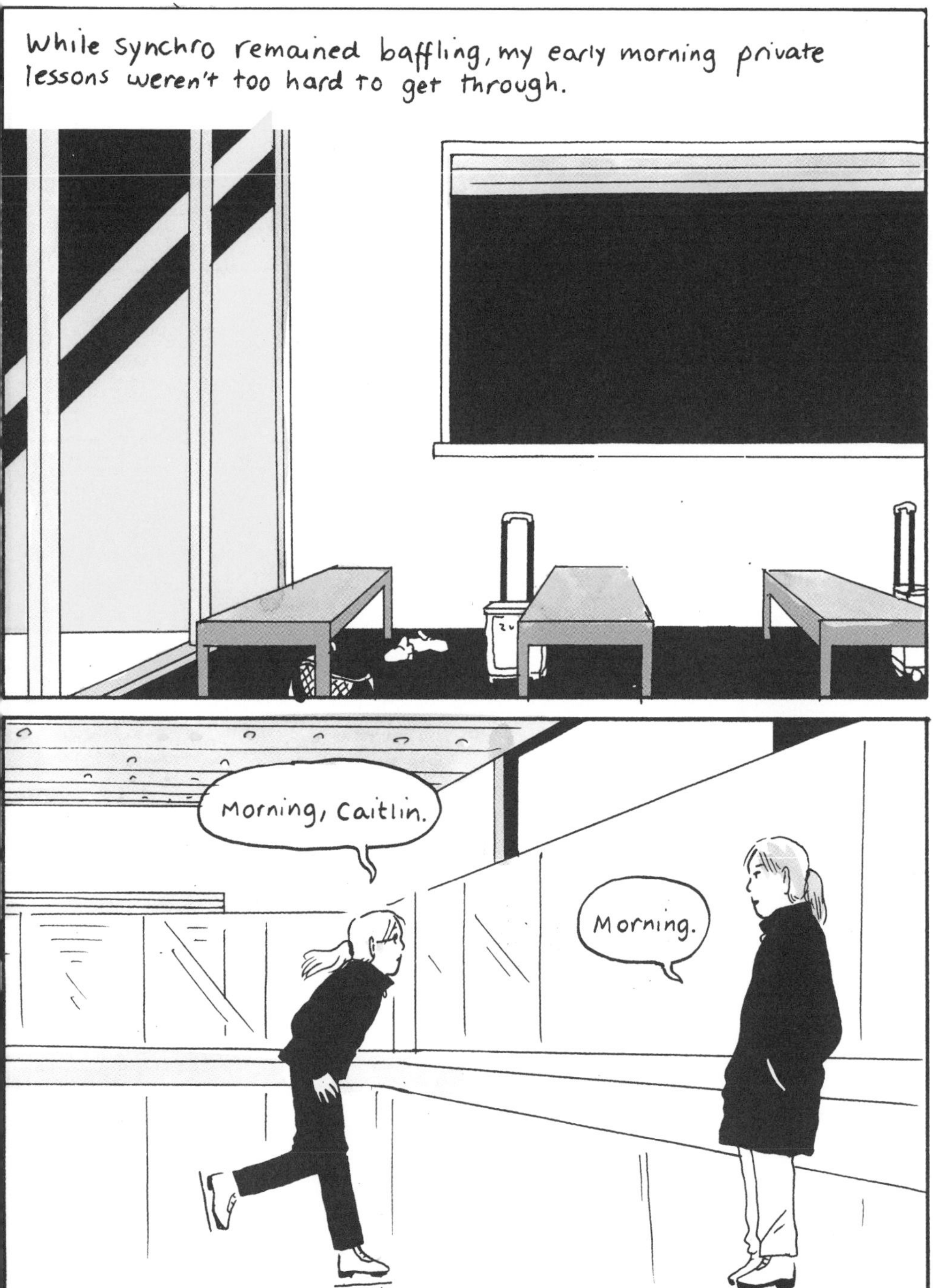
While synchro remained baffling, my early morning private lessons weren't too hard to get through.
Morning, Caitlin.
Morning.

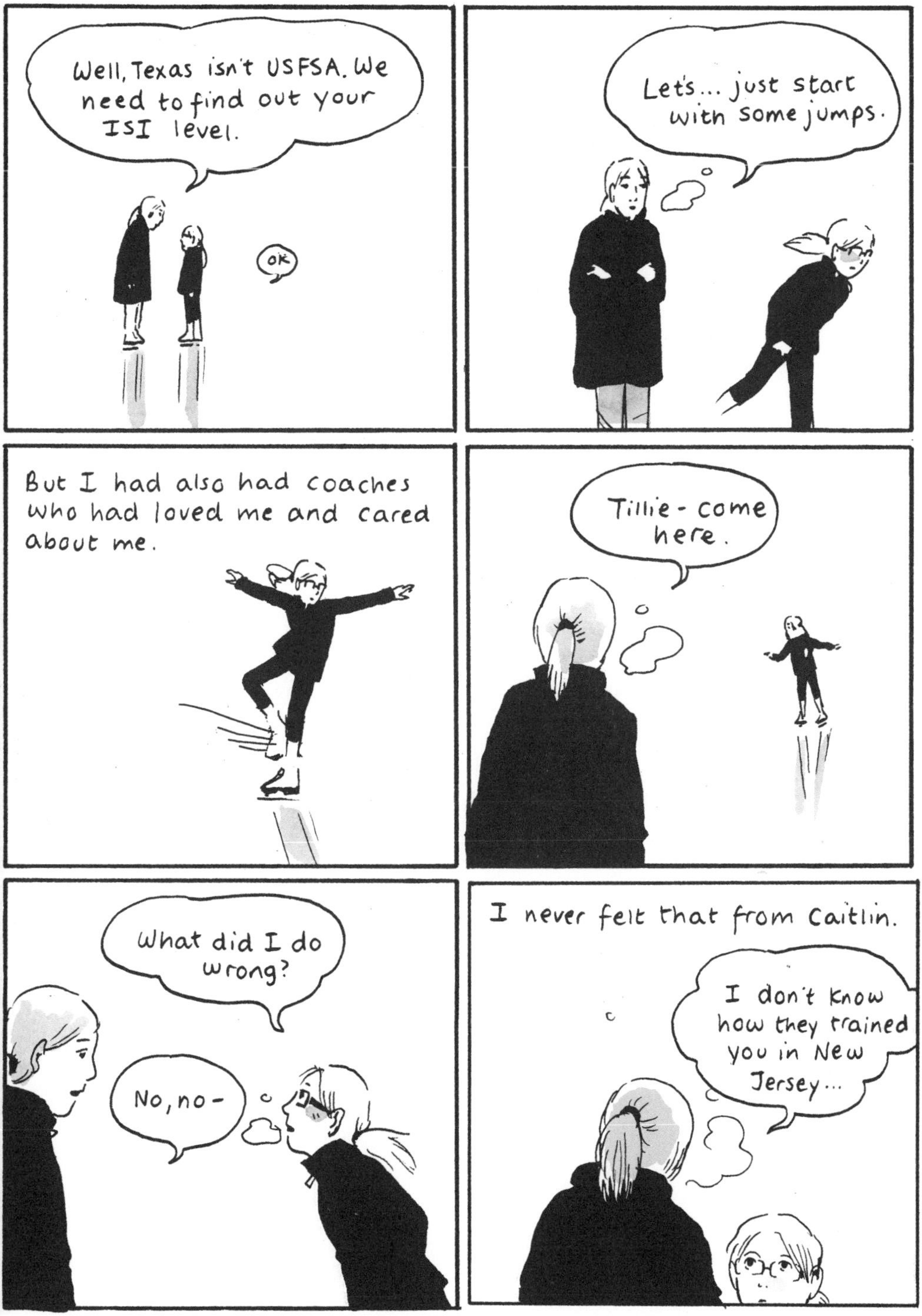
Well, Texas isn't USFSA. We need to find out your ISI level.
ok
Let's... just start with some jumps.
But I had also had coaches who had loved me and cared about me.
Tillie - come here.
What did I do wrong?
No, no-
I never felt that from Caitlin.
I don't know how they trained you in New Jersey...

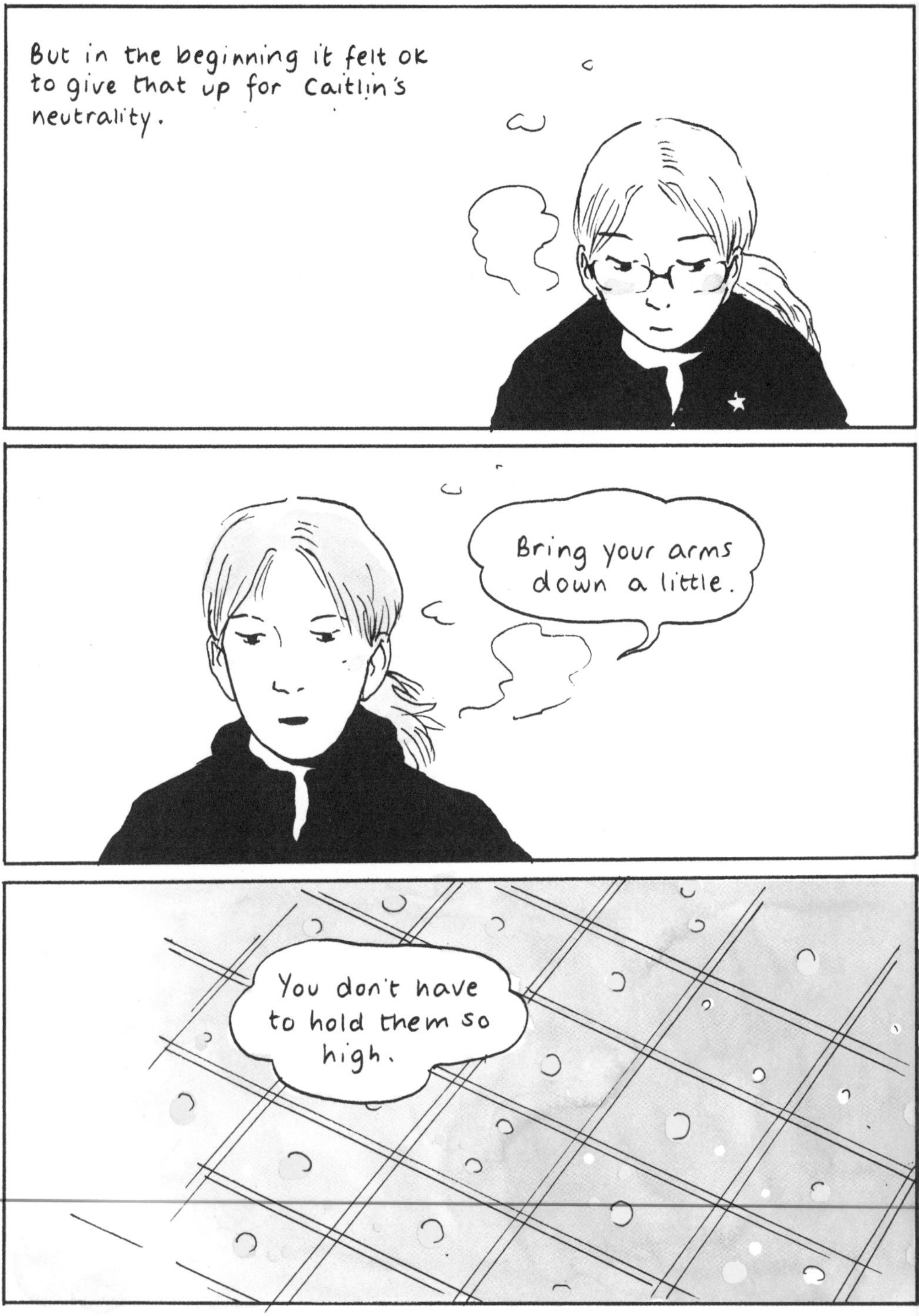
But in the beginning it felt ok to give that up for Caitlin's neutrality.
Bring your arms down a little.
You don't have to hold them so high.

After training with Caitlin for a
few months, I took my first Texas test at a
scrubby rink in Dallas.

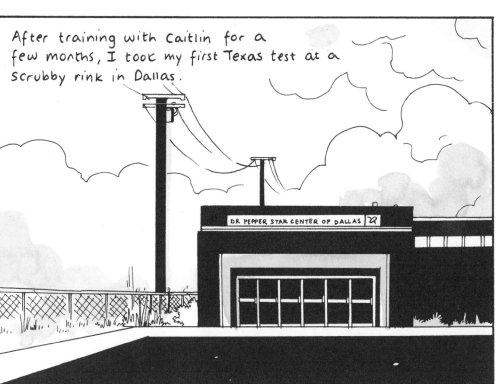

Testing determined my group at competition. It was also
an experience a skater always went through with their coach.
My first test with Caitlin felt like a milestone. She was
by my side now, and memories of old coaches no longer
had a place.

I'd perform five-six moves, pausing between each one.

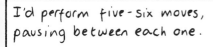

The pauses killed me. Silence would fill the rink.

The judges would have their heads down, scribbling their comments.

My coach, blurry and far away.

I'd feel my lungs swallowing frigid air, trying to keep up,

and my face and arms would prickle with cold sweat.

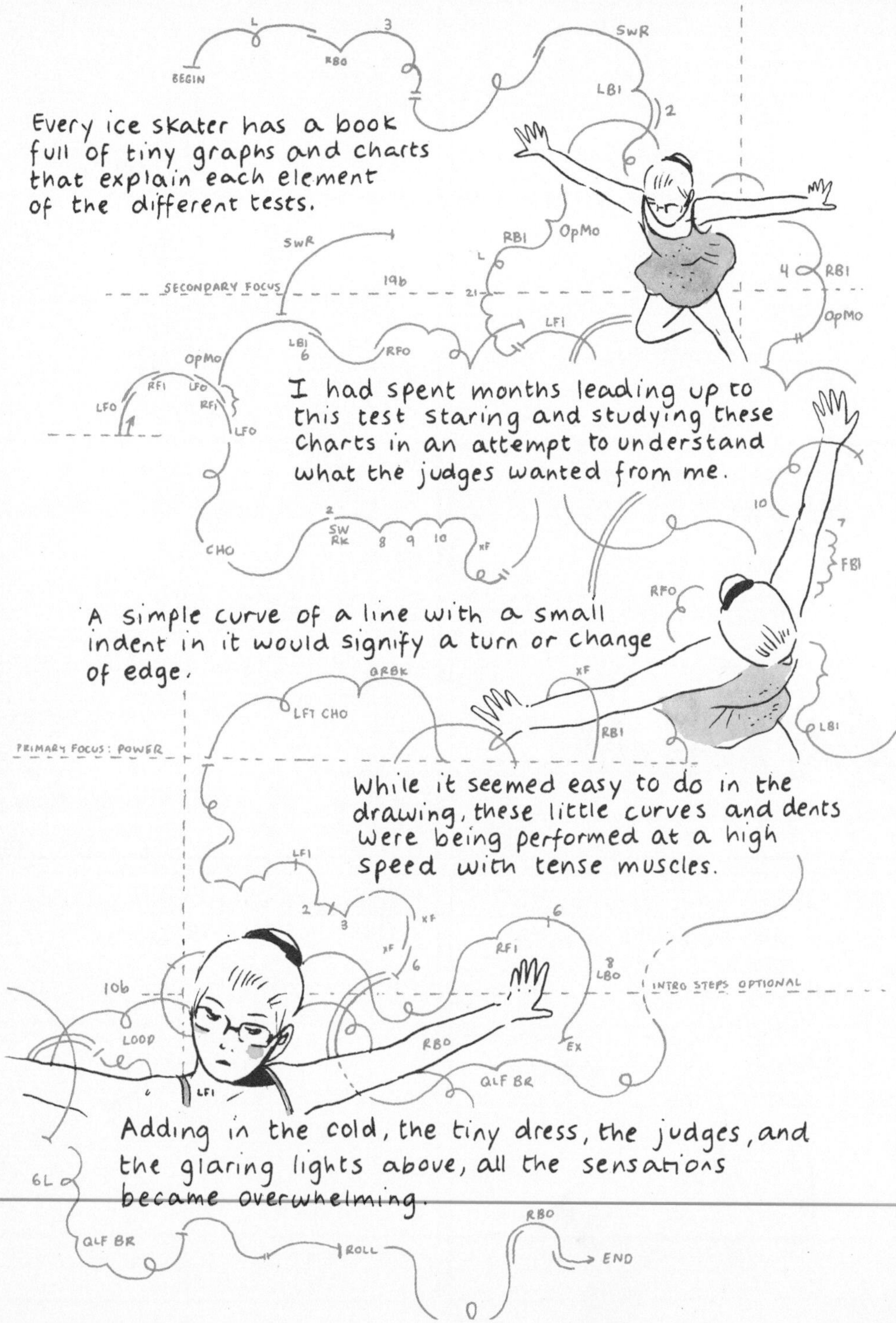
Every ice skater has a book full of tiny graphs and charts that explain each element of the different tests.
I had spent months leading up to this test staring and studying these charts in an attempt to understand what the judges wanted from me.
A simple curve of a line with a small indent in it would signify a turn or change of edge.
While it seemed easy to do in the drawing, these little curves and dents were being performed at a high speed with tense muscles.
Adding in the cold, the tiny dress, the judges, and the glaring lights above, all the sensations became overwhelming.
BEGIN
RBO
SWR
LBI
SECONDARY FOCUS
OpMo
RBI
LFI
RFO
LFO
CHO
PRIMARY FOCUS: POWER
LFT CHO
INTRO STEPS OPTIONAL
LOOP
QLF BR
ROLL
END

LCO
RFI
LFI
RBO
6B
OPMO
RBO
LFI
RBO
LFI
CHO
7x
LFI

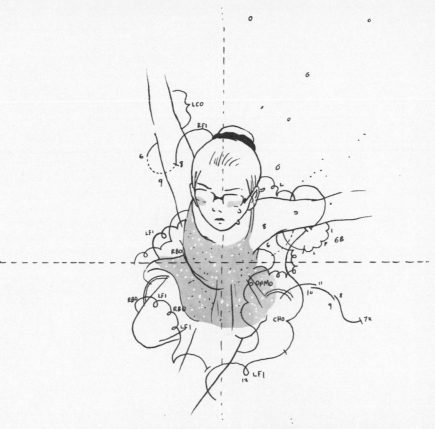

Testing felt like a prolonged spasm. My muscles were trying to recreate perfect shapes and angles while my mind churned through images and memories of the moves.

But that was how it felt. To me, that was ice skating. It wasn't large jumps or sweeping glides. It was intricate patterns and minute details under the veil of makeup and freezing air.

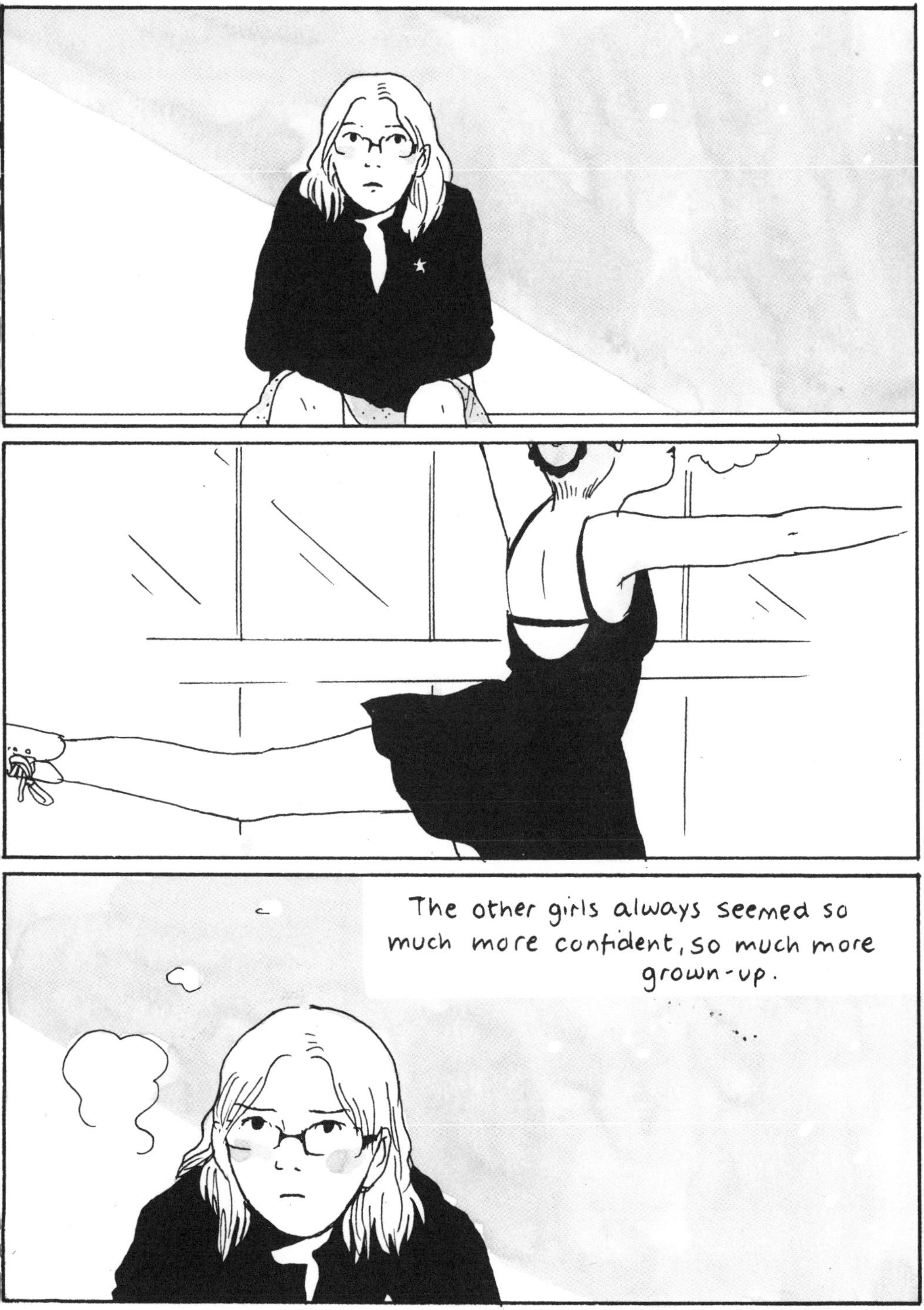
The other girls always seemed so much more confident, so much more grown-up.

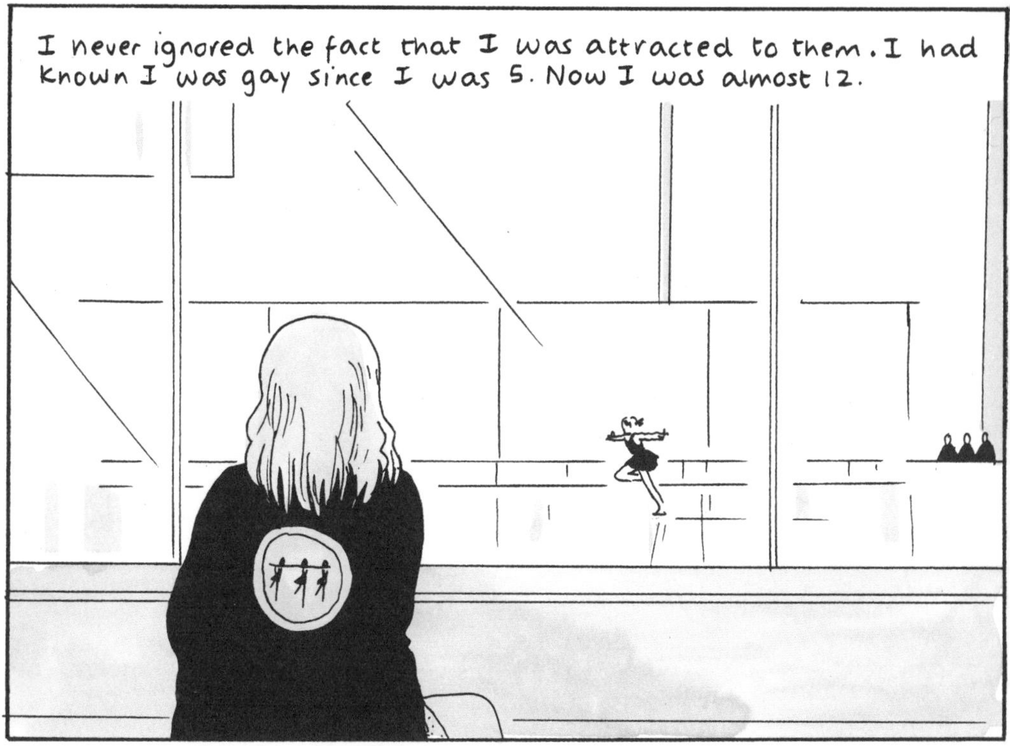
I never ignored the fact that I was attracted to them. I had Known I was gay since I was 5. Now I was almost 12.

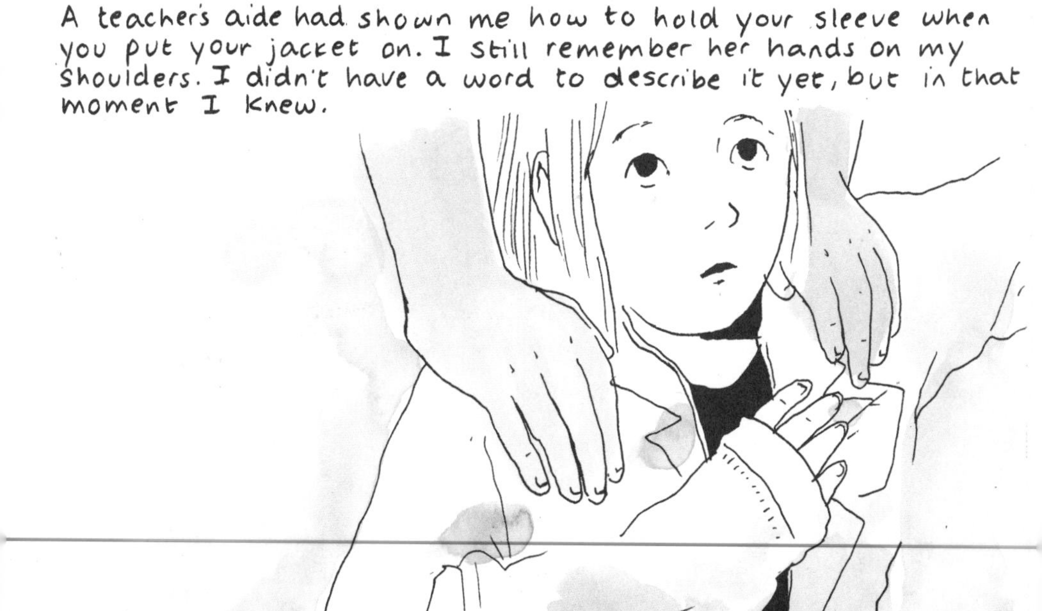
A teacher's aide had shown me how to hold your sleeve when you put your jacket on. I still remember her hands on my shoulders. I didn't have a word to describe it yet, but in that moment I Knew.

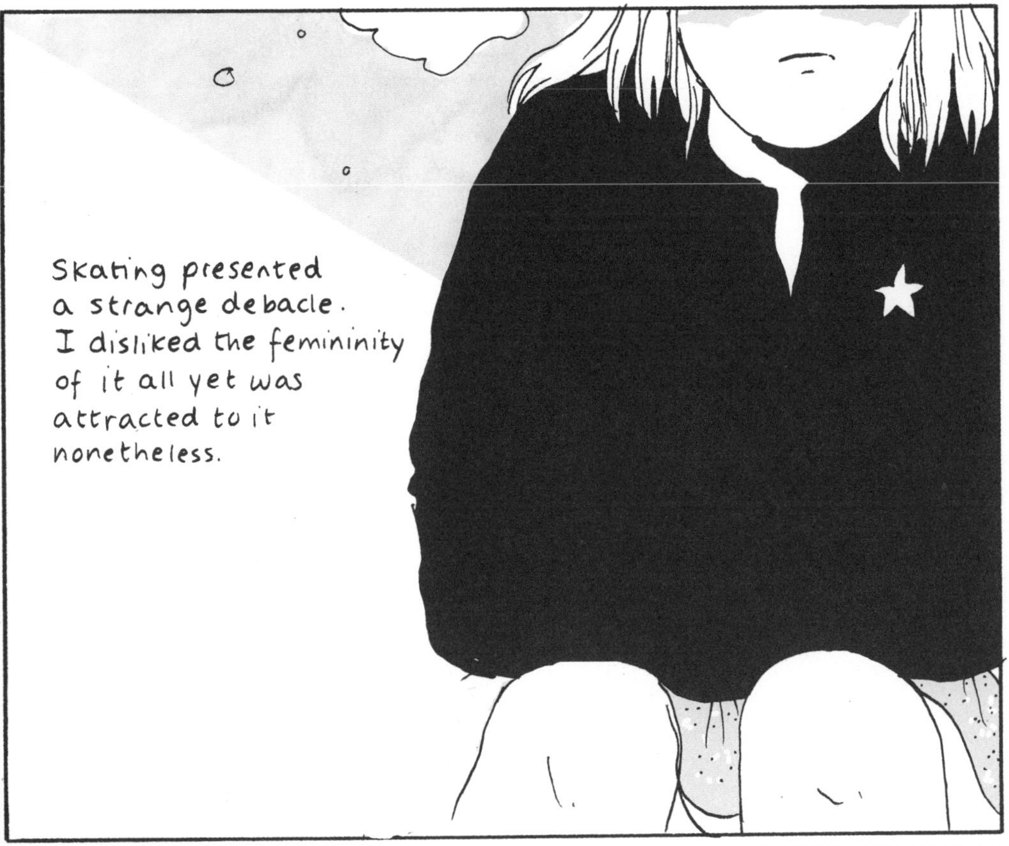
Skating presented a strange debacle. I disliked the femininity of it all yet was attracted to it nonetheless.

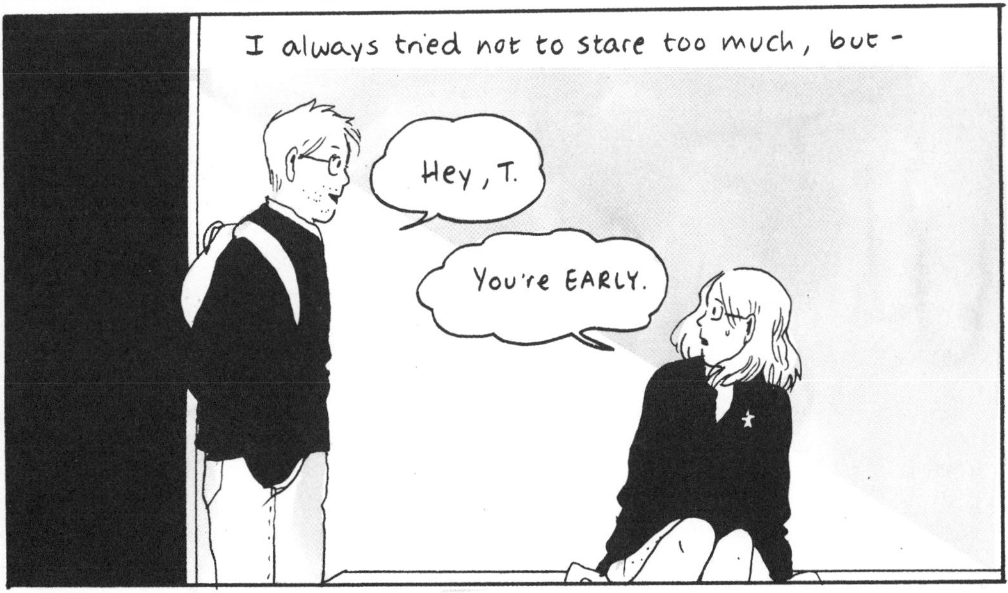
I always tried not to stare too much, but -
Hey, T.
You're EARLY.

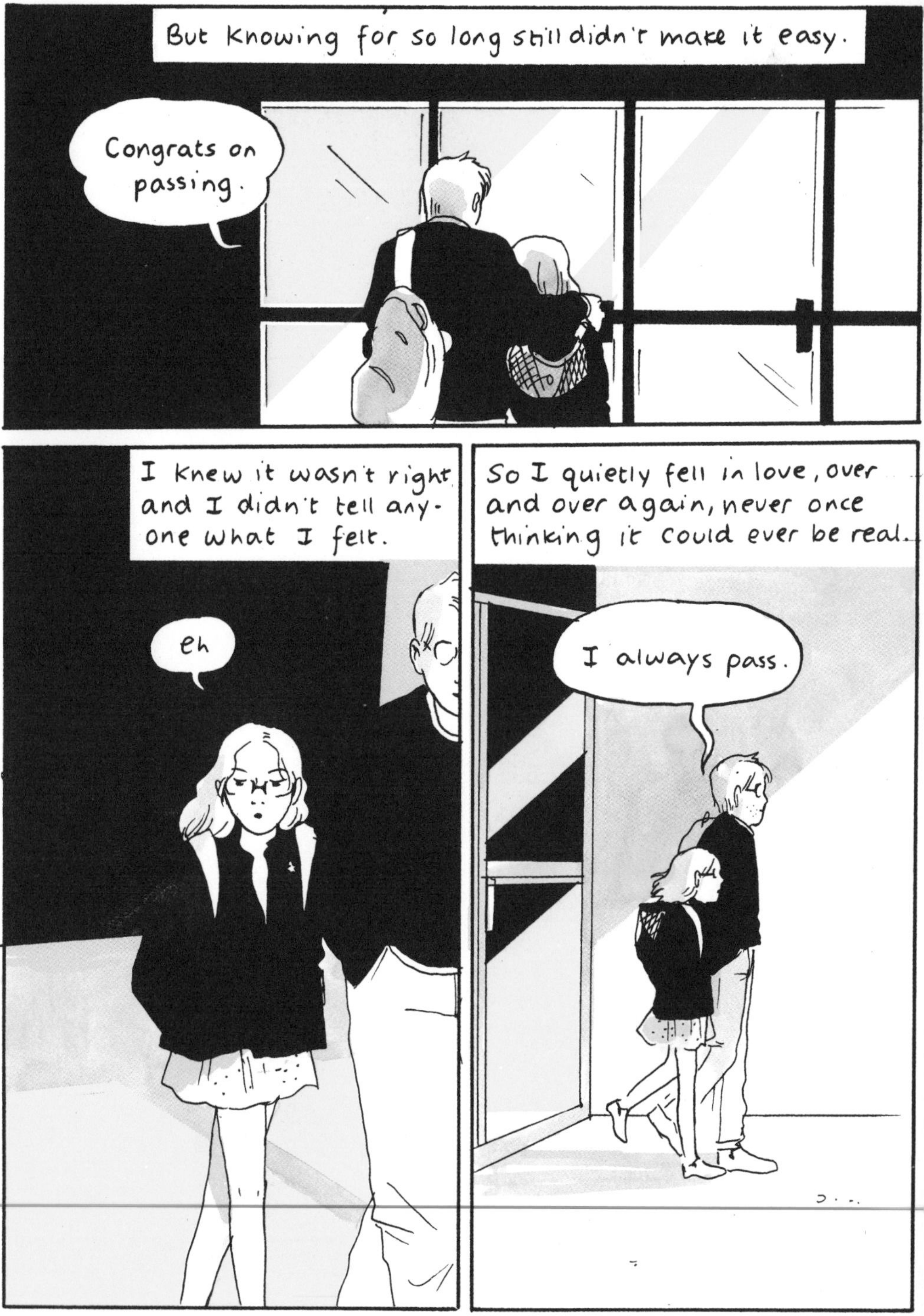
But knowing for so long still didn't make it easy.
Congrats on passing.
I knew it wasn't right and I didn't tell any-one what I felt.
eh
So I quietly fell in love, over and over again, never once thinking it could ever be real.
I always pass.

3

FLIP JUMP

I loved flips. You would launch
yourself into the air by slamming
the tip of your blade into the ice.

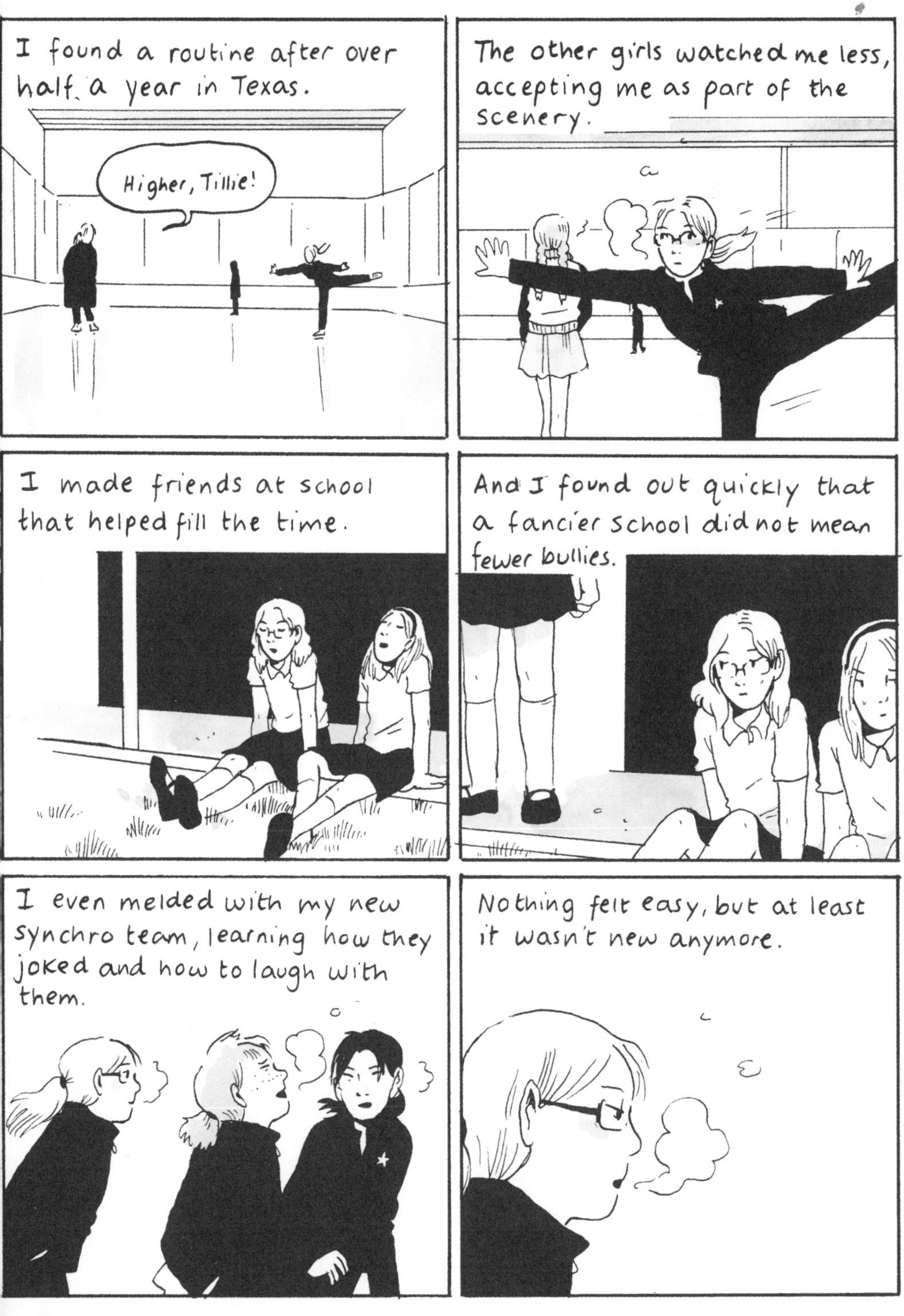
I found a routine after over half a year in Texas.
Higher, Tillie!
The other girls watched me less, accepting me as part of the scenery.
I made friends at school that helped fill the time.
And I found out quickly that a fancier school did not mean fewer bullies.
I even melded with my new synchro team, learning how they joked and how to laugh with them.
Nothing felt easy, but at least it wasn't new anymore.

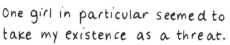
One girl in particular seemed to take my existence as a threat.

Grace.

CRACK

She was vicious to everyone, and in a tiny school there was no escape.

You okay?

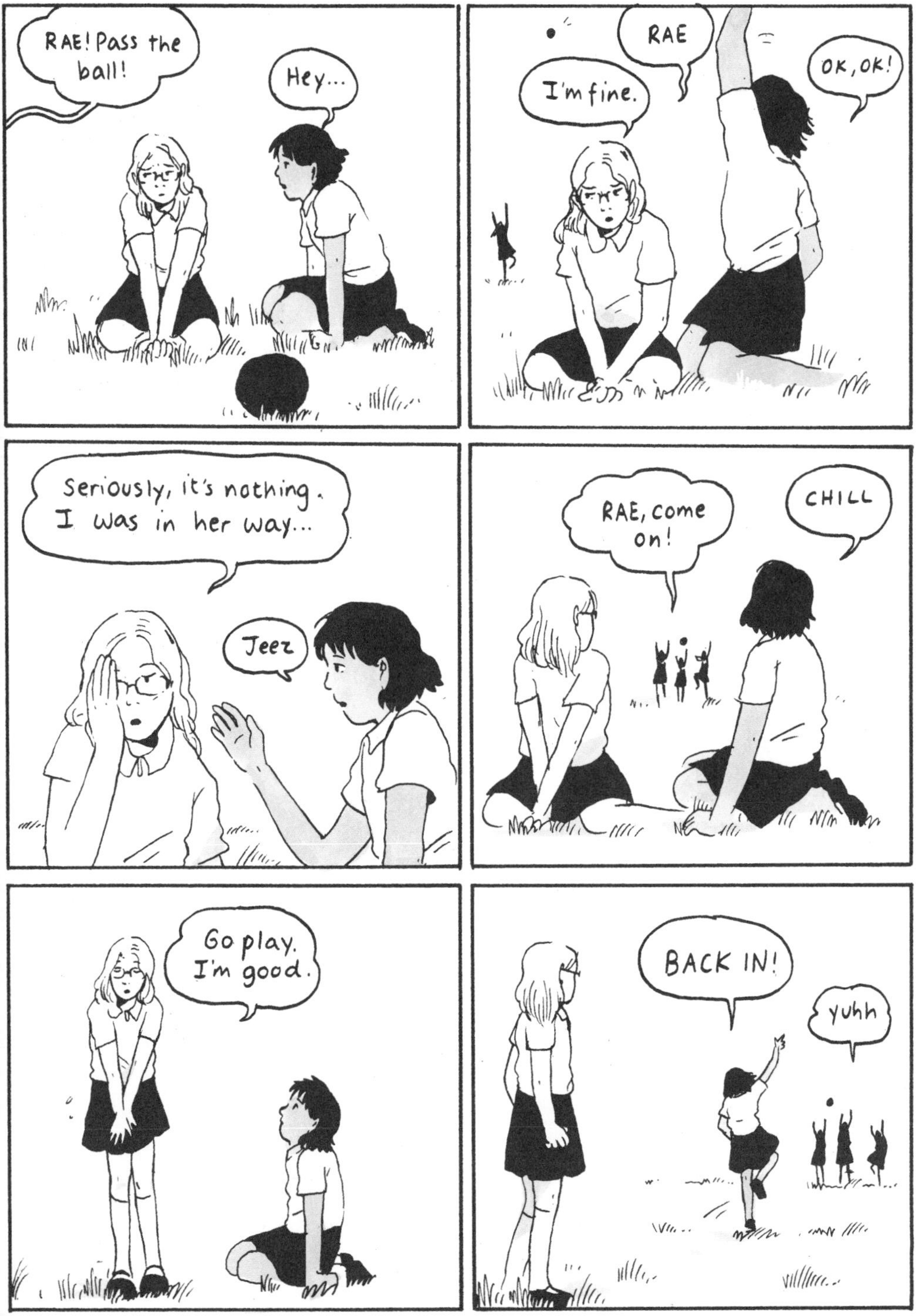
RAE! Pass the ball!
Hey...
RAE
I'm fine.
OK, OK!
Seriously, it's nothing. I was in her way...
Jeez
RAE, come on!
CHILL
Go play. I'm good.
BACK IN!
yuhh

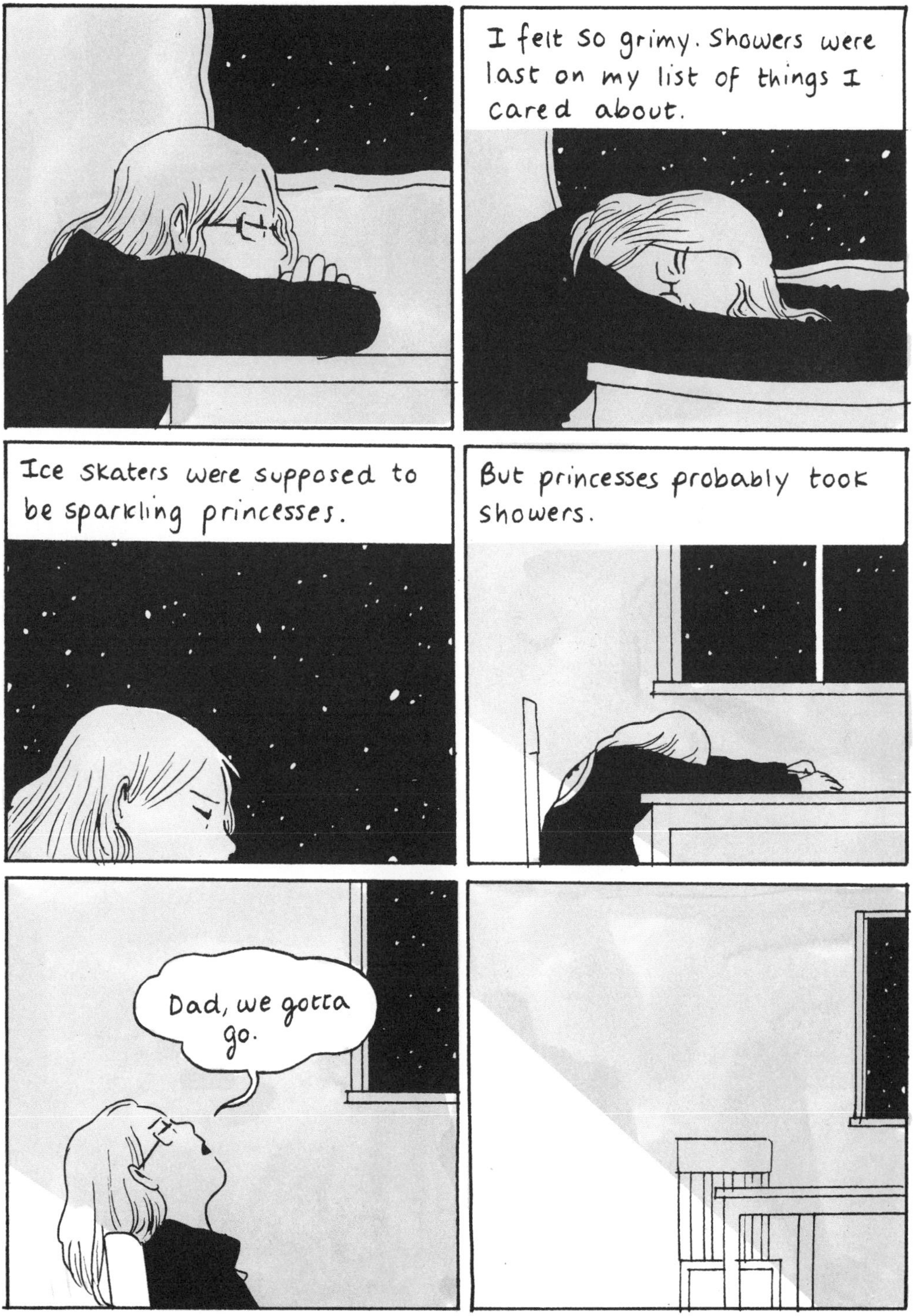
I felt so grimy. Showers were last on my list of things I cared about.
Ice skaters were supposed to be sparkling princesses.
But princesses probably took showers.
Dad, we gotta go.

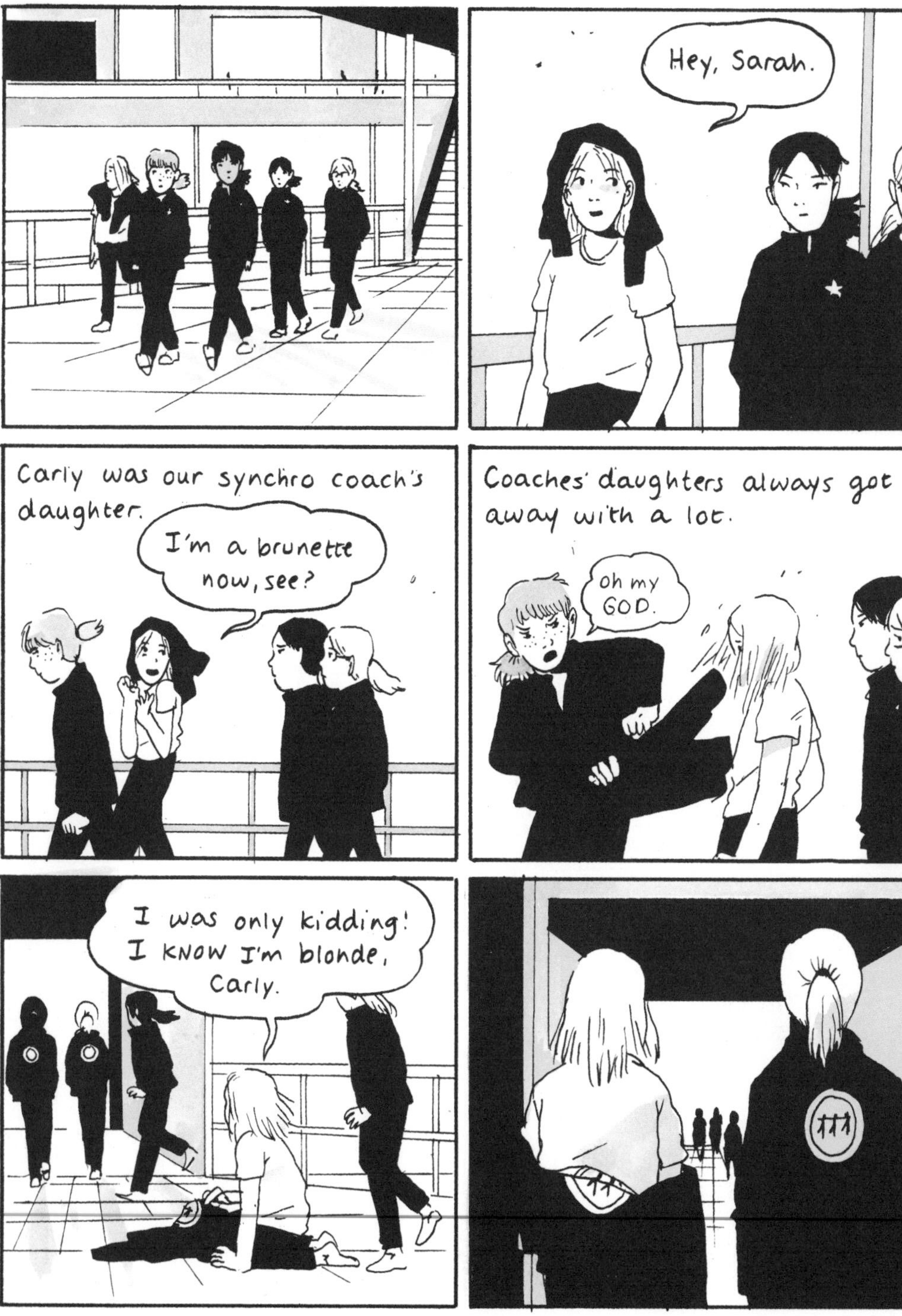
Hey, Sarah.
Carly was our synchro coach's daughter.
I'm a brunette now, see?
Coaches' daughters always got away with a lot.
oh my GOD.
I was only kidding! I KNOW I'm blonde, Carly.

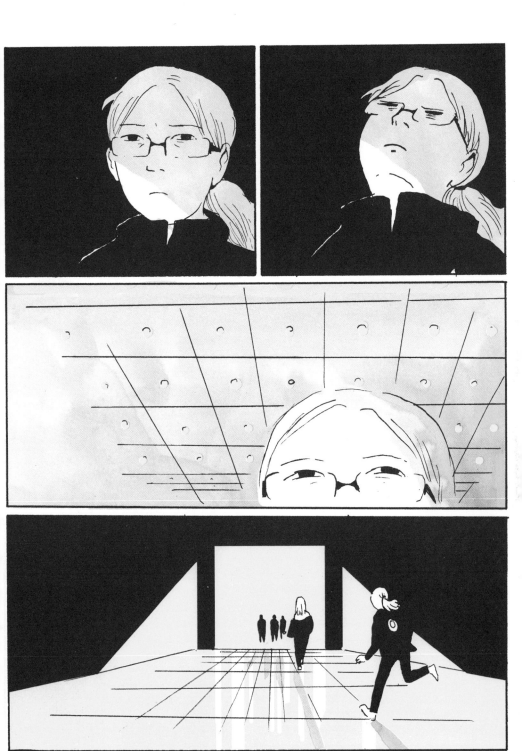

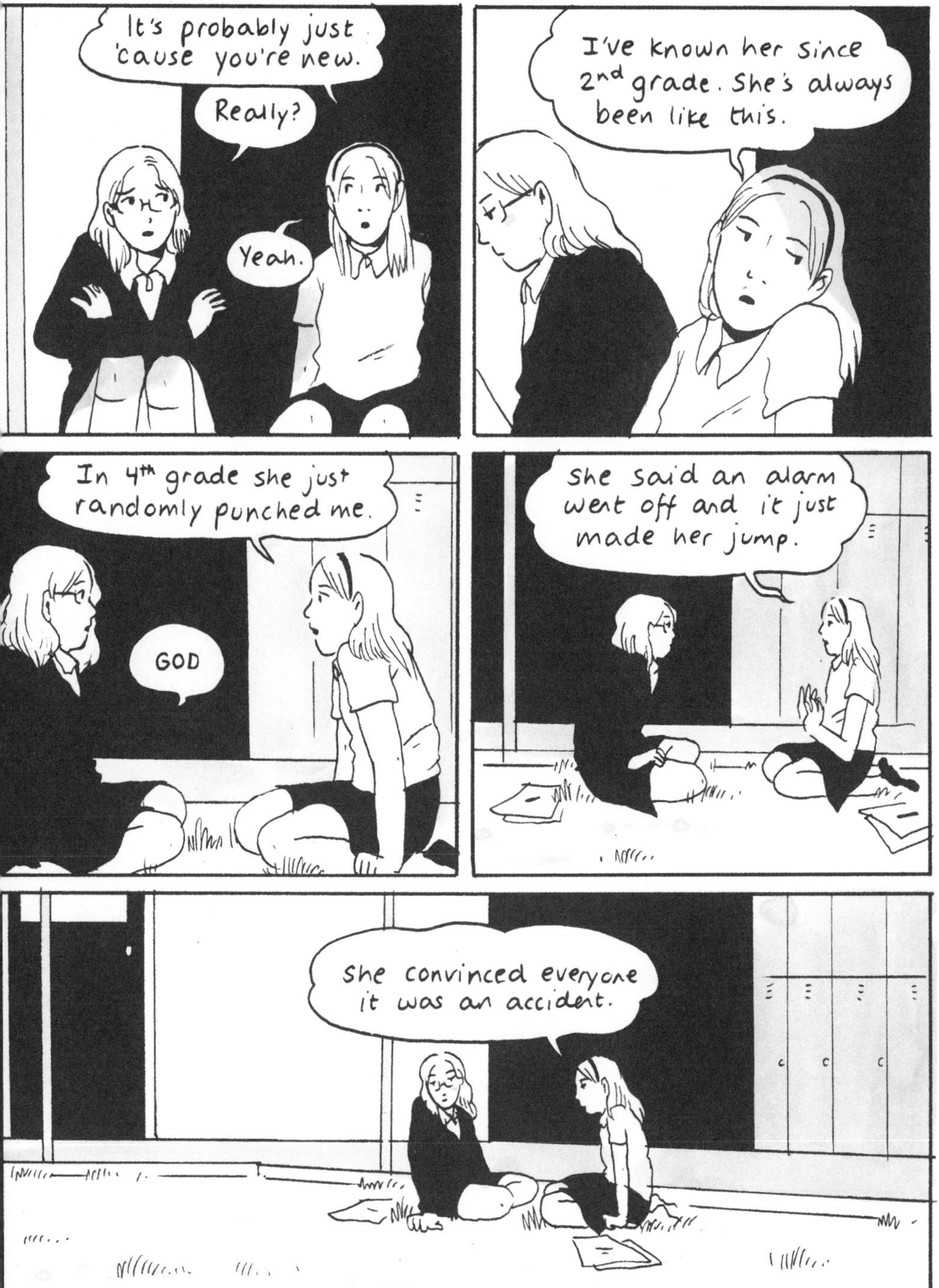
It's probably just 'cause you're new.
Really?
Yeah.
I've known her since 2nd grade. She's always been like this.
In 4th grade she just randomly punched me.
GOD
She said an alarm went off and it just made her jump.
She convinced everyone it was an accident.

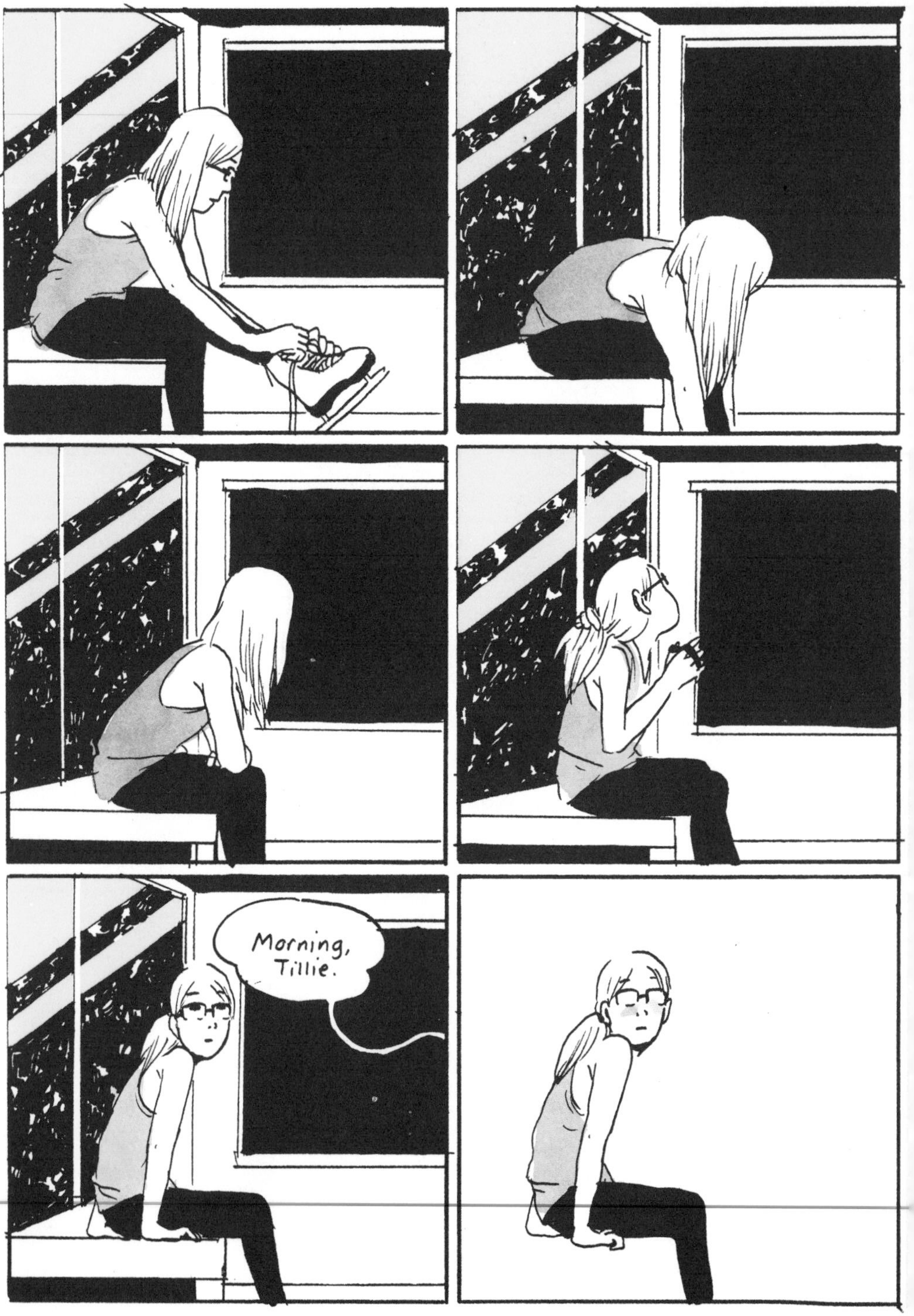
Morning, Tillie.

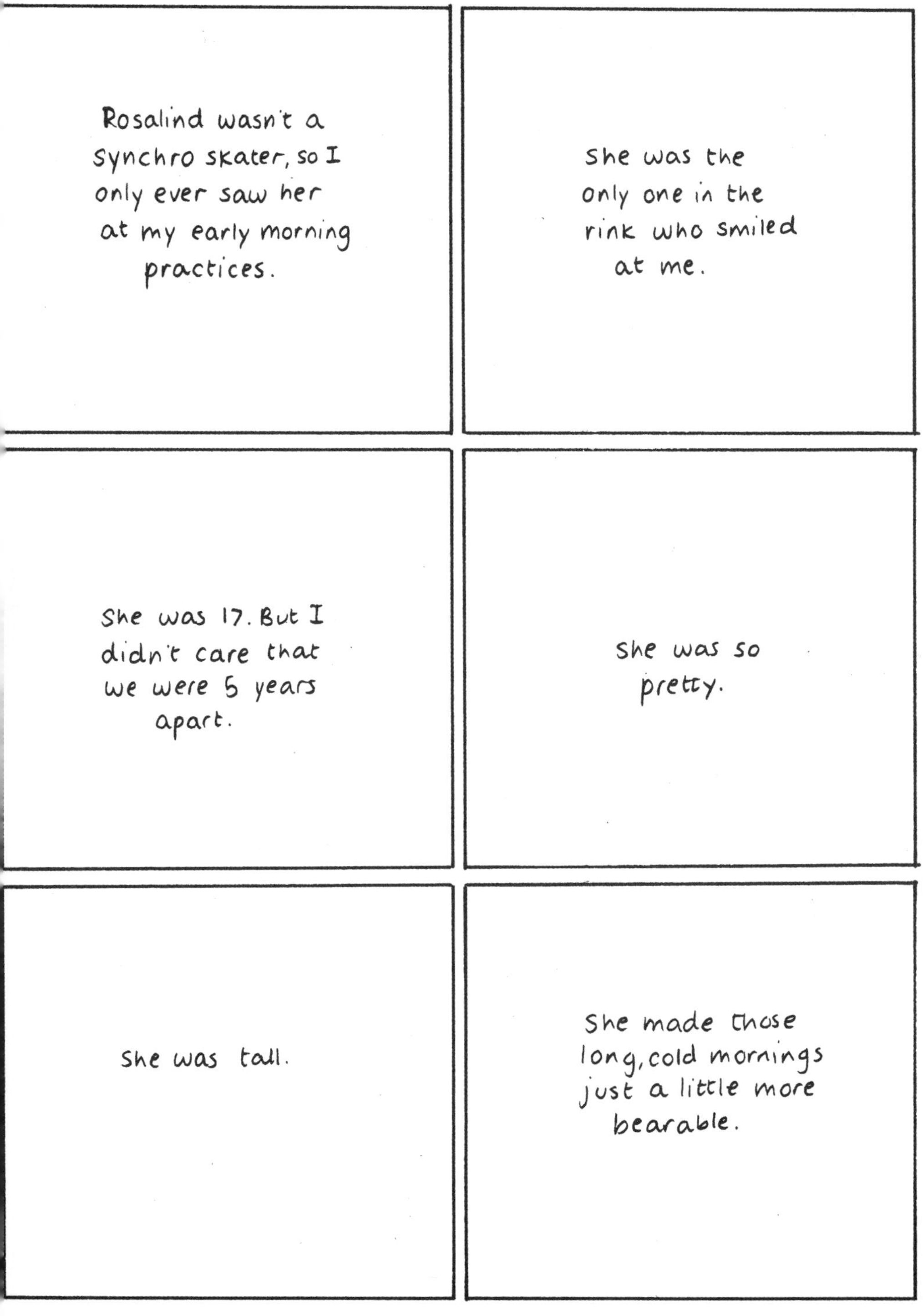
Rosalind wasn't a synchro skater, so I only ever saw her at my early morning practices.
She was the only one in the rink who smiled at me.
She was 17. But I didn't care that we were 5 years apart.
She was so pretty.
She was tall.
She made those long, cold mornings just a little more bearable.

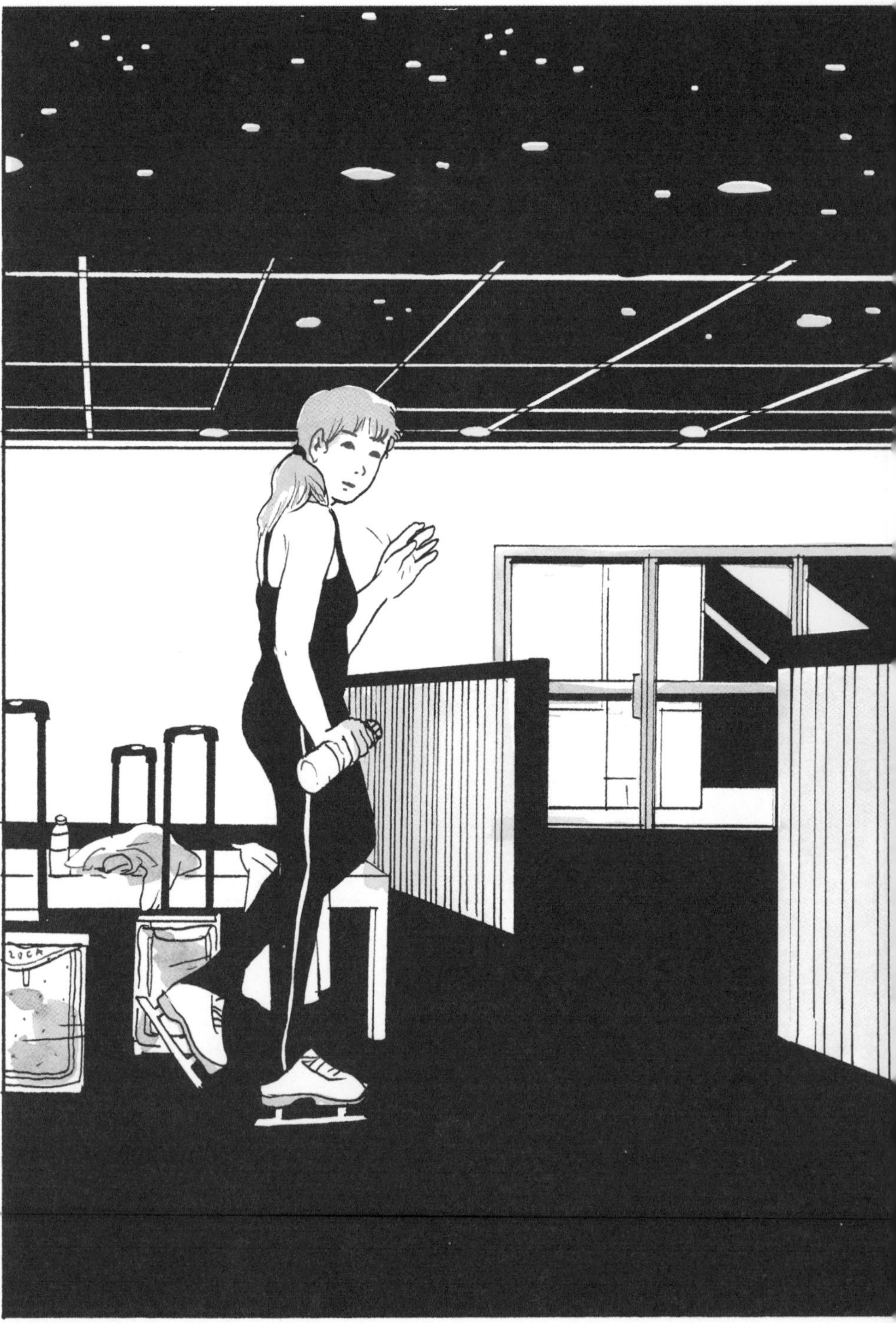

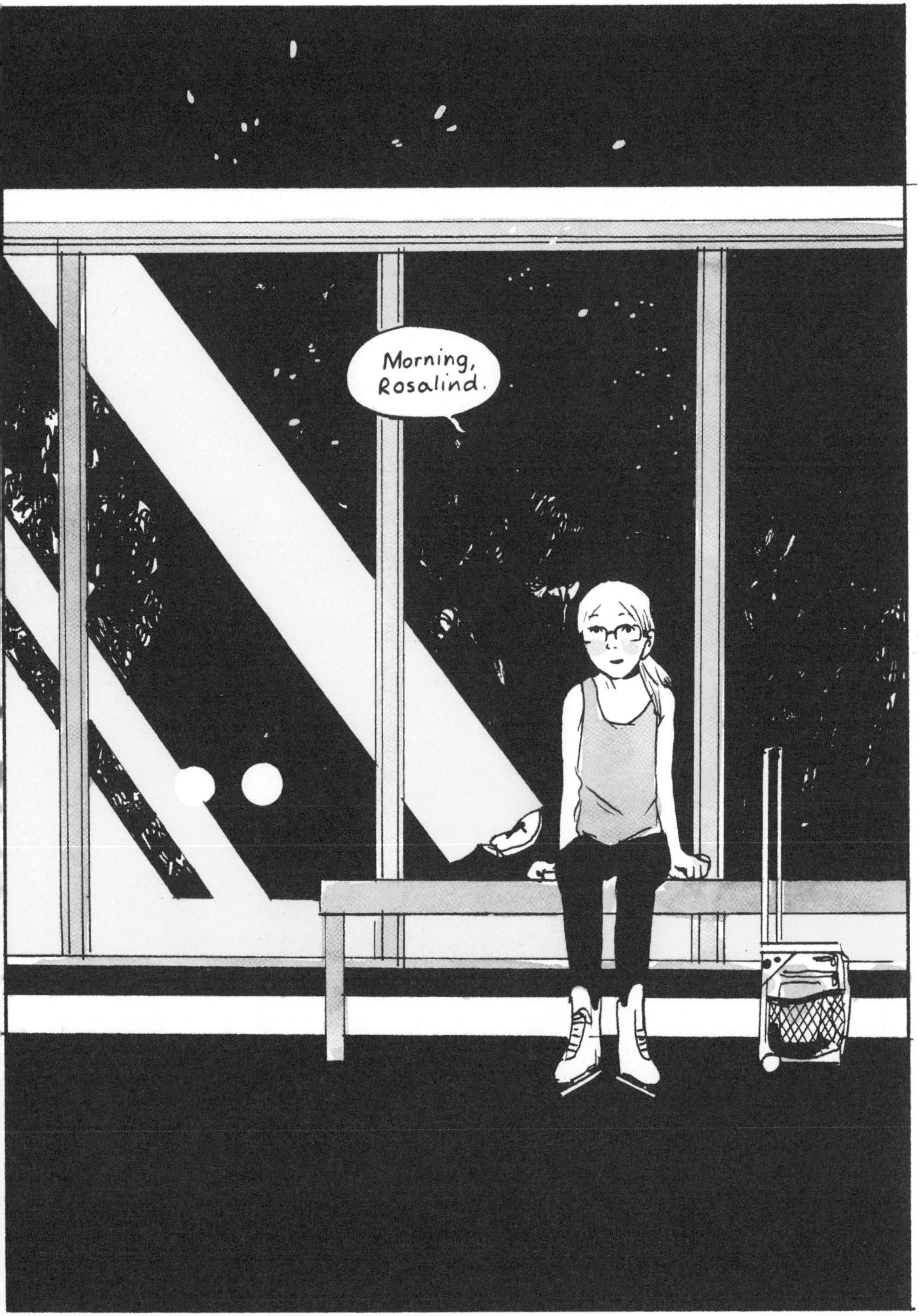
Morning,
Rosalind.

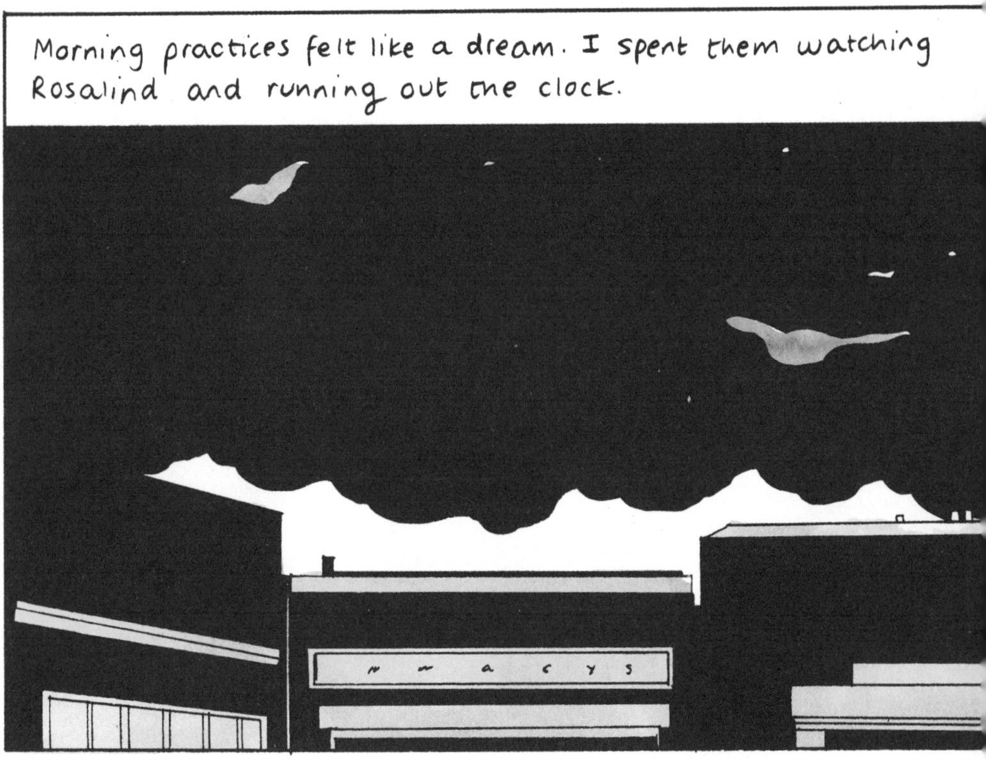
Morning practices felt like a dream. I spent them watching Rosalind and running out the clock.

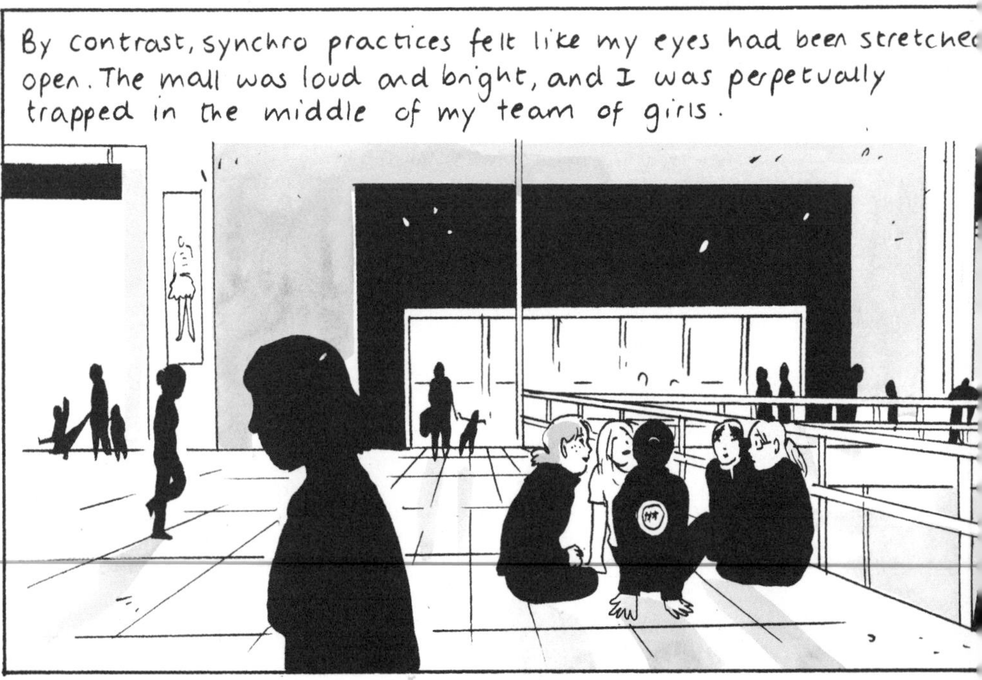
By contrast, synchro practices felt like my eyes had been stretched open. The mall was loud and bright, and I was perpetually trapped in the middle of my team of girls.

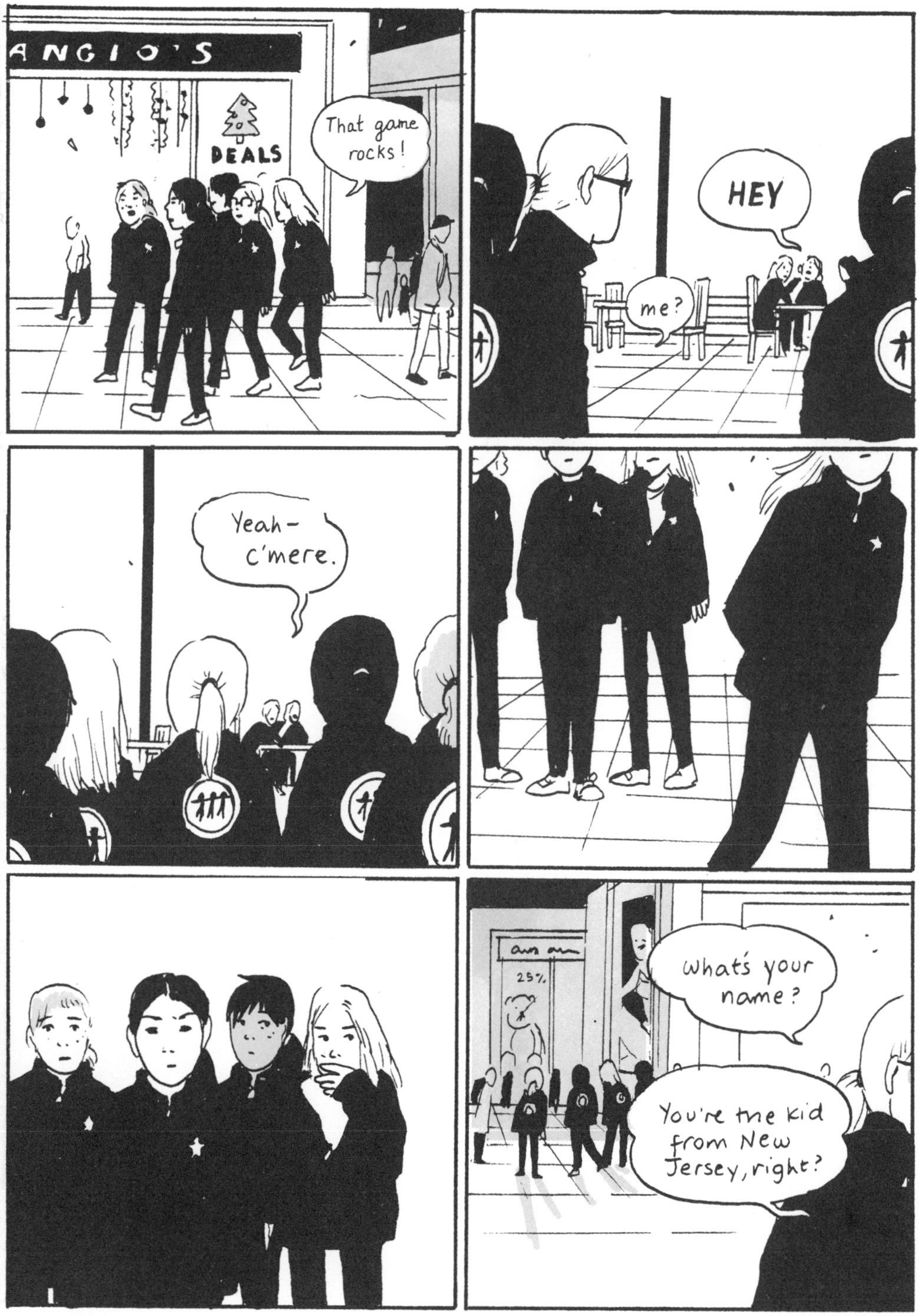
ANGIO'S
DEALS
That game rocks!
HEY
me?
Yeah-c'mere.
What's your name?
25%
You're the kid from New Jersey, right?

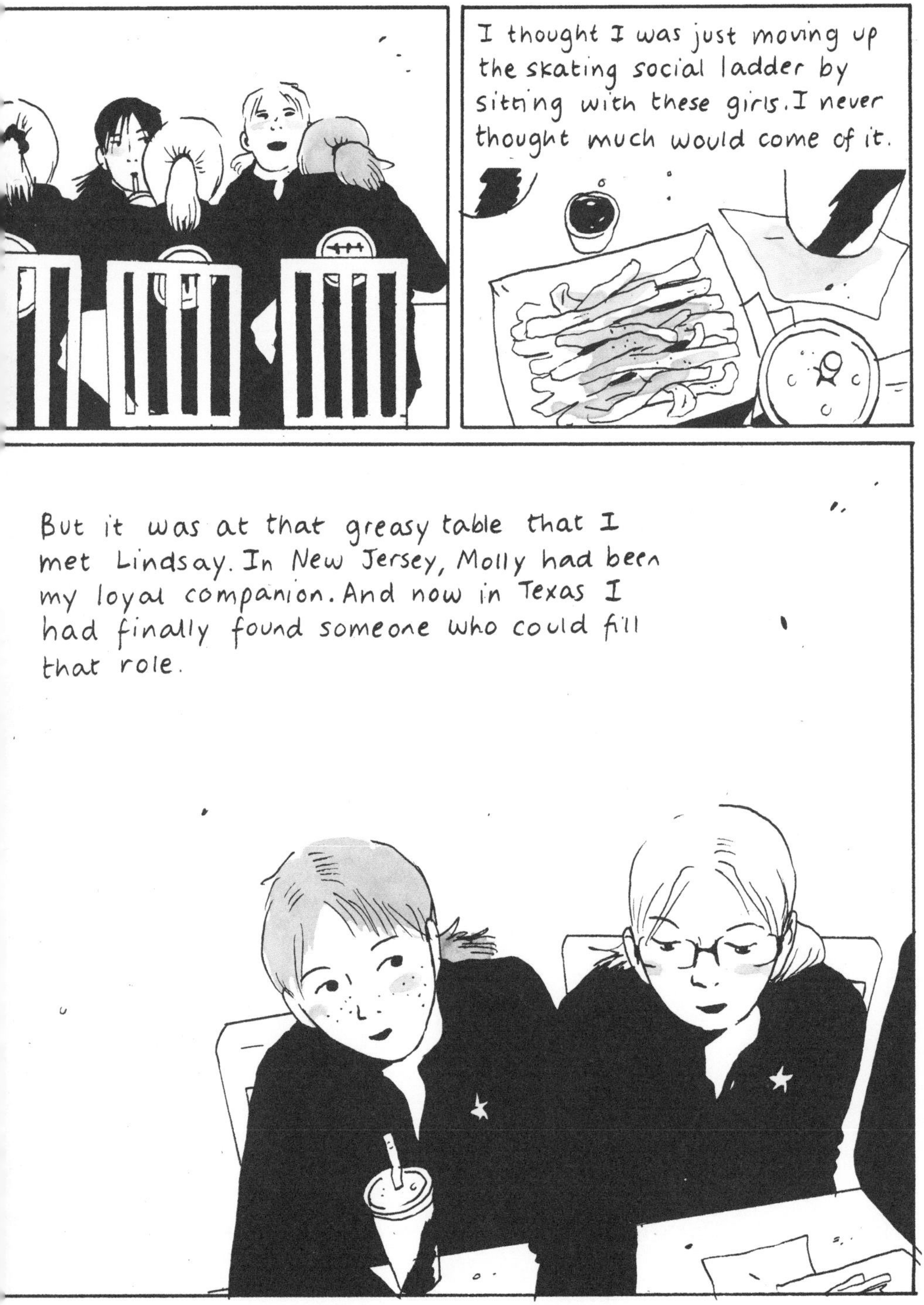
I thought I was just moving up the skating social ladder by sitting with these girls. I never thought much would come of it.
But it was at that greasy table that I met Lindsay. In New Jersey, Molly had been my loyal companion. And now in Texas I had finally found someone who could fill that role.

When Ms. Ramberg read aloud to us, it was the only time in school I felt perfectly at ease.

"Day was always over."

I didn't know why reading was so hard for me.

"Night was always coming."

So to hear a story with such ease was like magic.

"And aren't you always afraid, Apeman there? Or you, Mummy, that the sun will never rise again?

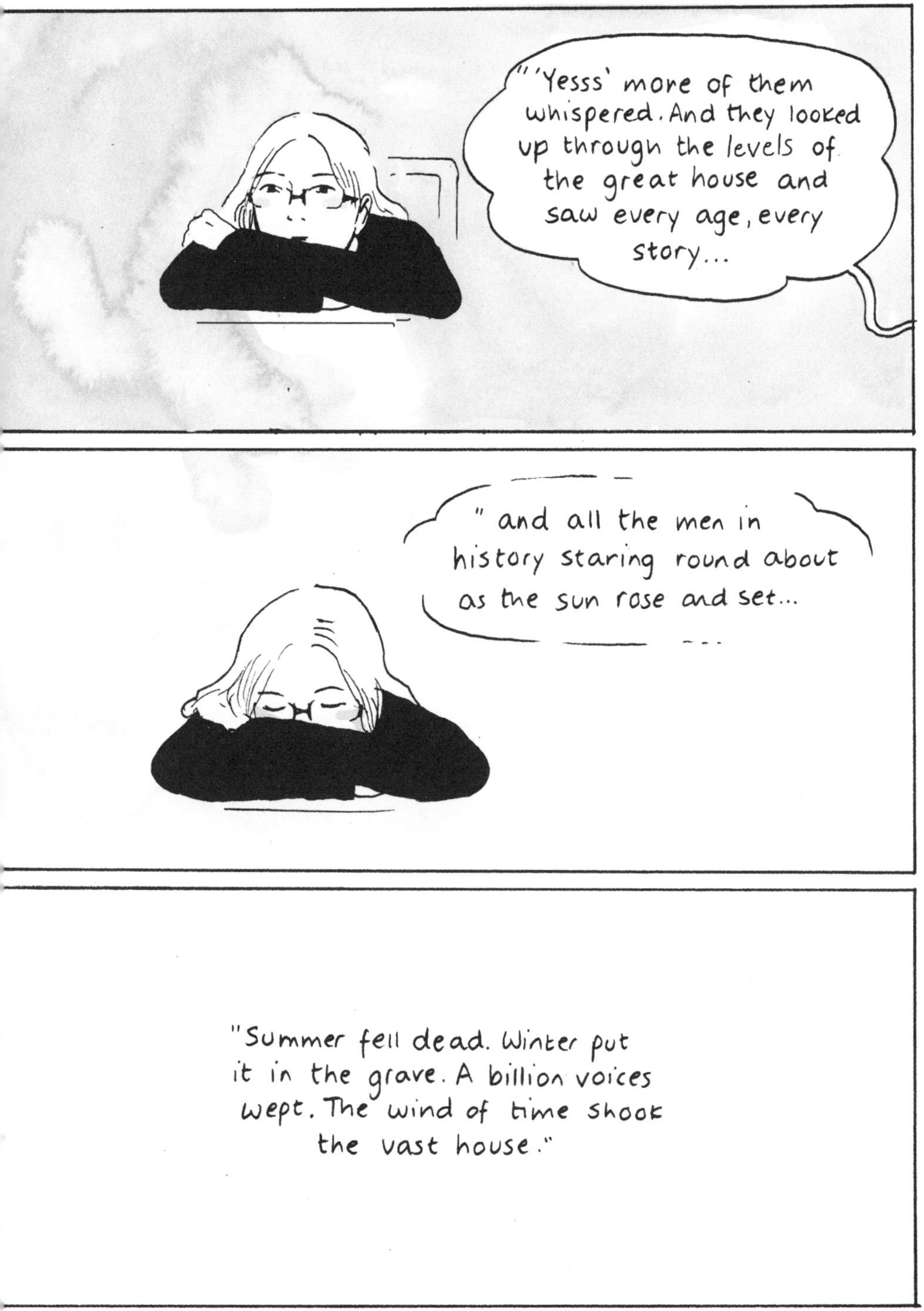
"'Yesss' more of them whispered. And they looked up through the levels of the great house and saw every age, every story...
" and all the men in history staring round about as the sun rose and set...
"Summer fell dead. Winter put it in the grave. A billion voices wept. The wind of time shook the vast house."

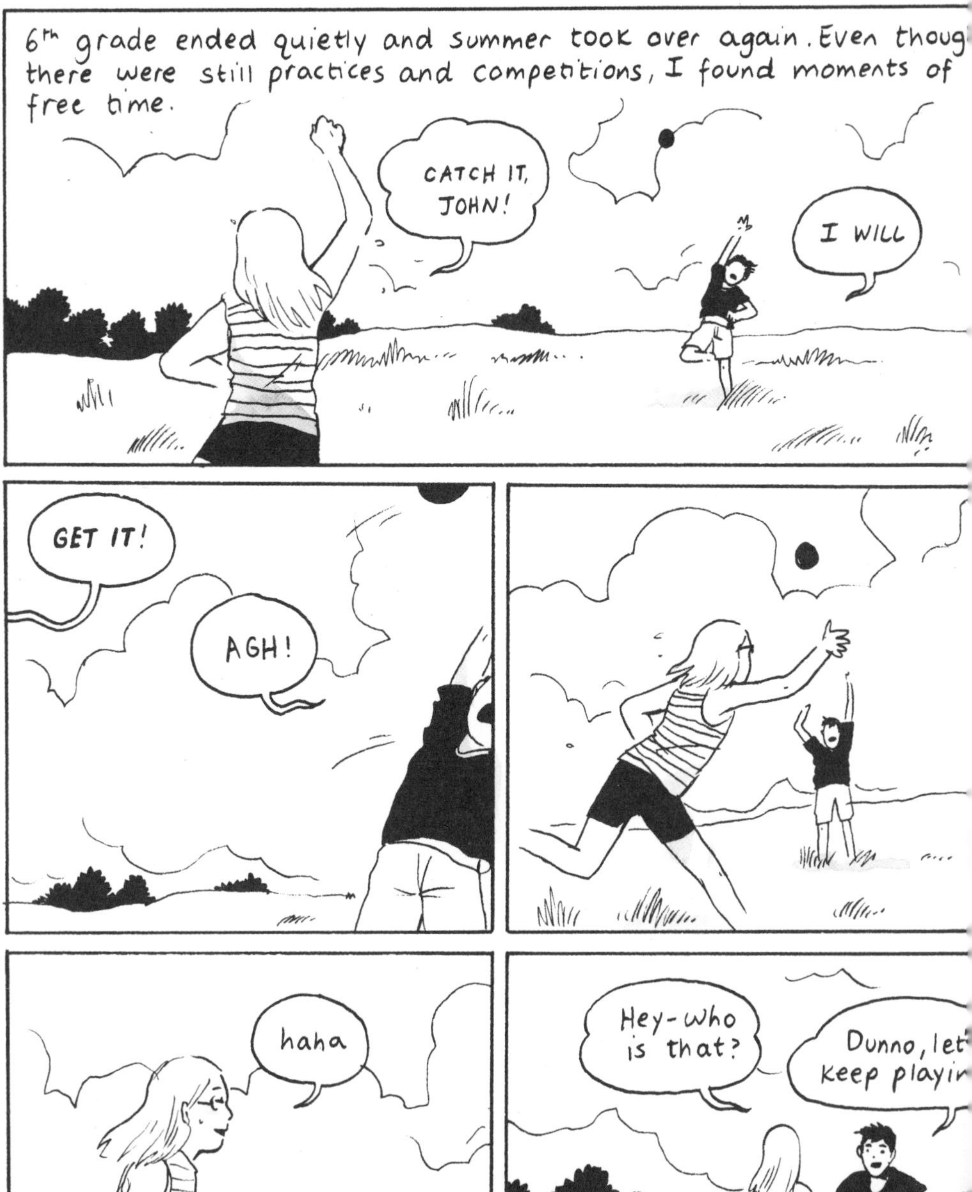
6th grade ended quietly and summer took over again. Even thoug
there were still practices and competitions, I found moments of
free time.
CATCH IT, JOHN!
I WILL
GET IT!
AGH!
haha
Hey-who is that?
Dunno, let
keep playin

99

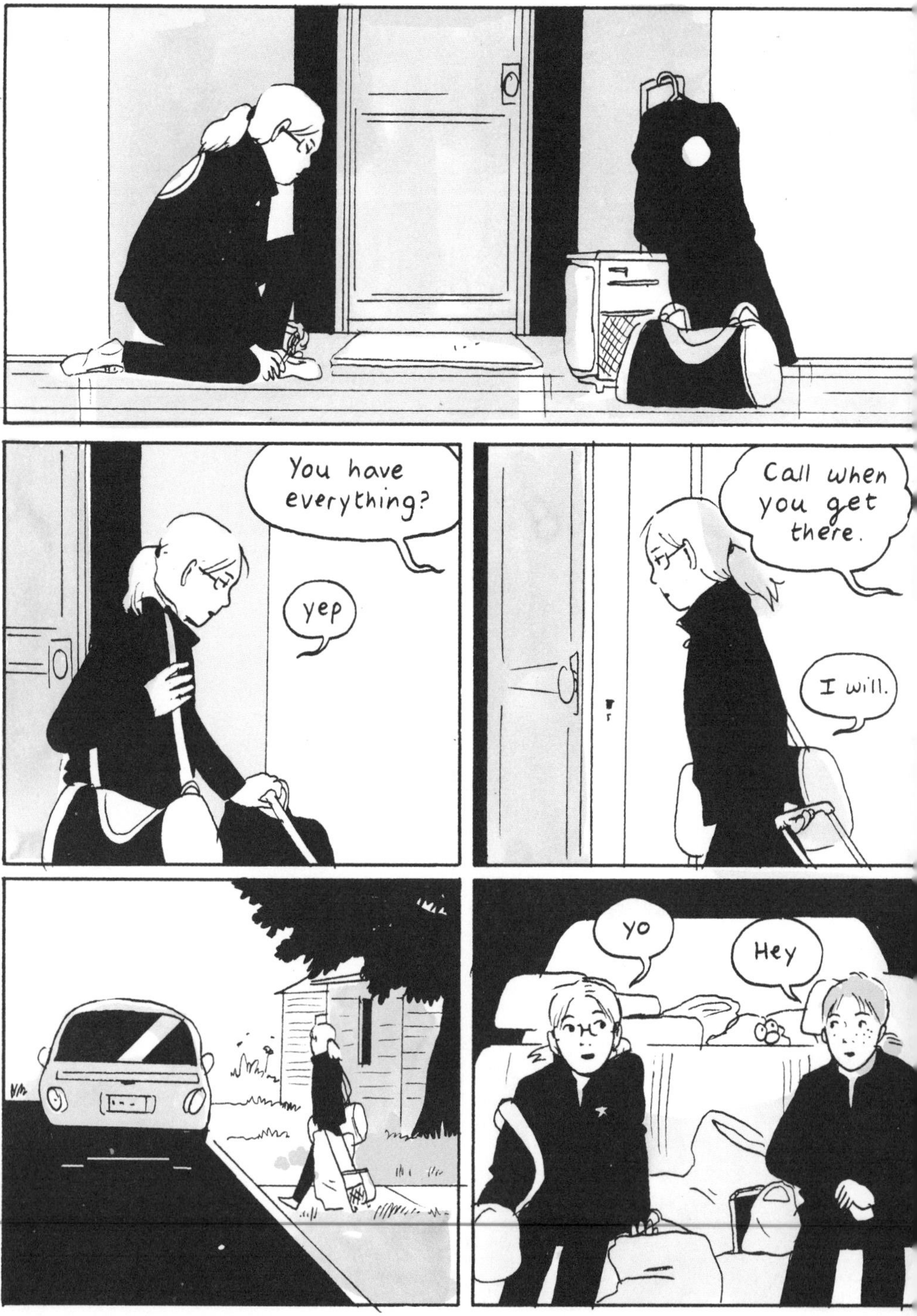
You have everything?
yep
Call when you get there.
I will.
yo
Hey

Traveling with Lindsay and Judy was always so peaceful.

They seemed so relaxed with one another, whereas I always felt so tense with my mom.

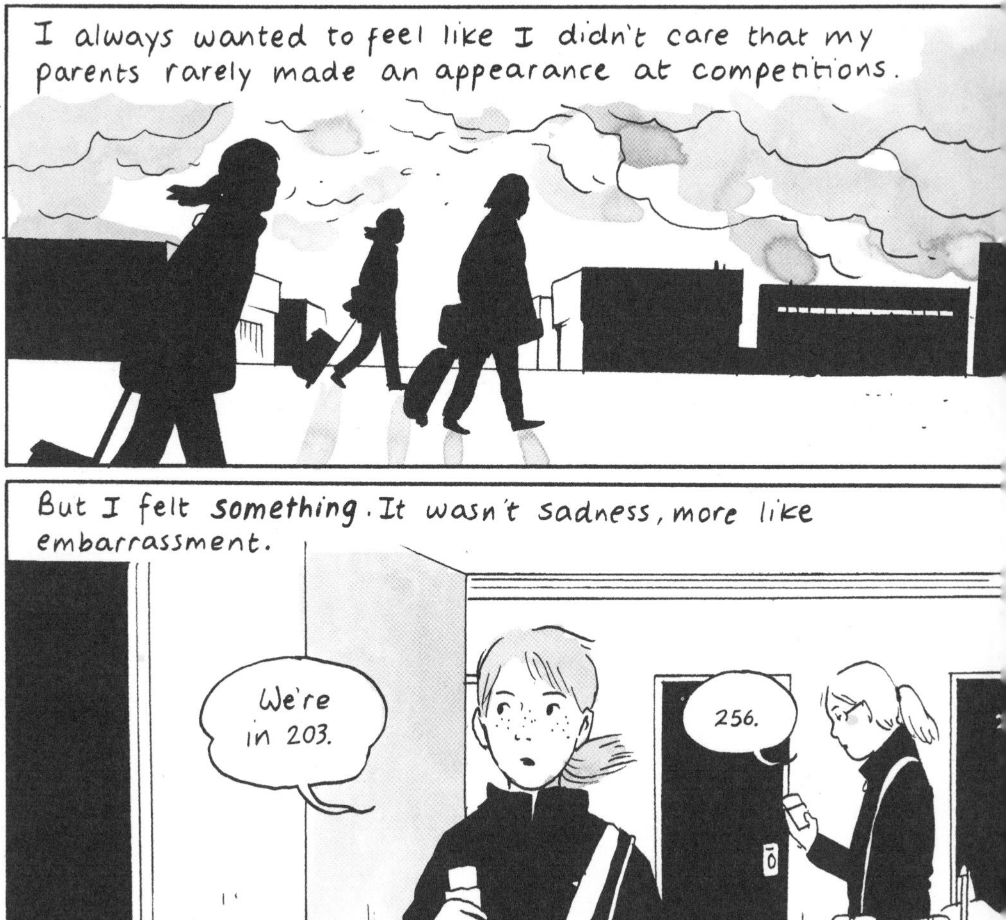
I always wanted to feel like I didn't care that my parents rarely made an appearance at competitions.
But I felt something. It wasn't sadness, more like embarrassment.
We're in 203.
256.
I was always the only girl in the locker room without a mom, the only one who didn't have family members lurking around the results area.

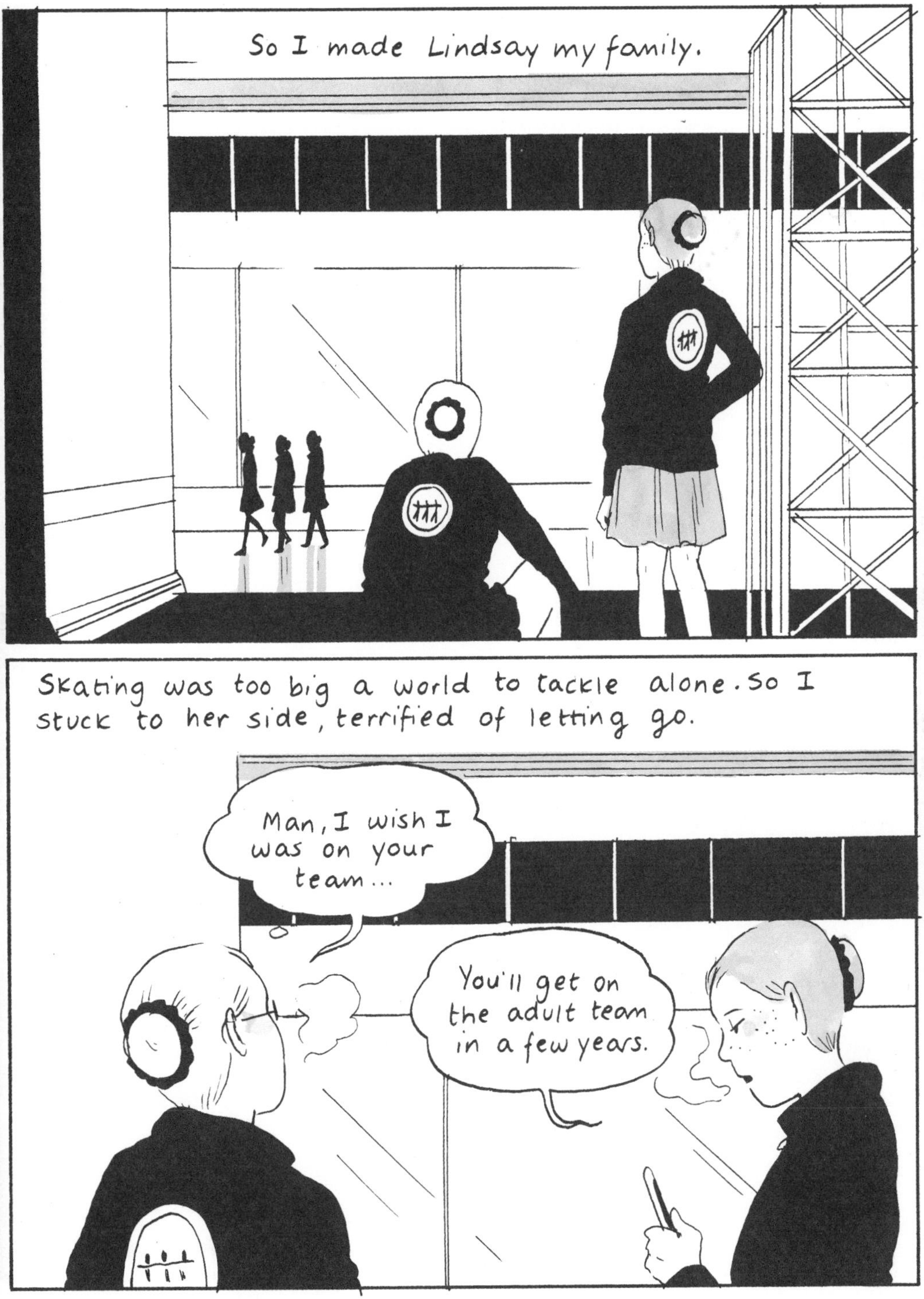
So I made Lindsay my family.
Skating was too big a world to tackle alone. So I stuck to her side, terrified of letting go.
Man, I wish I was on your team...
You'll get on the adult team in a few years.

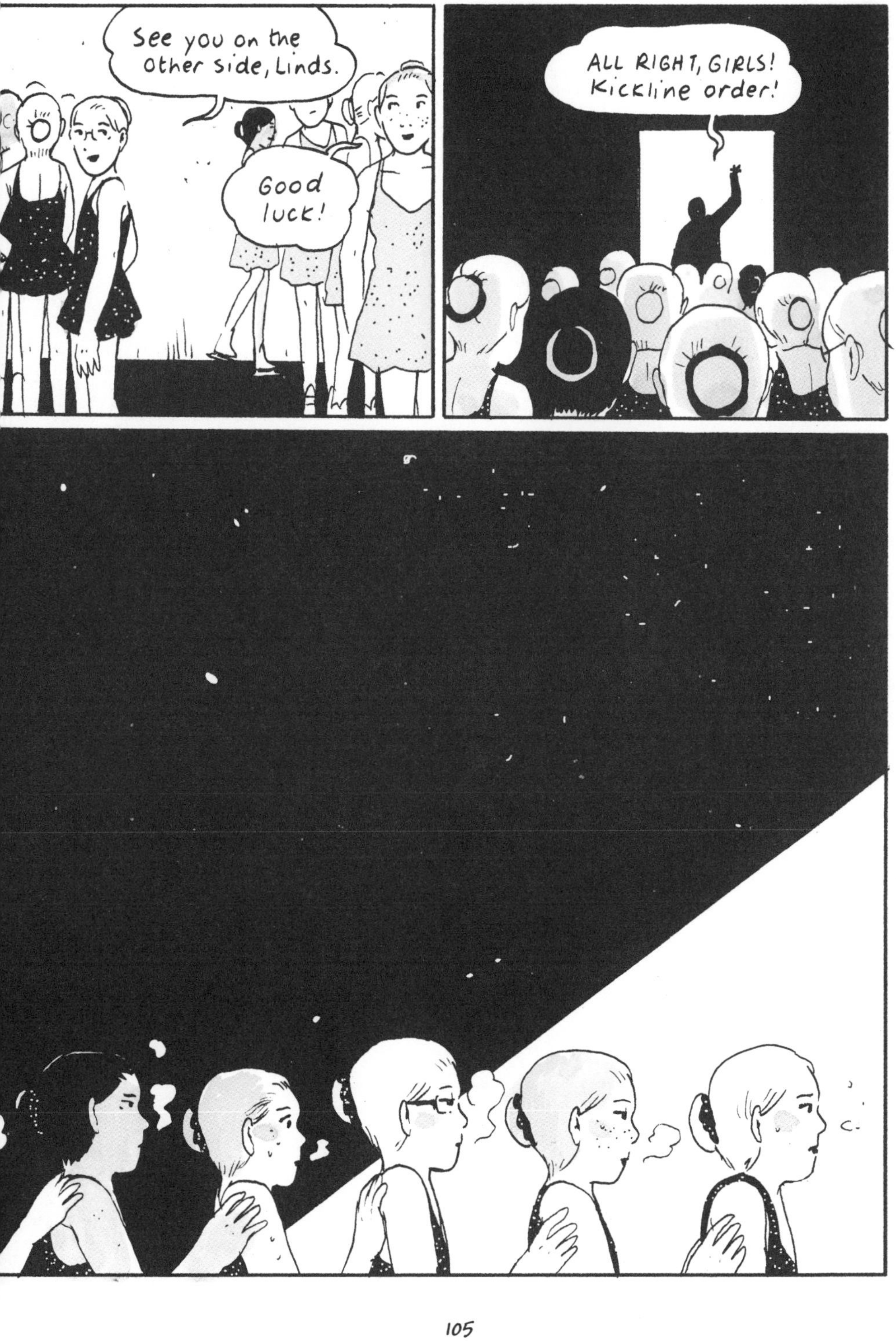
See you on the other side, Linds.
Good luck!
ALL RIGHT, GIRLS! Kickline order!

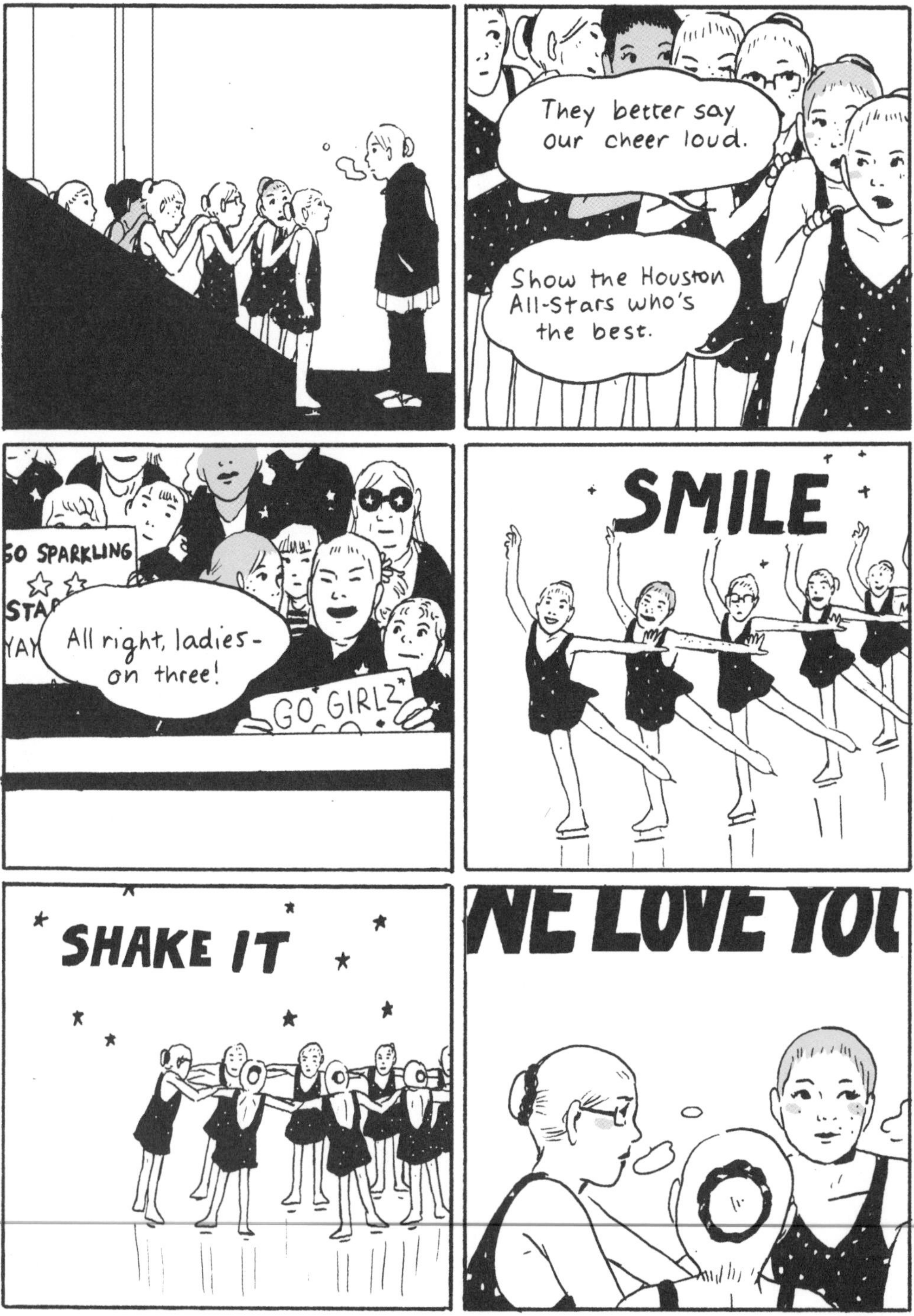
They better say our cheer loud.
Show the Houston All-Stars who's the best.
SO SPARKLING
STA
YAY
All right, ladies- on three!
GO GIRLZ
SMILE
SHAKE IT
WE LOVE YOU

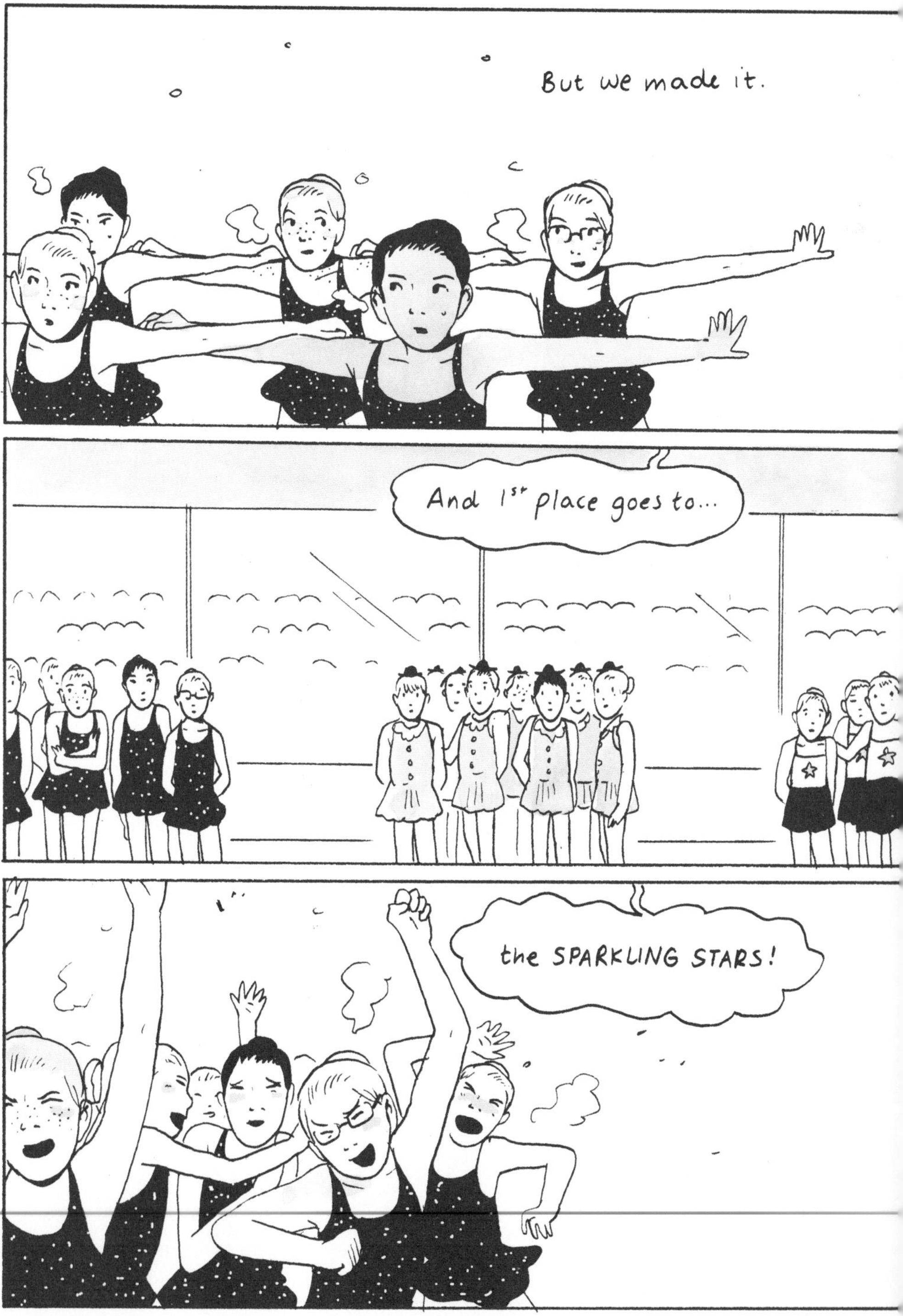

But we made it.
And 1st place goes to...
the SPARKLING STARS!

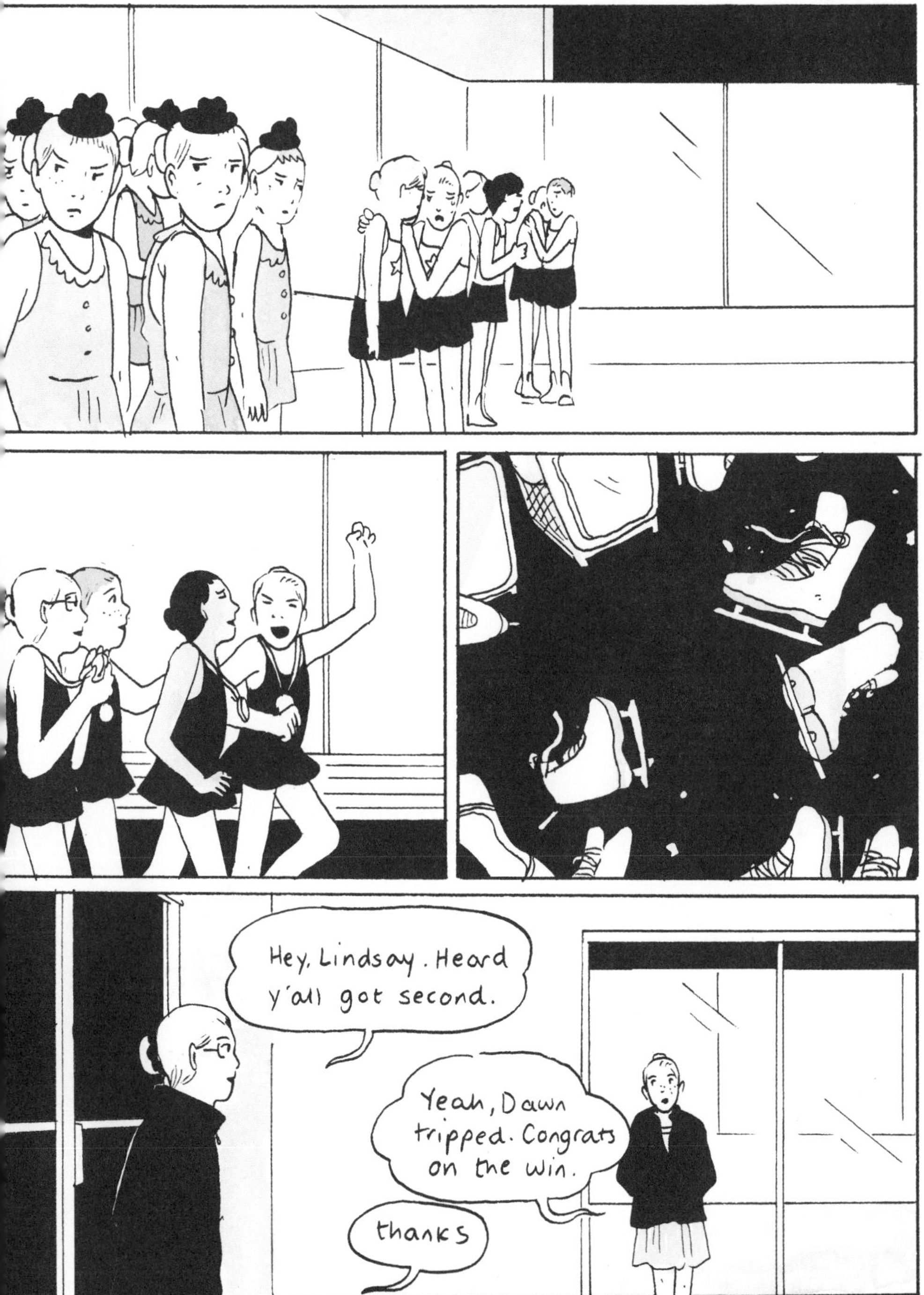
Hey, Lindsay. Heard y'all got second.
Yeah, Dawn tripped. Congrats on the win.
thanks

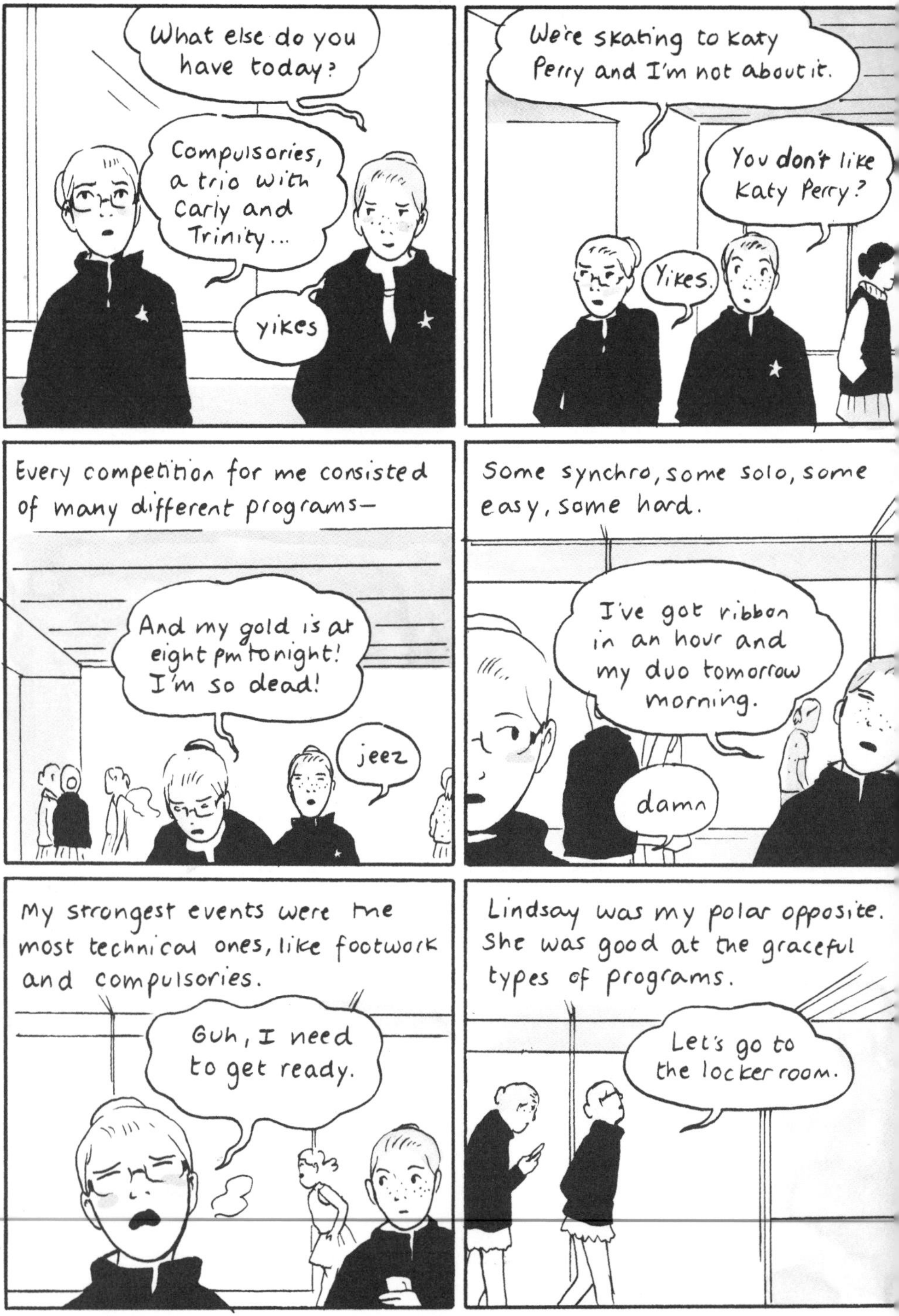
What else do you have today?
Compulsories, a trio with Carly and Trinity...
yikes
We're skating to Katy Perry and I'm not about it.
You don't like Katy Perry?
Yikes.
Every competition for me consisted of many different programs—
And my gold is at eight pm tonight! I'm so dead!
jeez
Some synchro, some solo, some easy, some hard.
I've got ribbon in an hour and my duo tomorrow morning.
damn
My strongest events were the most technical ones, like footwork and compulsories.
Guh, I need to get ready.
Lindsay was my polar opposite. She was good at the graceful types of programs.
Let's go to the locker room.

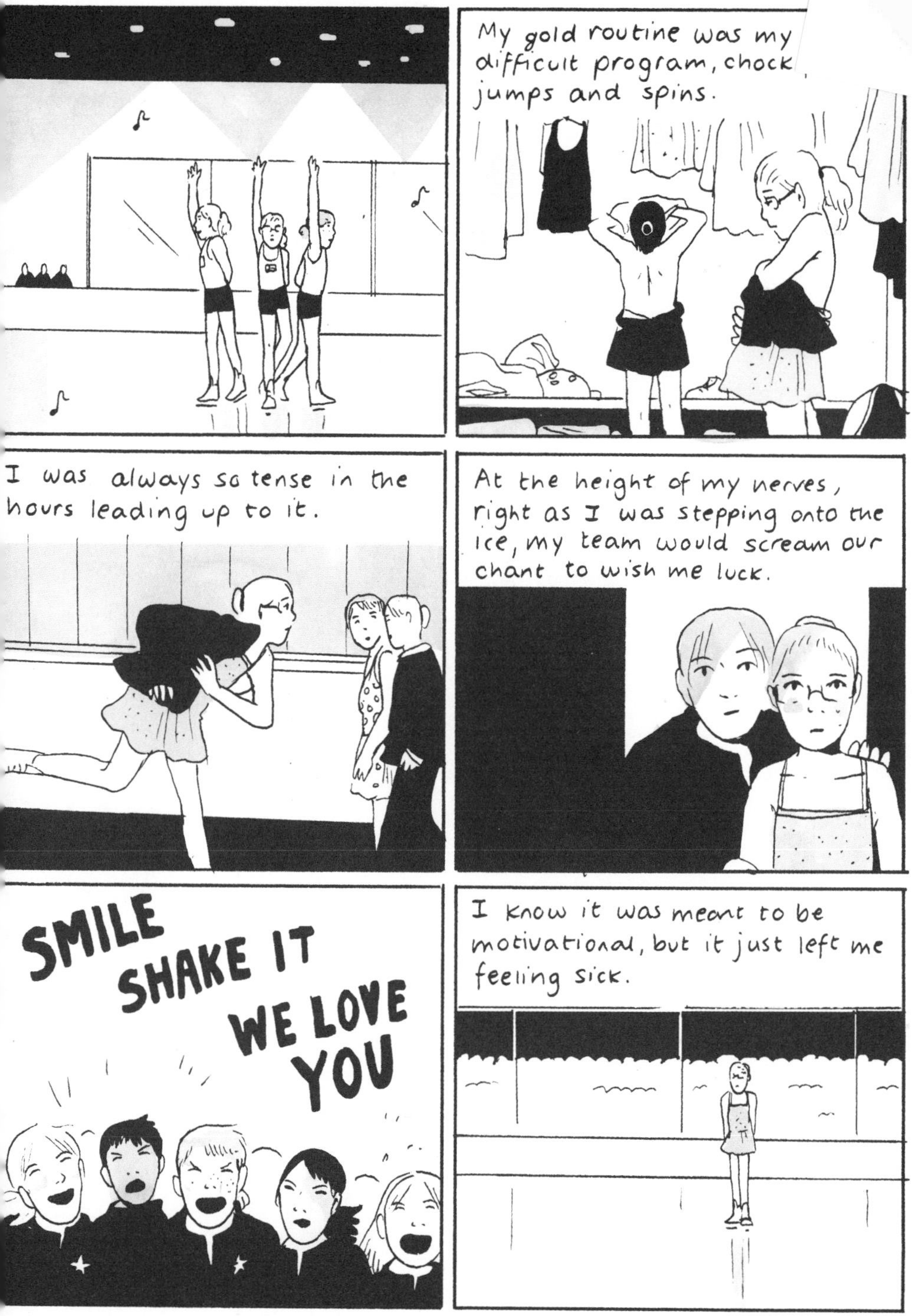
My gold routine was my difficult program, chock jumps and spins.
I was always so tense in the hours leading up to it.
At the height of my nerves, right as I was stepping onto the ice, my team would scream our chant to wish me luck.
SMILE SHAKE IT WE LOVE YOU
I know it was meant to be motivational, but it just left me feeling sick.

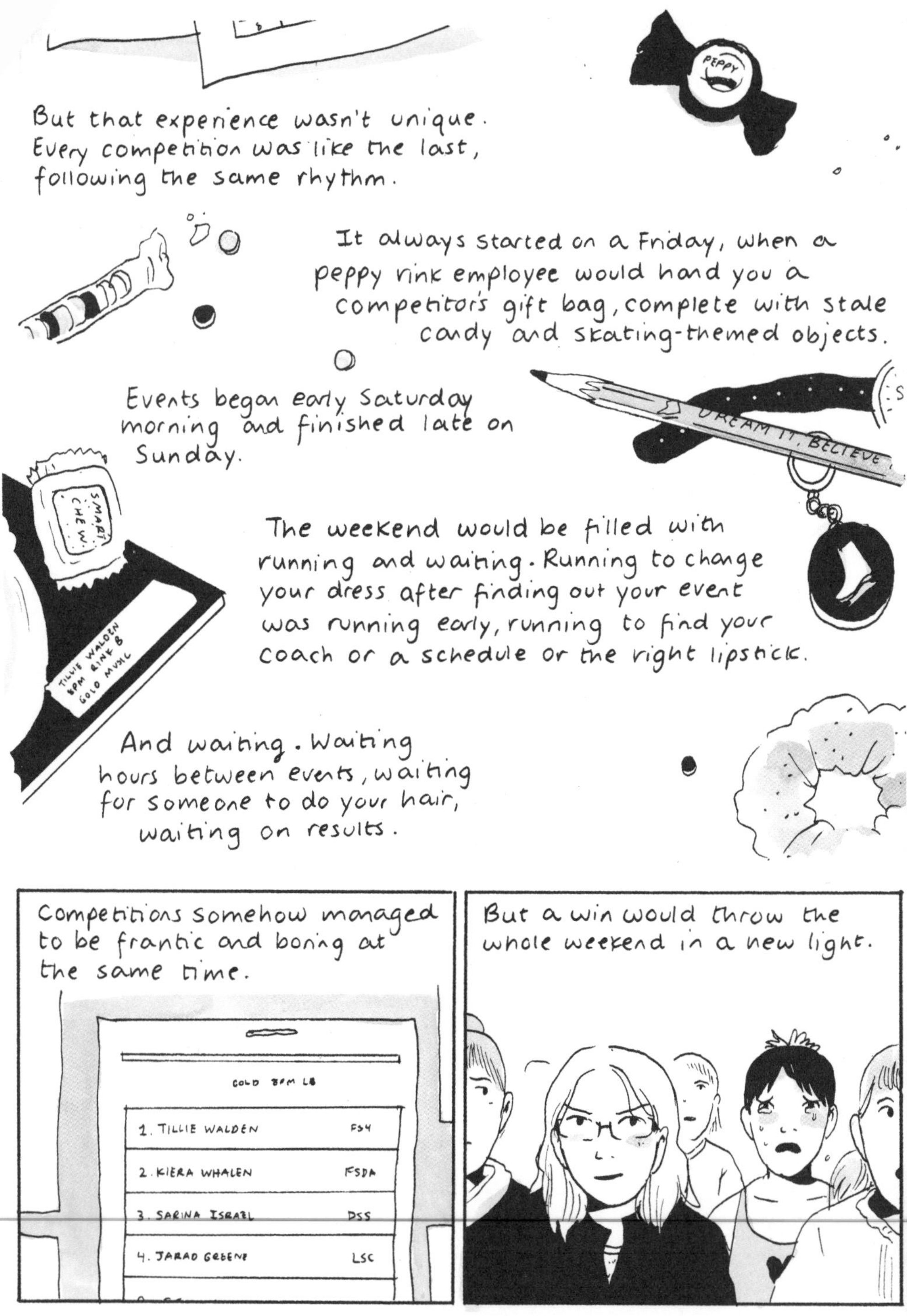
PEPPY
But that experience wasn't unique. Every competition was like the last, following the same rhythm.
It always started on a Friday, when a peppy rink employee would hand you a competitor's gift bag, complete with stale candy and skating-themed objects.
Events began early Saturday morning and finished late on Sunday.
DREAM IT, BELIEVE
SMART CHEW
The weekend would be filled with running and waiting. Running to change your dress after finding out your event was running early, running to find your coach or a schedule or the right lipstick.
TILLIE WALDEN
8PM RINK B
GOLD MUSIC
And waiting. Waiting hours between events, waiting for someone to do your hair, waiting on results.
Competitions somehow managed to be frantic and boring at the same time.
GOLD 8PM LB
1. TILLIE WALDEN FSG
2. KIERA WHALEN FSDA
3. SARINA ISRAEL DSS
4. JARAD GREENE LSC
But a win would throw the whole weekend in a new light.

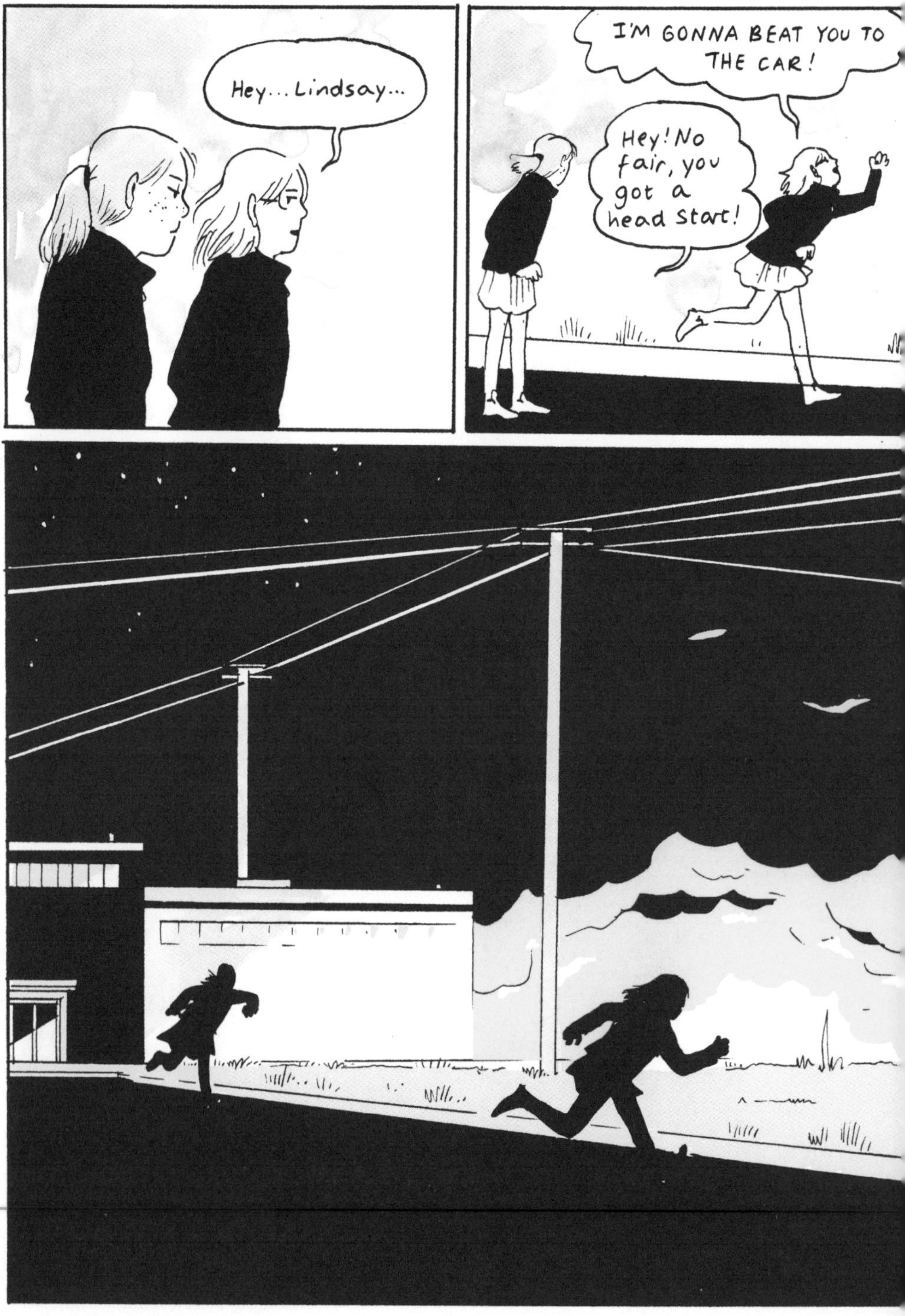
Hey... Lindsay...
I'M GONNA BEAT YOU TO THE CAR!
Hey! No fair, you got a head start!

4

AXEL

I have never known a more
frustrating jump.

I remember going into it, gliding
backwards and holding my breath.

As I would turn to go into it I
would wish and hope with
everything I had that this time it
would work.

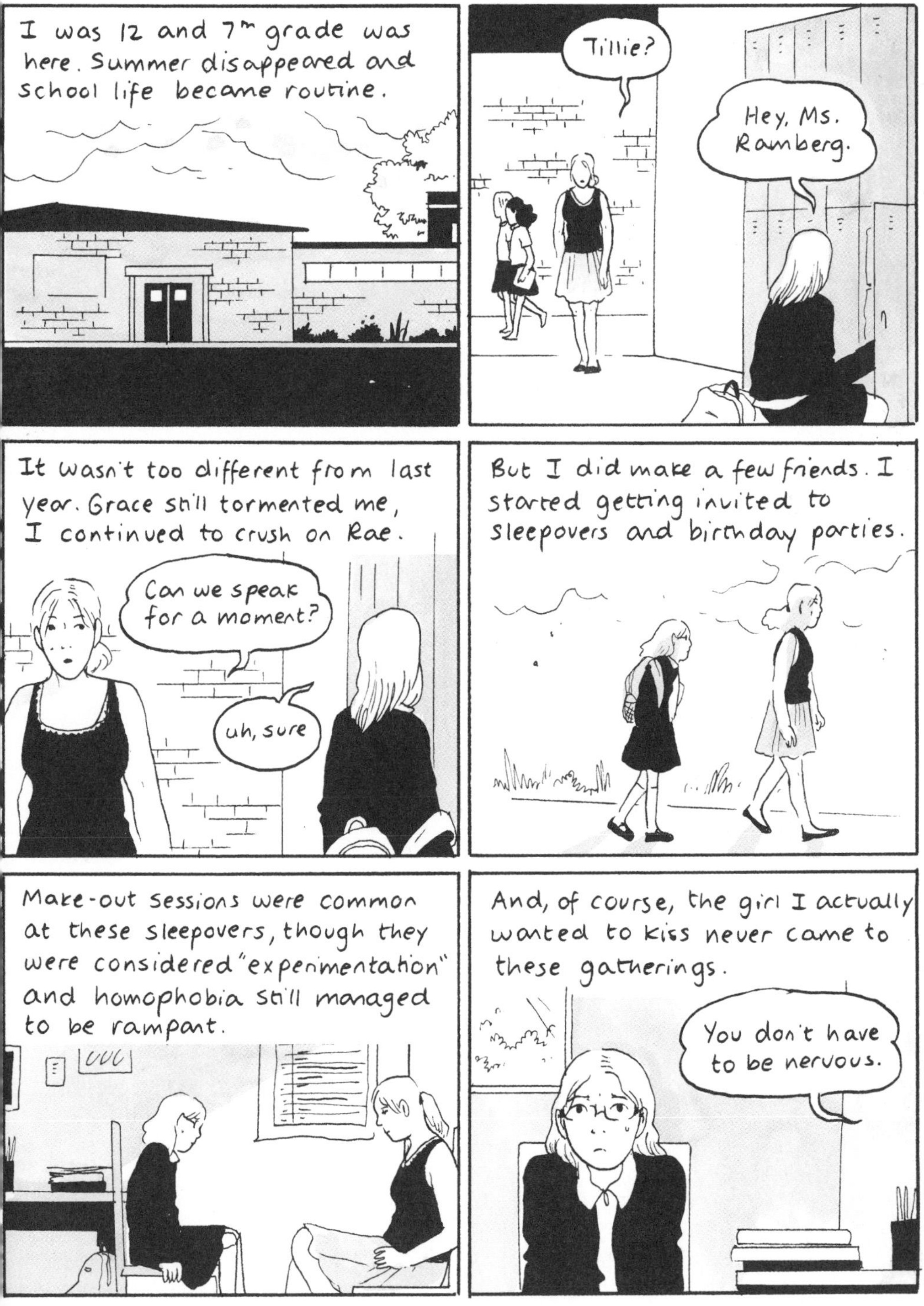
I was 12 and 7th grade was here. Summer disappeared and school life became routine.
Tillie?
Hey, Ms. Ramberg.
It wasn't too different from last year. Grace still tormented me, I continued to crush on Rae.
Can we speak for a moment?
uh, sure
But I did make a few friends. I started getting invited to sleepovers and birthday parties.
Make-out sessions were common at these sleepovers, though they were considered "experimentation" and homophobia still managed to be rampant.
And, of course, the girl I actually wanted to kiss never came to these gatherings.
You don't have to be nervous.

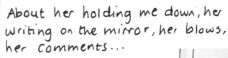

Occasionally Lindsay and I would land on the same early morning session.

She made everything so much warmer.

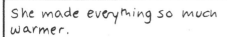

morning

hey

Talking to her was so easy because I didn't have to be afraid she'd make fun of me.

brrr

She was the kindest person I'd ever met.

How are you?

OK. Rather be here than home.

Yeah?

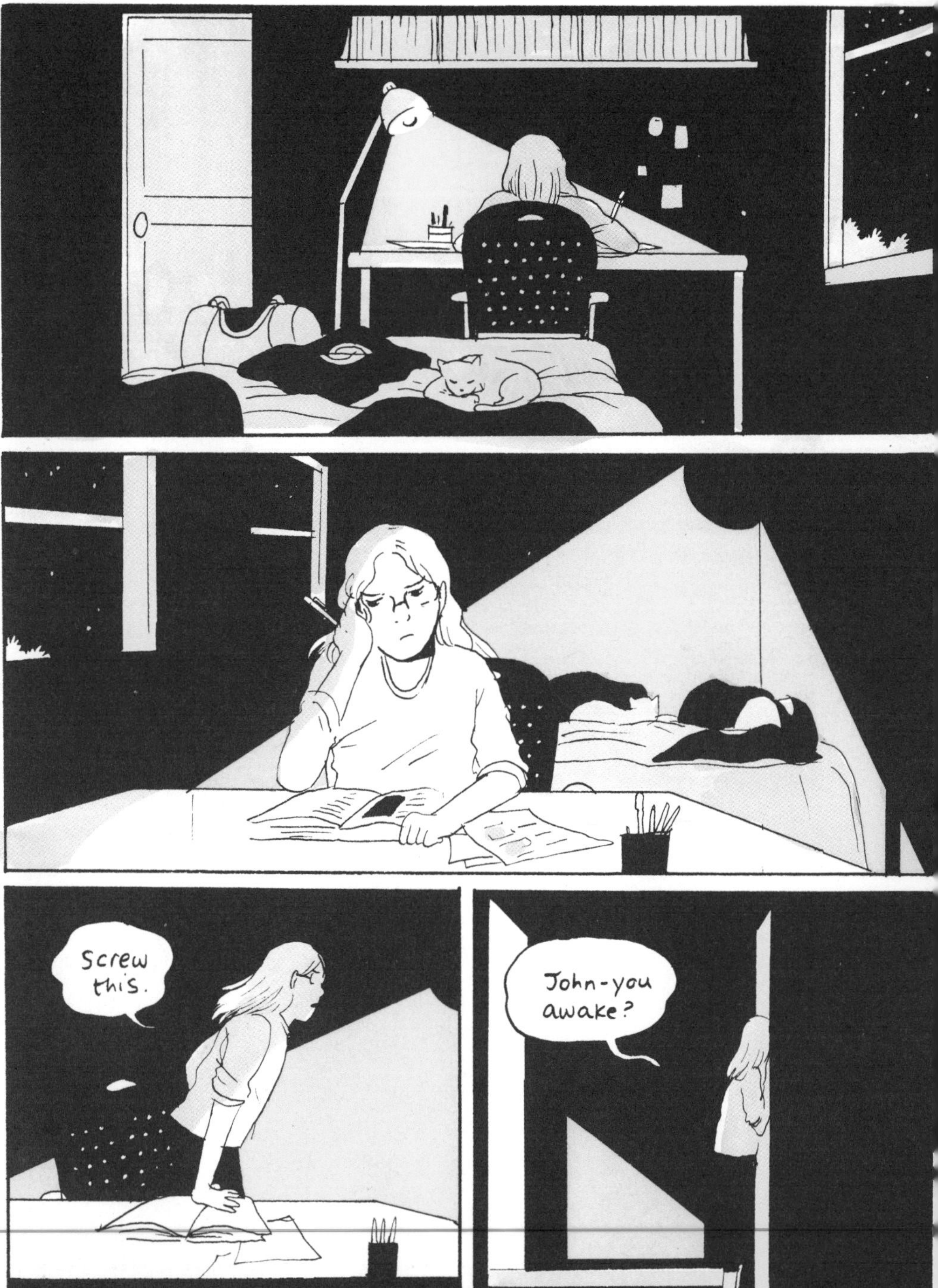
Screw this.
John-you awake?

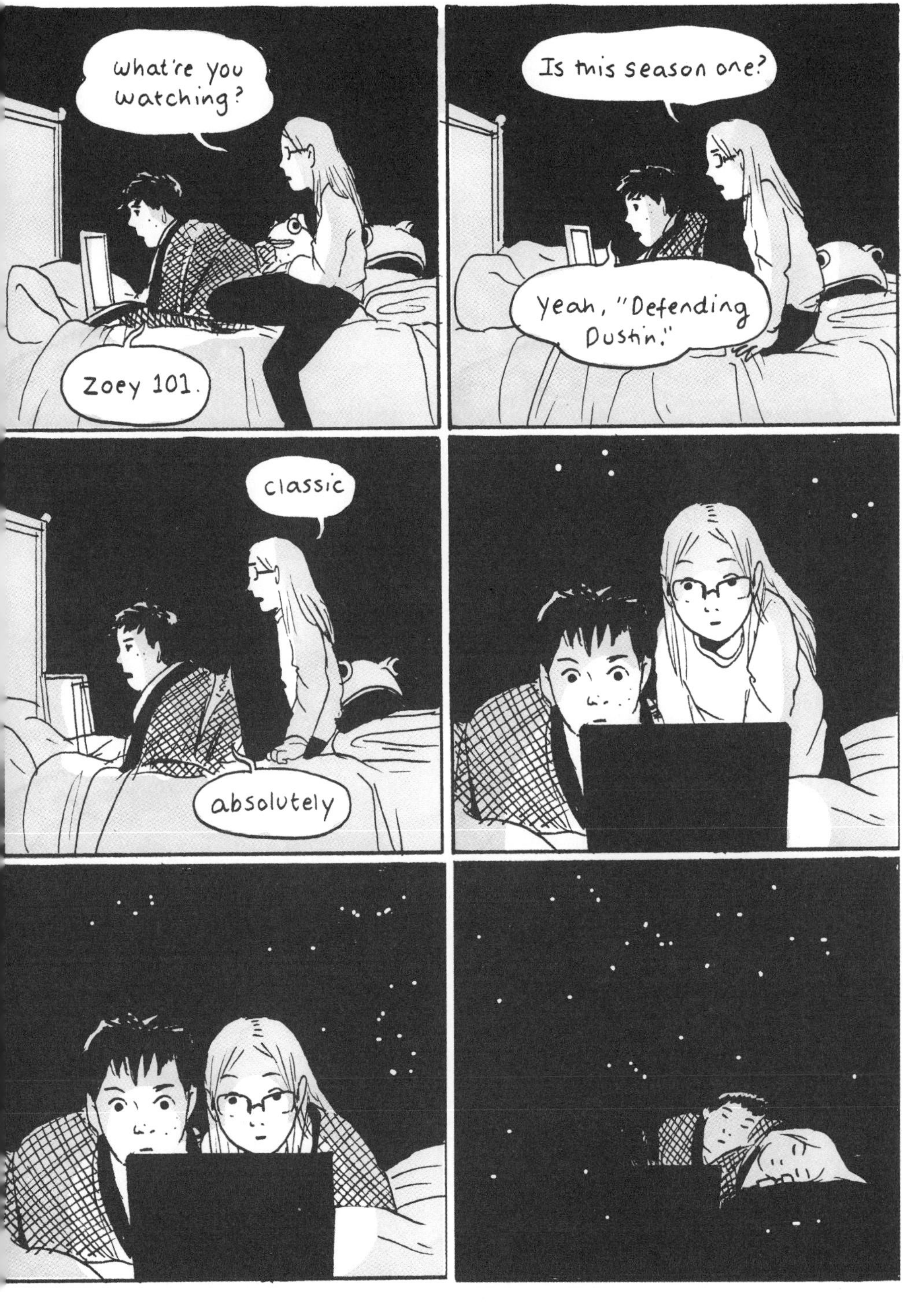
what're you watching?
Zoey 101.
Is this season one?
Yeah, "Defending Dustin."
classic
absolutely

In New Jersey, we had traveled all over the country for competitions. Yet living in Austin it seemed like the farthest we ever got to go was the outskirts of Dallas.

127

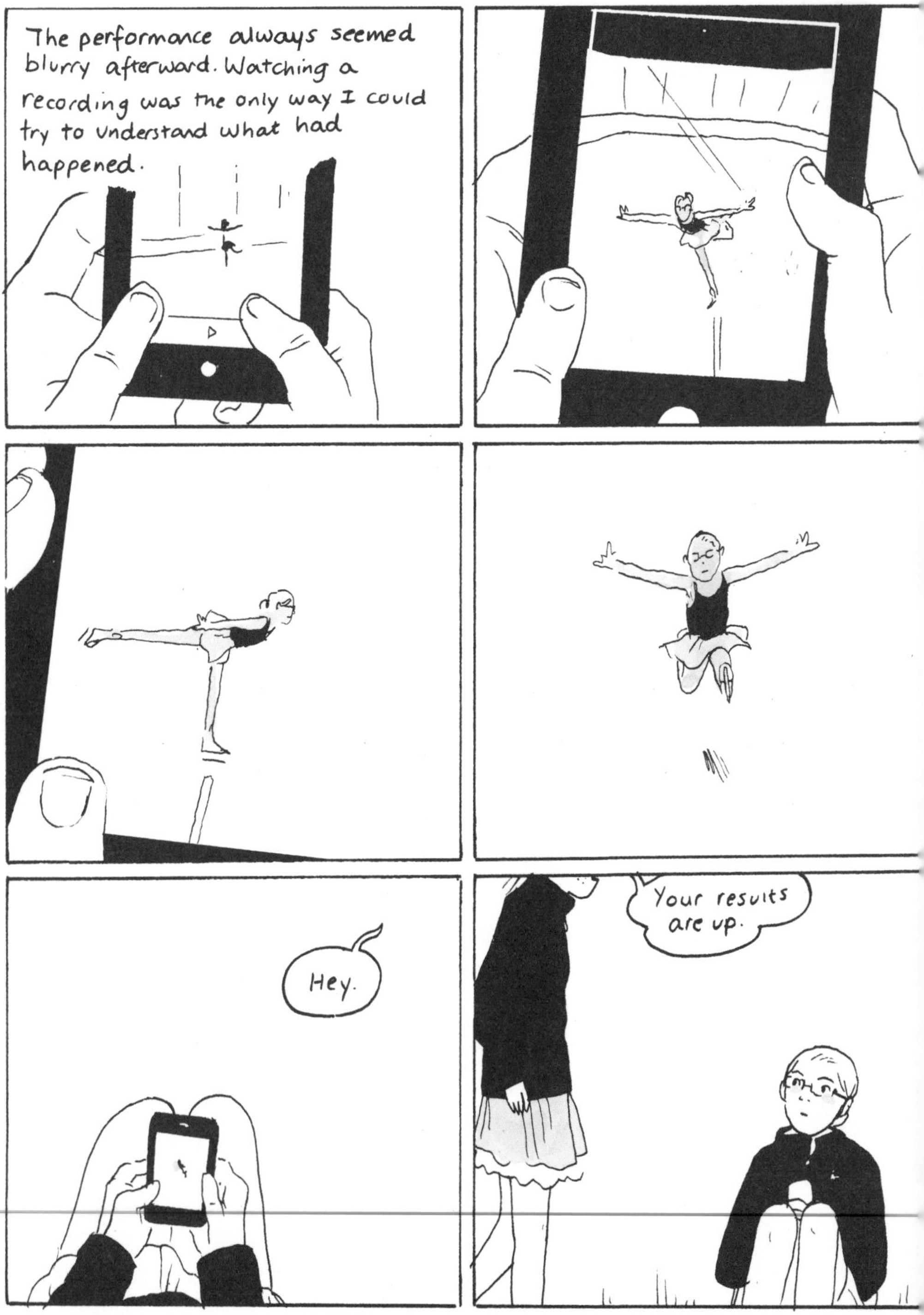
The performance always seemed blurry afterward. Watching a recording was the only way I could try to understand what had happened.
Hey.
Your results are up.

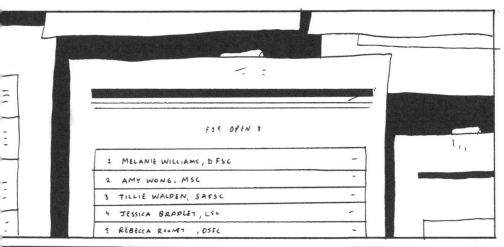

F35 OPEN 8

1	MELANIE WILLIAMS, DFSC	—
2	AMY WONG, MSC	—
3	TILLIE WALDEN, SAFSC	—
4	JESSICA BRADLEY, LSC	—
5	REBECCA ROONEY, DSFC	—

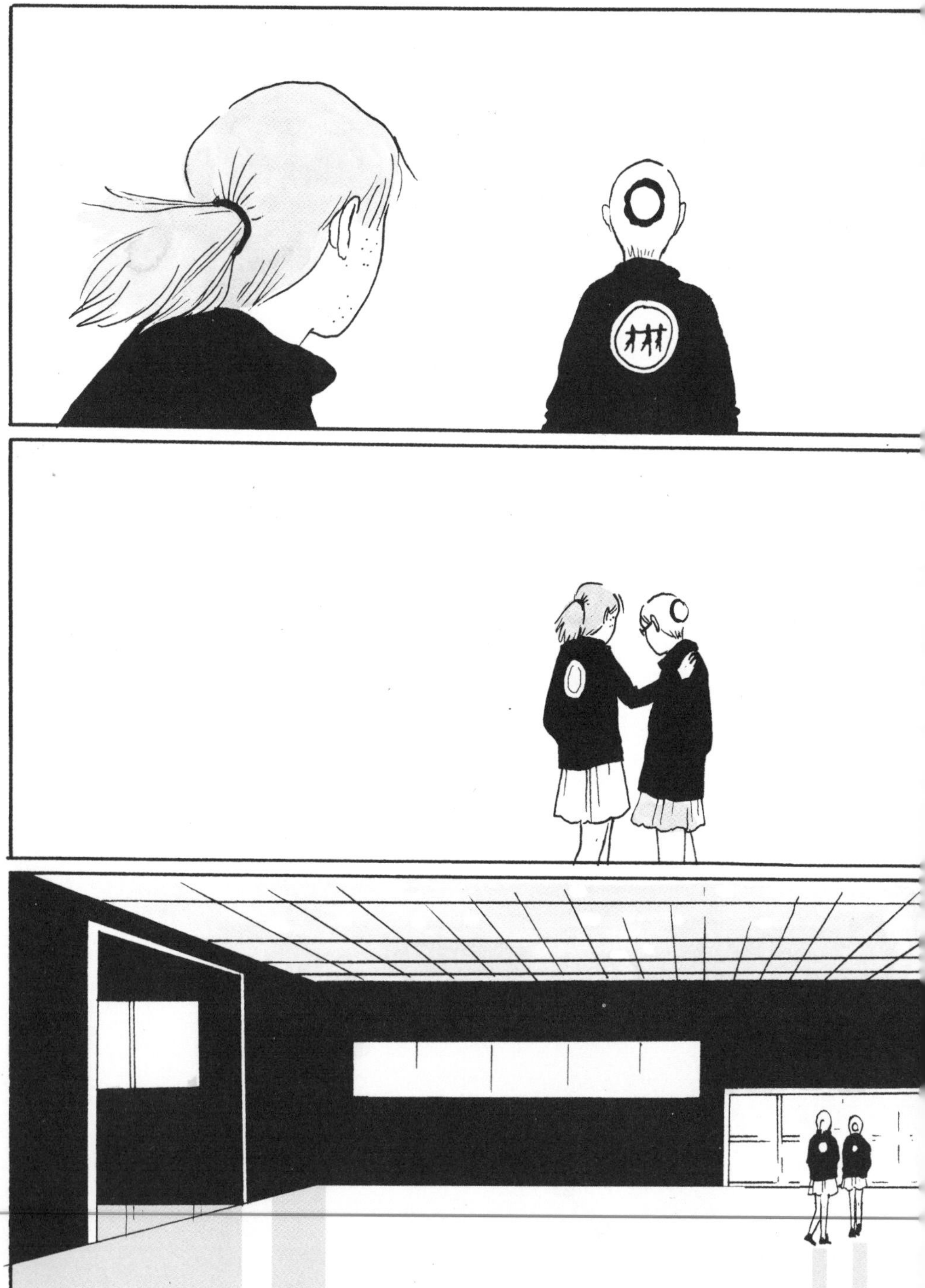

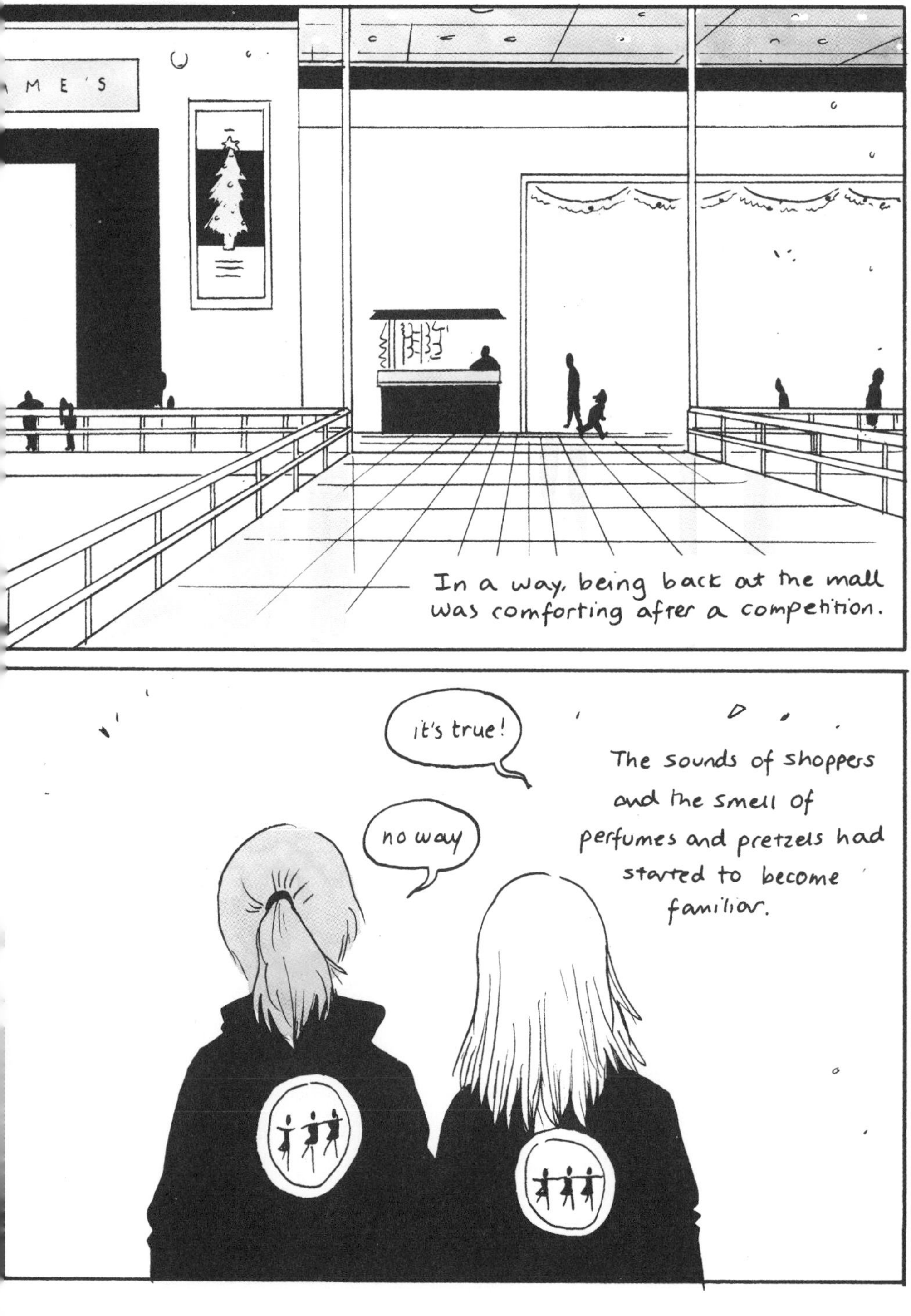
In a way, being back at the mall was comforting after a competition.
it's true!
no way
The sounds of shoppers and the smell of perfumes and pretzels had started to become familiar.

134

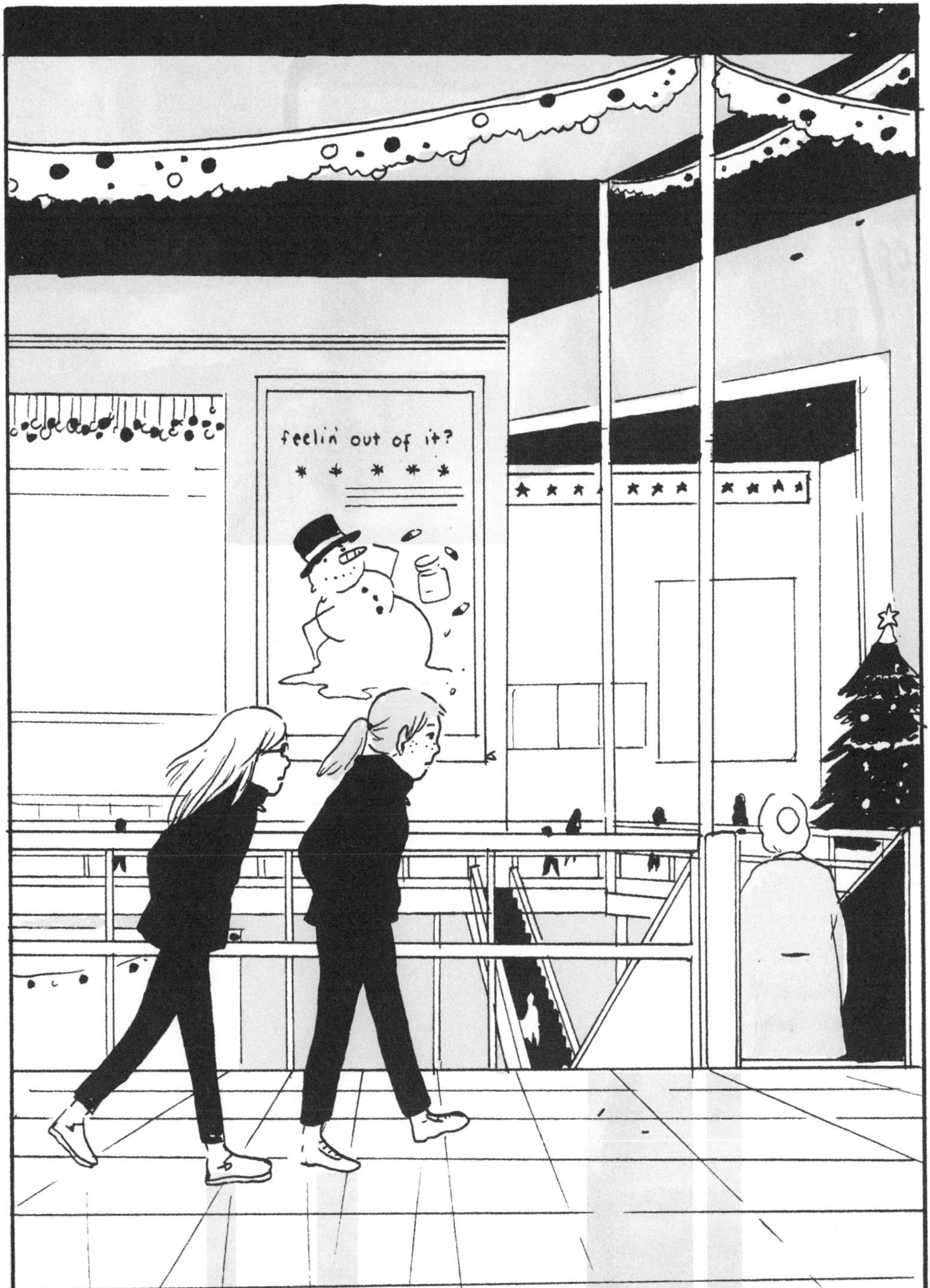
feelin' out of it?

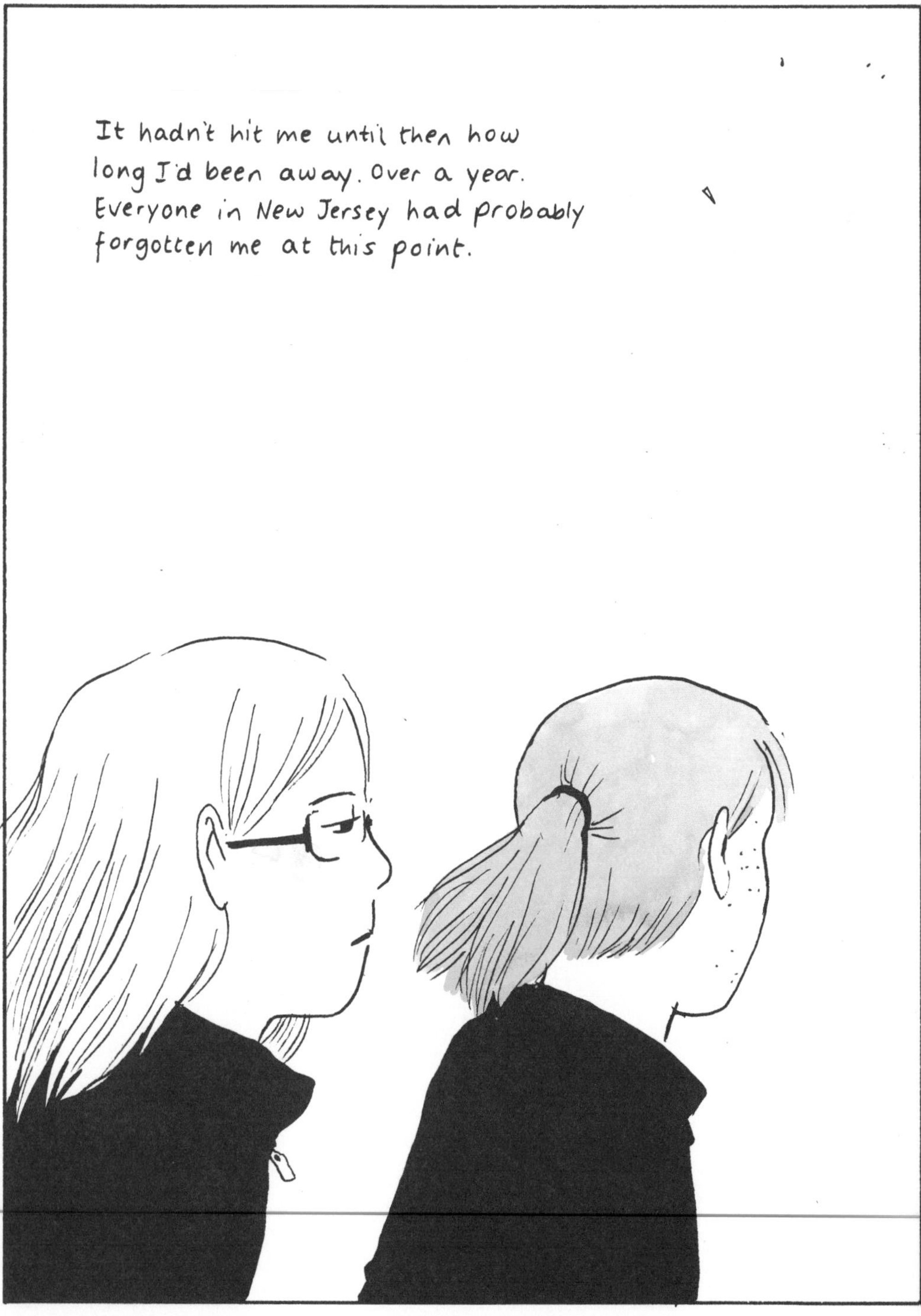
It hadn't hit me until then how long I'd been away. Over a year. Everyone in New Jersey had probably forgotten me at this point.

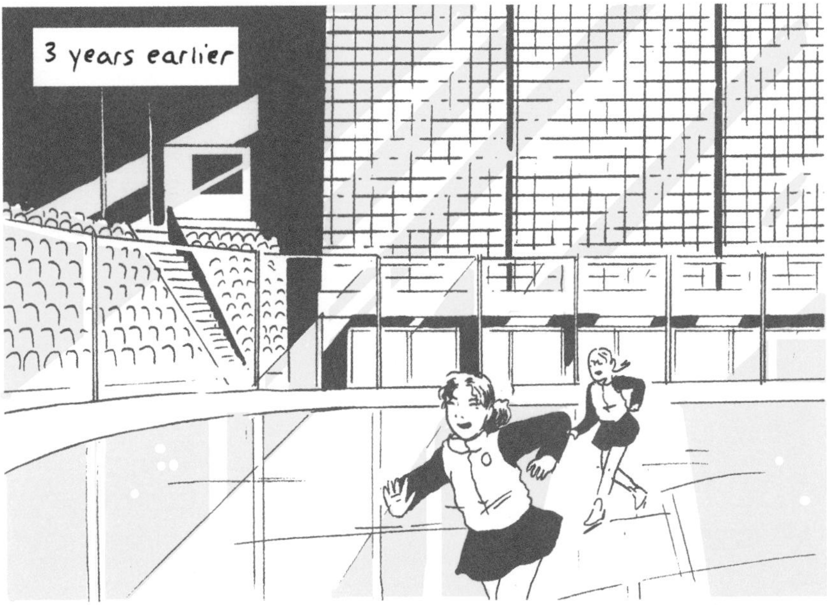
3 years earlier

I missed Molly and I didn't understand why. We were constantly bickering and driving each other crazy. But I missed it. I missed being in that beautiful rink with her.

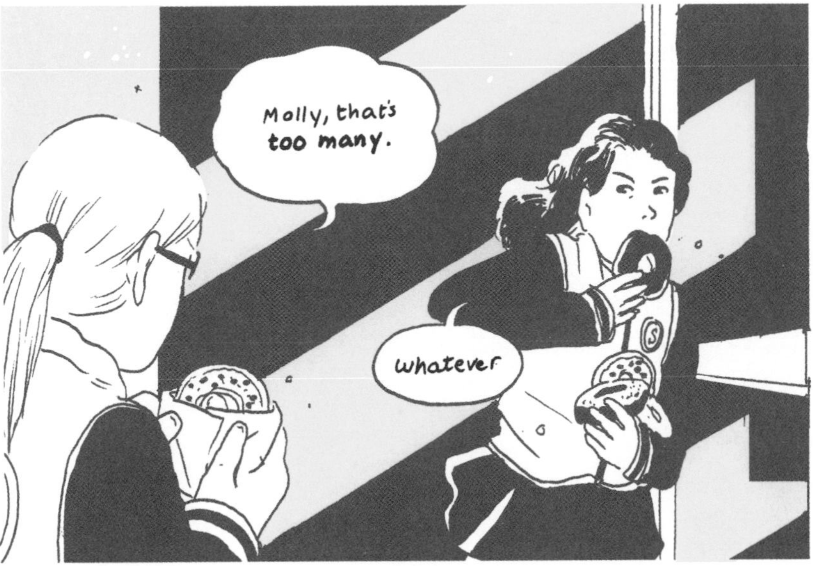
Molly, that's **too many.**
whatever

I hadn't forgotten the brutality of practices there, and I didn't miss getting yelled at. But there was something wonderful about it all. That feeling of freedom when practice was done and romping around the rink like we owned the place.

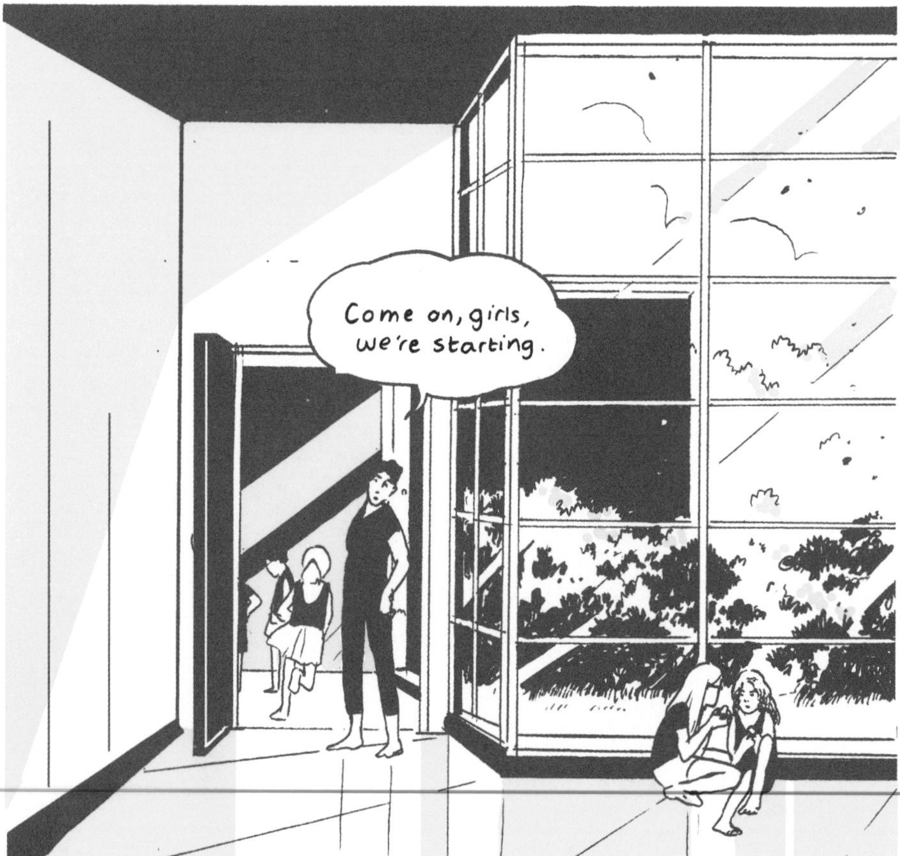
Come on, girls, we're starting.

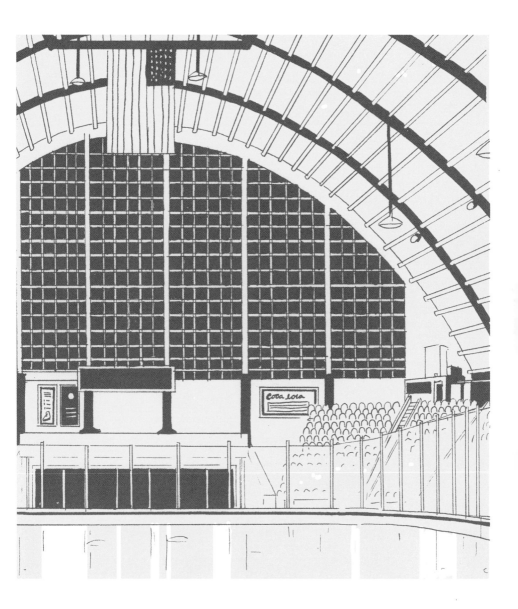

Skating changed when I came to Texas.
It wasn't strict or beautiful or energizing
anymore. Now it just felt dull and
exhausting. I couldn't understand why
I should keep skating after it lost all its shine.

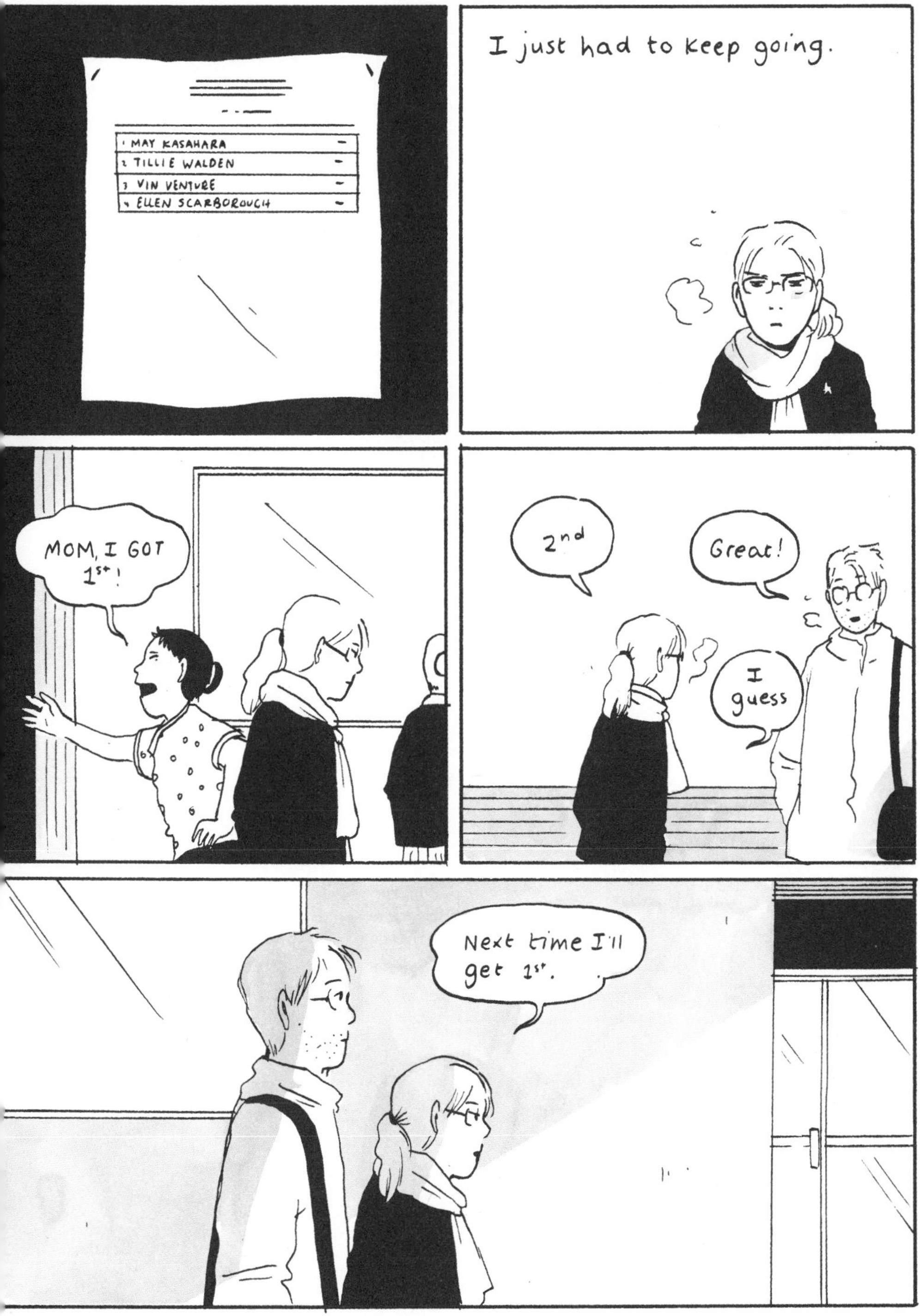
1 MAY KASAHARA
2 TILLIE WALDEN
3 VIN VENTURE
4 ELLEN SCARBOROUGH
I just had to keep going.
MOM, I GOT 1st!
2nd
Great!
I guess
Next time I'll get 1st.

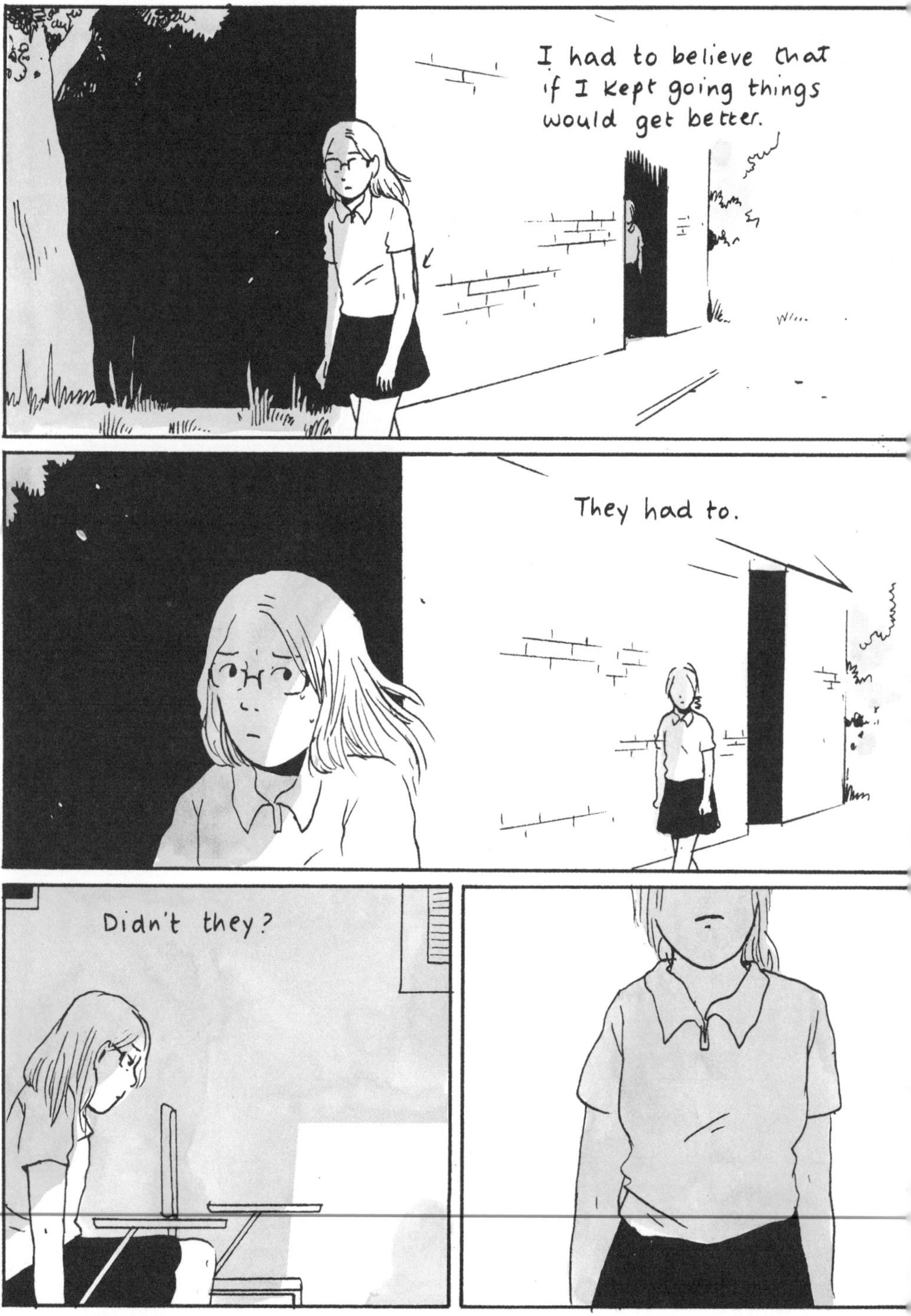
I had to believe that if I kept going things would get better.
They had to.
Didn't they?

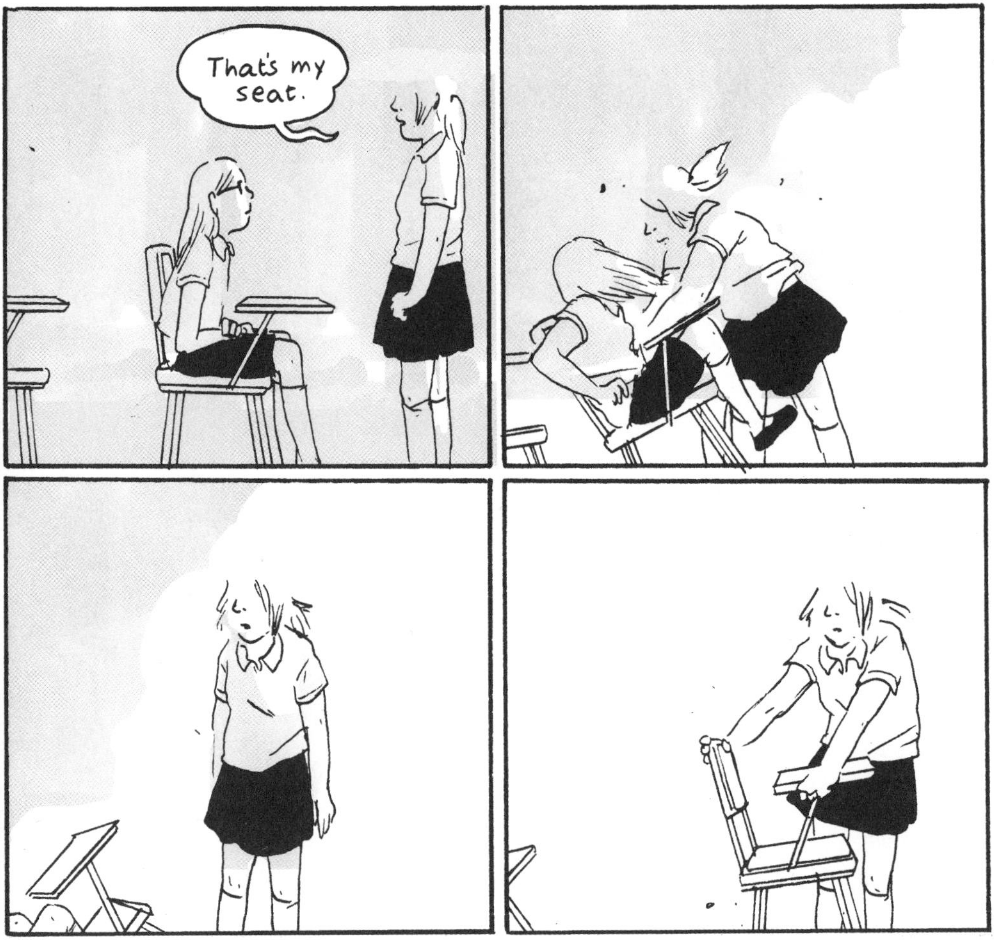
That's my seat.

It was when I hit the floor that I noticed someone sitting in the corner of the room.

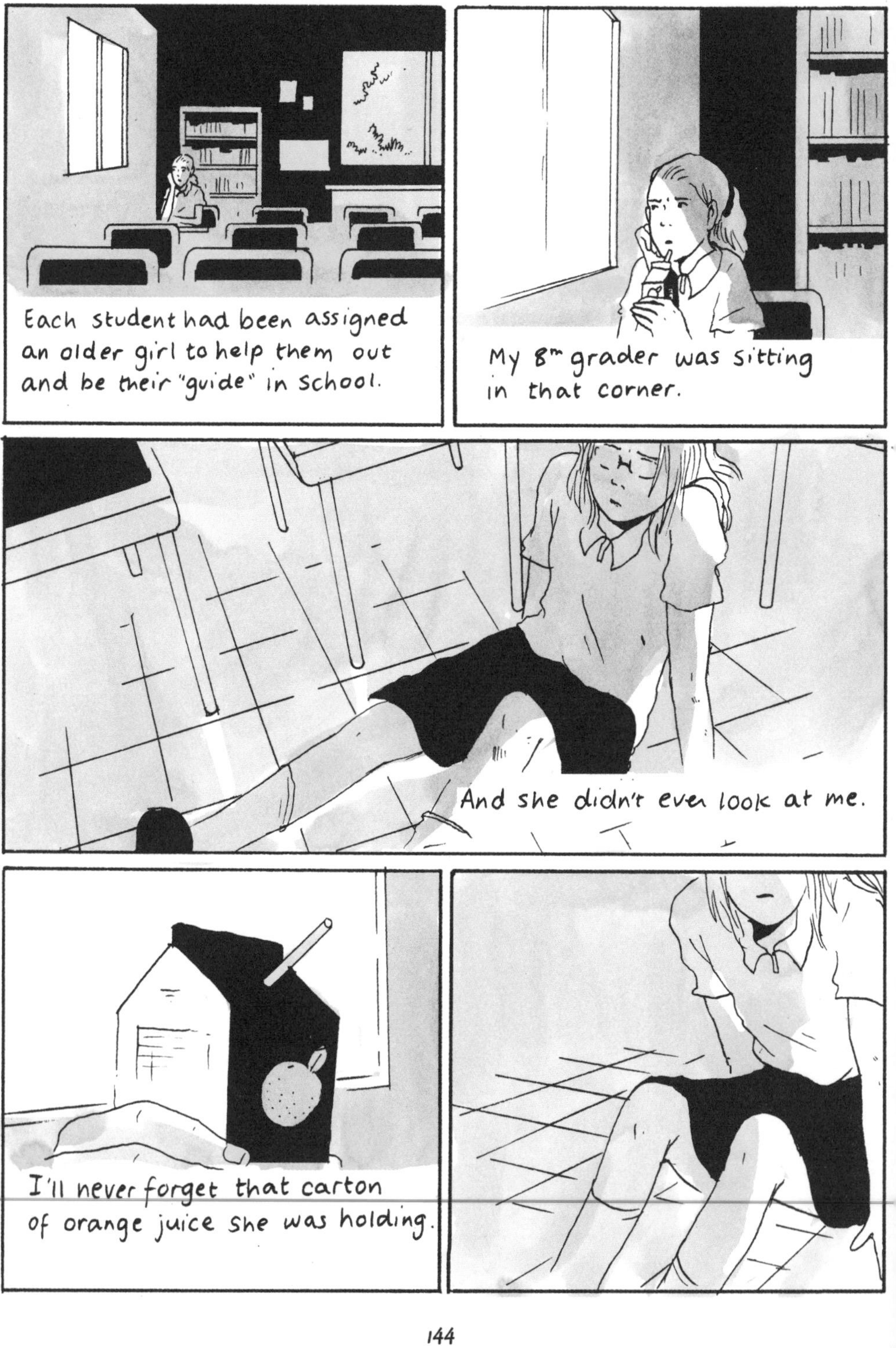
Each student had been assigned an older girl to help them out and be their "guide" in school.
My 8th grader was sitting in that corner.
And she didn't even look at me.
I'll never forget that carton of orange juice she was holding.

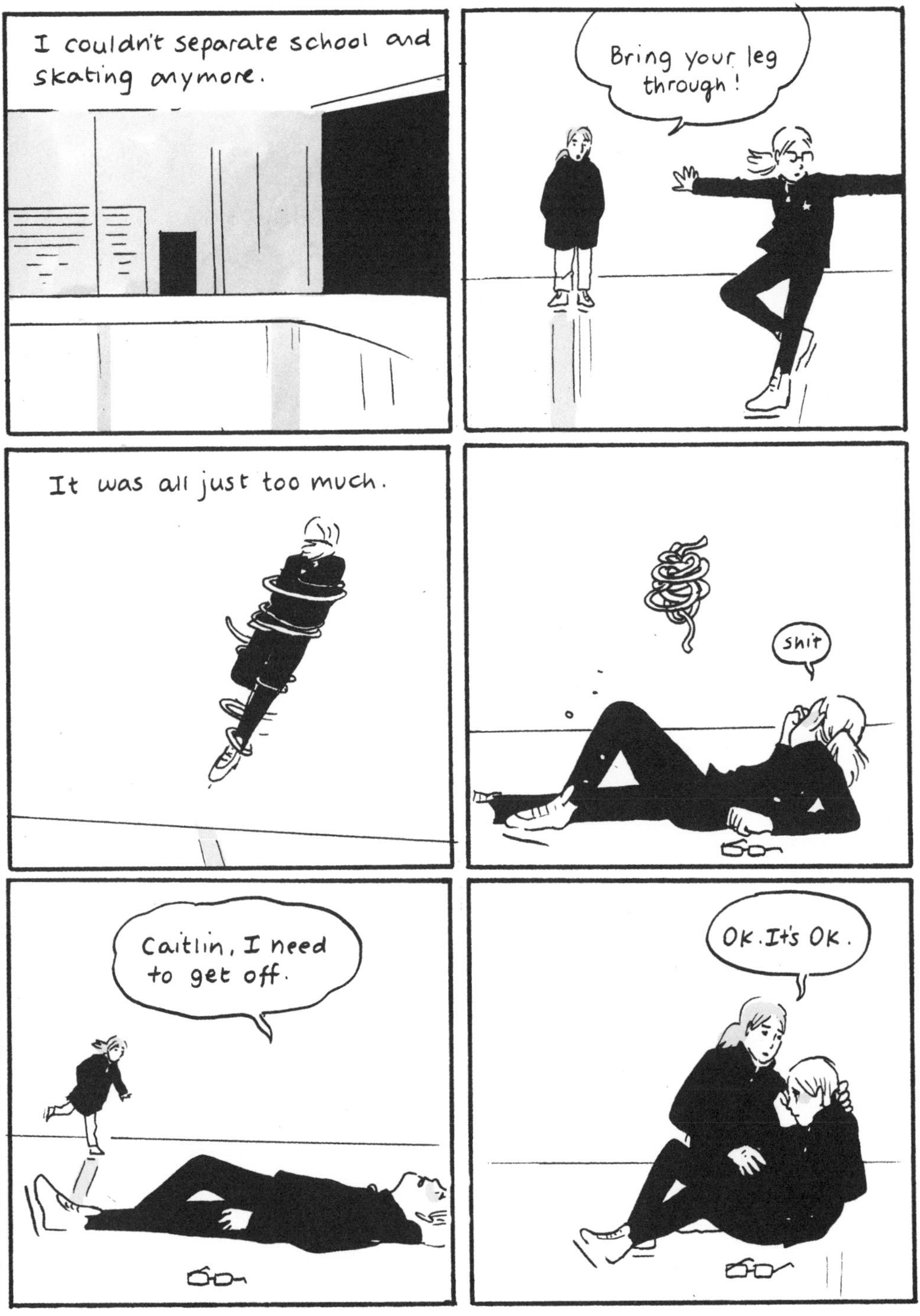
I couldn't separate school and skating anymore.
Bring your leg through!
It was all just too much.
shit
Caitlin, I need to get off.
OK. It's OK.

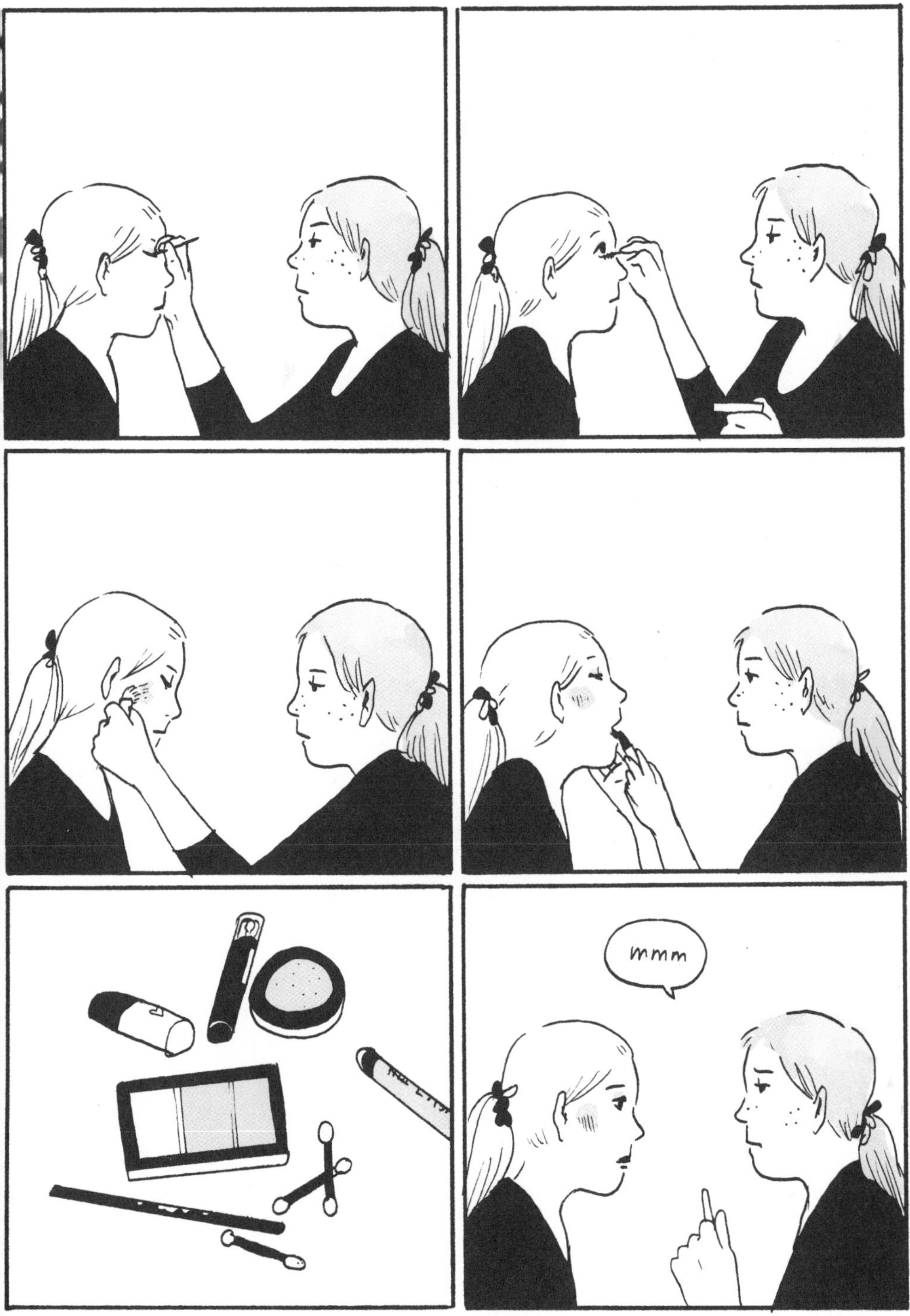
mmm

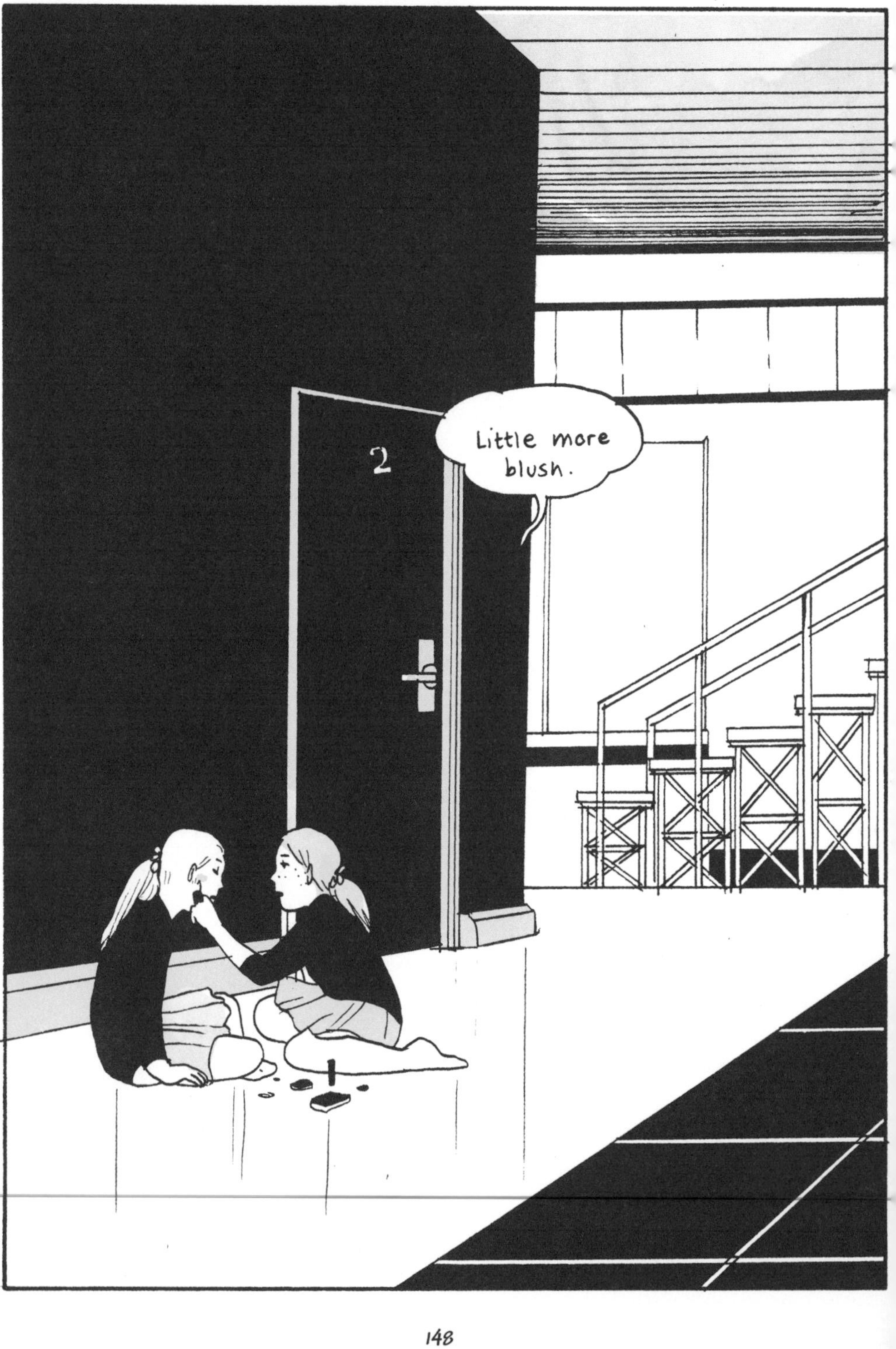
2
Little more blush.

5

SPIRAL

The only hard part of a spiral was finding your momentum. Once you were moving fast enough and your leg was in the air, it felt like you could go on forever.

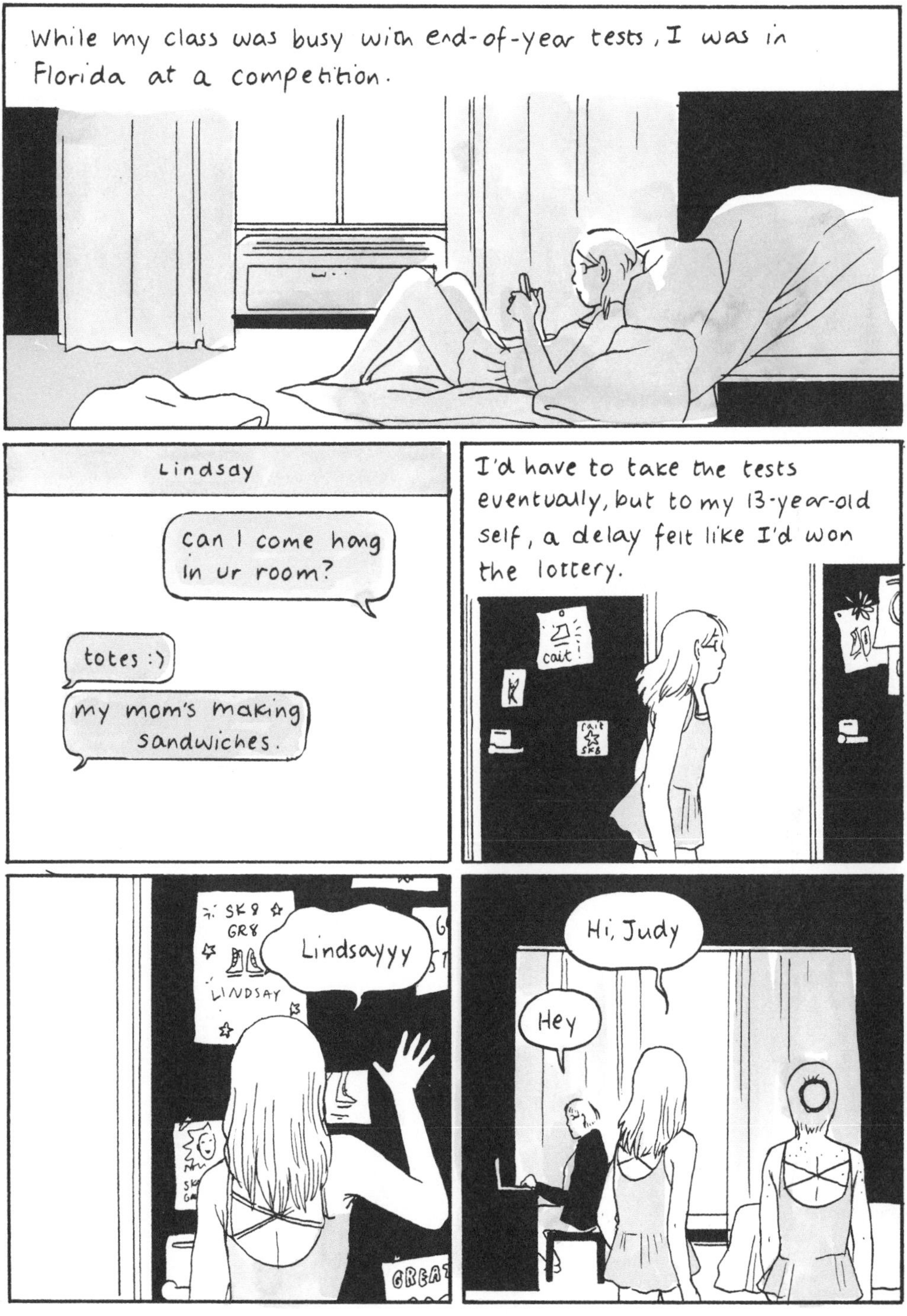
While my class was busy with end-of-year tests, I was in Florida at a competition.
Lindsay
can I come hang in ur room?
totes :)
my mom's making sandwiches.
I'd have to take the tests eventually, but to my 13-year-old self, a delay felt like I'd won the lottery.
cait
SK8 GR8
LINDSAY
Lindsayyy
Hi, Judy
Hey

152

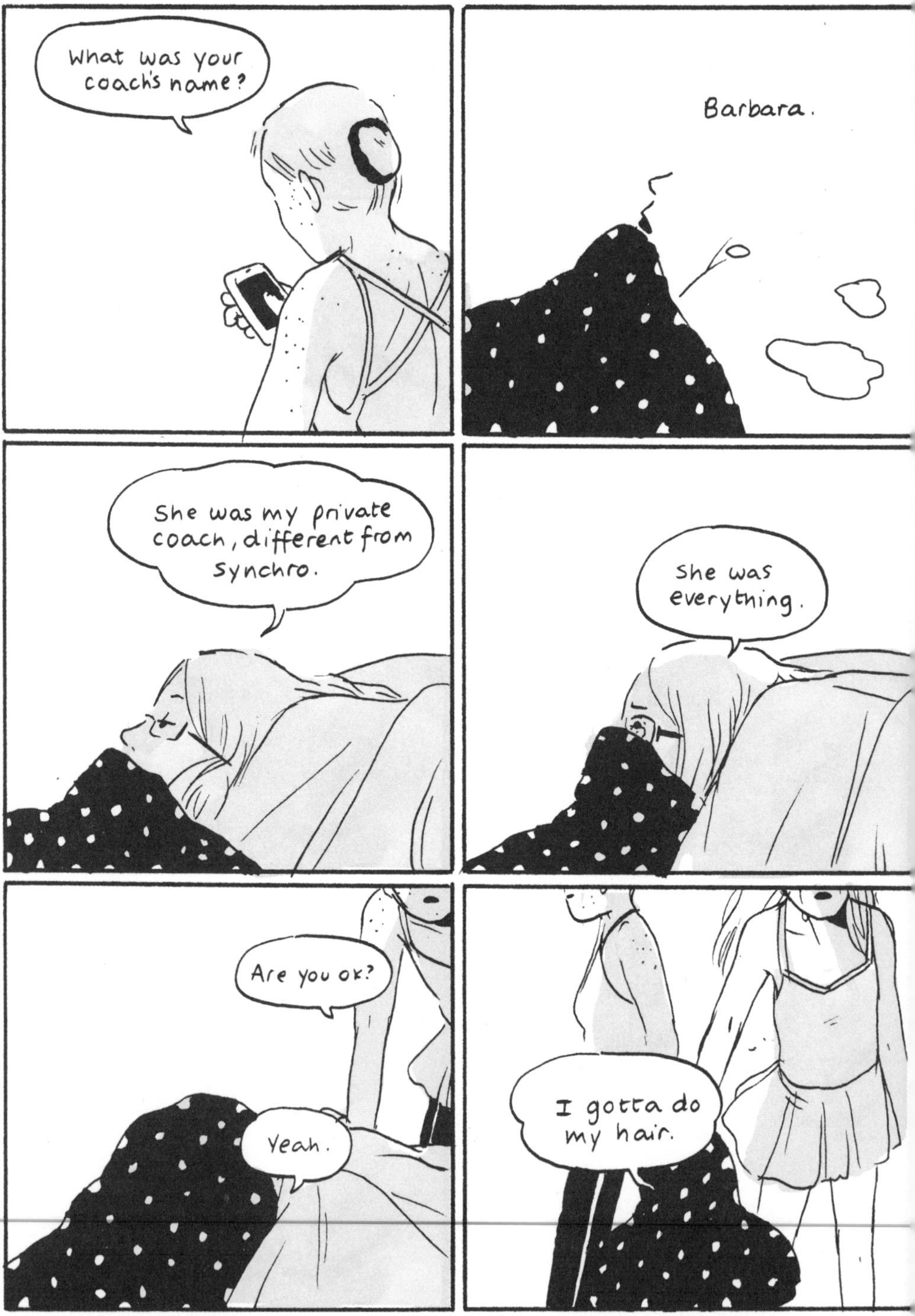
What was your coach's name?
Barbara.
She was my private coach, different from synchro.
She was everything.
Are you ok?
Yeah.
I gotta do my hair.

Barbara had been
my first coach. She
was the one who
held my hand when
I first stepped
onto the ice.

But teaching
me to ice skate
never meant
much to me.

I came to her
lessons just to
be in her arms.

As a little kid, I
was desperate for
any affection or
attention

and she gave
it all to me.

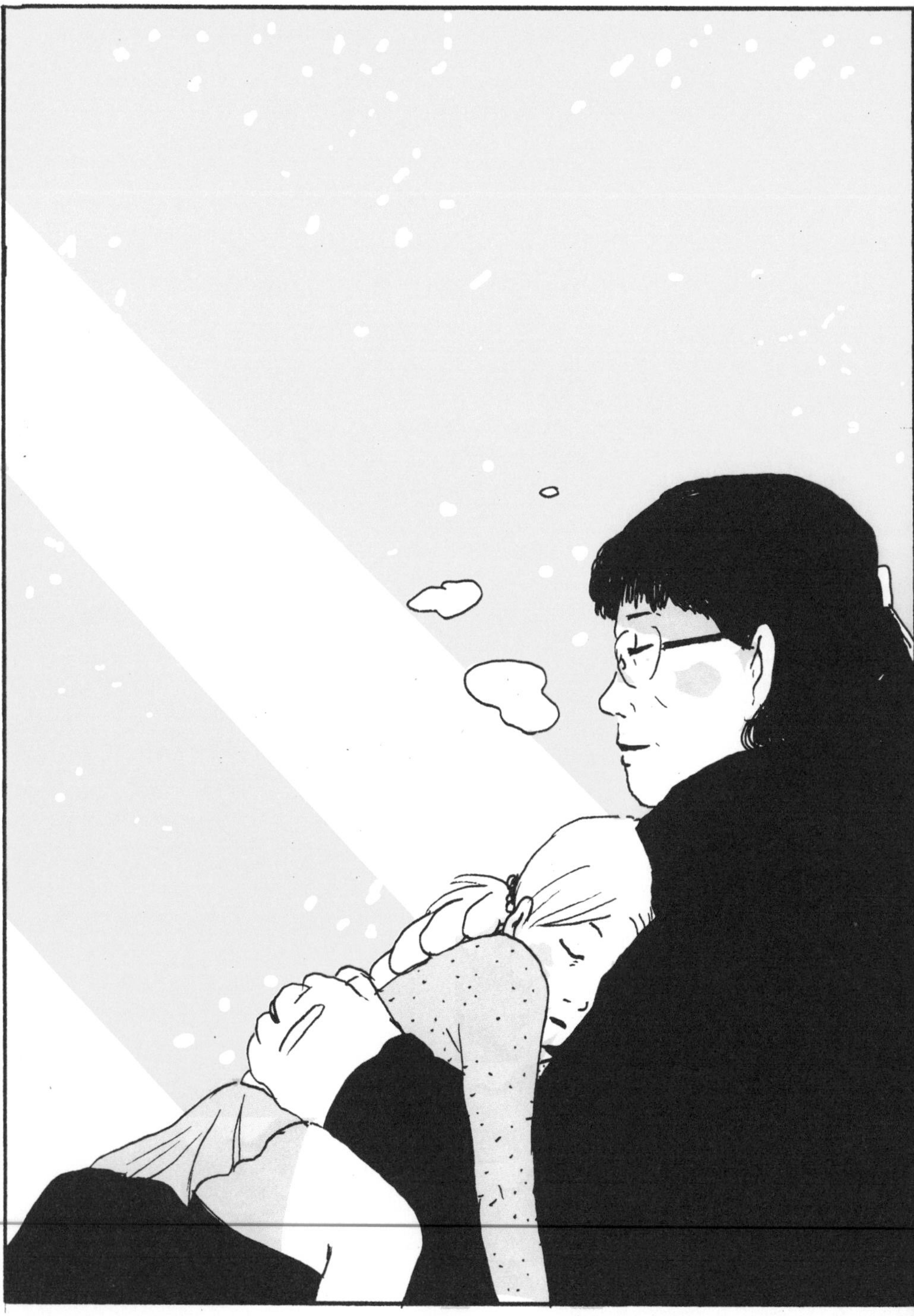

158

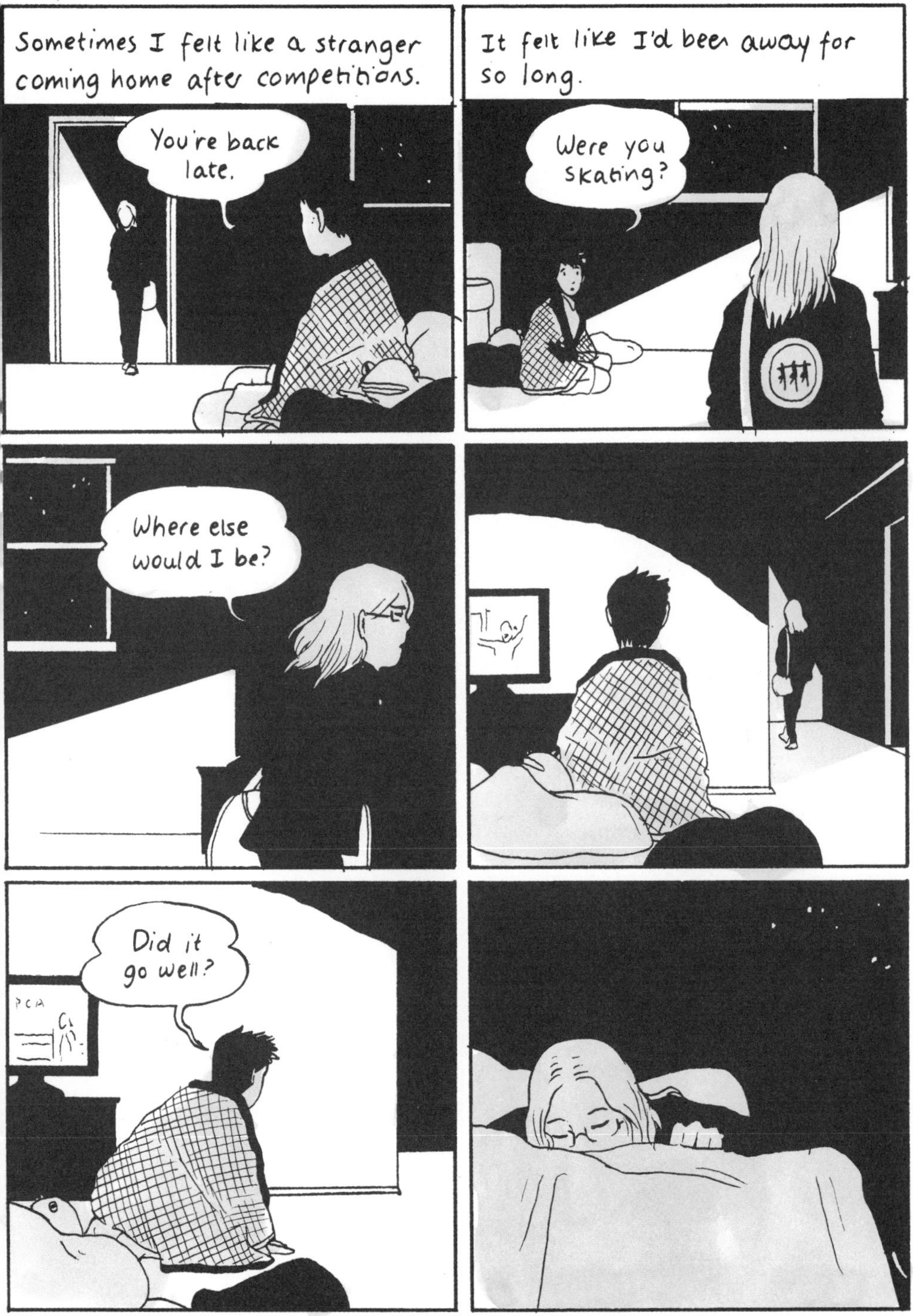
Sometimes I felt like a stranger coming home after competitions.
You're back late.
It felt like I'd been away for so long.
Were you skating?
Where else would I be?
Did it go well?

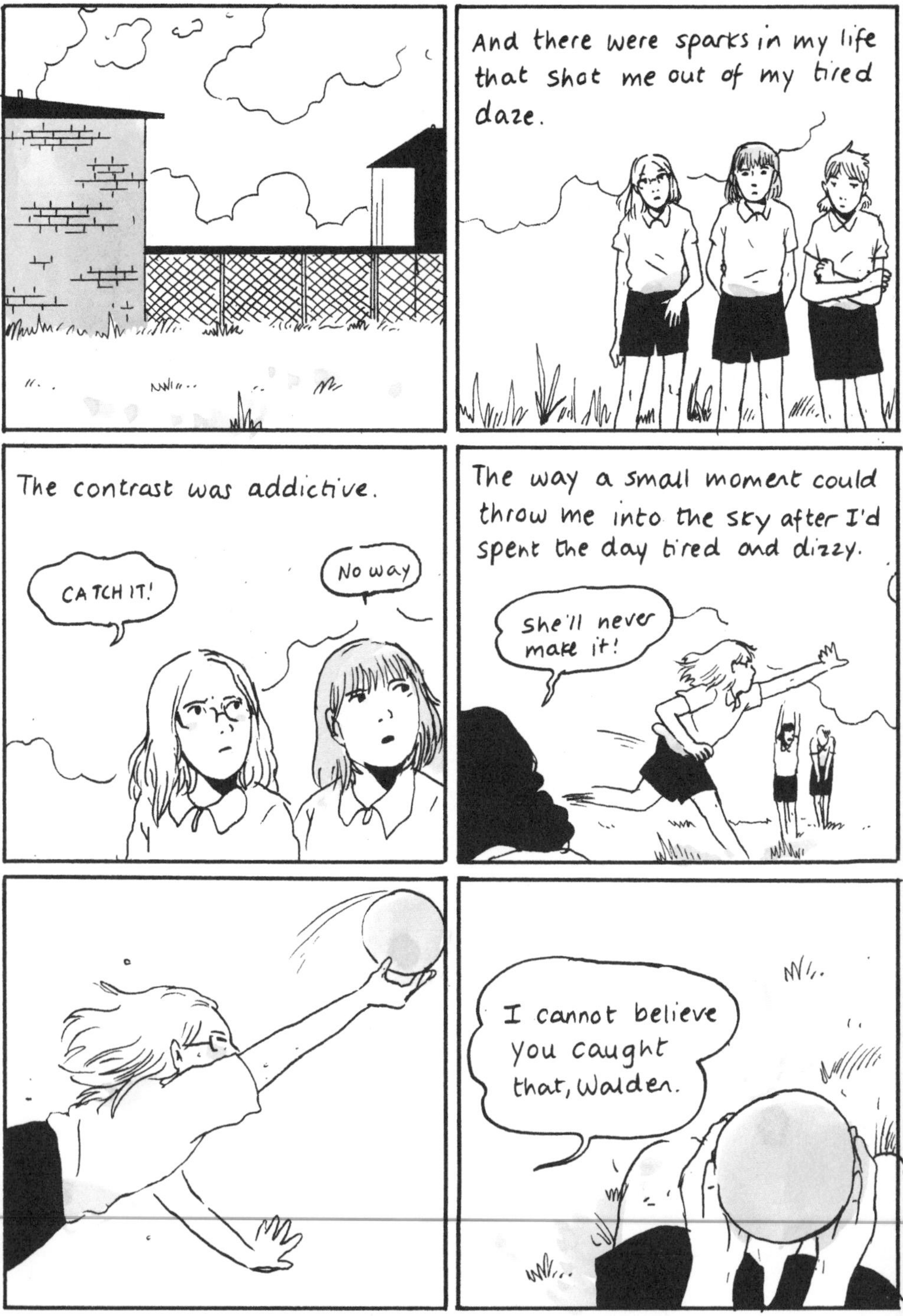
And there were sparks in my life that shot me out of my tired daze.
The contrast was addictive.
CATCH IT!
No way
The way a small moment could throw me into the sky after I'd spent the day tired and dizzy.
She'll never make it!
I cannot believe you caught that, Walden.

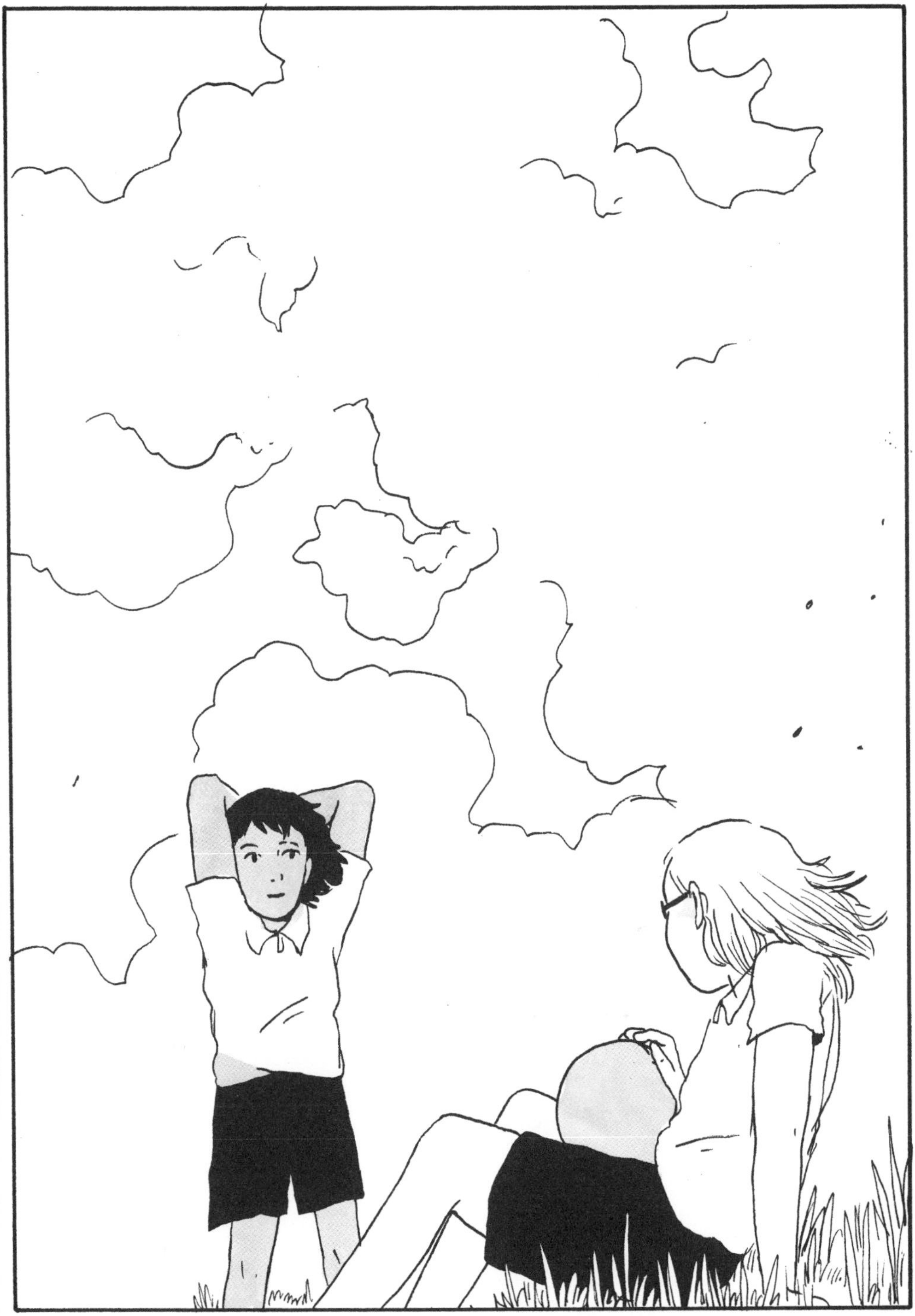

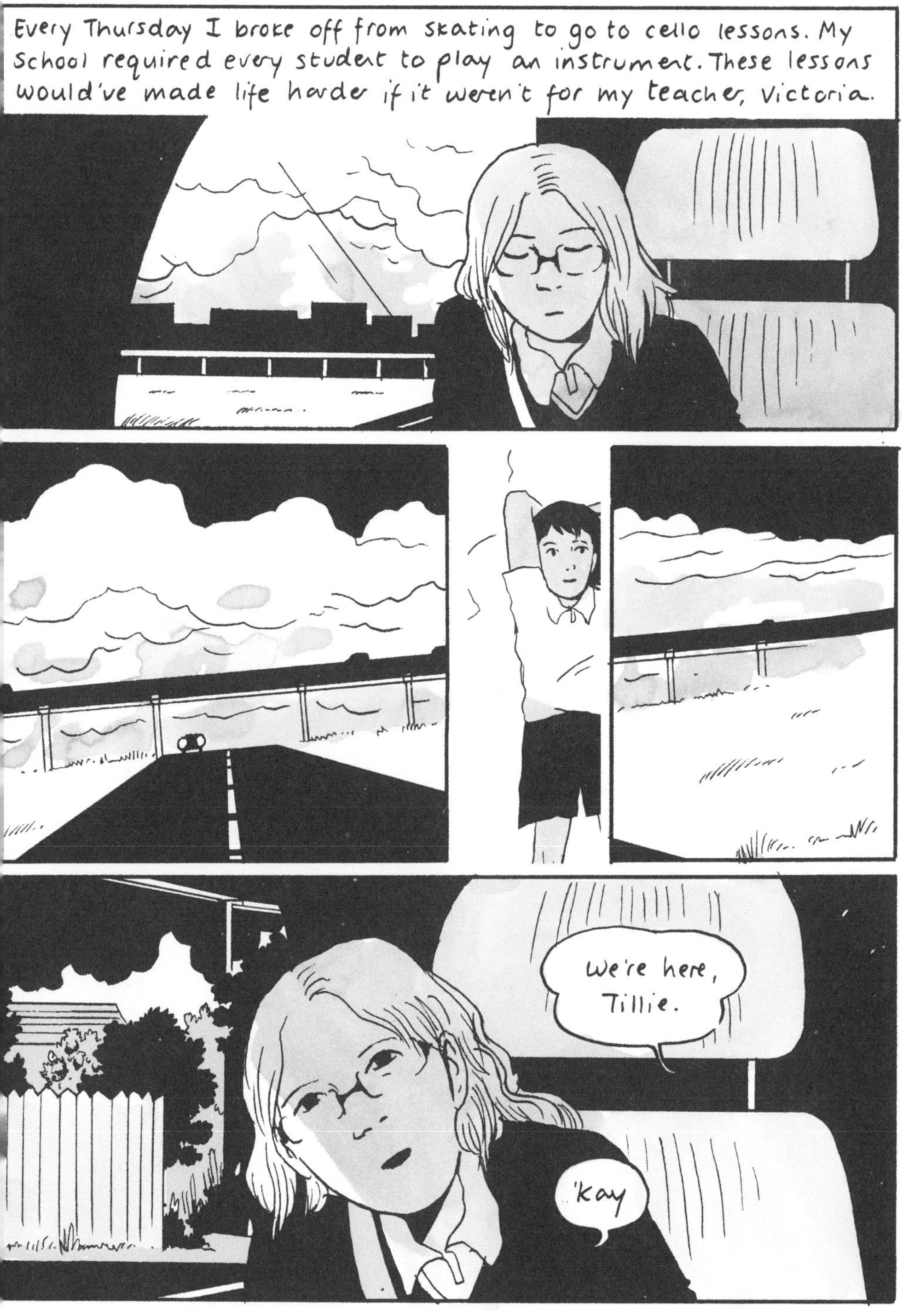
Every Thursday I broke off from skating to go to cello lessons. My School required every student to play an instrument. These lessons would've made life harder if it weren't for my teacher, Victoria.
We're here, Tillie.
'Kay

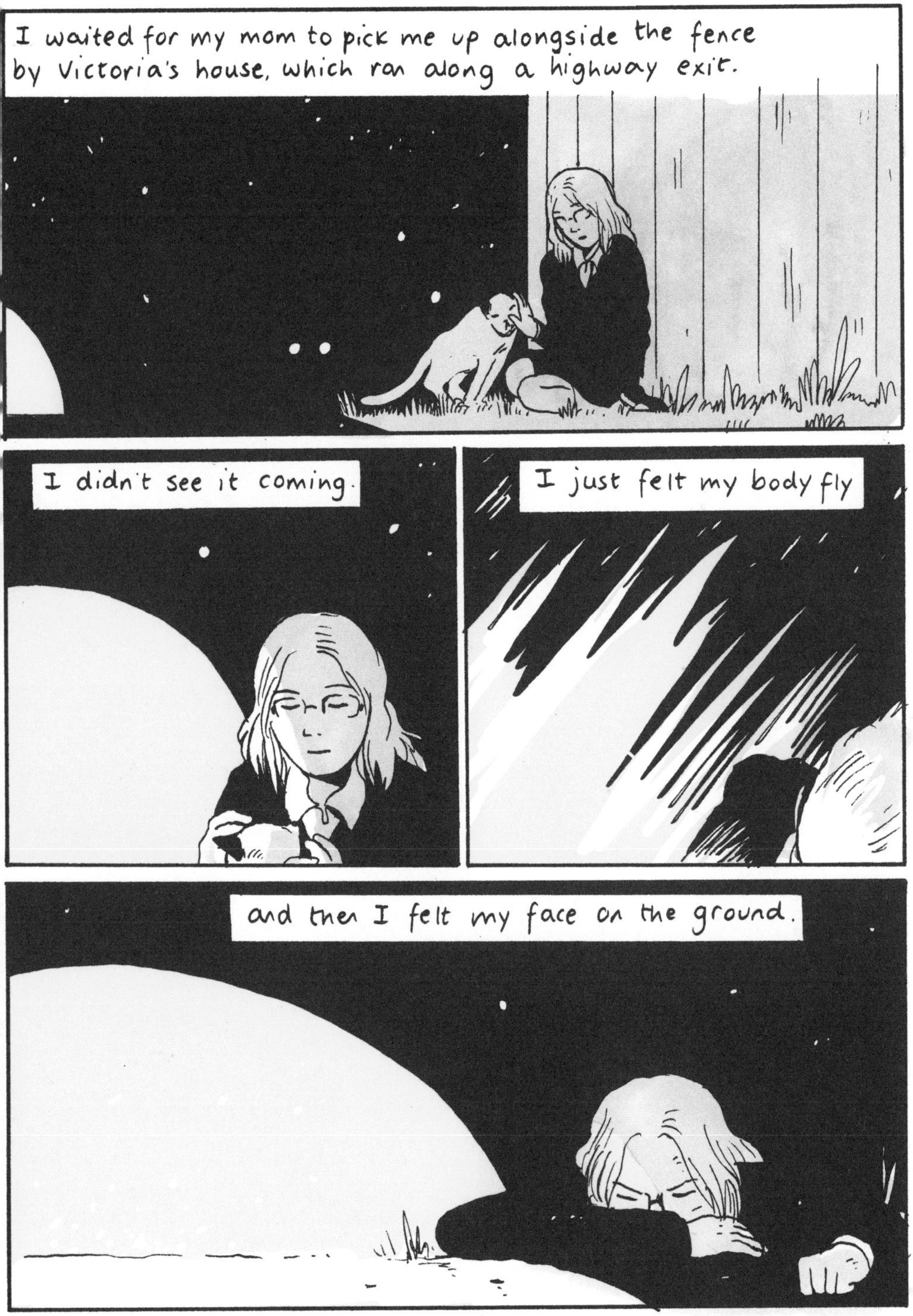
I waited for my mom to pick me up alongside the fence by Victoria's house, which ran along a highway exit.
I didn't see it coming.
I just felt my body fly
and then I felt my face on the ground.

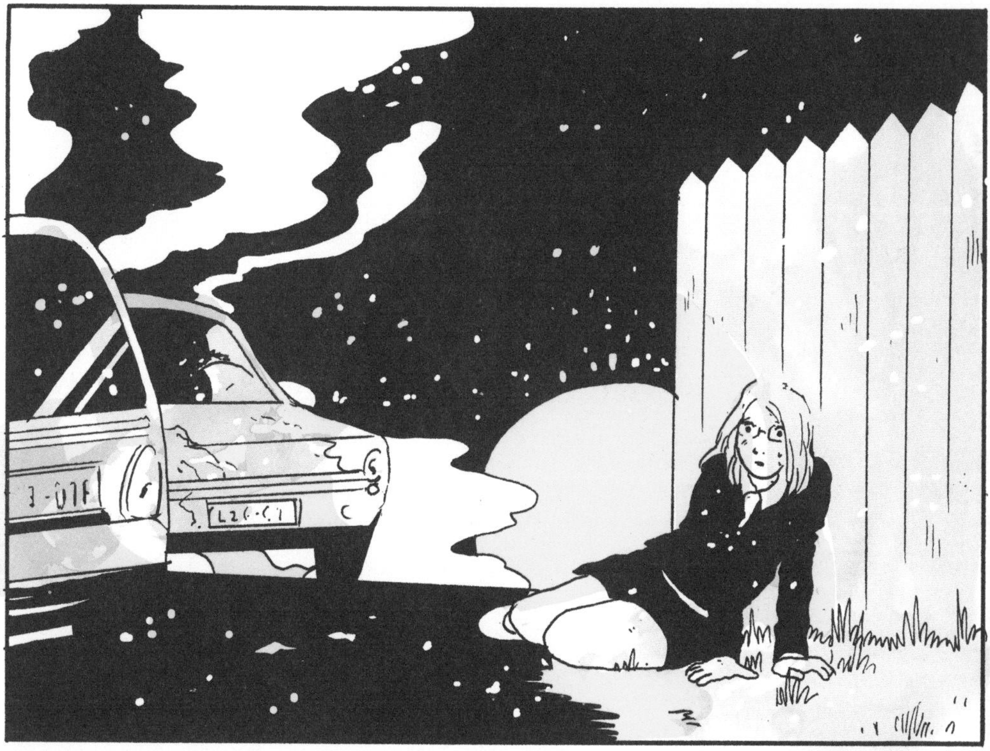

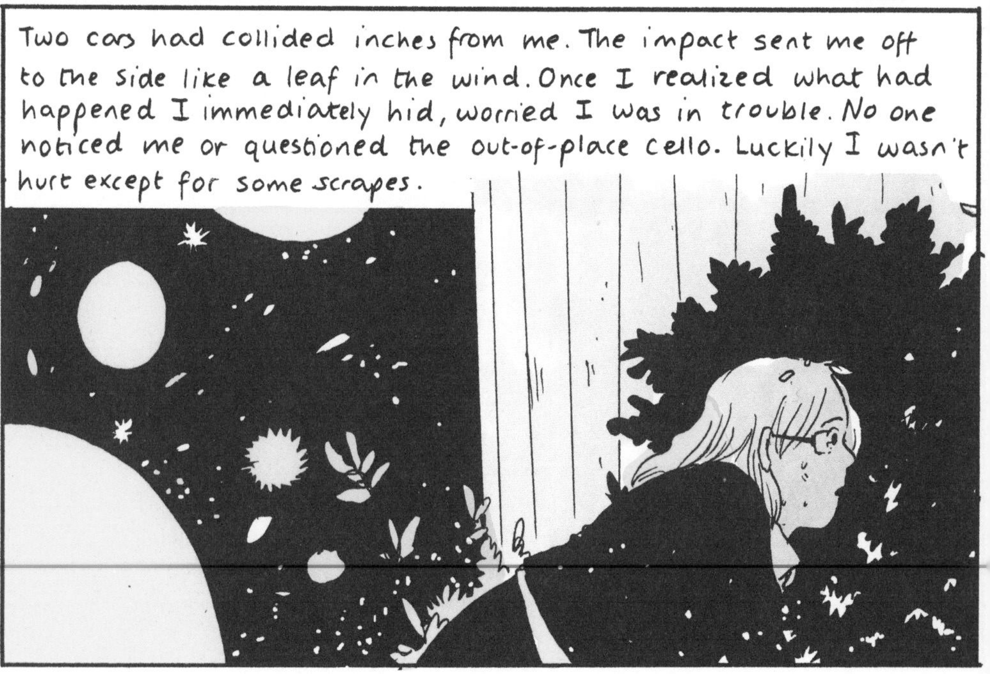
Two cars had collided inches from me. The impact sent me off to the side like a leaf in the wind. Once I realized what had happened I immediately hid, worried I was in trouble. No one noticed me or questioned the out-of-place cello. Luckily I wasn't hurt except for some scrapes.

Something changed in me that night.

It was like I had swallowed my voice.

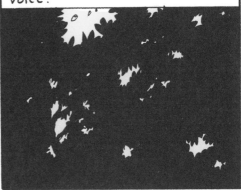

I wanted to scream and cry but nothing came out.

Even after my heartbeat had slowed down, I knew that the words were gone.

This silence spread over everything.

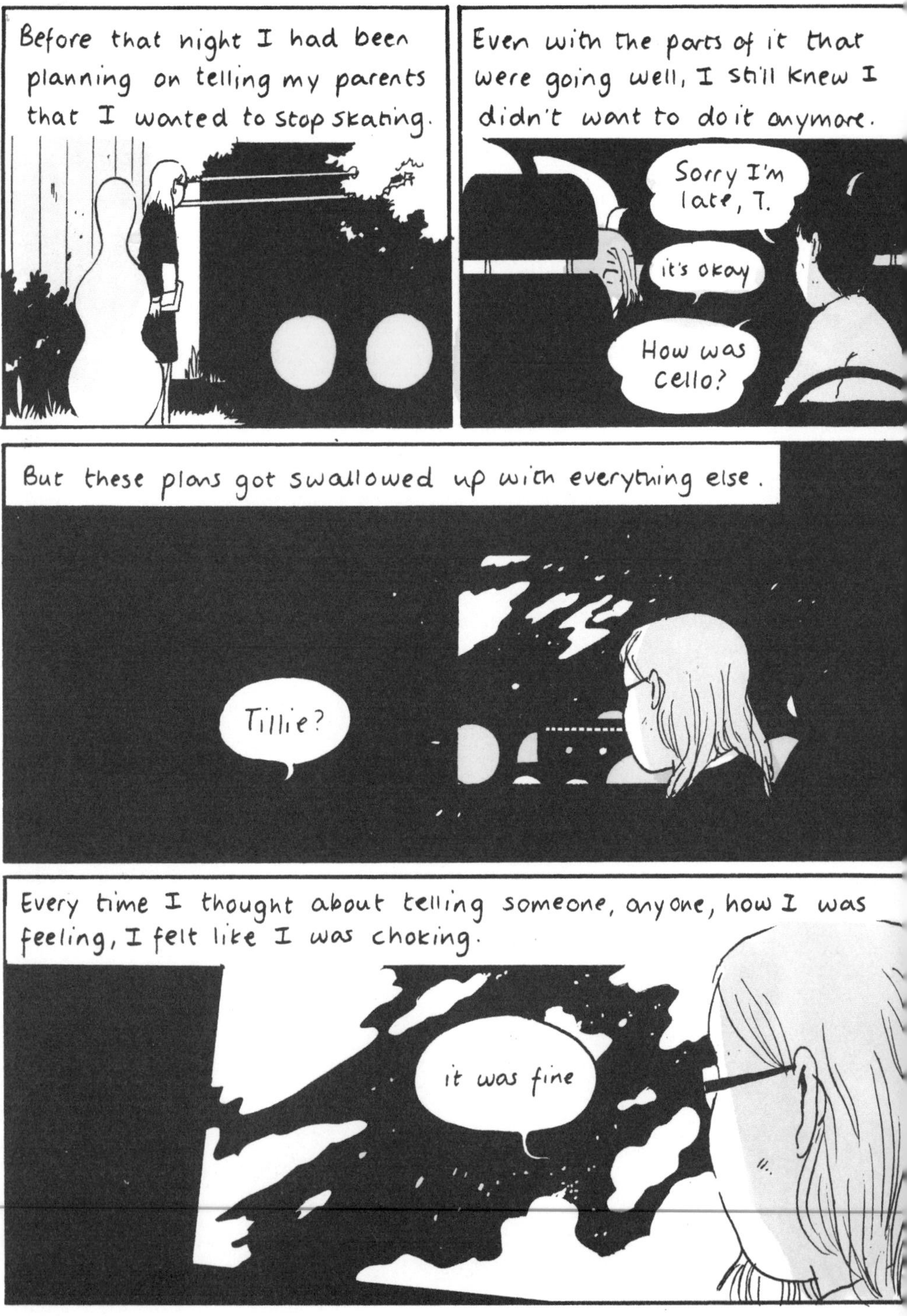
Before that night I had been planning on telling my parents that I wanted to stop skating.
Even with the parts of it that were going well, I still knew I didn't want to do it anymore.
Sorry I'm late, T.
it's okay
How was cello?
But these plans got swallowed up with everything else.
Tillie?
Every time I thought about telling someone, anyone, how I was feeling, I felt like I was choking.
it was fine

I tried to distract myself. But all I could feel were the scrapes on my palms.
I was so scared. I didn't want to get close to anything like that ever again.
click
Cloudy
mrow
mrow
The next morning I found out that something else had changed.

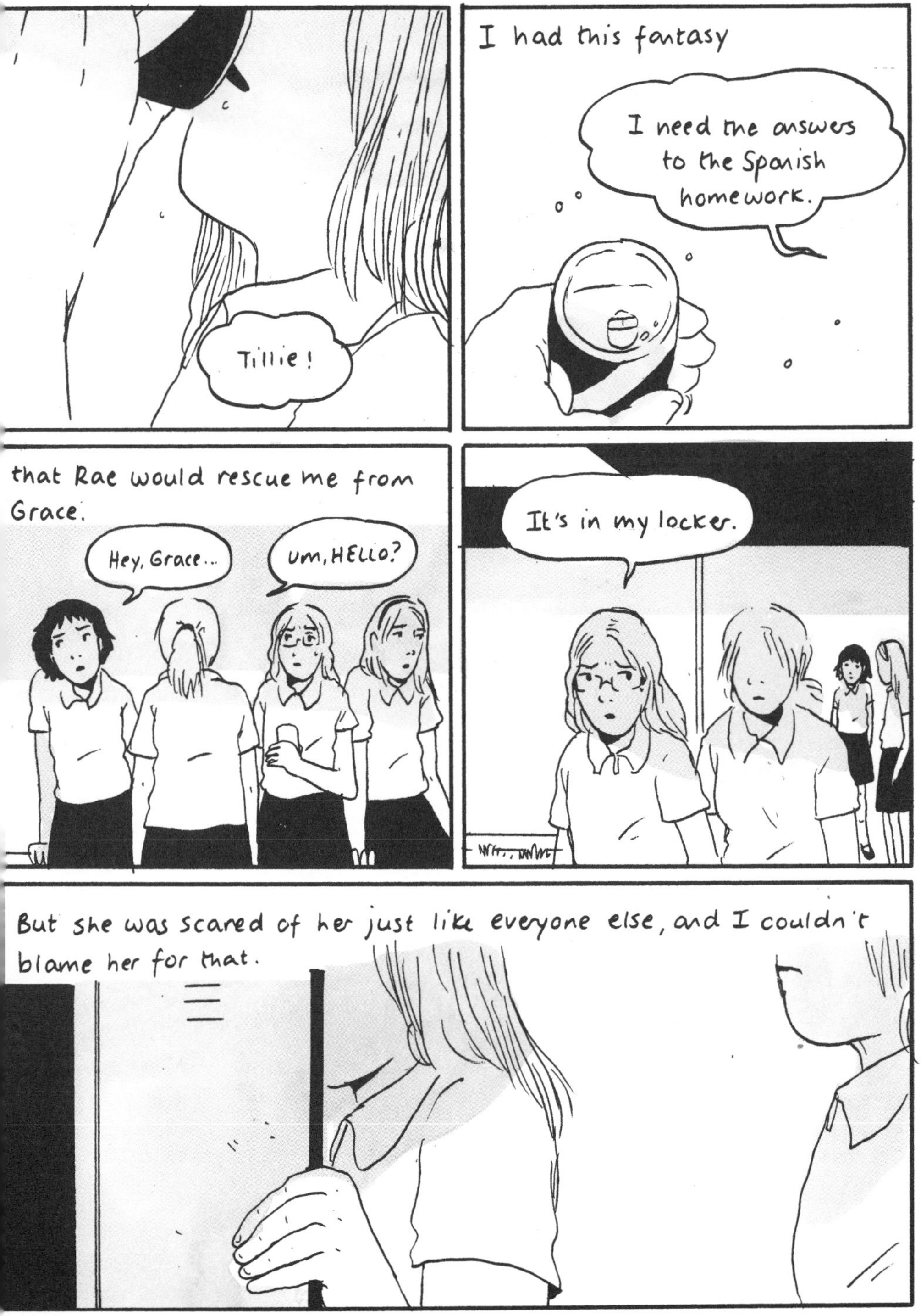
Tillie!
I had this fantasy
I need the answers to the Spanish homework.
that Rae would rescue me from Grace.
Hey, Grace...
um, HELLO?
It's in my locker.
But she was scared of her just like everyone else, and I couldn't blame her for that.

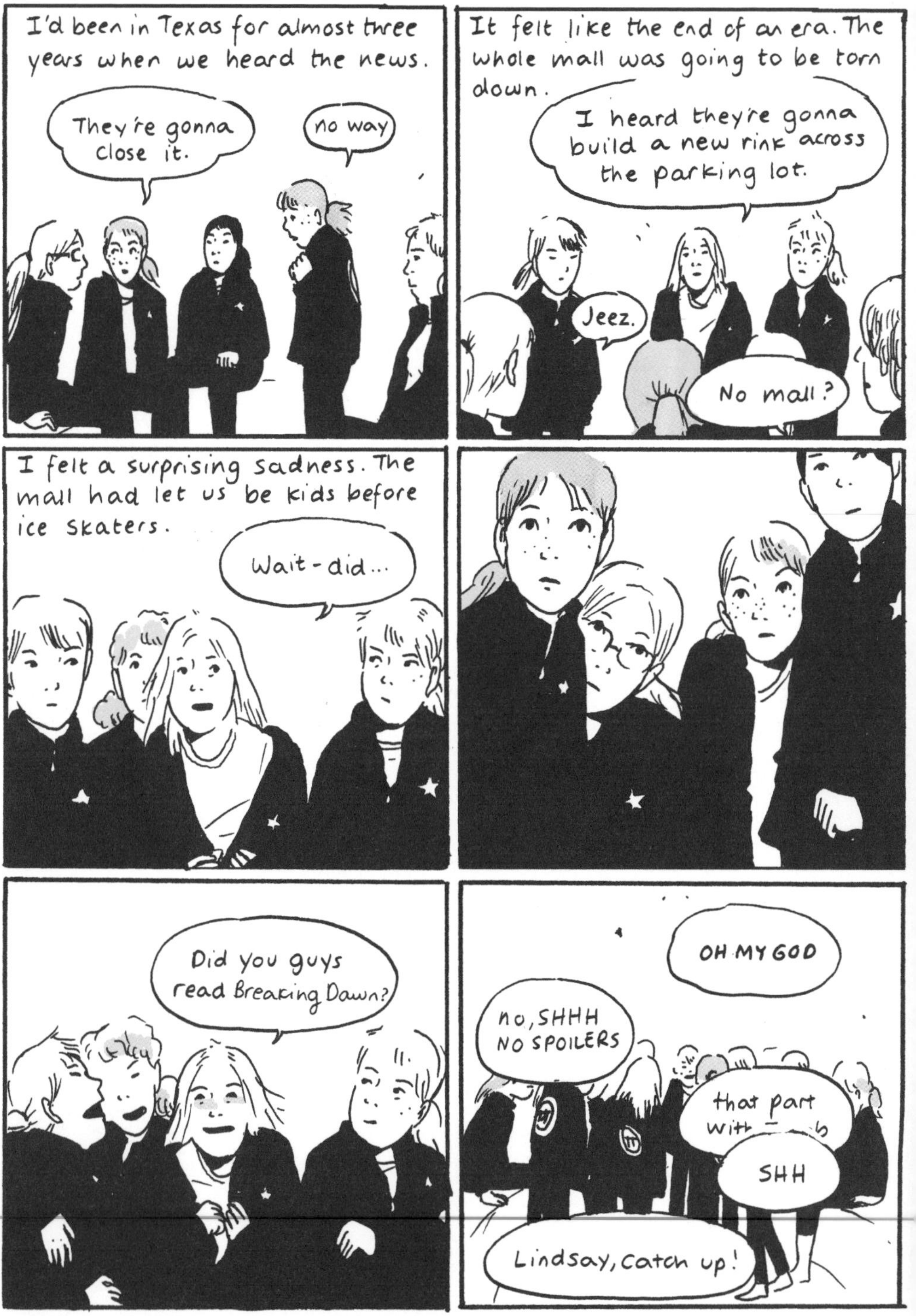
I'd been in Texas for almost three years when we heard the news.
They're gonna close it.
no way
It felt like the end of an era. The whole mall was going to be torn down.
I heard they're gonna build a new rink across the parking lot.
Jeez.
No mall?
I felt a surprising sadness. The mall had let us be kids before ice skaters.
Wait-did...
Did you guys read Breaking Dawn?
OH MY GOD
no, SHHH NO SPOILERS
that part
SHH
Lindsay, catch up!

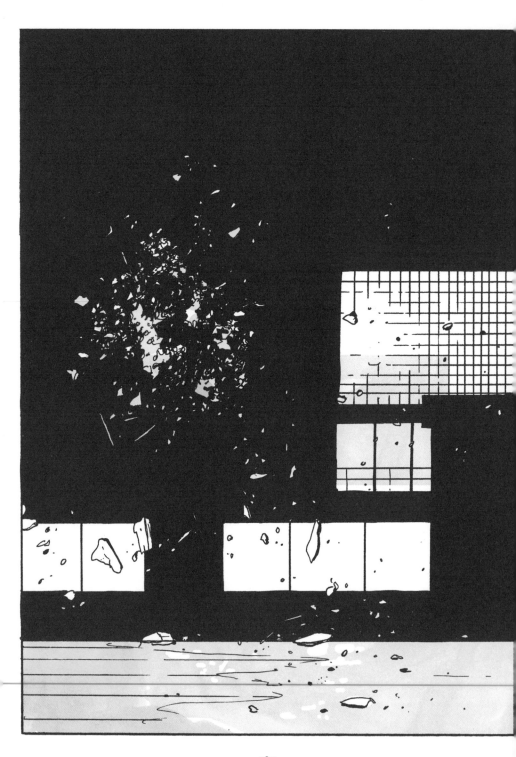

 I wouldn't forget any of it.

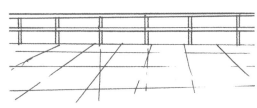

But it was time to leave it behind and push forward.

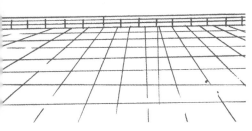 

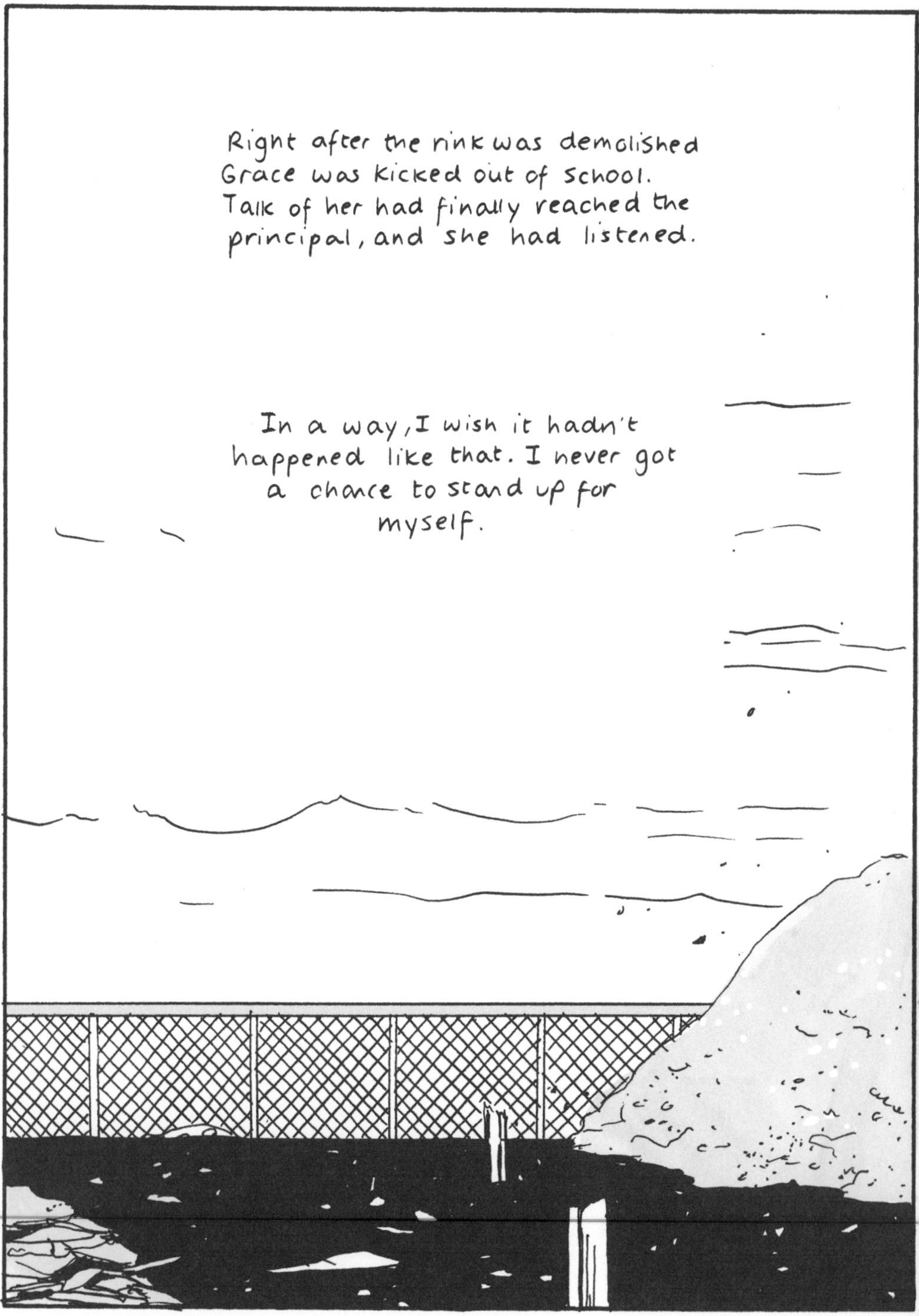
Right after the rink was demolished Grace was kicked out of school. Talk of her had finally reached the principal, and she had listened.
In a way, I wish it hadn't happened like that. I never got a chance to stand up for myself.

6

CAMEL SPIN

A camel spin is basically a
spinning spiral. It was a dizzying
move and always sent my glasses
flying off my face.

Everything was speeding up. The new rink was done and ready to be explored, and school was flying by.

It felt like there was an energy growing inside of me, itching to come out.

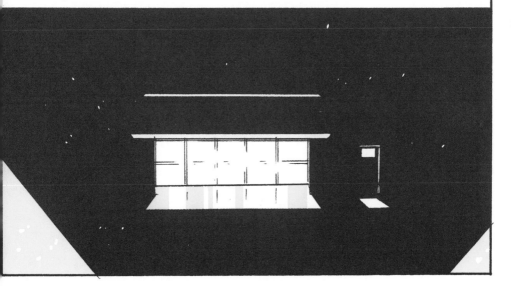

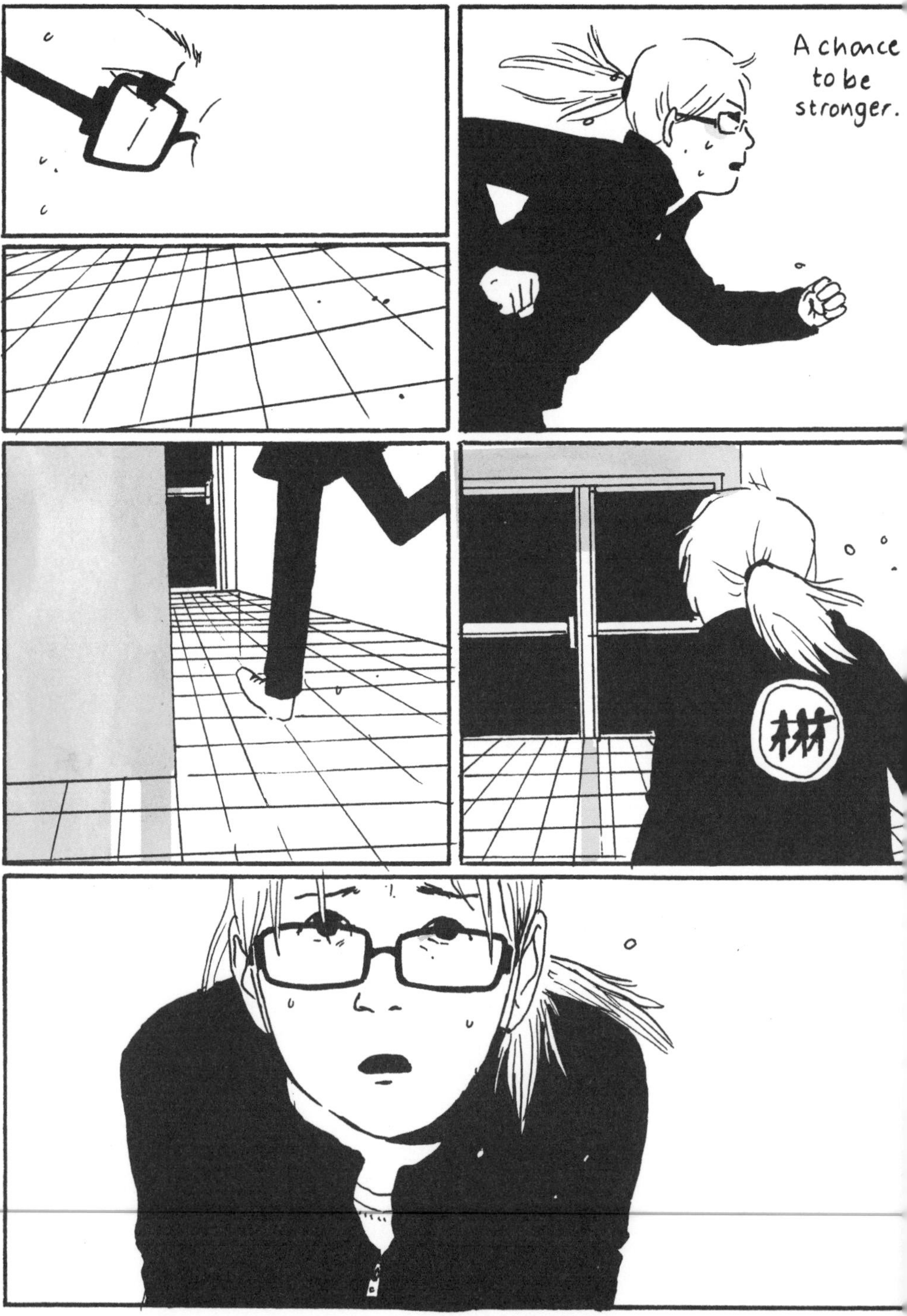
A chance to be stronger.

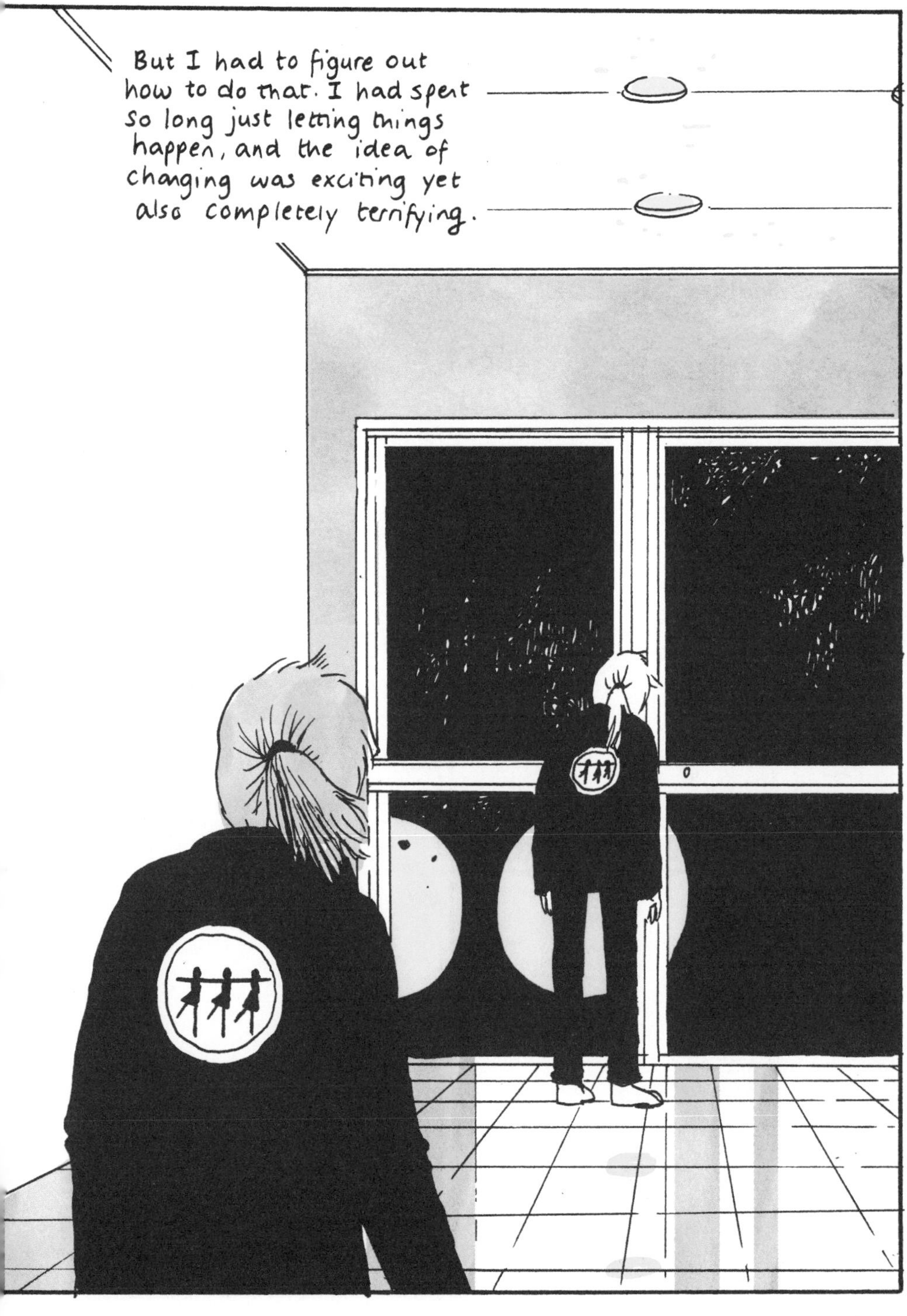
But I had to figure out how to do that. I had spent so long just letting things happen, and the idea of changing was exciting yet also completely terrifying.

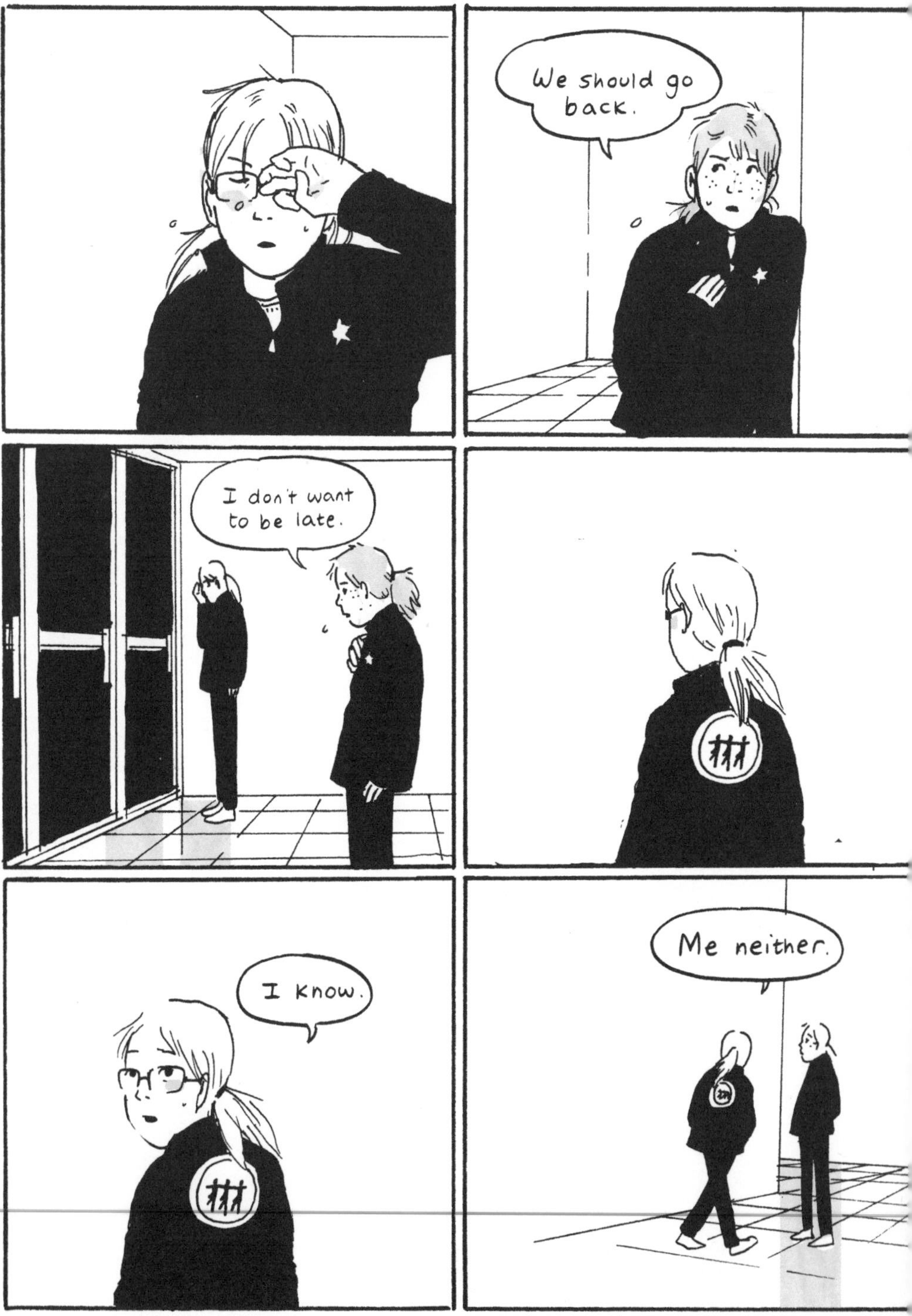
We should go back.
I don't want to be late.
I know.
Me neither.

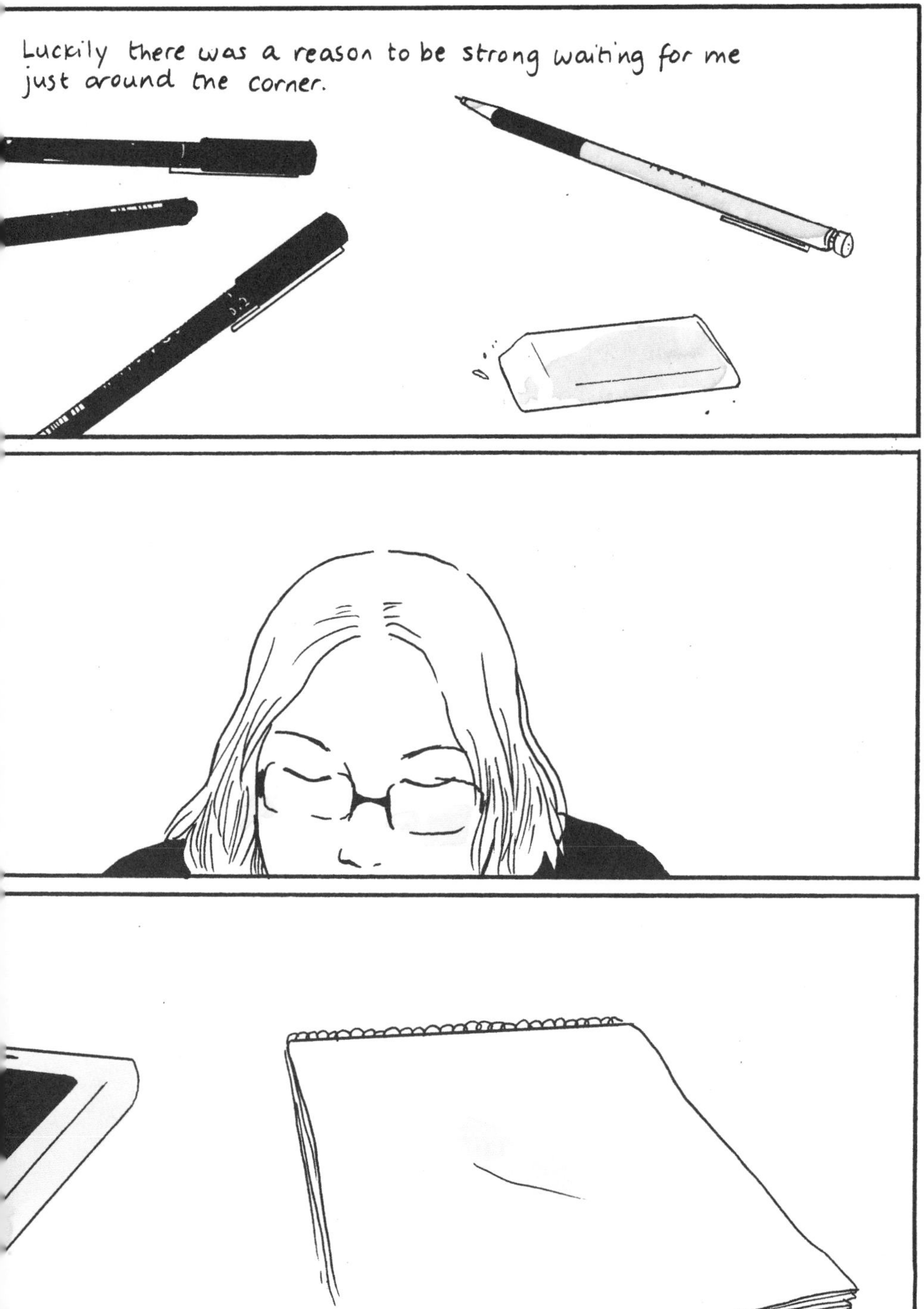
Luckily there was a reason to be strong waiting for me just around the corner.

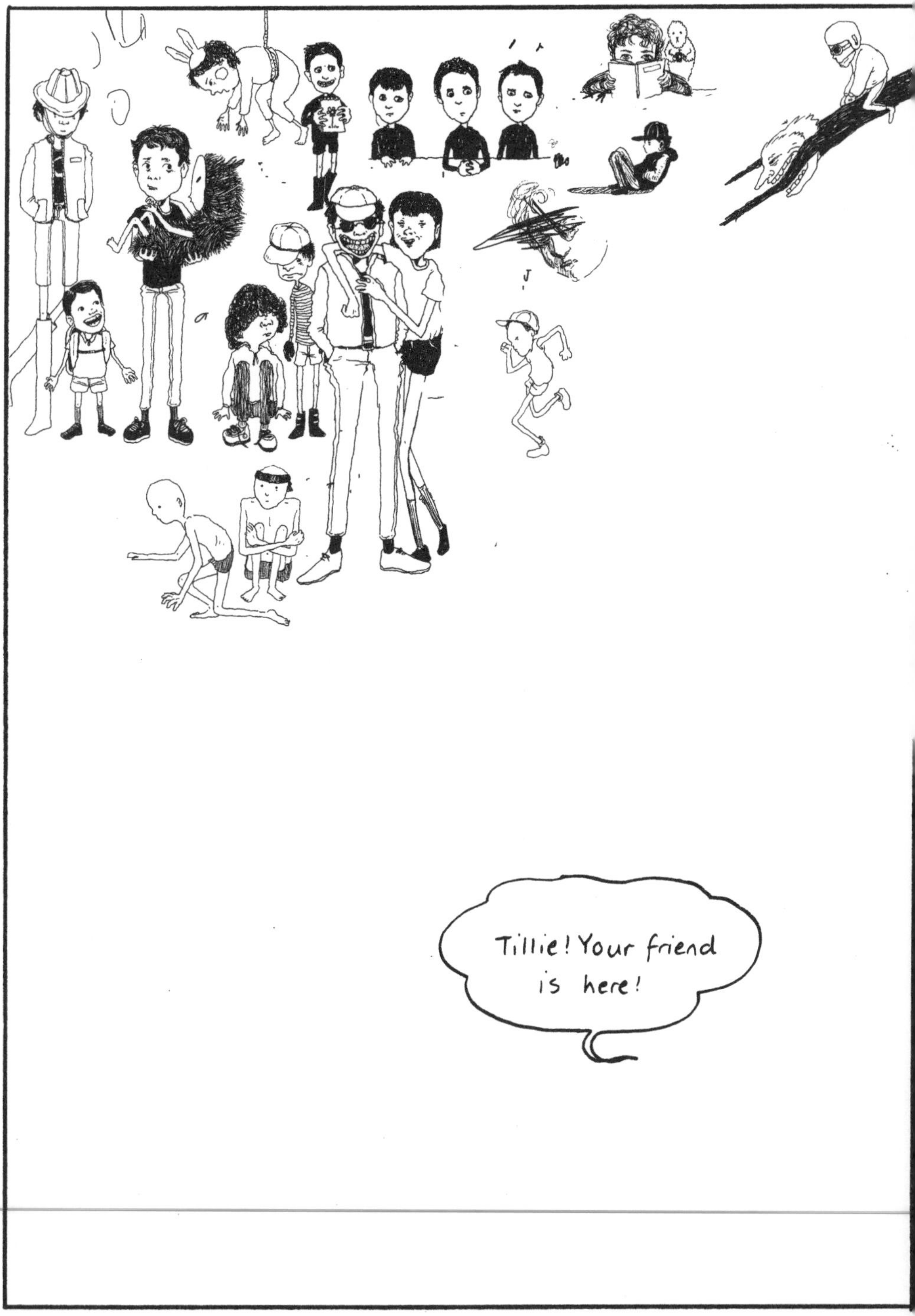
Tillie! Your friend is here!

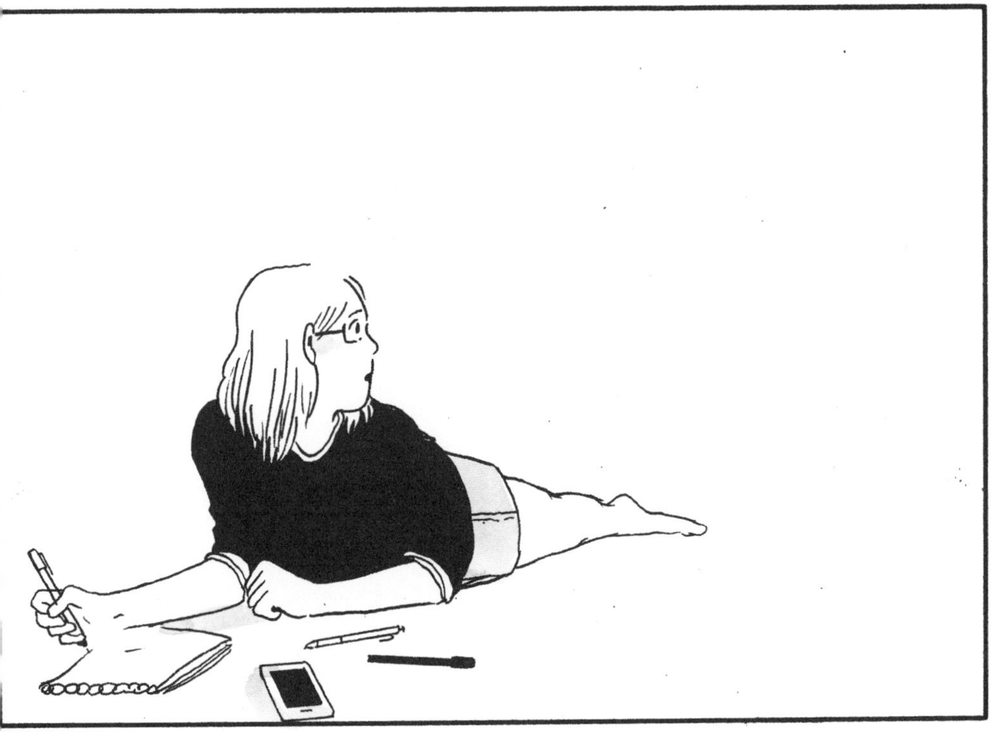

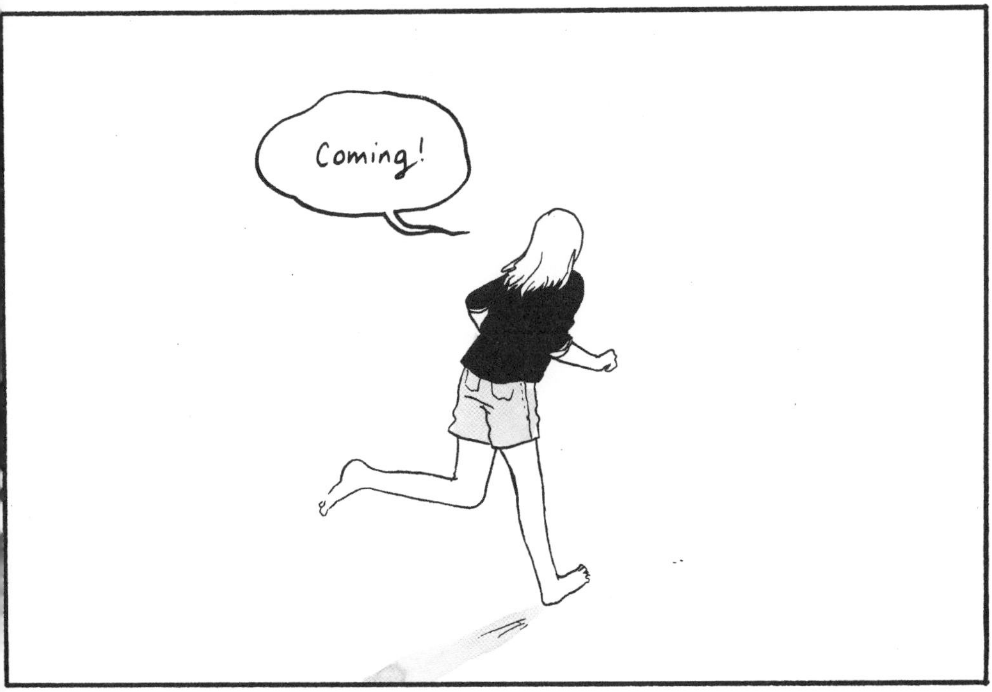
Coming!

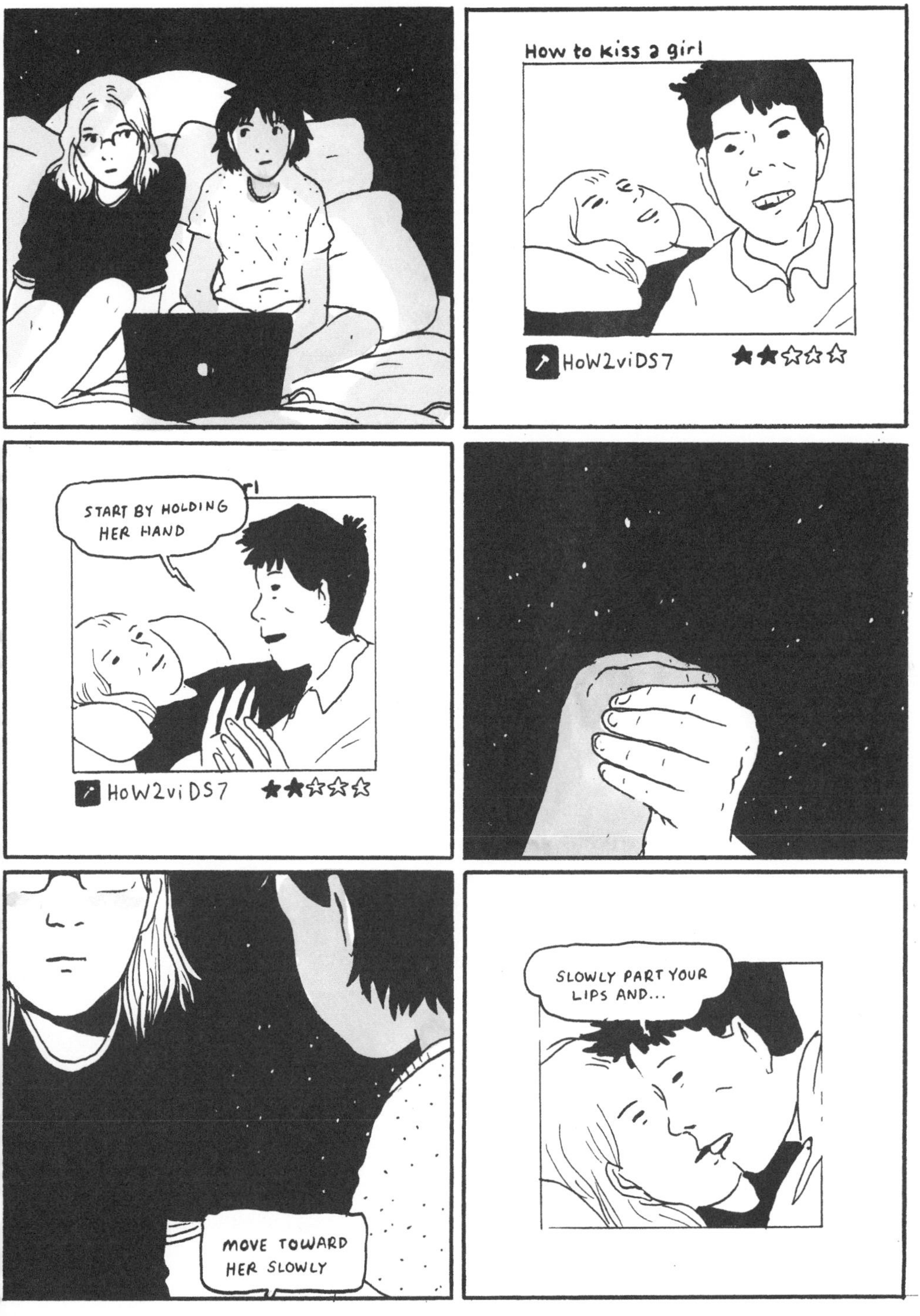
How to kiss a girl
HoW2viDS7
START BY HOLDING HER HAND
HoW2viDS7
MOVE TOWARD HER SLOWLY
SLOWLY PART YOUR LIPS AND...

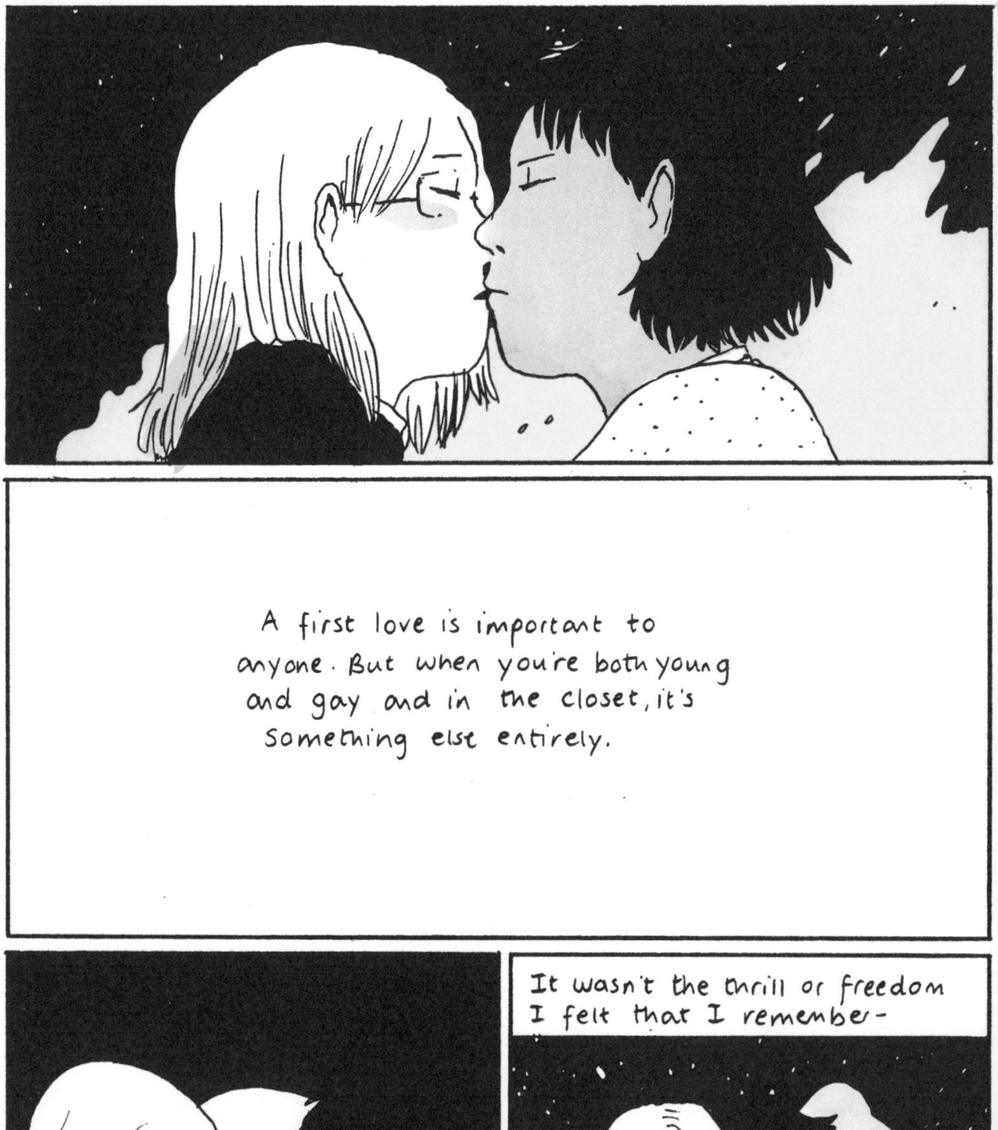
A first love is important to anyone. But when you're both young and gay and in the closet, it's something else entirely.
It wasn't the thrill or freedom I felt that I remember-

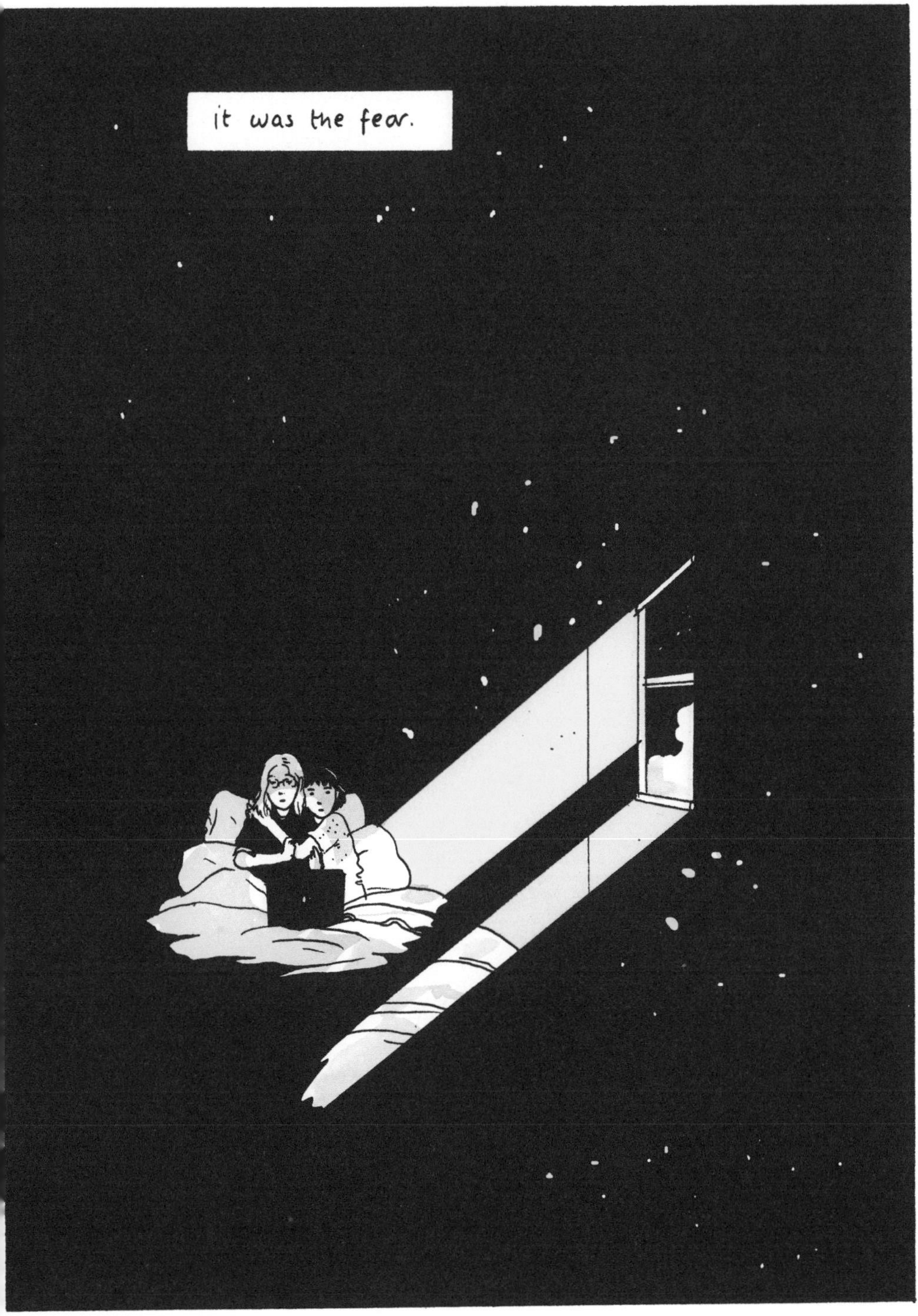
it was the fear.

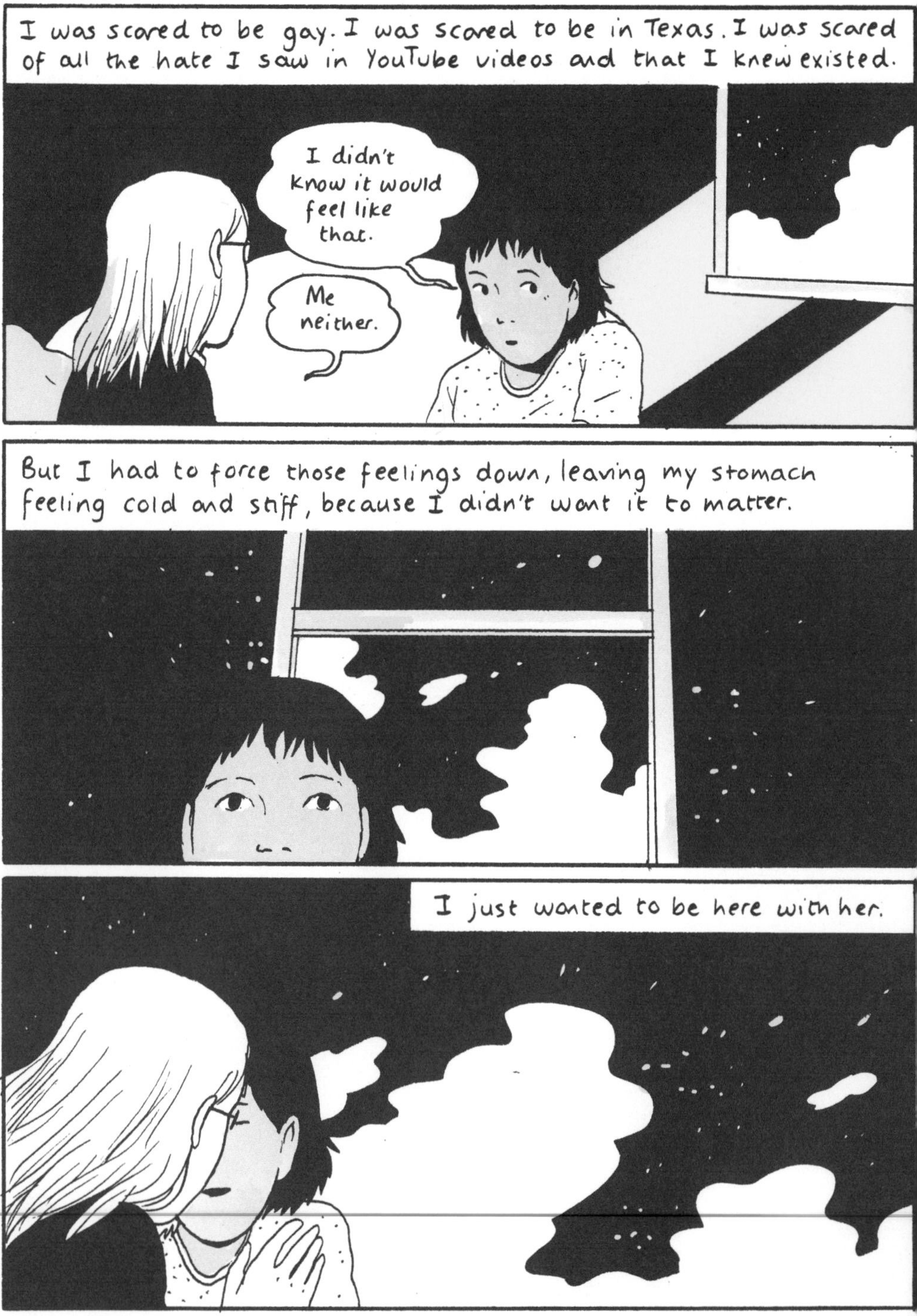

I was scared to be gay. I was scared to be in Texas. I was scared of all the hate I saw in YouTube videos and that I knew existed.
I didn't know it would feel like that.
Me neither.
But I had to force those feelings down, leaving my stomach feeling cold and stiff, because I didn't want it to matter.
I just wanted to be here with her.

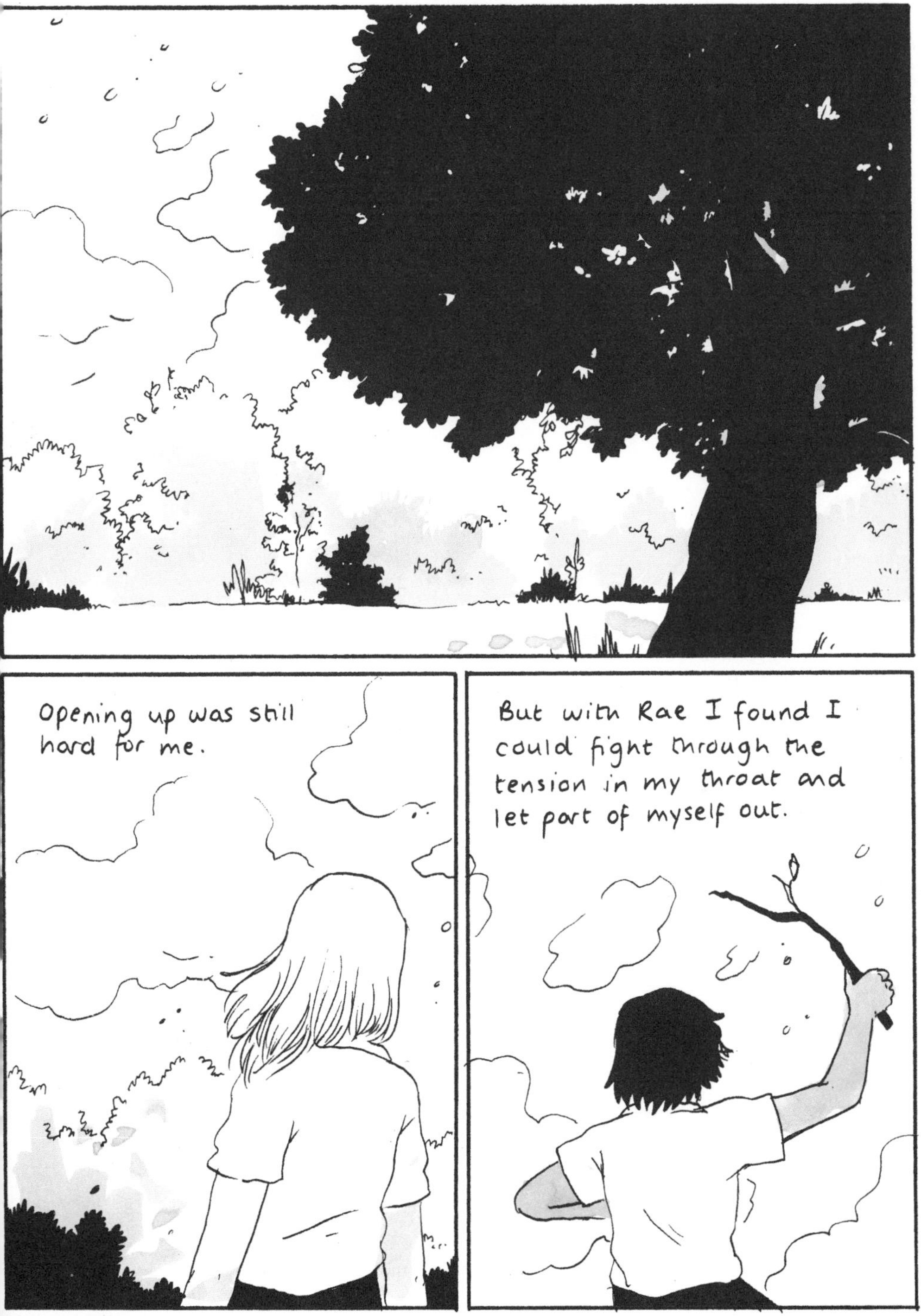
Opening up was still hard for me.
But with Rae I found I could fight through the tension in my throat and let part of myself out.

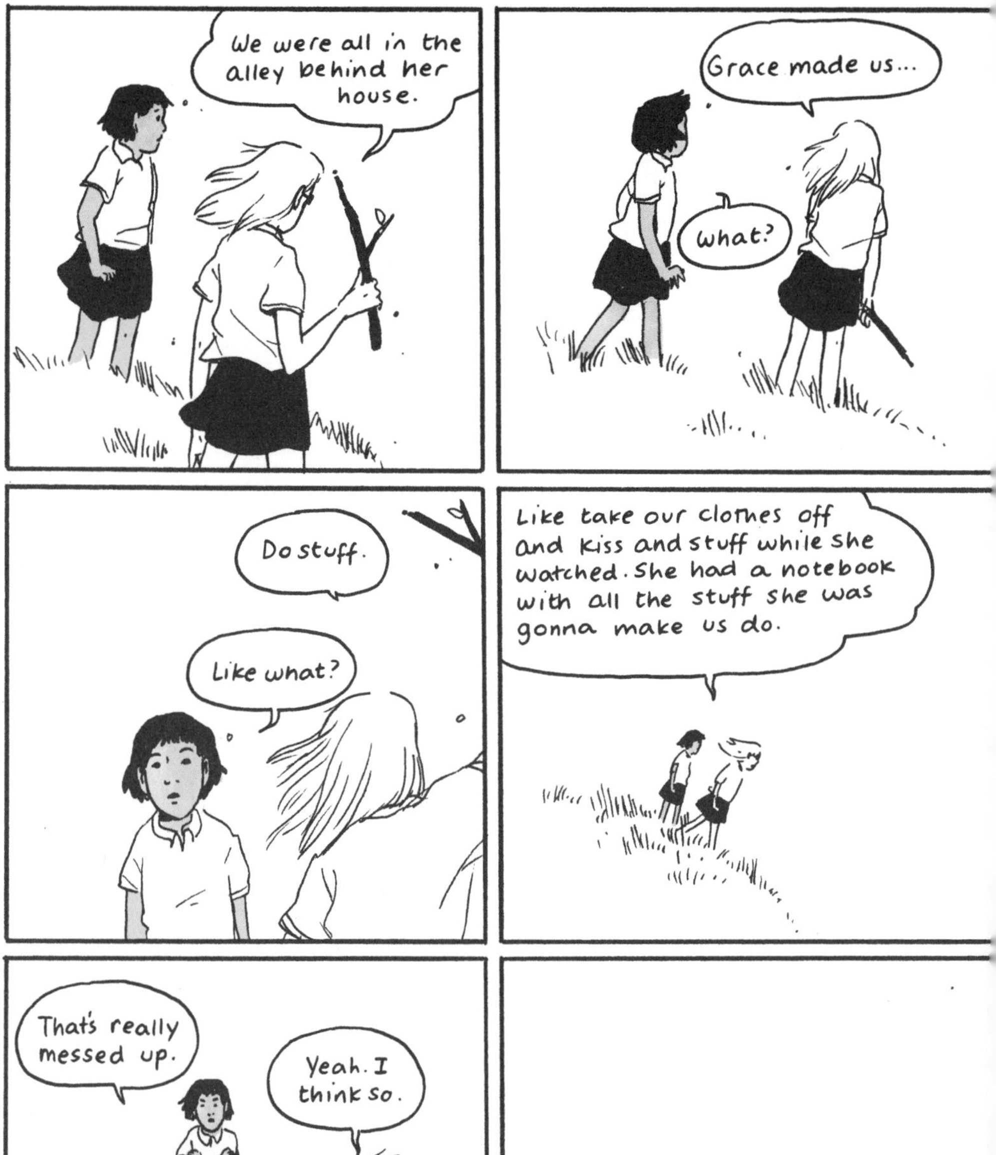
We were all in the alley behind her house.
Grace made us...
What?
Do stuff.
Like what?
Like take our clothes off and kiss and stuff while she watched. She had a notebook with all the stuff she was gonna make us do.
That's really messed up.
Yeah. I think so.

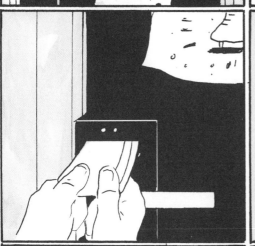

Competitions used to make me nothing but tense.

And while the performance anxiety never faded, I started to enjoy my time alone in hotels.

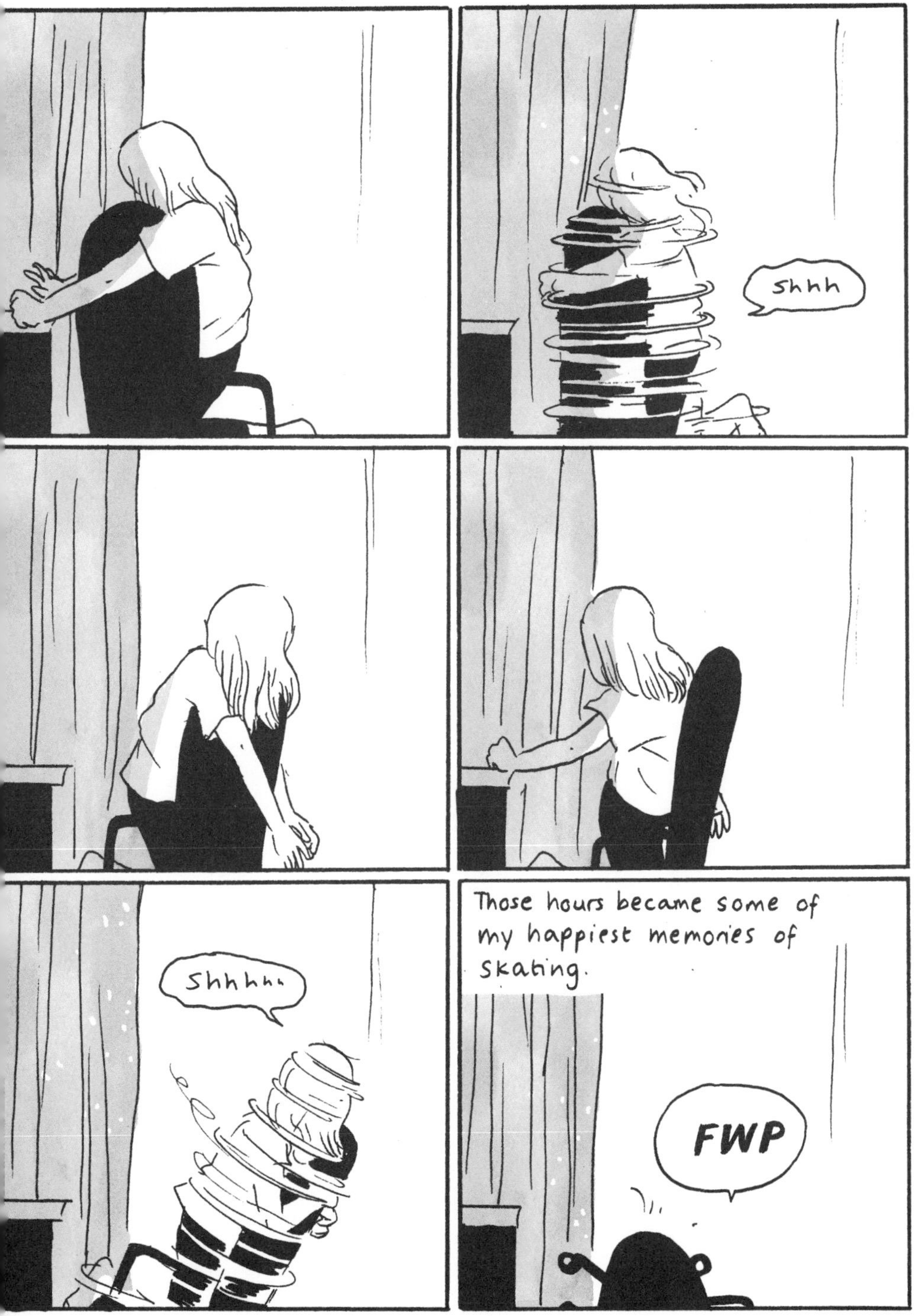
Shhh
Shhhh
Those hours became some of my happiest memories of skating.
FWP

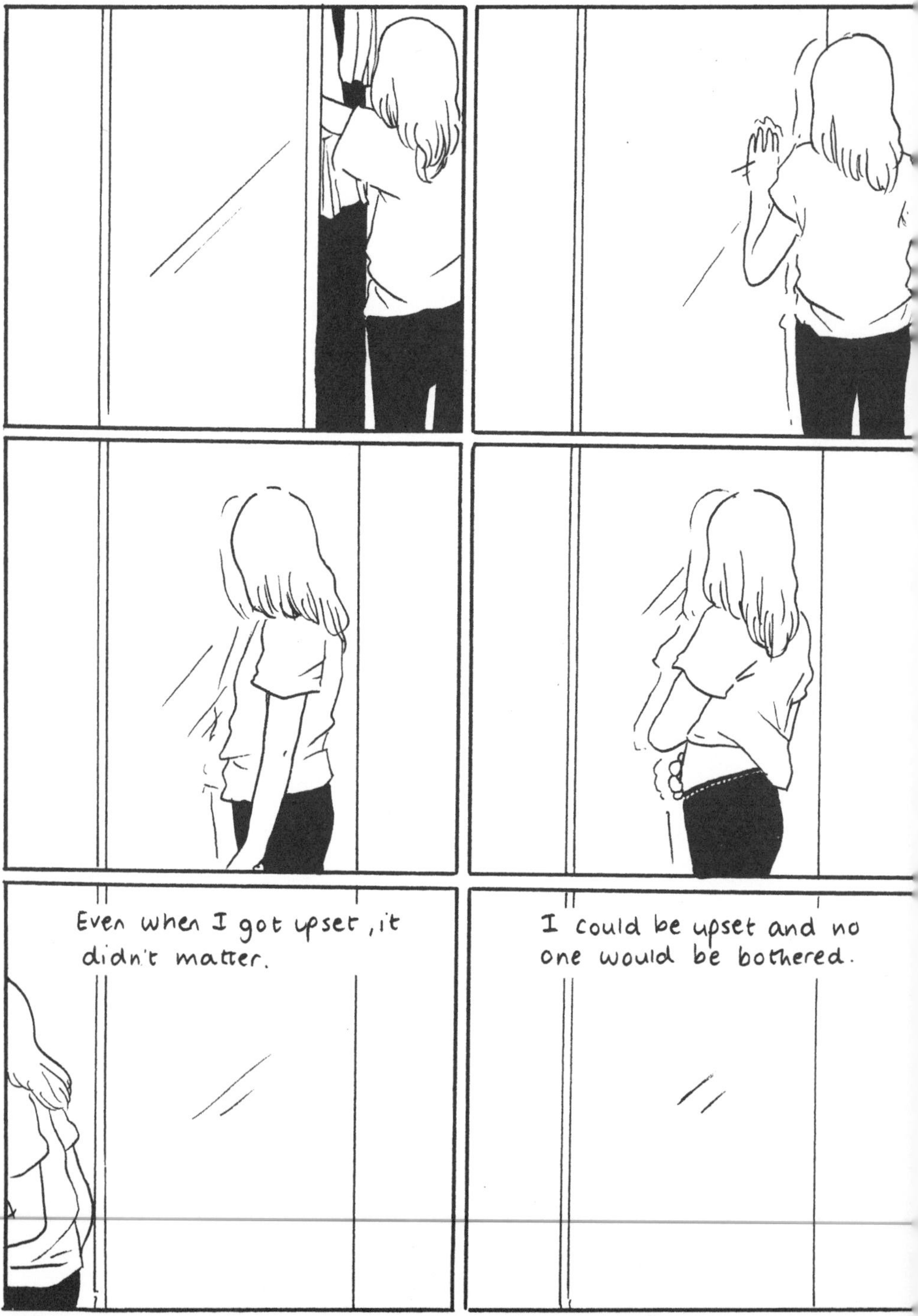
Even when I got upset, it didn't matter.
I could be upset and no one would be bothered.

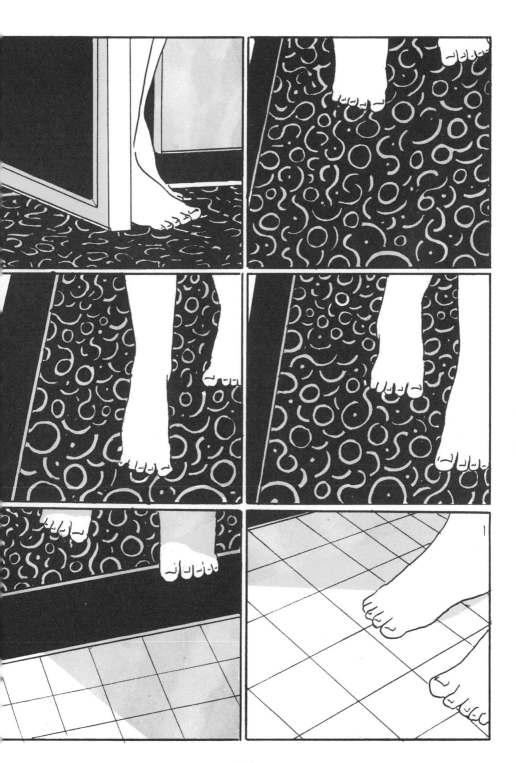

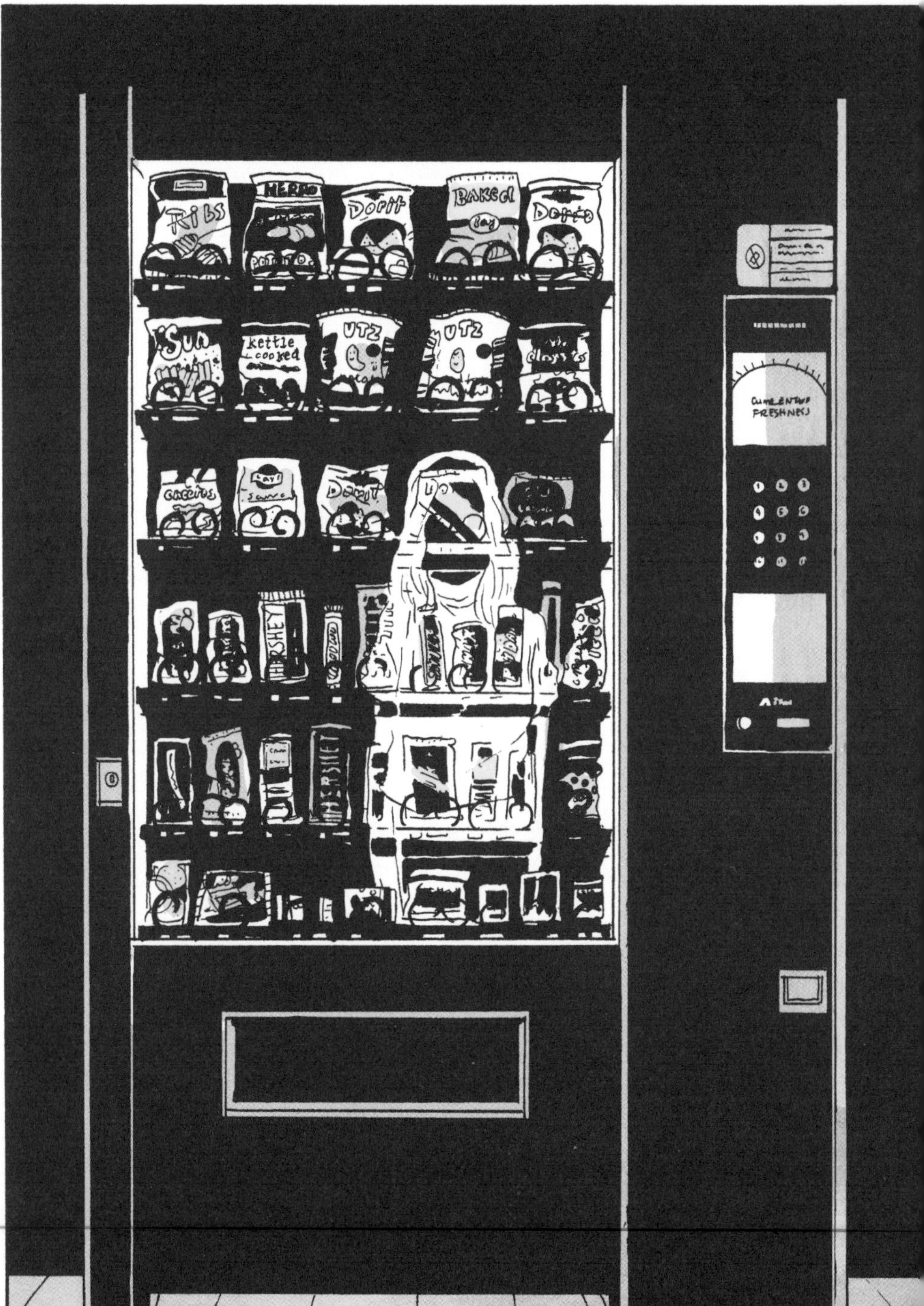
Ribs
Baked
kettle cooked
UTZ
UTZ
CURRENT FRESHNESS

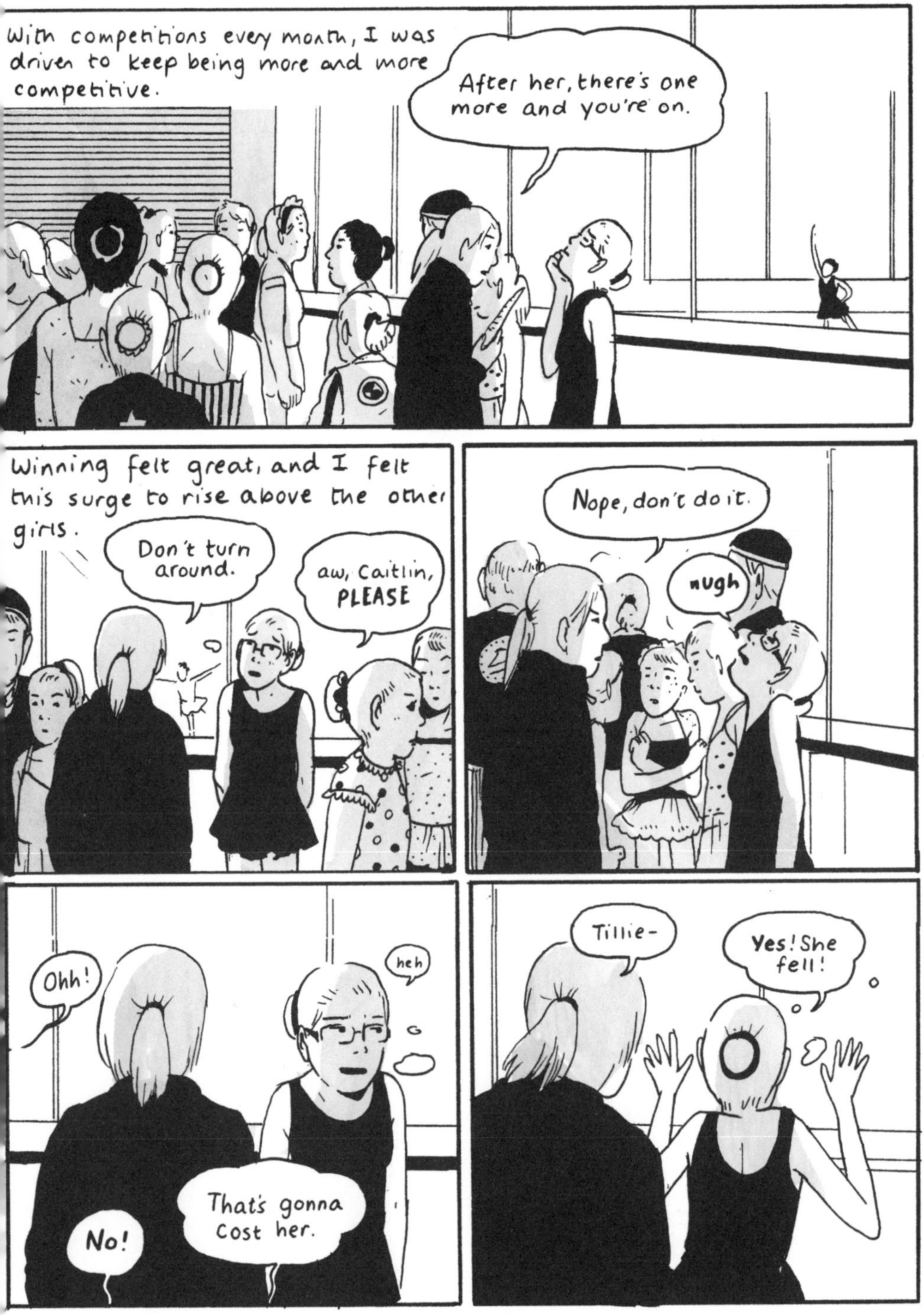

With competitions every month, I was driven to keep being more and more competitive.
After her, there's one more and you're on.
Winning felt great, and I felt this surge to rise above the other girls.
Don't turn around.
aw, Caitlin, PLEASE
Nope, don't do it.
nugh
Ohh!
heh
No!
That's gonna cost her.
Tillie-
Yes! She fell!

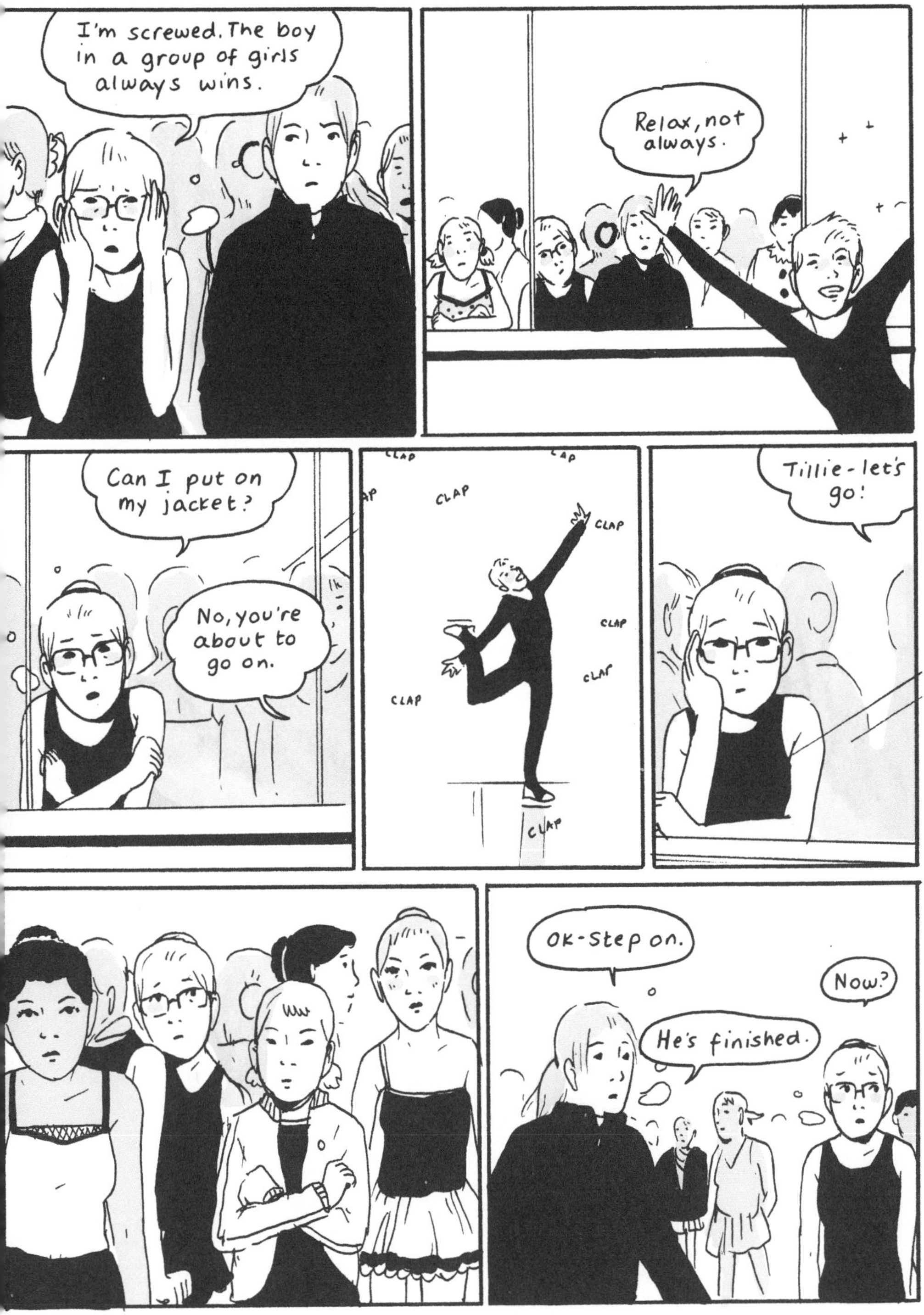
I'm screwed. The boy in a group of girls always wins.
Relax, not always.
Can I put on my jacket?
No, you're about to go on.
CLAP
CLAP
CLAP
CLAP
CLAP
CLAP
Tillie - let's go!
OK - Step on.
Now?
He's finished.

212

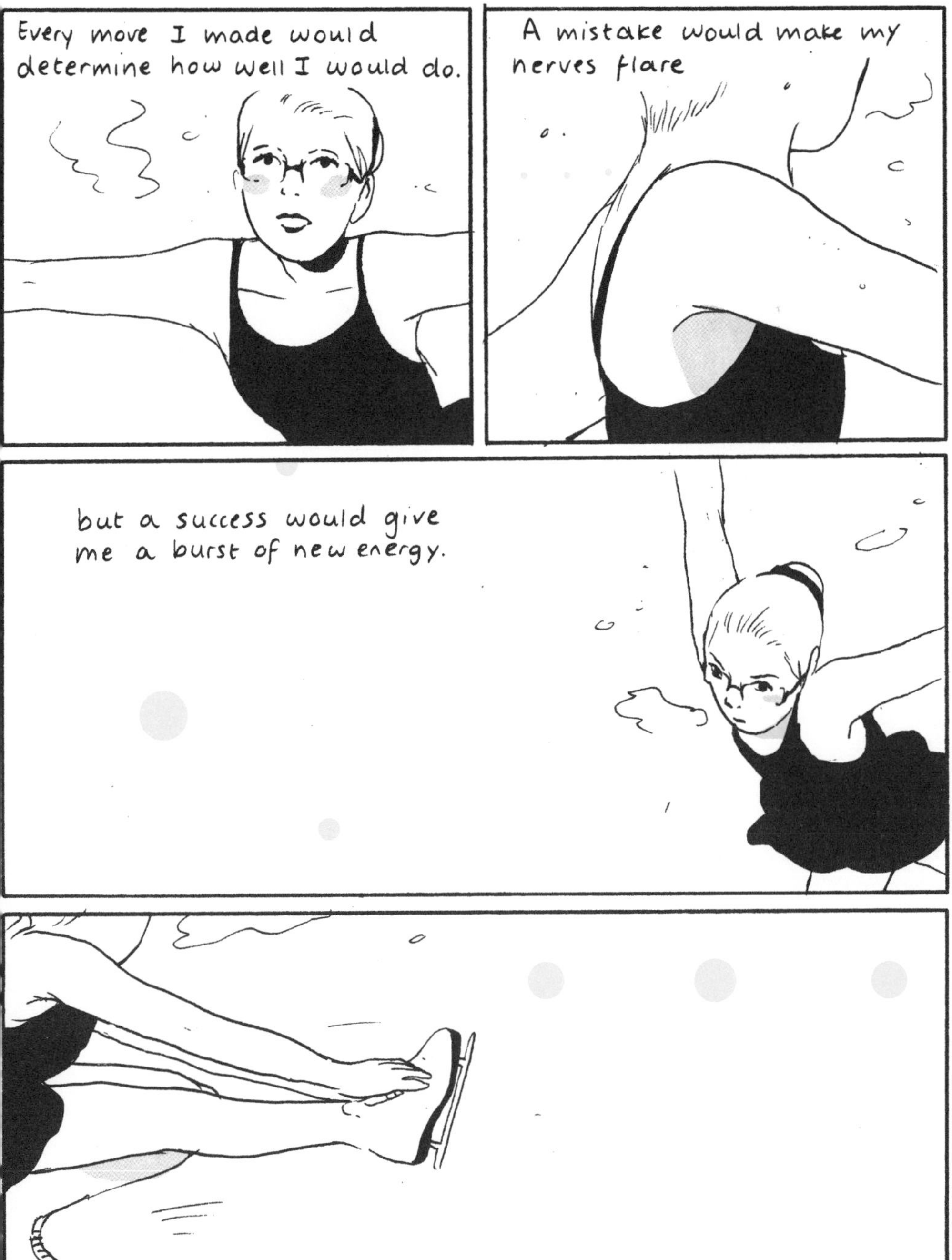
Every move I made would determine how well I would do.
A mistake would make my nerves flare
but a success would give me a burst of new energy.
My programs were only ever about three minutes long.

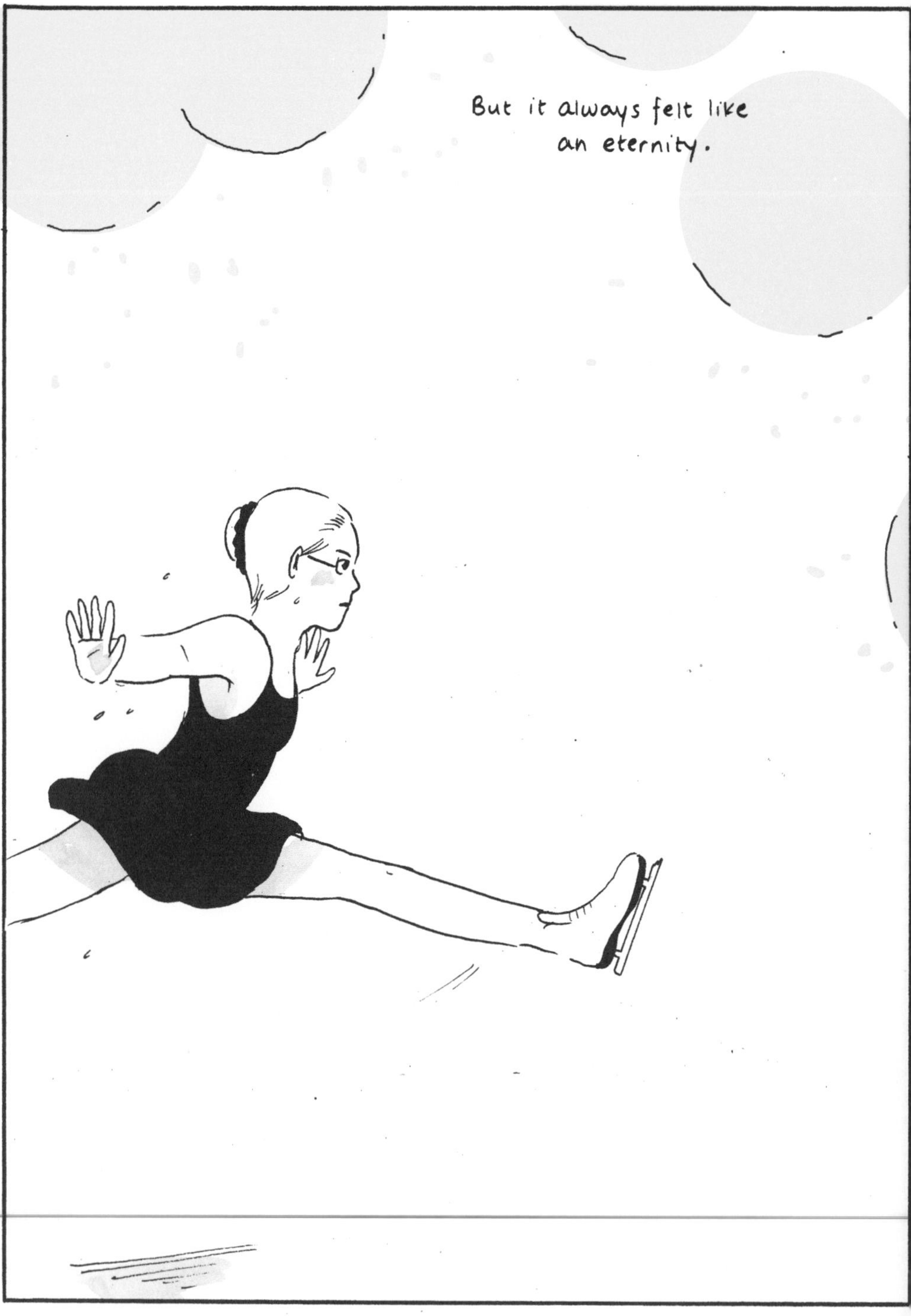
But it always felt like
an eternity.

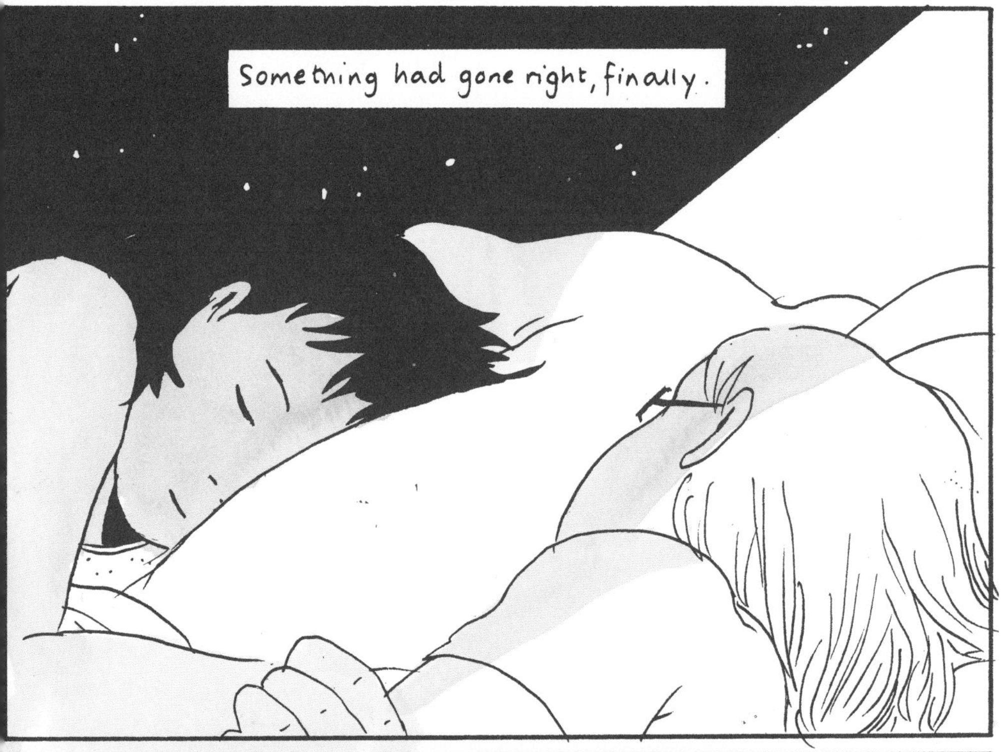
Something had gone right, finally.

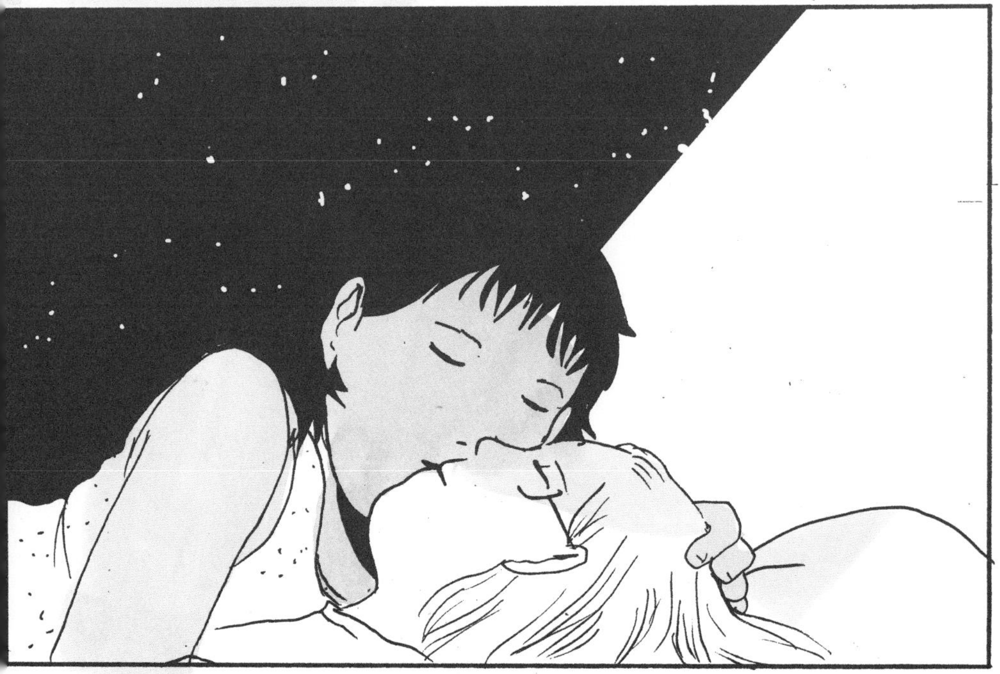

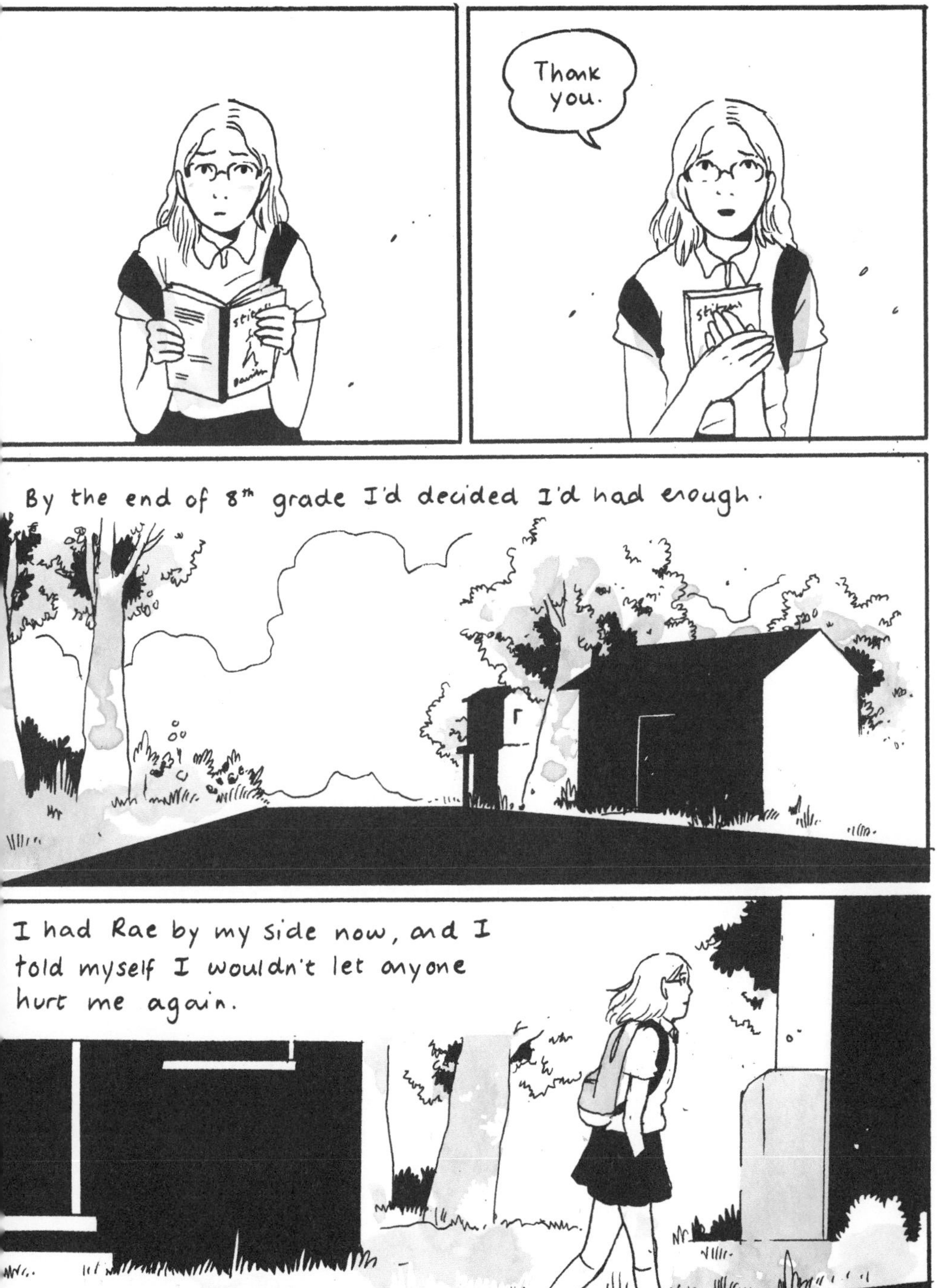
Thank you.
By the end of 8th grade I'd decided I'd had enough.
I had Rae by my side now, and I told myself I wouldn't let anyone hurt me again.

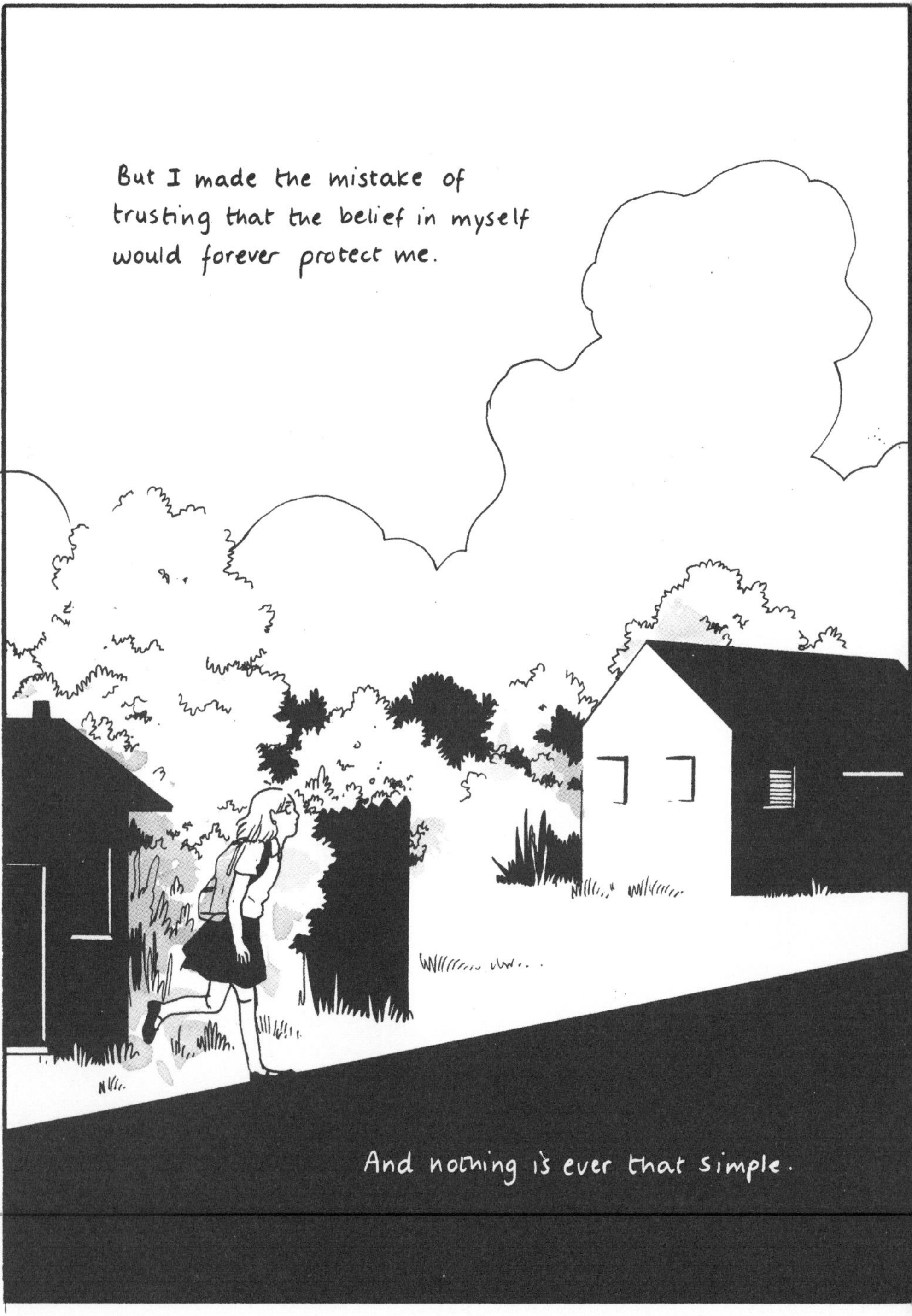
But I made the mistake of trusting that the belief in myself would forever protect me.
And nothing is ever that simple.

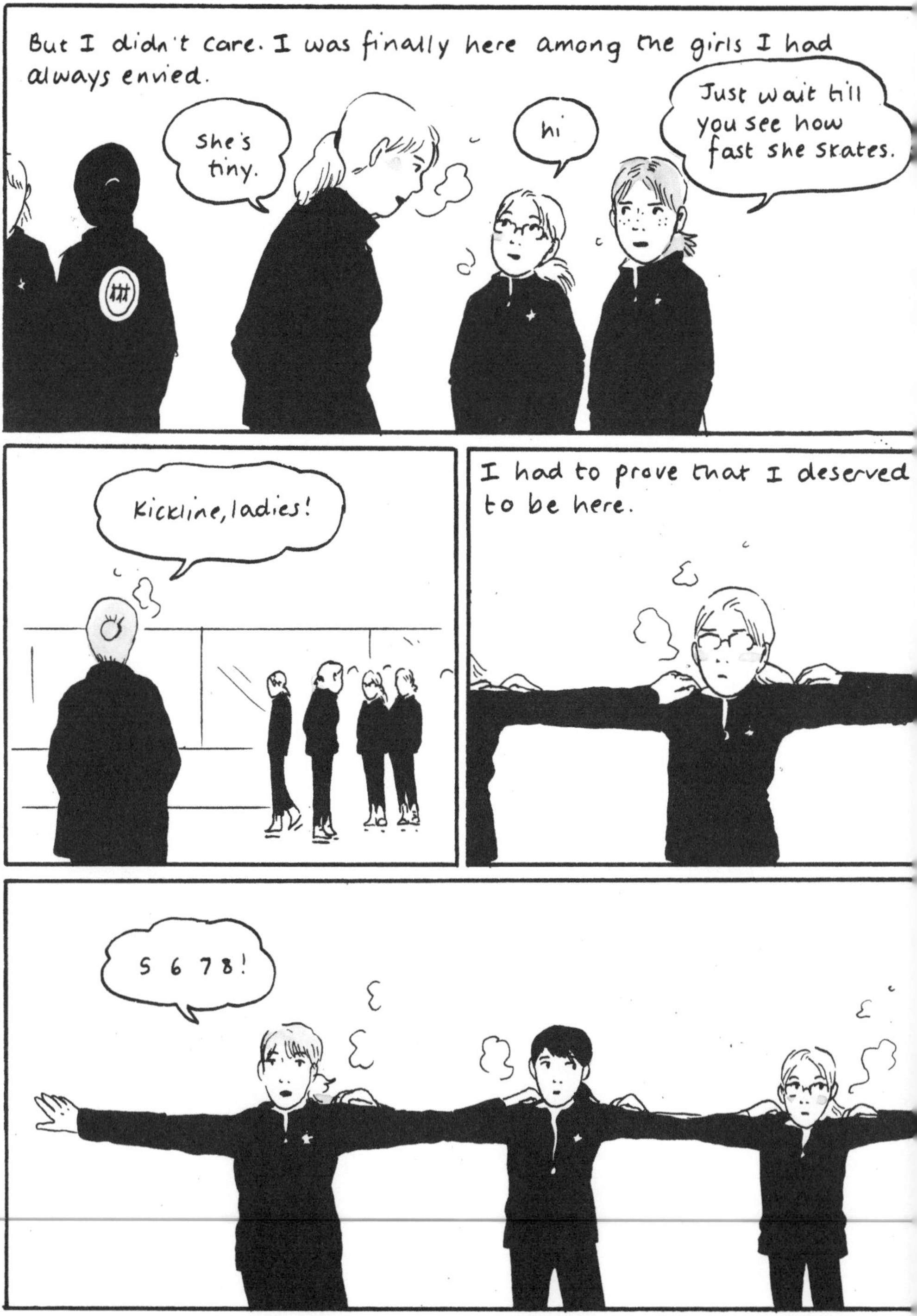
But I didn't care. I was finally here among the girls I had always envied.
She's tiny.
hi
Just wait till you see how fast she skates.
Kickline, ladies!
I had to prove that I deserved to be here.
5 6 7 8!

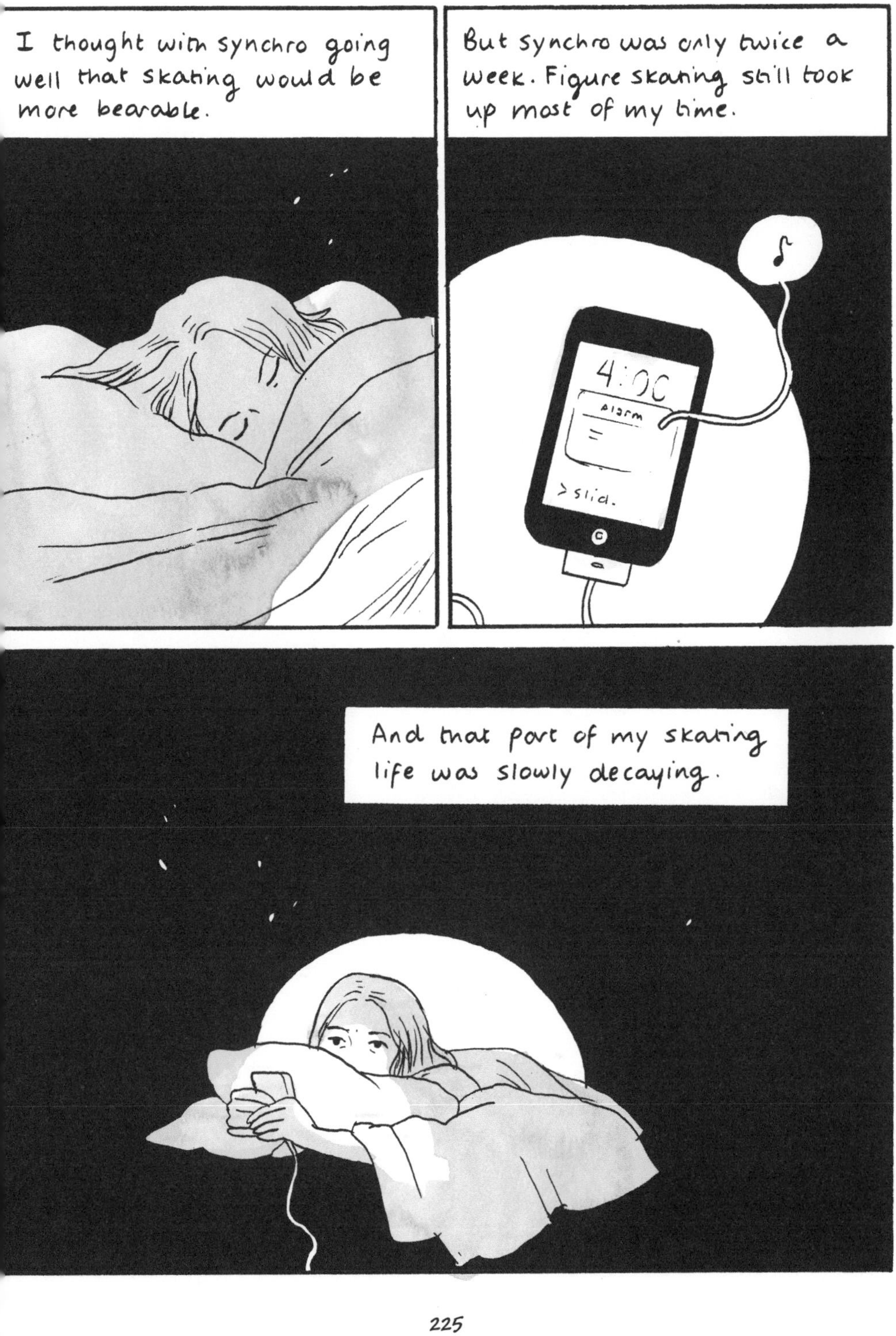
I thought with synchro going well that skating would be more bearable.
But synchro was only twice a week. Figure skating still took up most of my time.
4:00
alarm
> slid.
And that part of my skating life was slowly decaying.

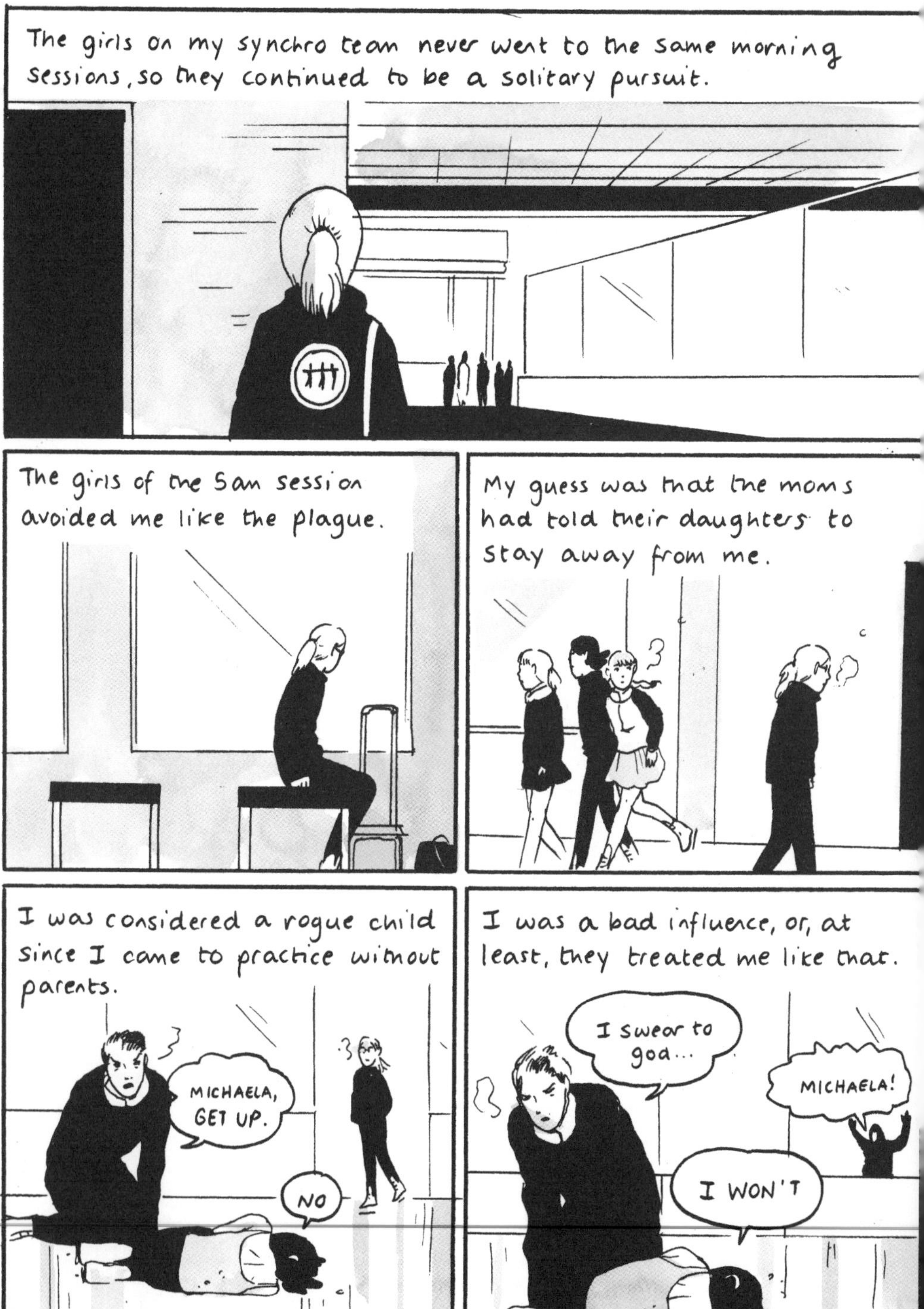
The girls on my synchro team never went to the same morning sessions, so they continued to be a solitary pursuit.
The girls of the 5am session avoided me like the plague.
My guess was that the moms had told their daughters to stay away from me.
I was considered a rogue child since I came to practice without parents.
MICHAELA, GET UP.
NO
I was a bad influence, or, at least, they treated me like that.
I swear to god...
MICHAELA!
I WON'T

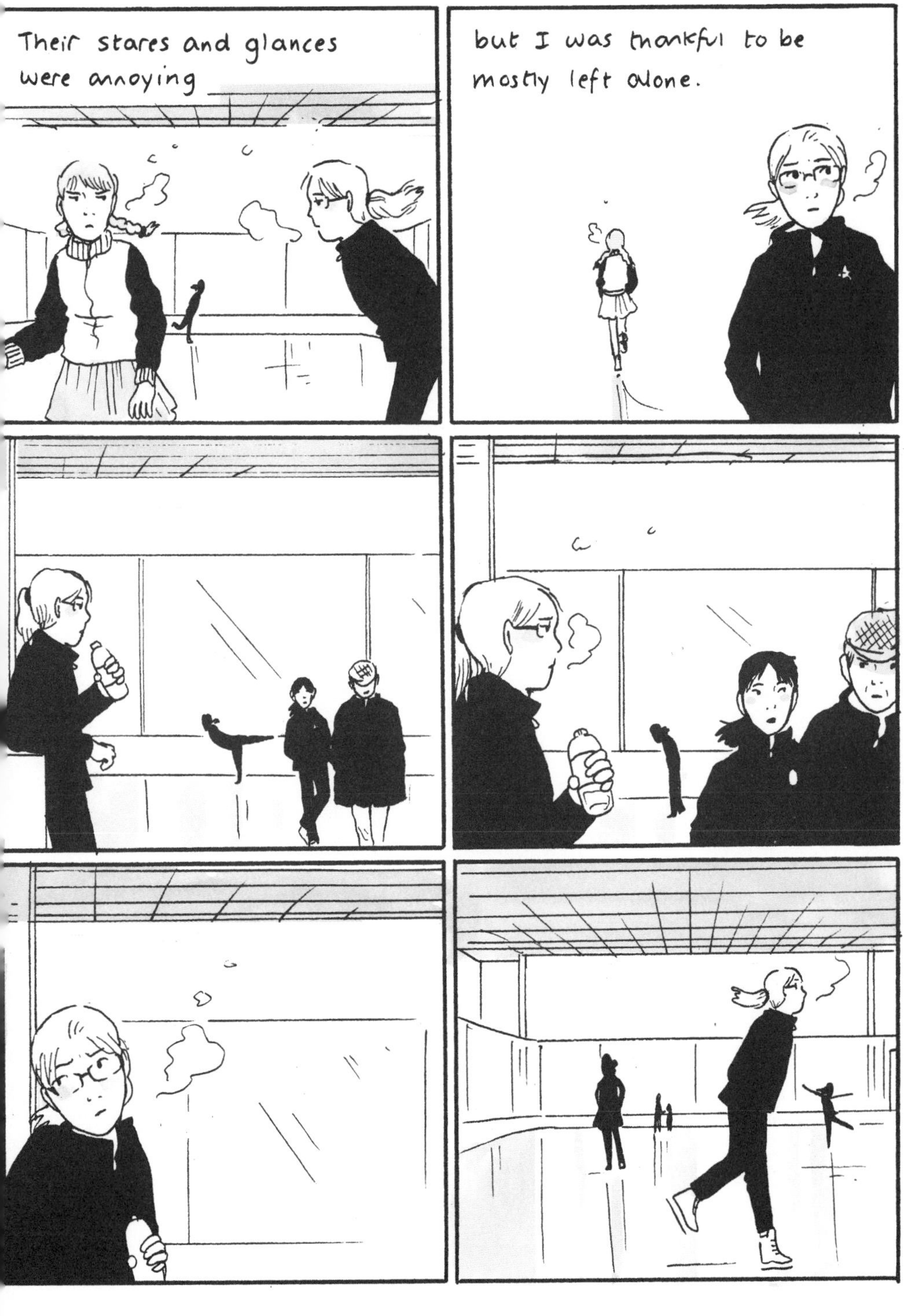
Their stares and glances were annoying
but I was thankful to be mostly left alone.

I needed to find a way to deal with the early-morning practices. Getting up was getting harder and harder.

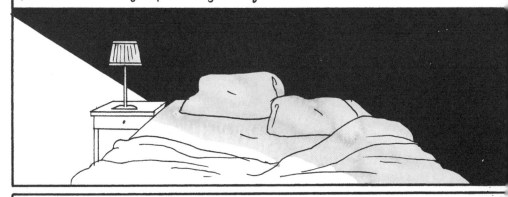

So I made a plan. The best one a 14-year-old could come up with

I would put on my clothes for practice the night before

and lie on top of my bed.

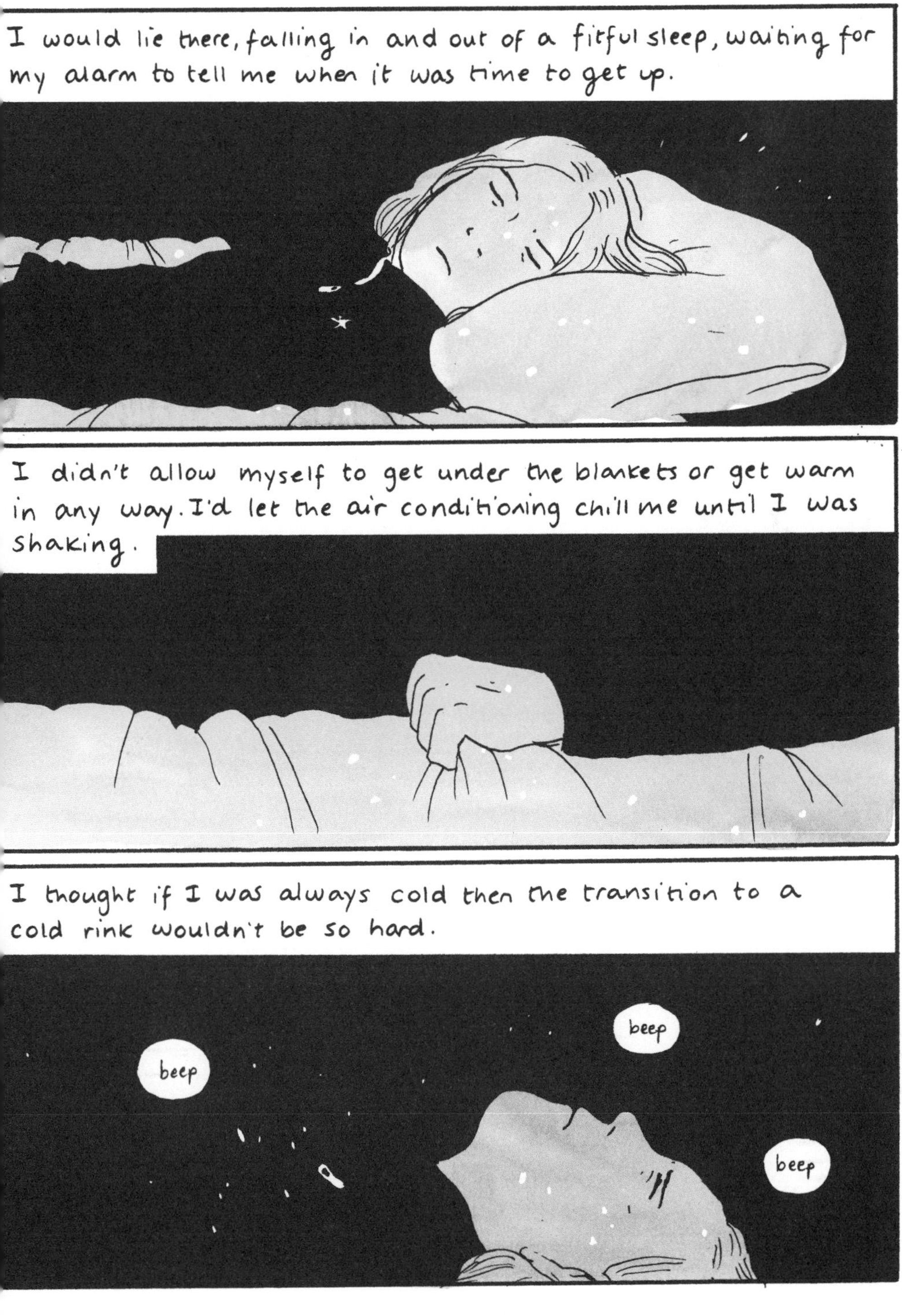
I would lie there, falling in and out of a fitful sleep, waiting for my alarm to tell me when it was time to get up.
I didn't allow myself to get under the blankets or get warm in any way. I'd let the air conditioning chill me until I was shaking.
I thought if I was always cold then the transition to a cold rink wouldn't be so hard.
beep
beep
beep

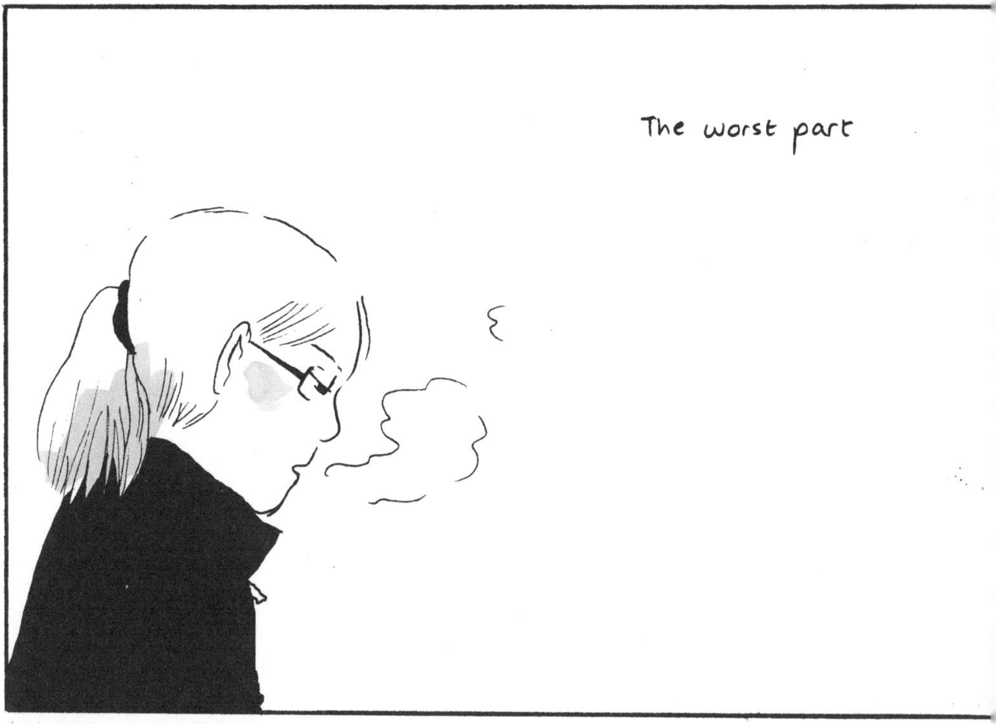
The worst part

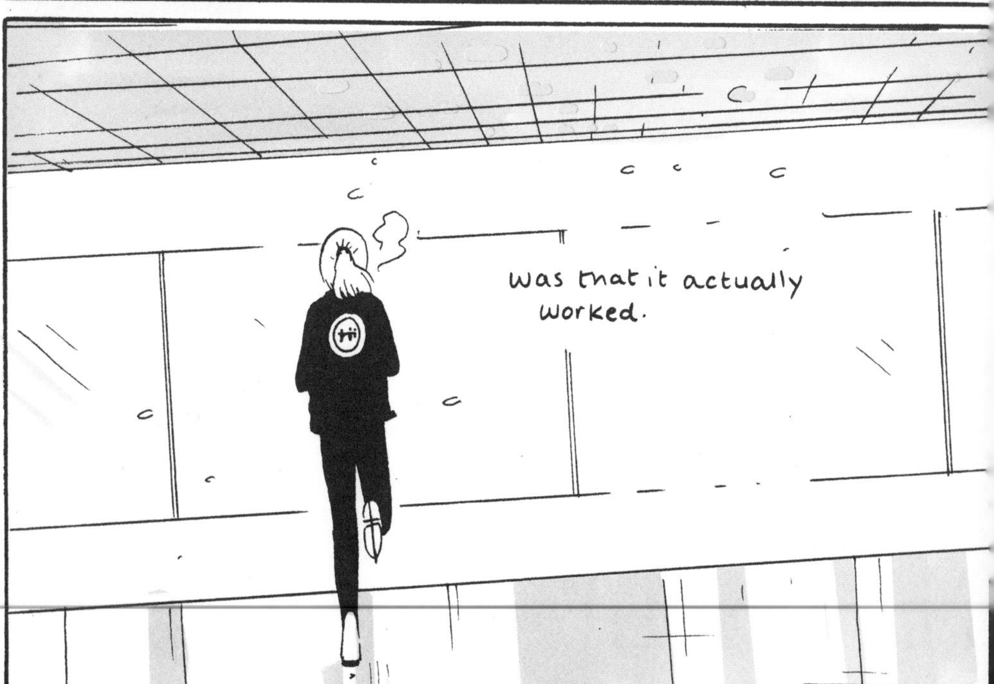
was that it actually worked.

7

SPREAD EAGLE

what it's supposed to look like

my attempt

I have never been able to
do a spread eagle. My coach in
New Jersey had the girls who
couldn't do it stand and push
their feet against a wall
until they stretched out.

But no amount of torture helped
me do it. My body just wasn't
built that way.

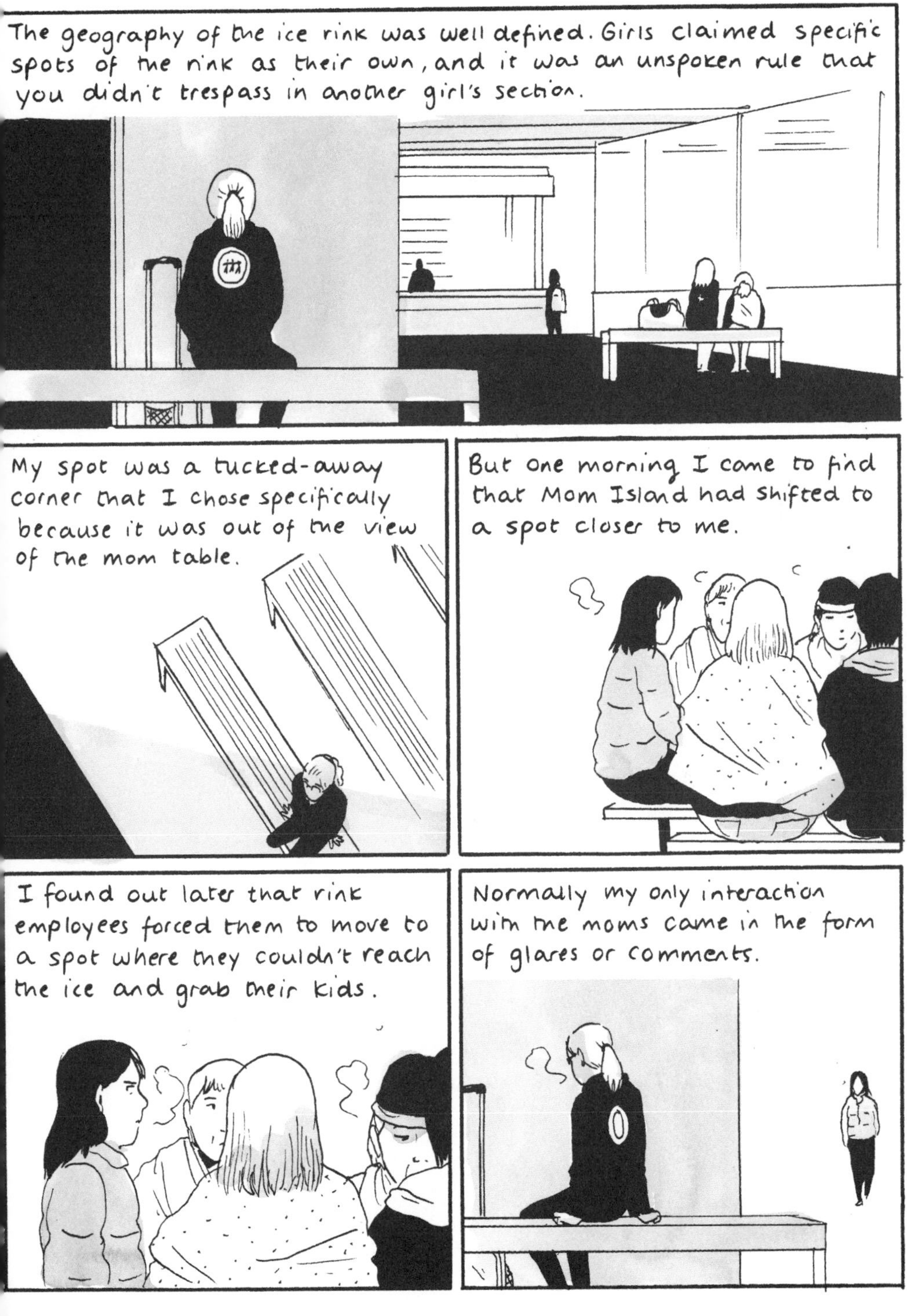
The geography of the ice rink was well defined. Girls claimed specific spots of the rink as their own, and it was an unspoken rule that you didn't trespass in another girl's section.
My spot was a tucked-away corner that I chose specifically because it was out of the view of the mom table.
But one morning I came to find that Mom Island had shifted to a spot closer to me.
I found out later that rink employees forced them to move to a spot where they couldn't reach the ice and grab their kids.
Normally my only interaction with the moms came in the form of glares or comments.

235

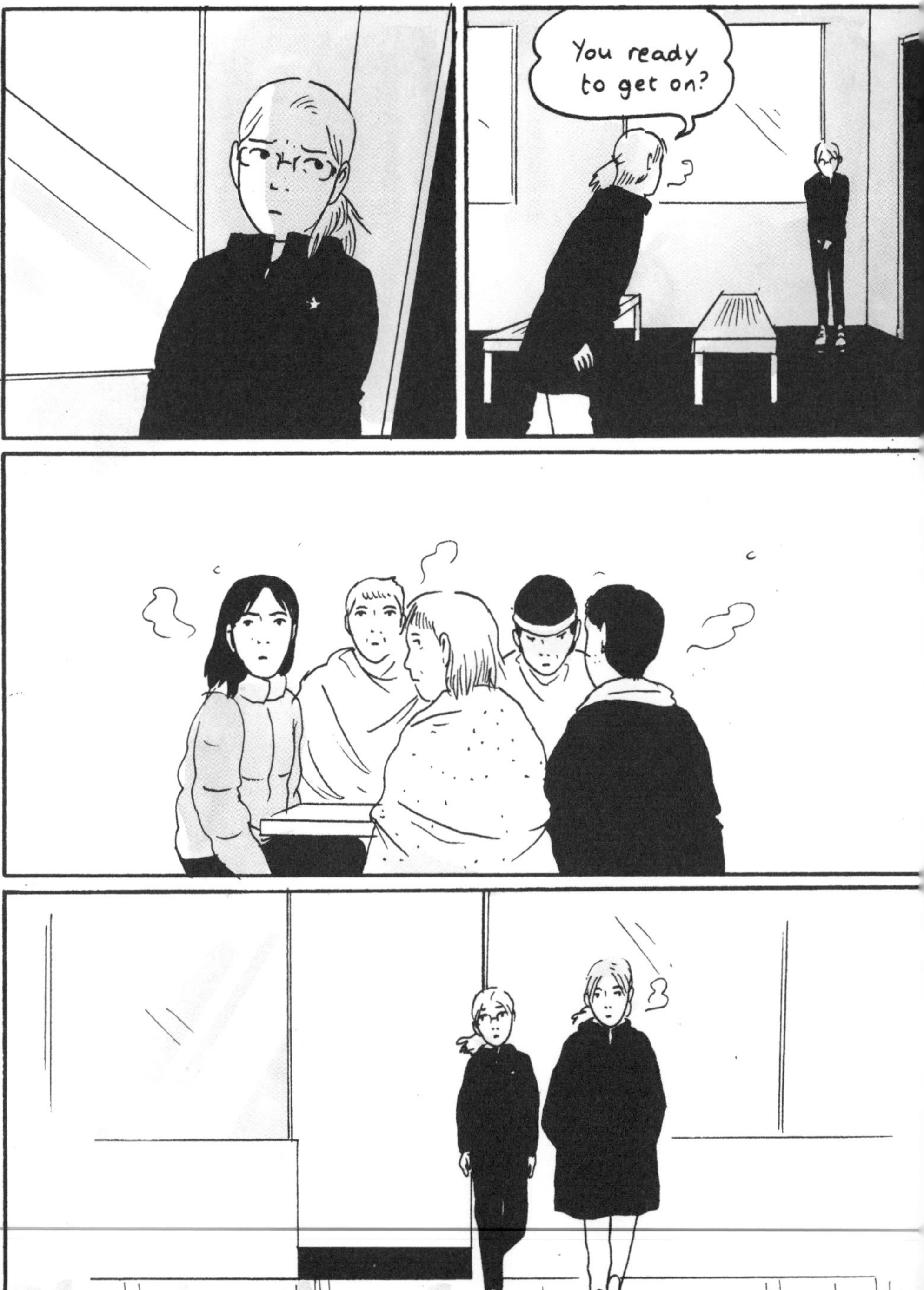
You ready to get on?

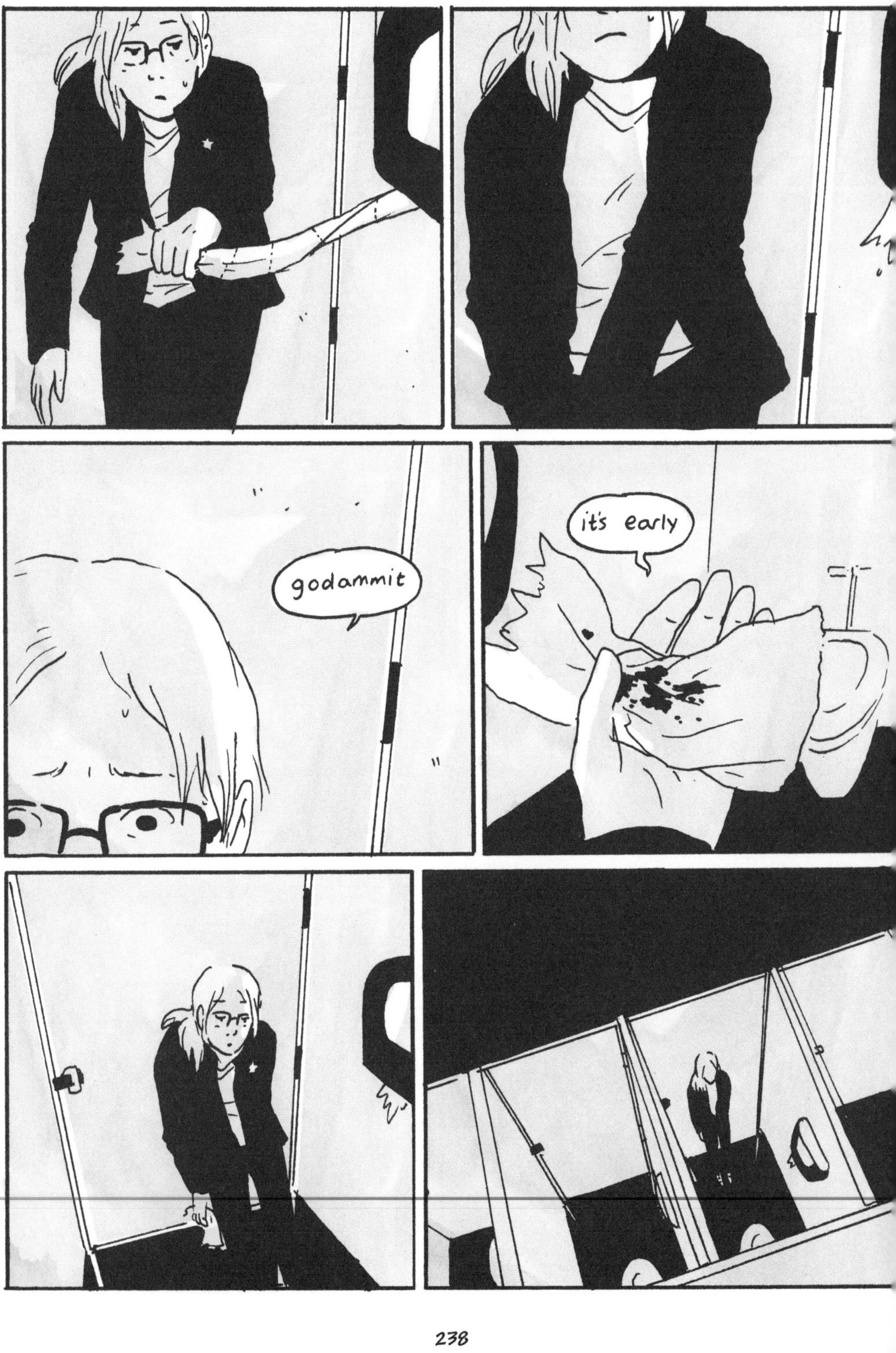
godammit
it's early

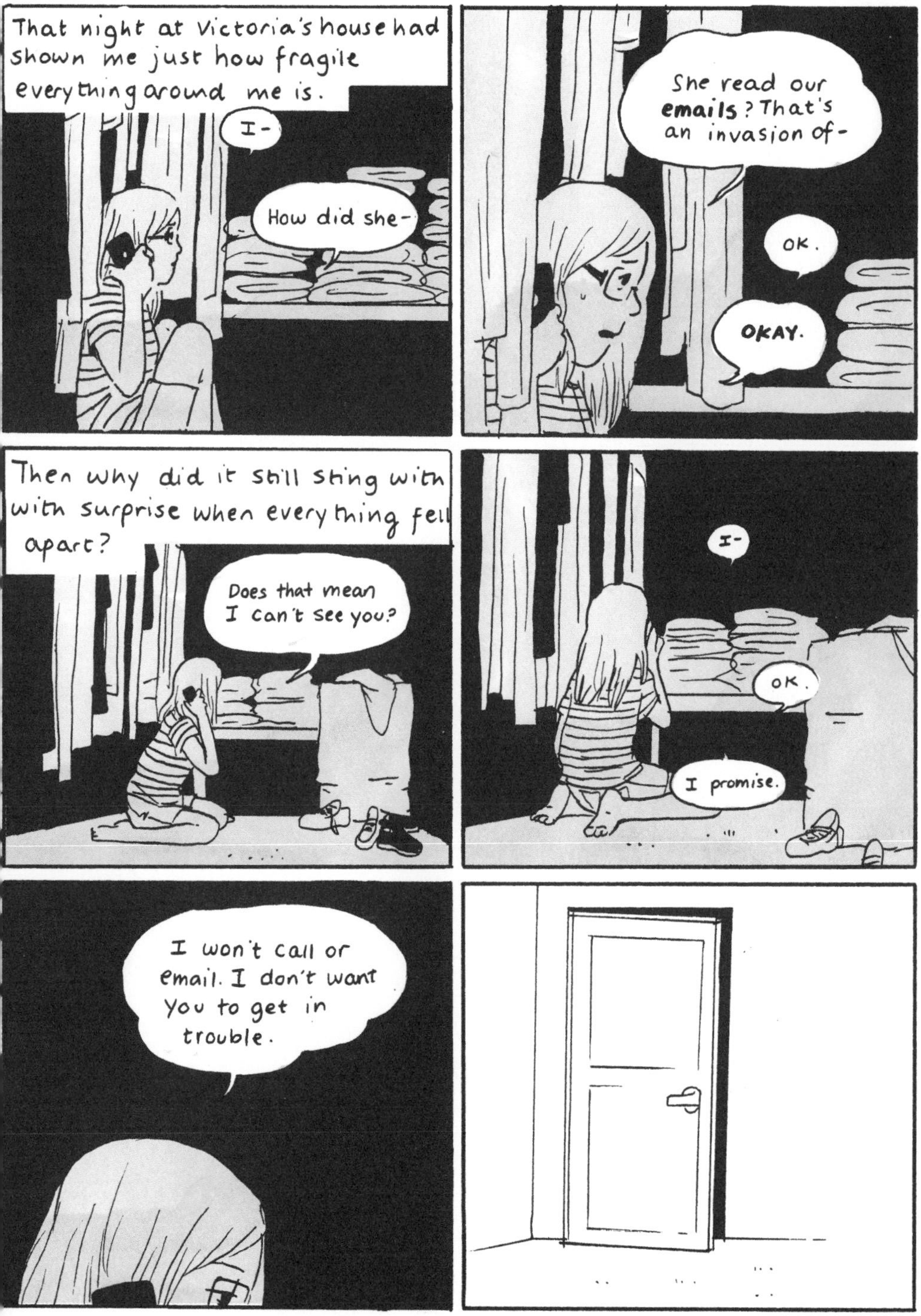
That night at Victoria's house had shown me just how fragile everything around me is.
I-
How did she-
She read our **emails**? That's an invasion of-
OK.
OKAY.
Then why did it still sting with with surprise when everything fell apart?
Does that mean I can't see you?
I-
OK.
I promise.
I won't call or email. I don't want you to get in trouble.

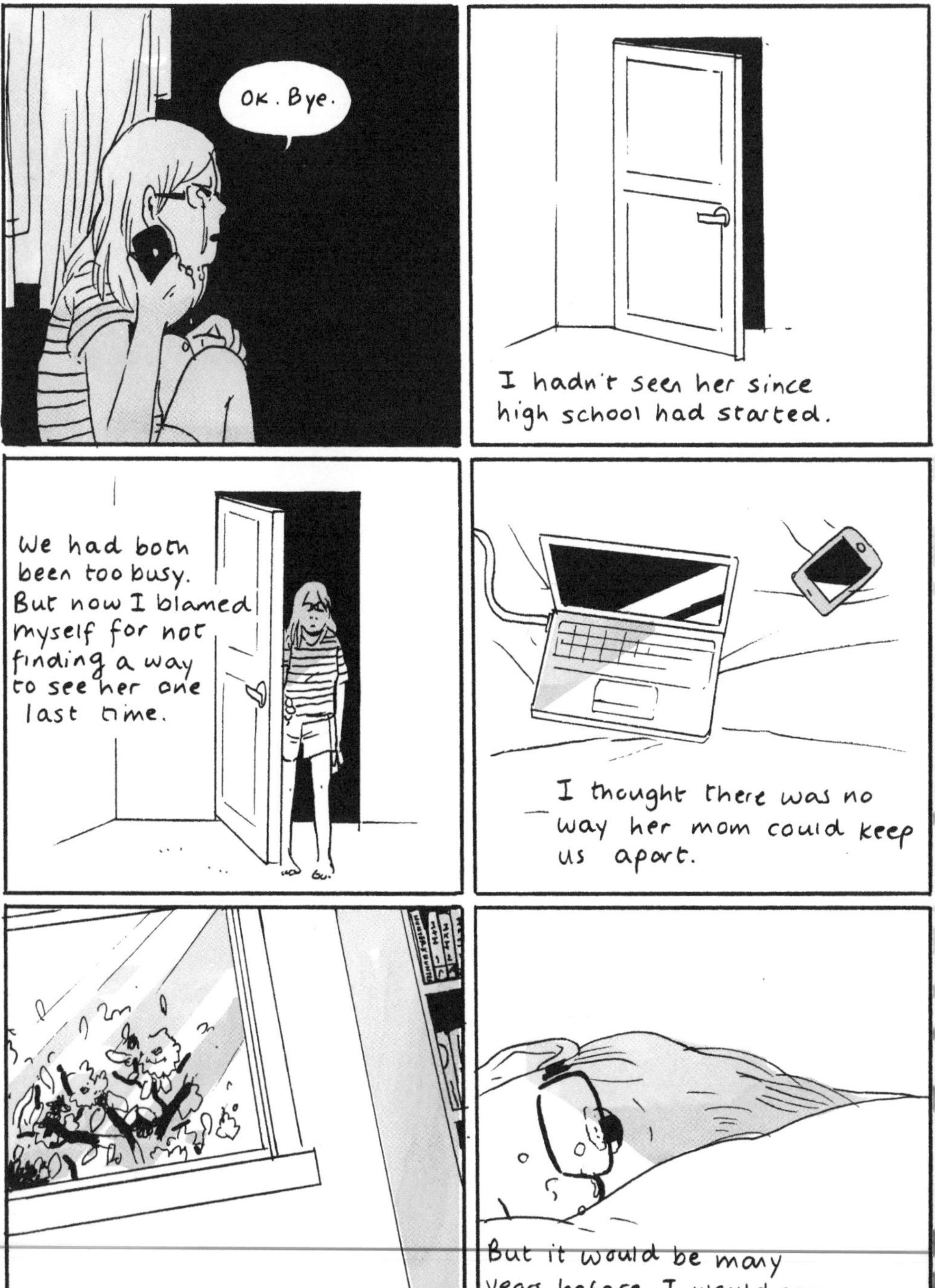
OK. Bye.
I hadn't seen her since high school had started.
We had both been too busy. But now I blamed myself for not finding a way to see her one last time.
I thought there was no way her mom could keep us apart.
But it would be many years before I would see Rae again.

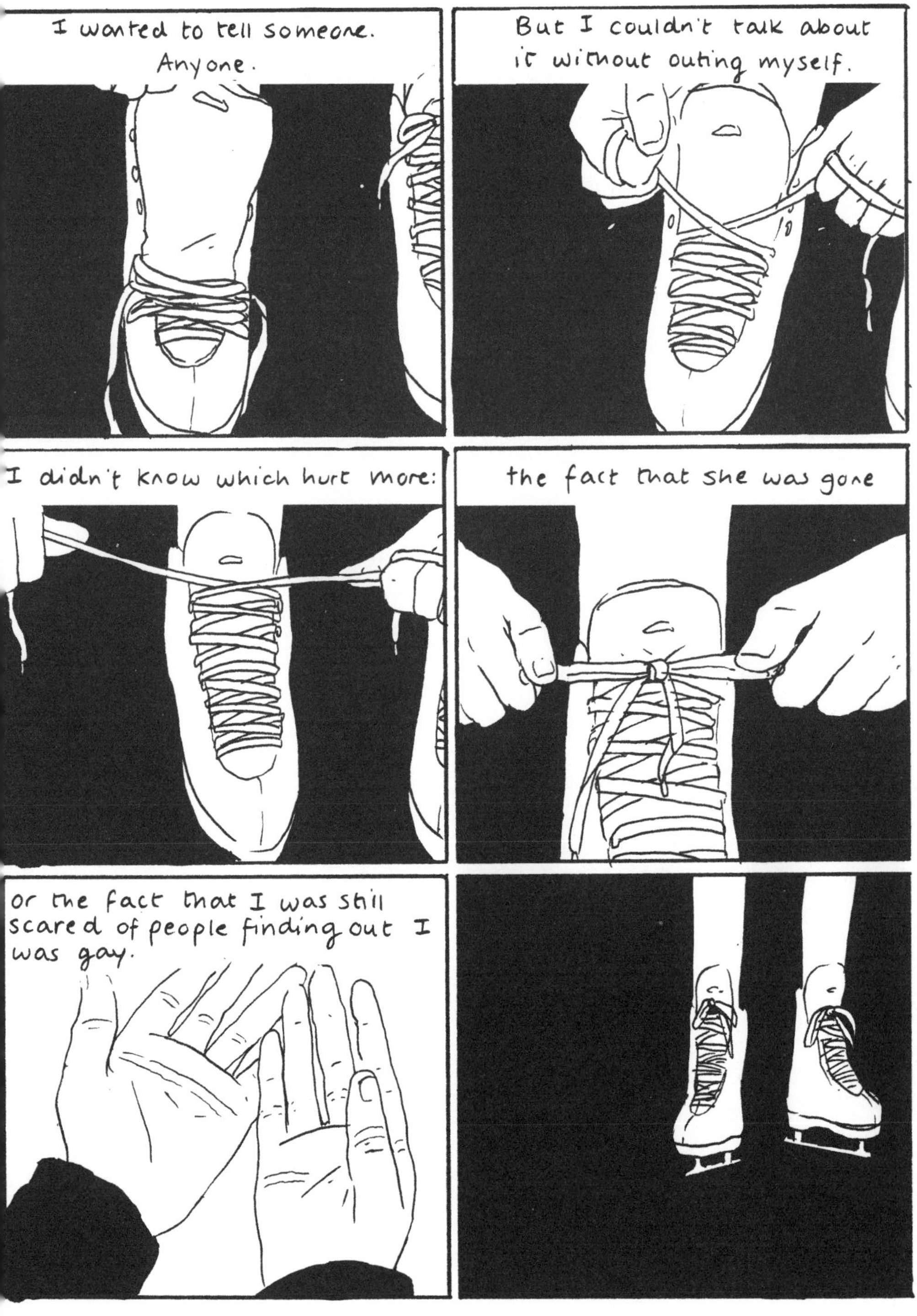
I wanted to tell someone.
Anyone.
But I couldn't talk about it without outing myself.
I didn't know which hurt more:
the fact that she was gone
or the fact that I was still scared of people finding out I was gay.

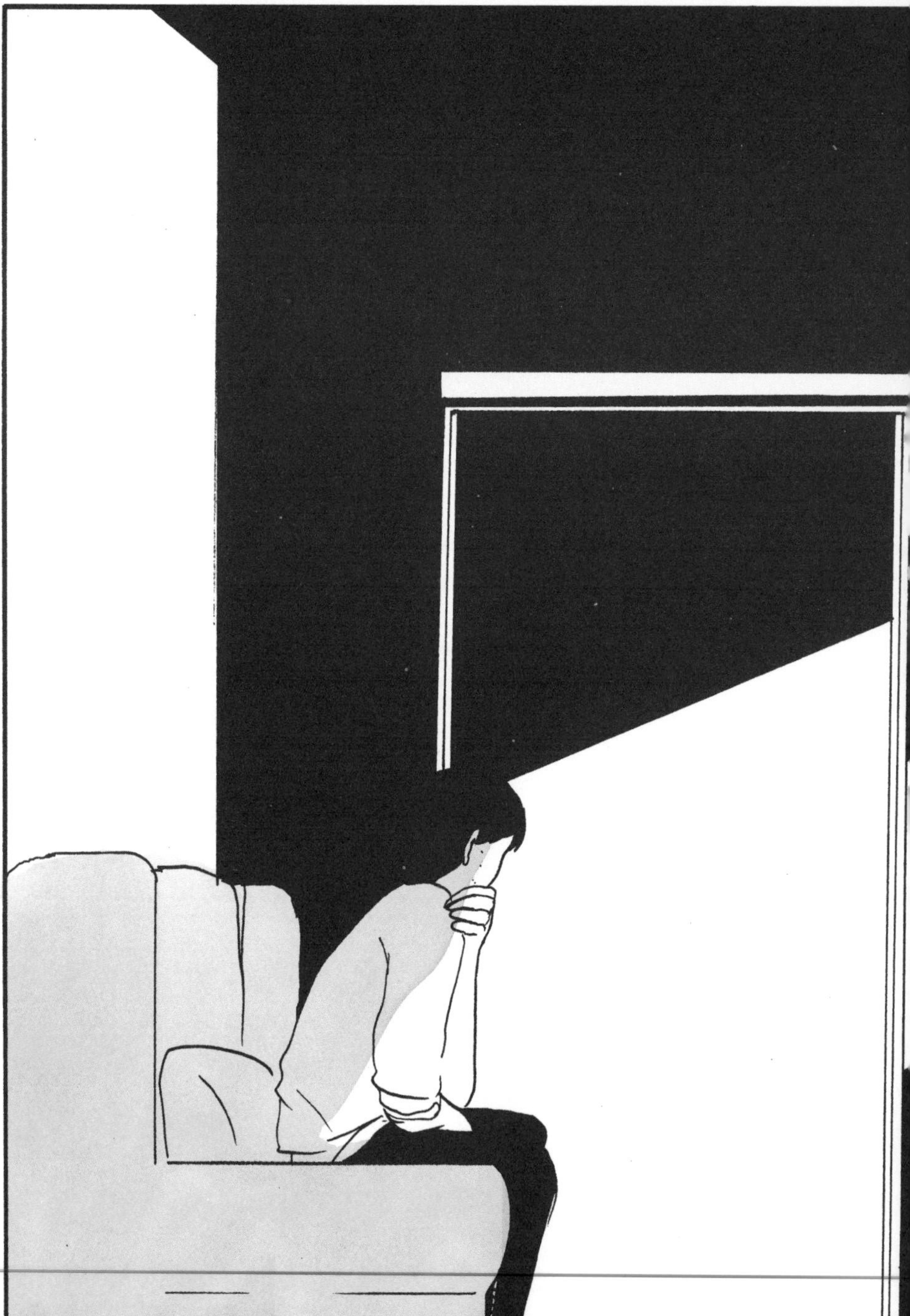

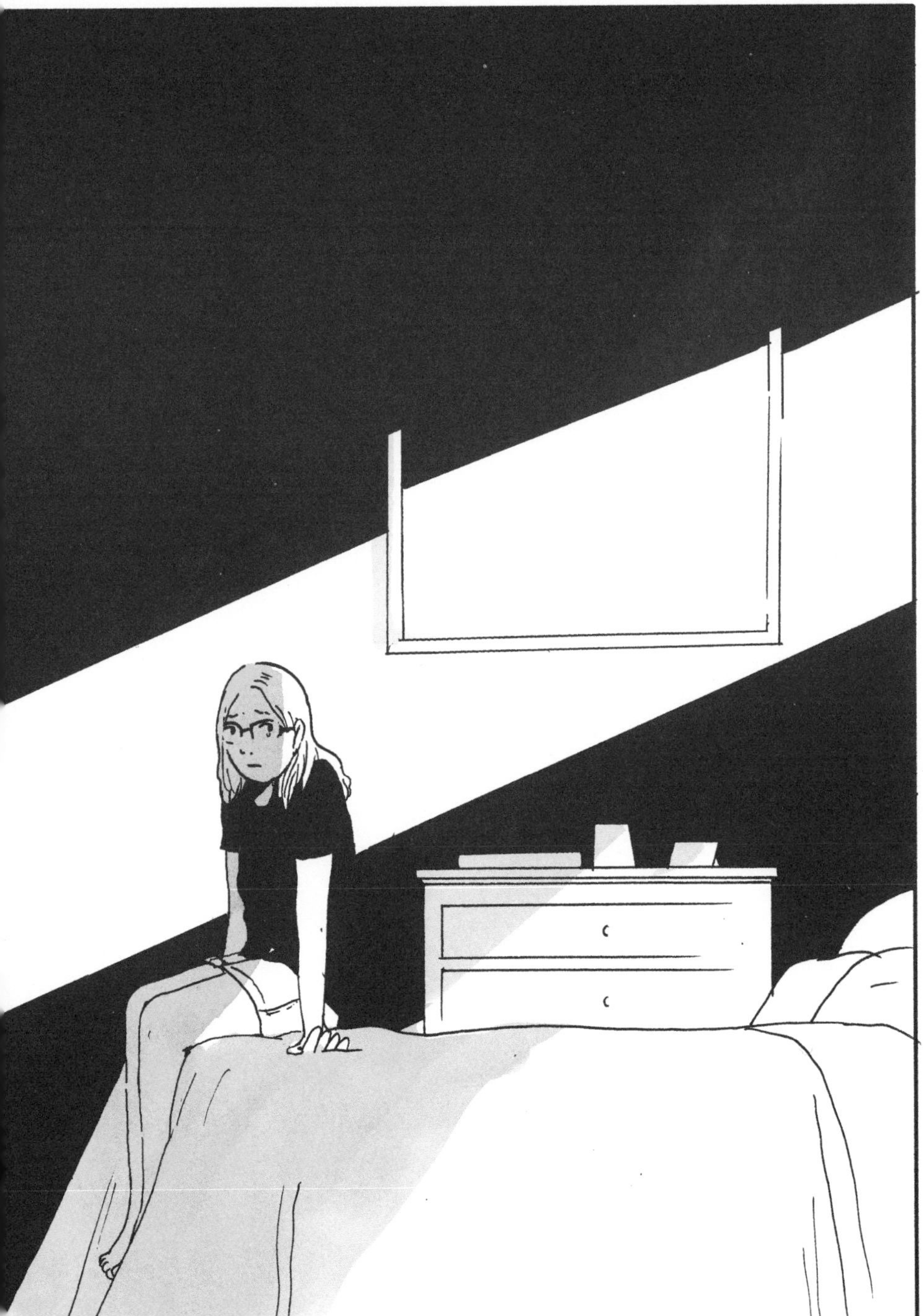

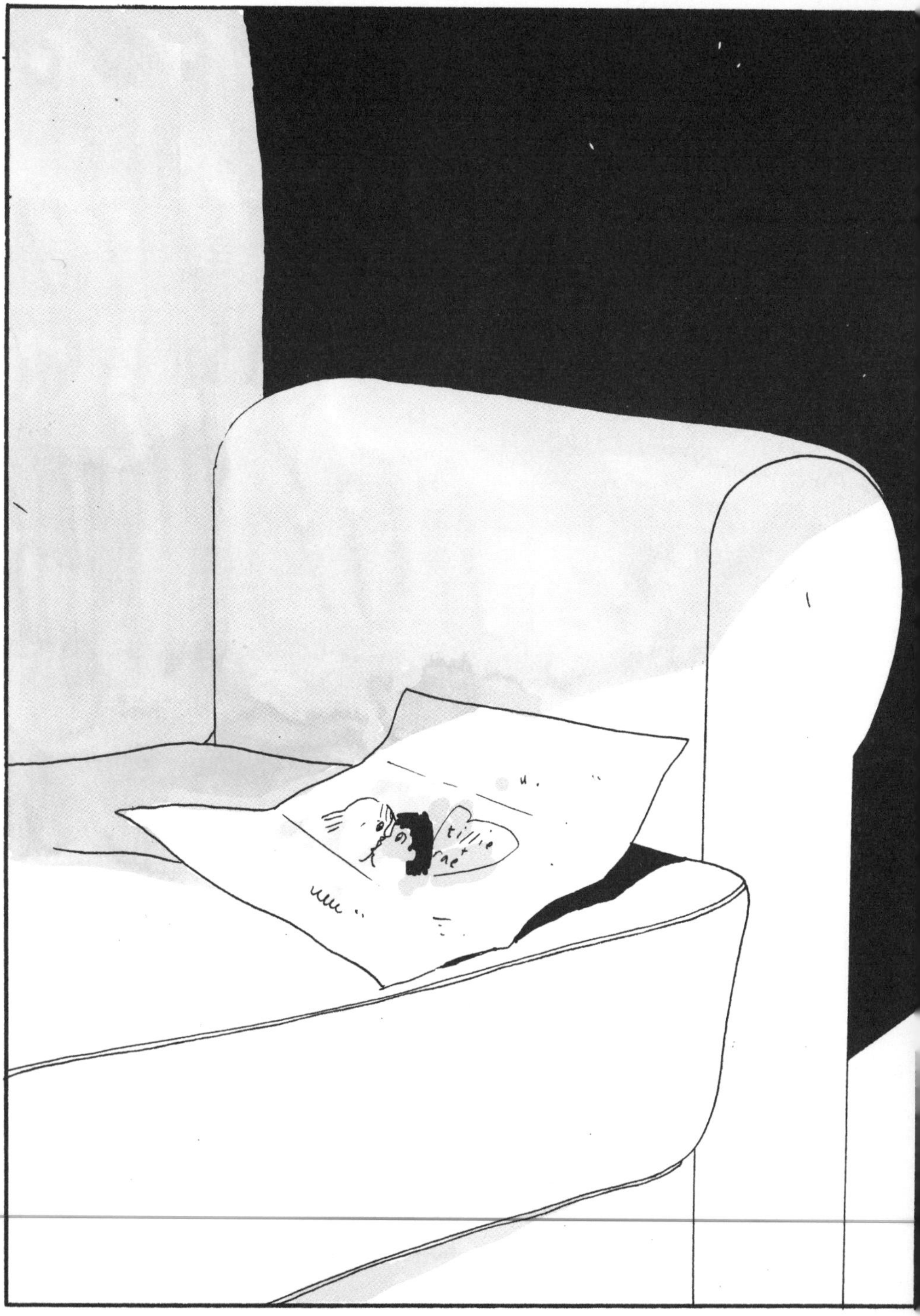
tillie
+
rae

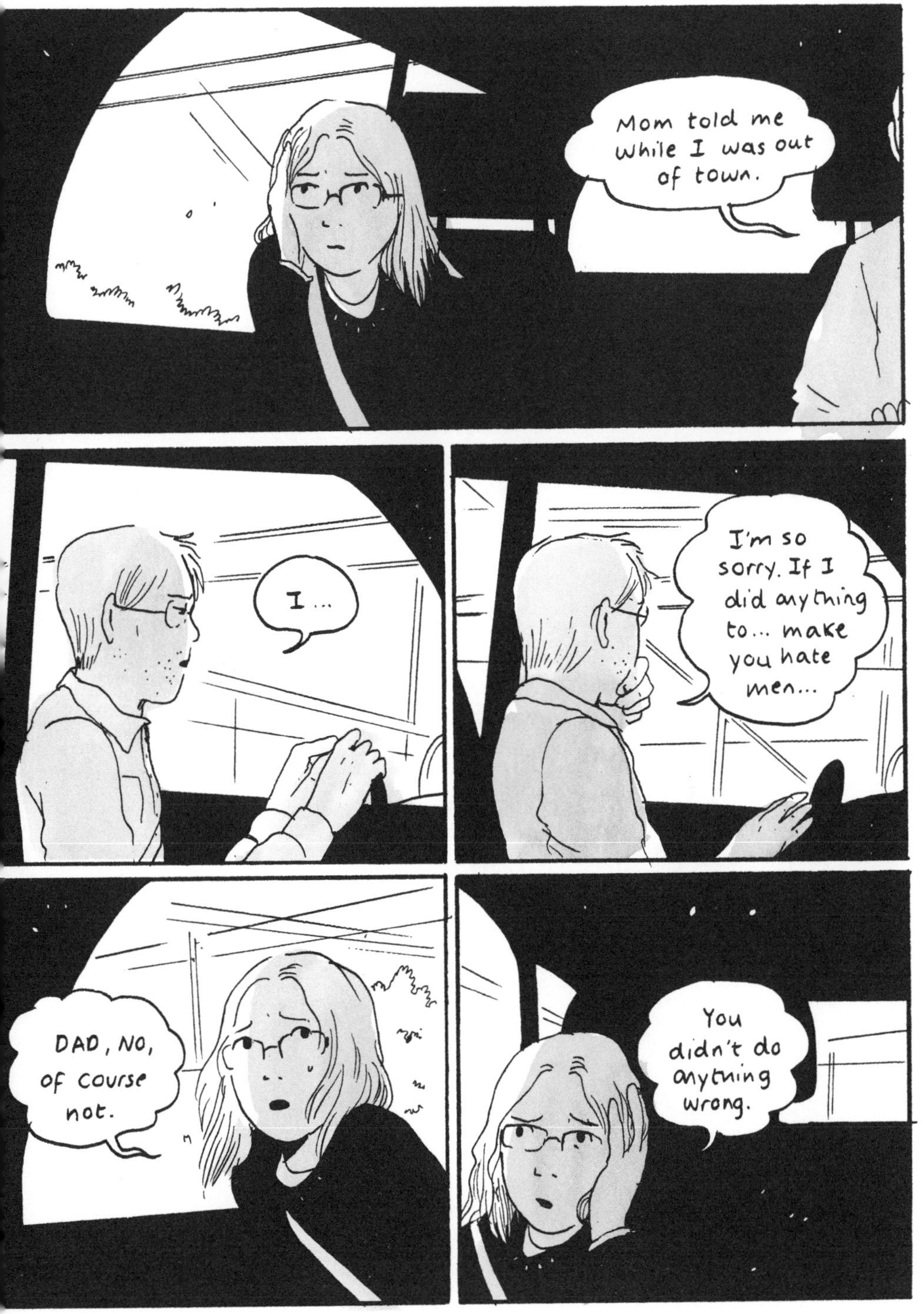

Mom told me while I was out of town.
I...
I'm so sorry. If I did anything to... make you hate men...
DAD, NO, of course not.
You didn't do anything wrong.

250

252

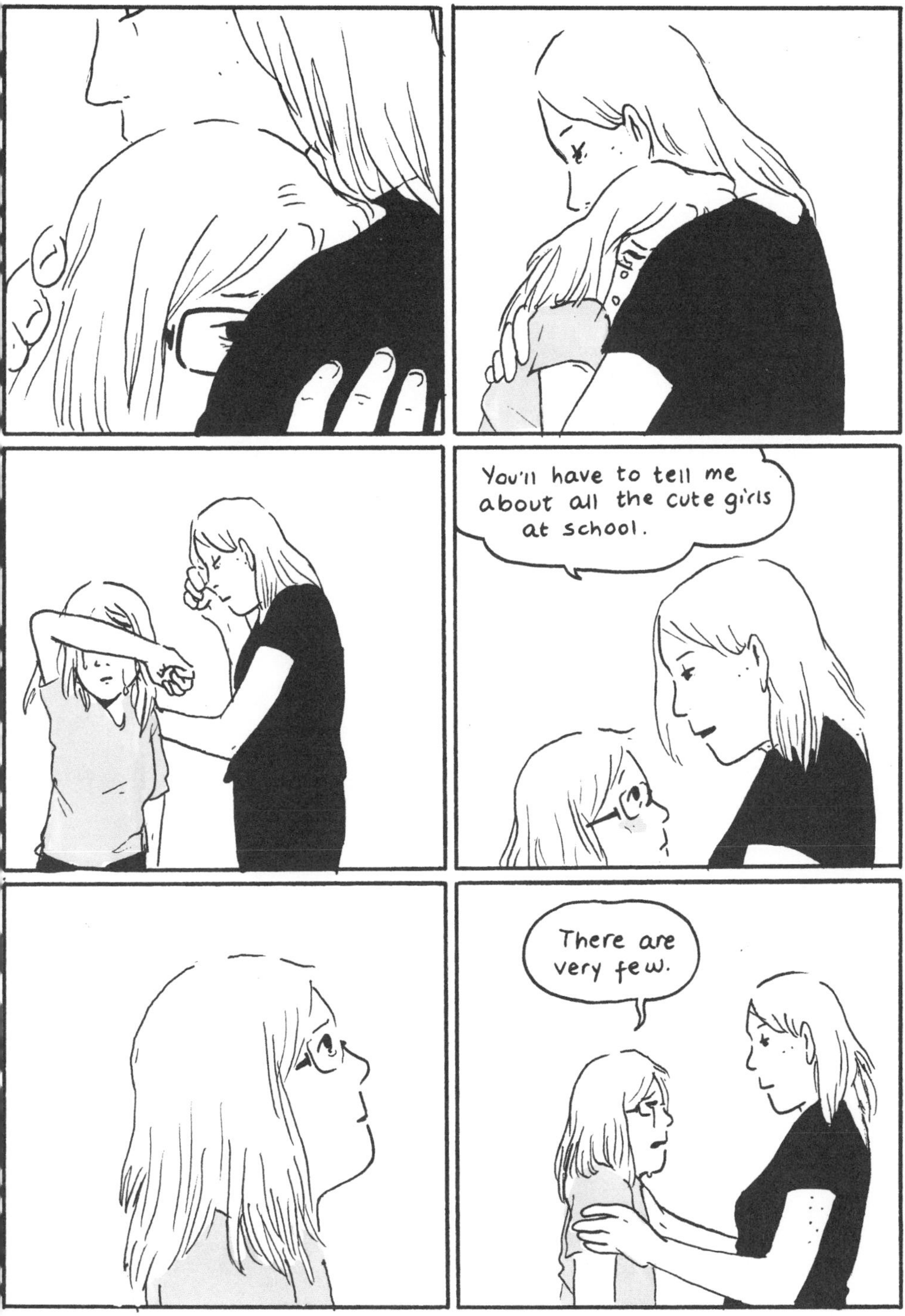
You'll have to tell me about all the cute girls at school.
There are very few.

Art was slowly becoming a bigger part of my life. I signed up for printmaking in my sophomore year because everyone said the teacher, Mr. Williams, was cool.

The class was in a tiny portable on the edge of campus.

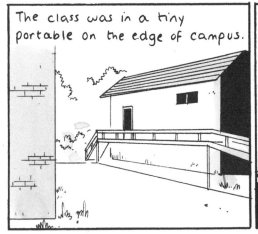

That portable became my home at school.

Mr. Williams let a group of us take over the backroom with the press and drying racks.

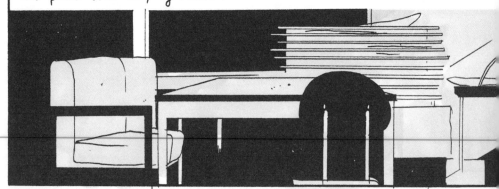

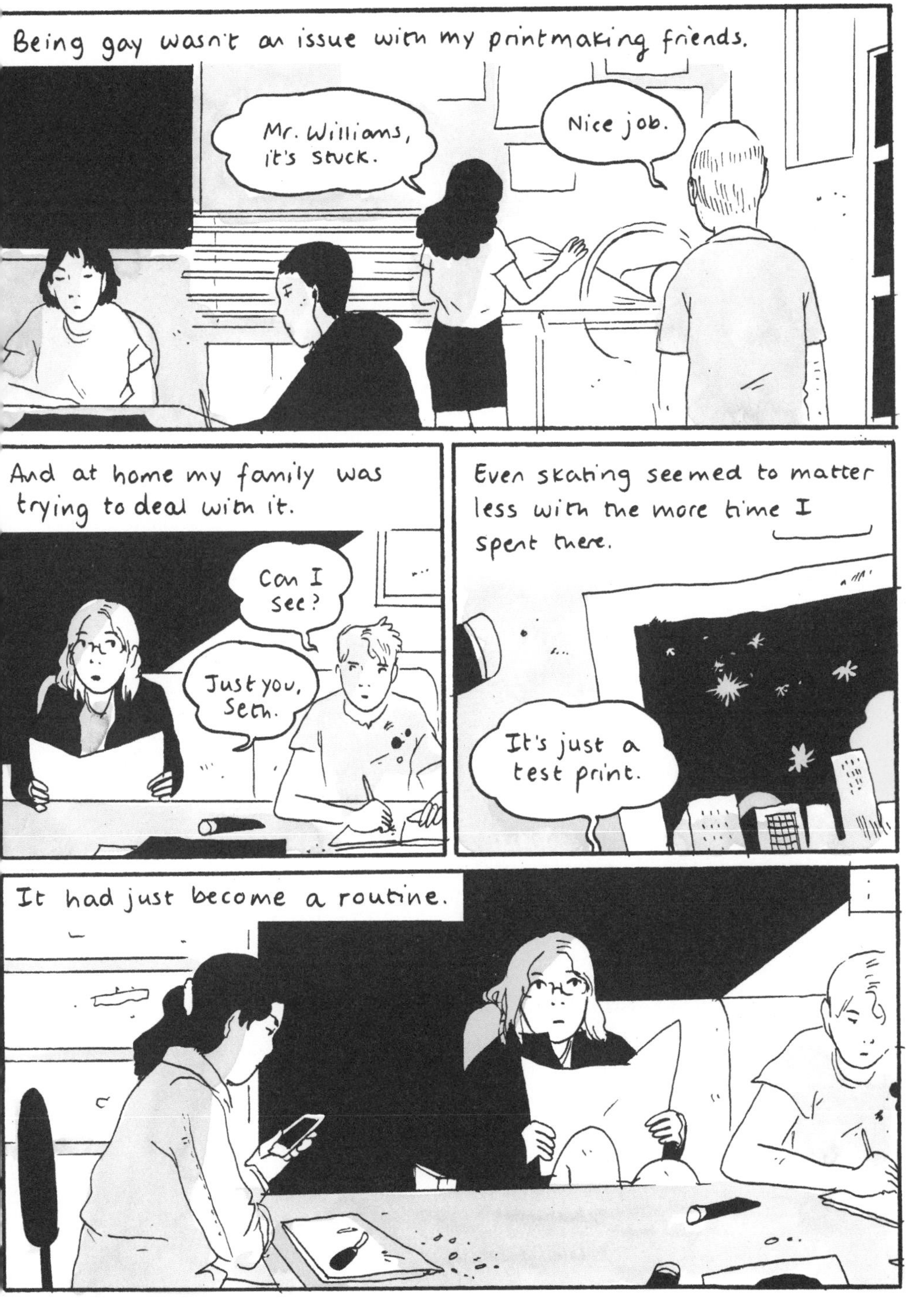

Being gay wasn't an issue with my printmaking friends.
Mr. Williams, it's stuck.
Nice job.
And at home my family was trying to deal with it.
Can I see?
Just you, Seth.
Even skating seemed to matter less with the more time I spent there.
It's just a test print.
It had just become a routine.

259

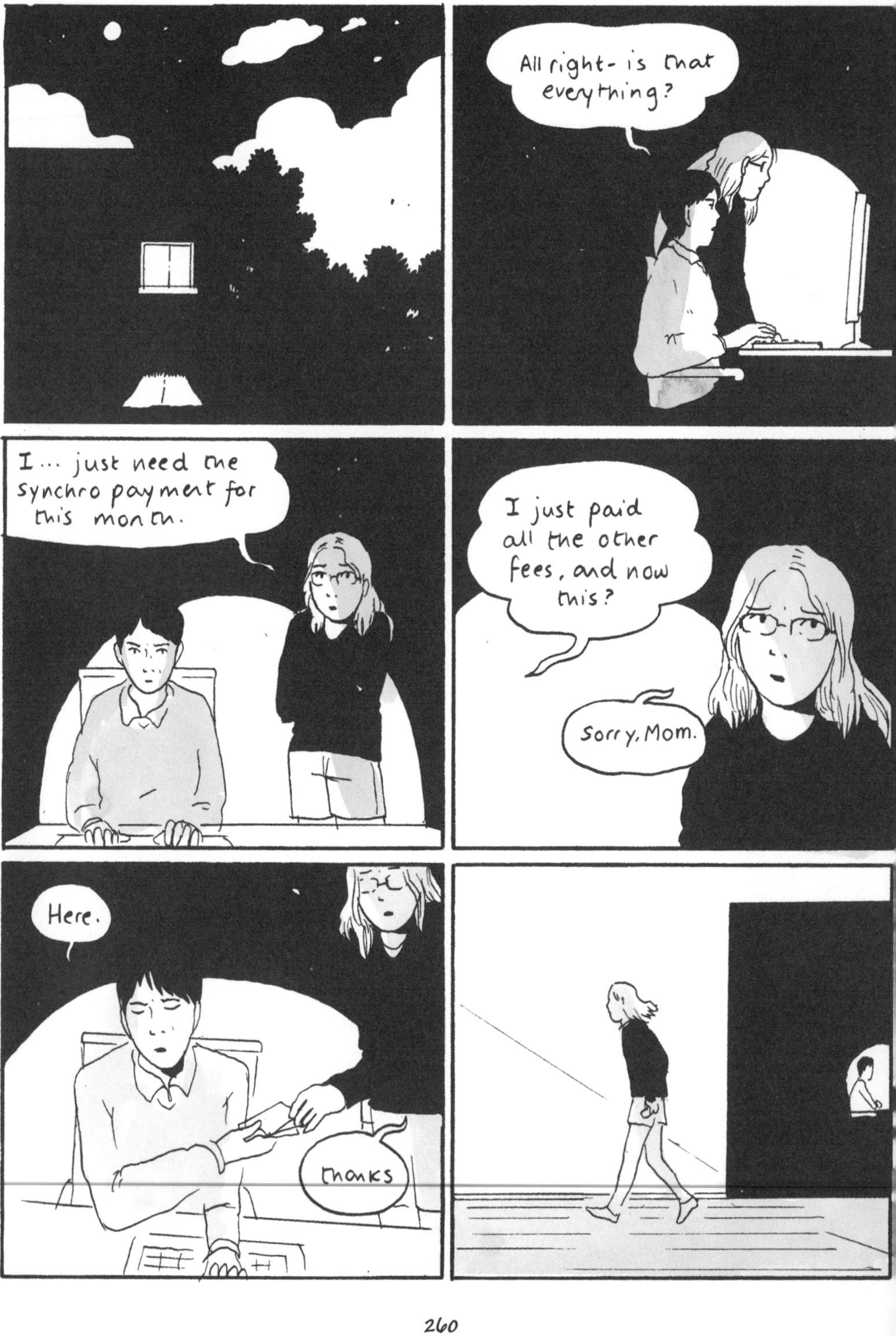
All right- is that everything?
I... just need the synchro payment for this month.
I just paid all the other fees, and now this?
Sorry, Mom.
Here.
thanks

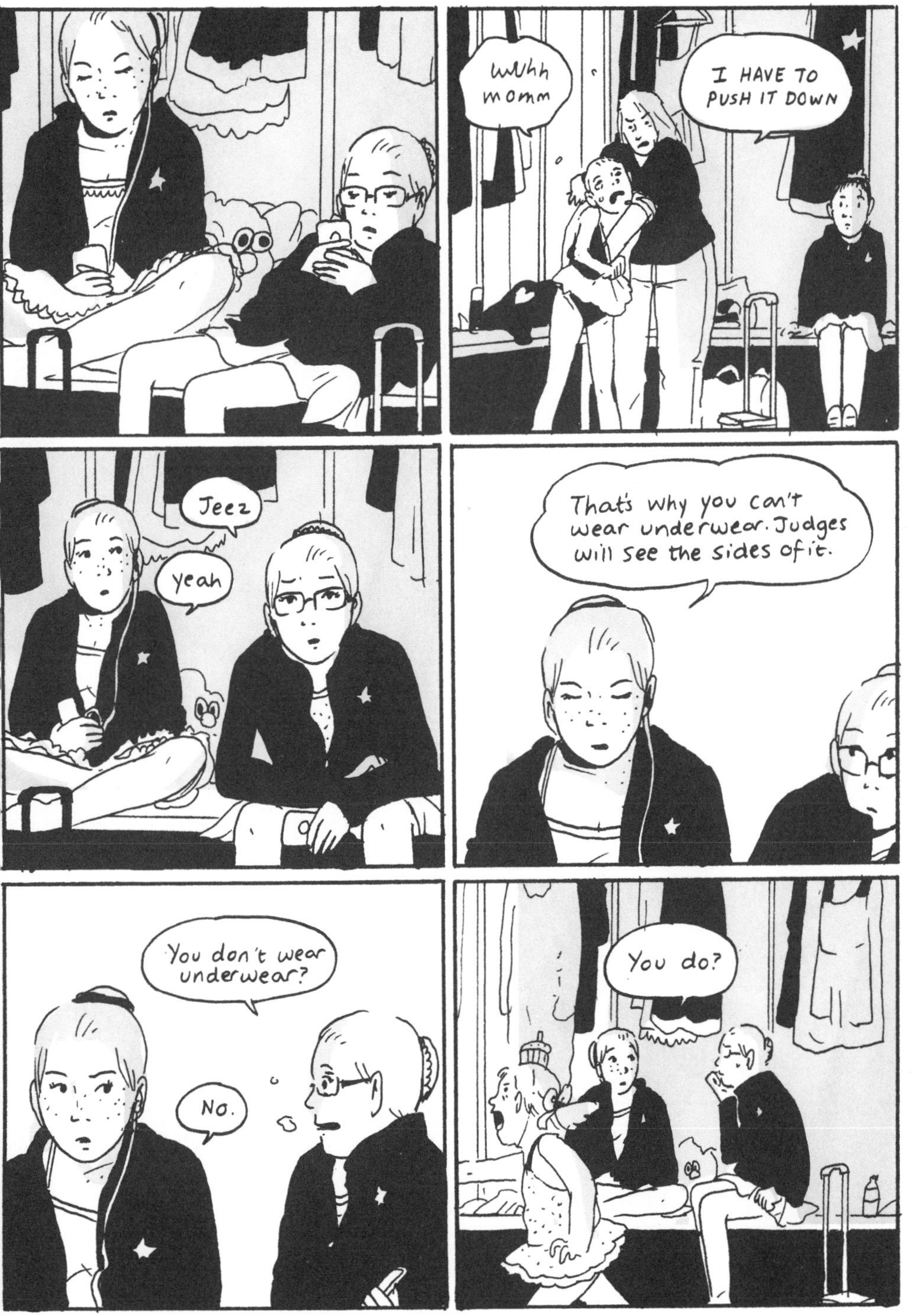

wuhh momm
I HAVE TO PUSH IT DOWN
Jeez
yeah
That's why you can't wear underwear. Judges will see the sides of it.
You don't wear underwear?
No.
You do?

I was starting to realize that skating wasn't what it seemed.

I always thought of it as simply a sport.

But with that sport came a lifestyle. And it wasn't optional.

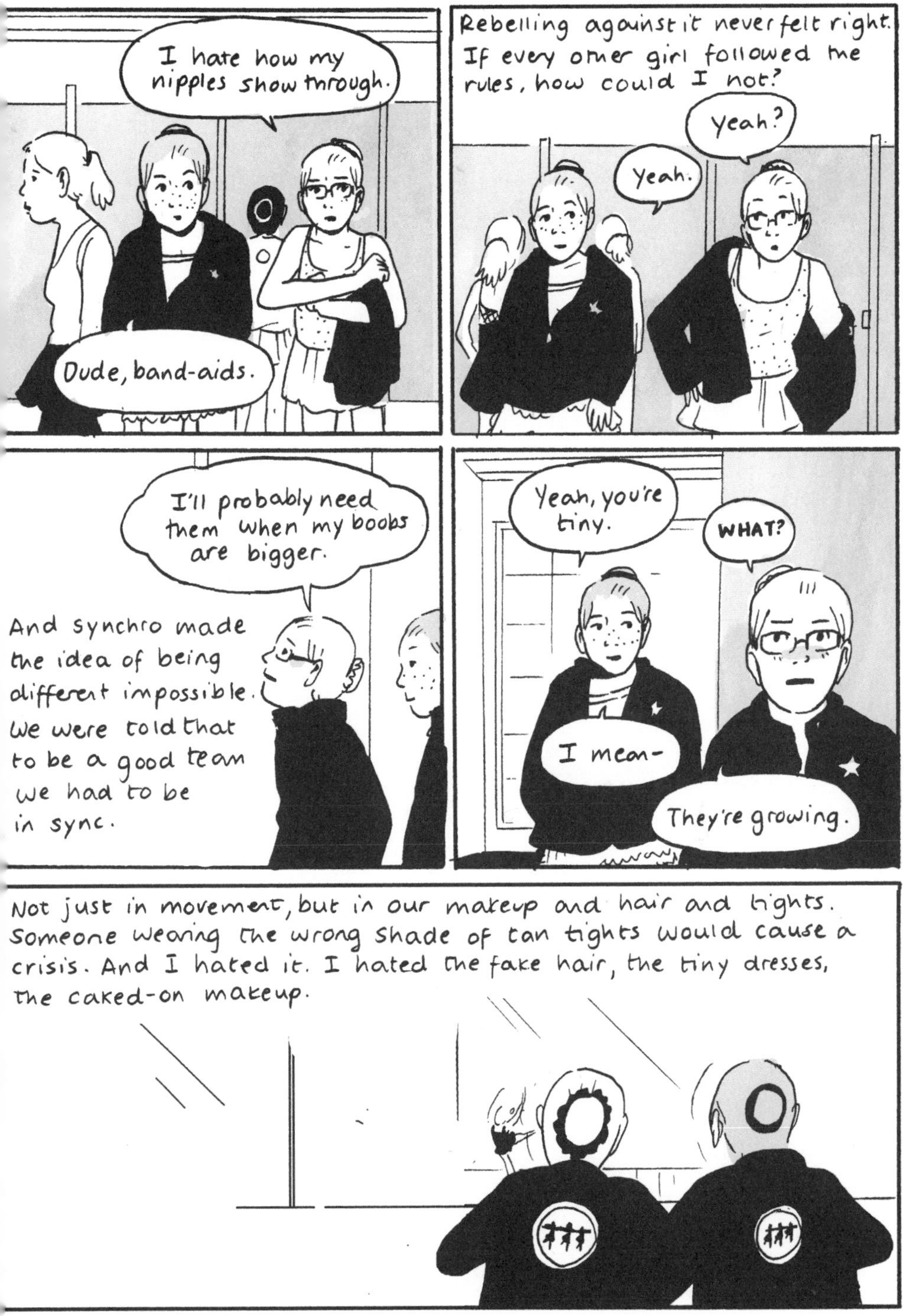
I hate how my nipples show through.
Dude, band-aids.
Rebelling against it never felt right. If every other girl followed the rules, how could I not?
Yeah.
Yeah?
I'll probably need them when my boobs are bigger.
And synchro made the idea of being different impossible. We were told that to be a good team we had to be in sync.
Yeah, you're tiny.
WHAT?
I mean-
They're growing.
Not just in movement, but in our makeup and hair and tights. Someone wearing the wrong shade of tan tights would cause a crisis. And I hated it. I hated the fake hair, the tiny dresses, the caked-on makeup.

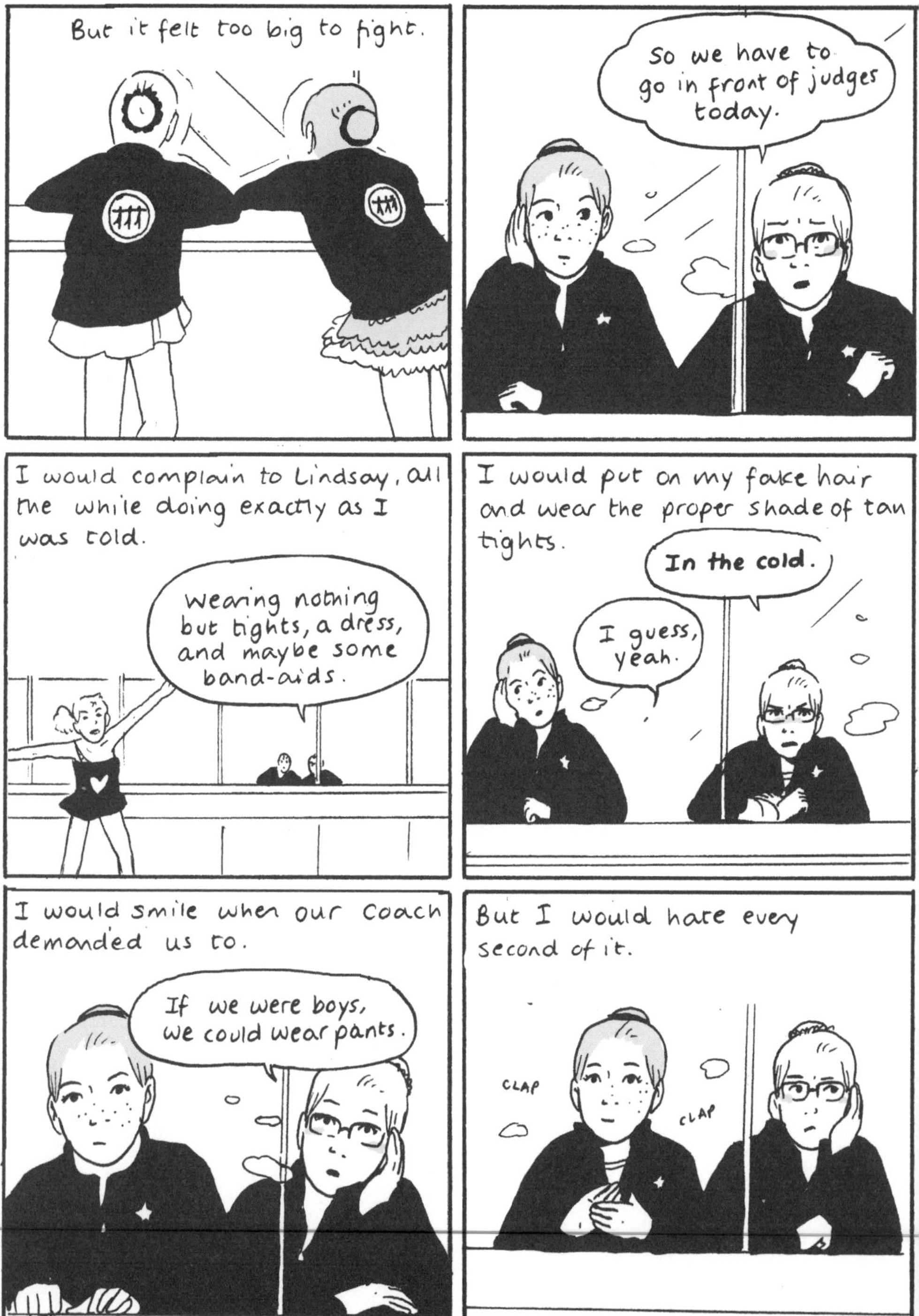

But it felt too big to fight.
So we have to go in front of judges today.
I would complain to Lindsay, all the while doing exactly as I was told.
Wearing nothing but tights, a dress, and maybe some band-aids.
I would put on my fake hair and wear the proper shade of tan tights.
In the cold.
I guess, yeah.
I would smile when our coach demanded us to.
If we were boys, we could wear pants.
But I would hate every second of it.
CLAP
CLAP

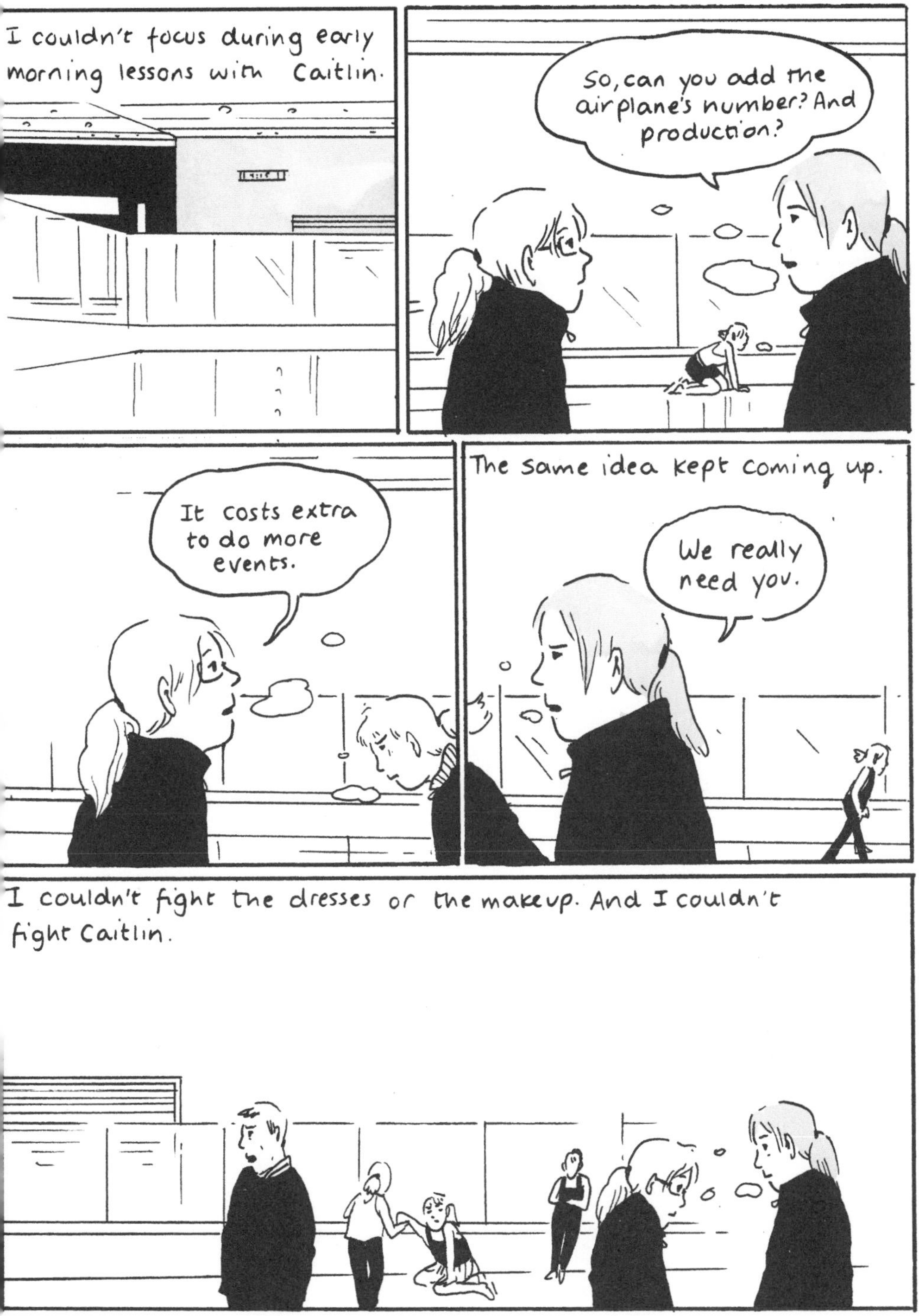
I couldn't focus during early morning lessons with Caitlin.
So, can you add the airplane's number? And production?
It costs extra to do more events.
The same idea kept coming up.
We really need you.
I couldn't fight the dresses or the makeup. And I couldn't fight Caitlin.

8

COUNTER

A counter is a one-foot turn
where your entry and exit are on
opposite curves. A perfect counter
makes a very specific mark on
the ice. After doing a few I
would always retrace my steps,
searching for the perfect cut
in the ice.

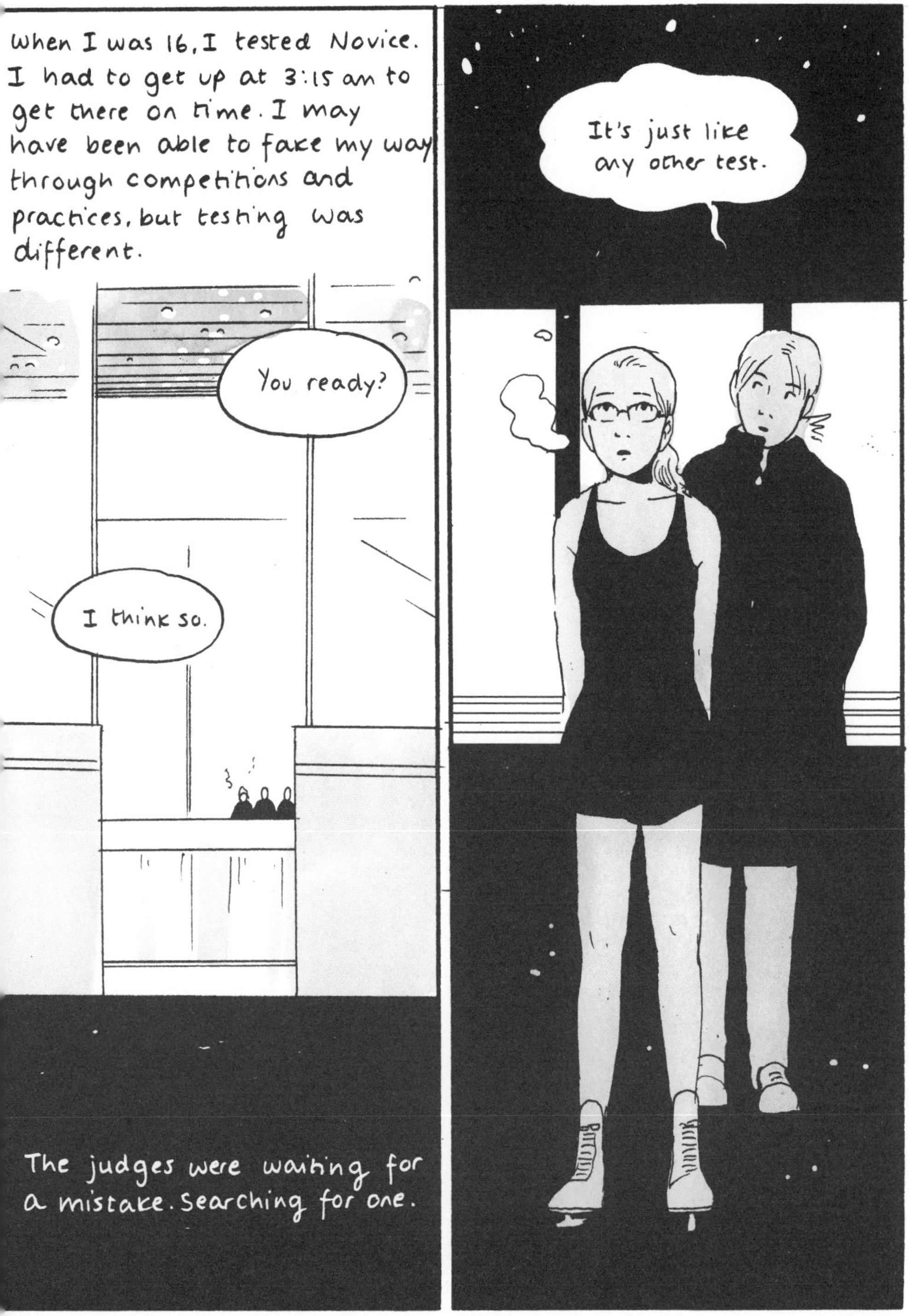
When I was 16, I tested Novice. I had to get up at 3:15 am to get there on time. I may have been able to fake my way through competitions and practices, but testing was different.
You ready?
I think so.
The judges were waiting for a mistake. Searching for one.
It's just like any other test.

There was no music to tell me when to start.

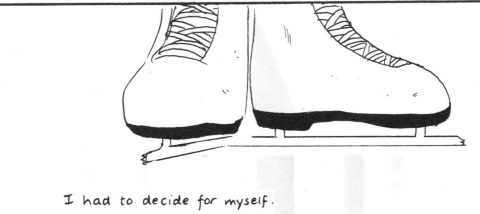

I had to decide for myself.

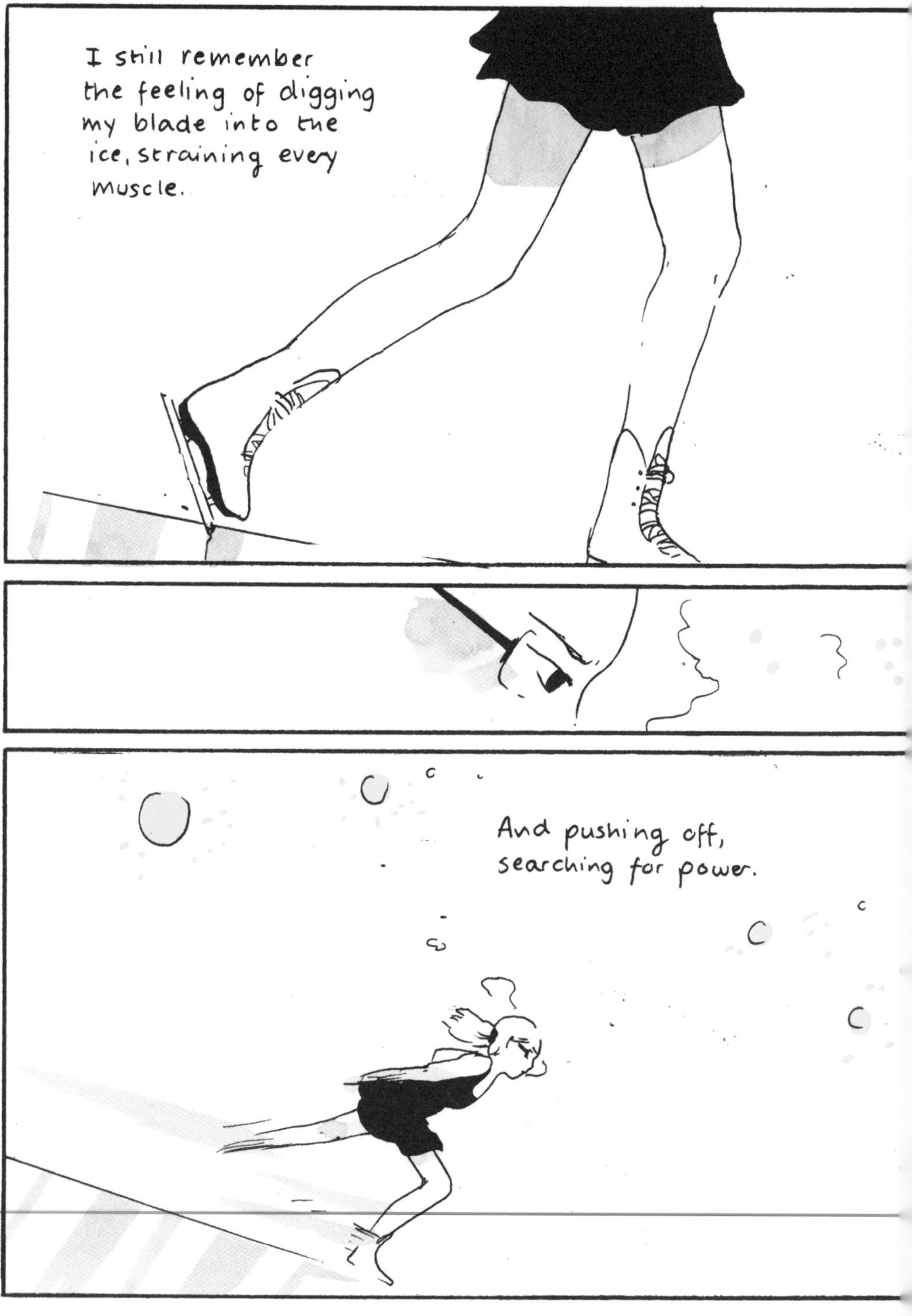
I still remember the feeling of digging my blade into the ice, straining every muscle.
And pushing off, searching for power.

But sometimes, no matter how much strength or speed I thought was inside me...

I couldn't reach it.

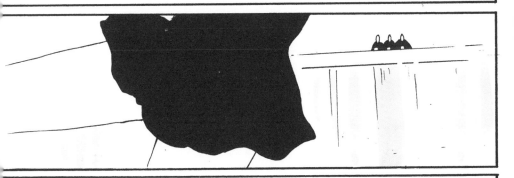

And so I'd have to skate through, knowing the whole time that this weakness wasn't all that I was.

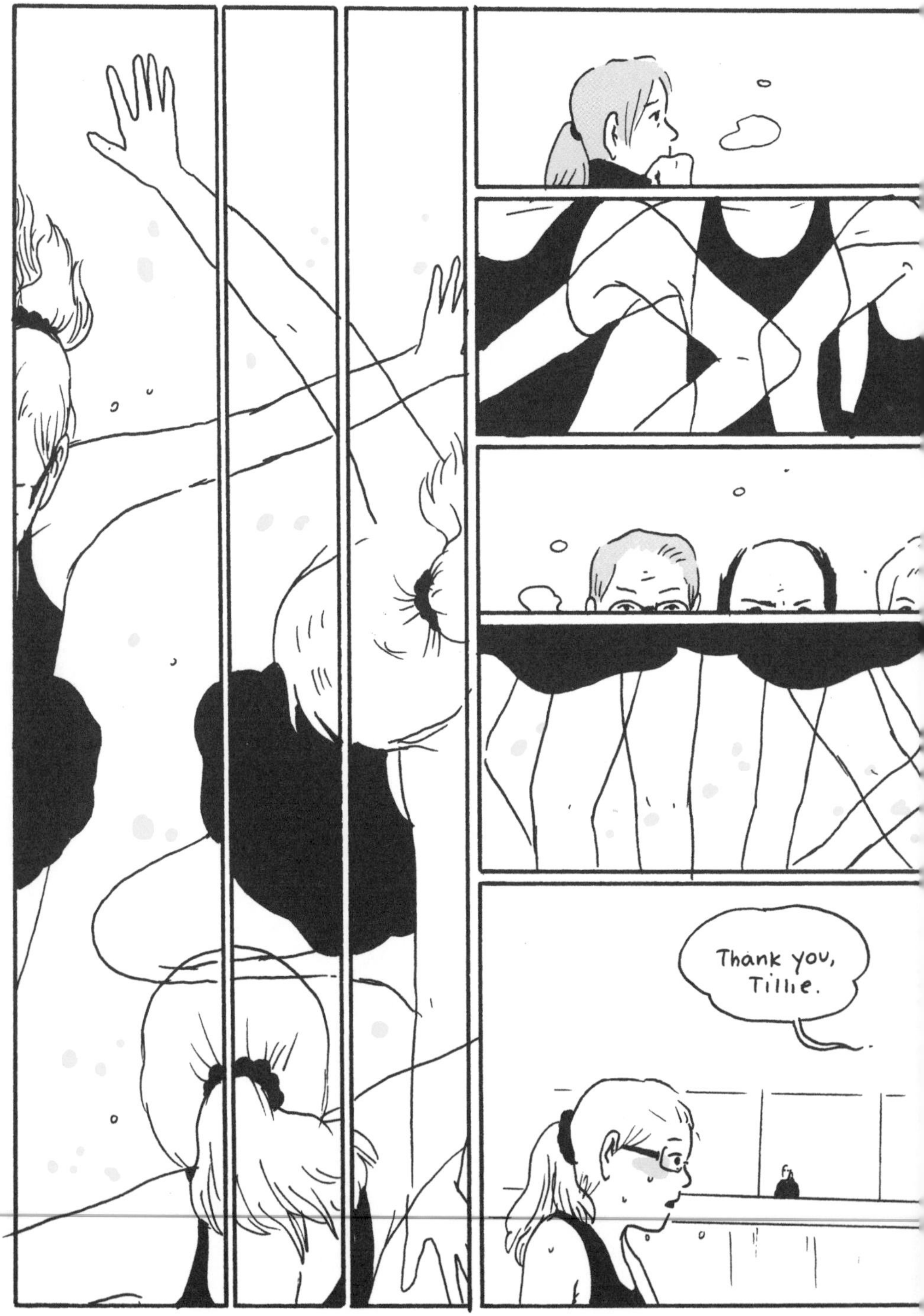
Thank you, Tillie.

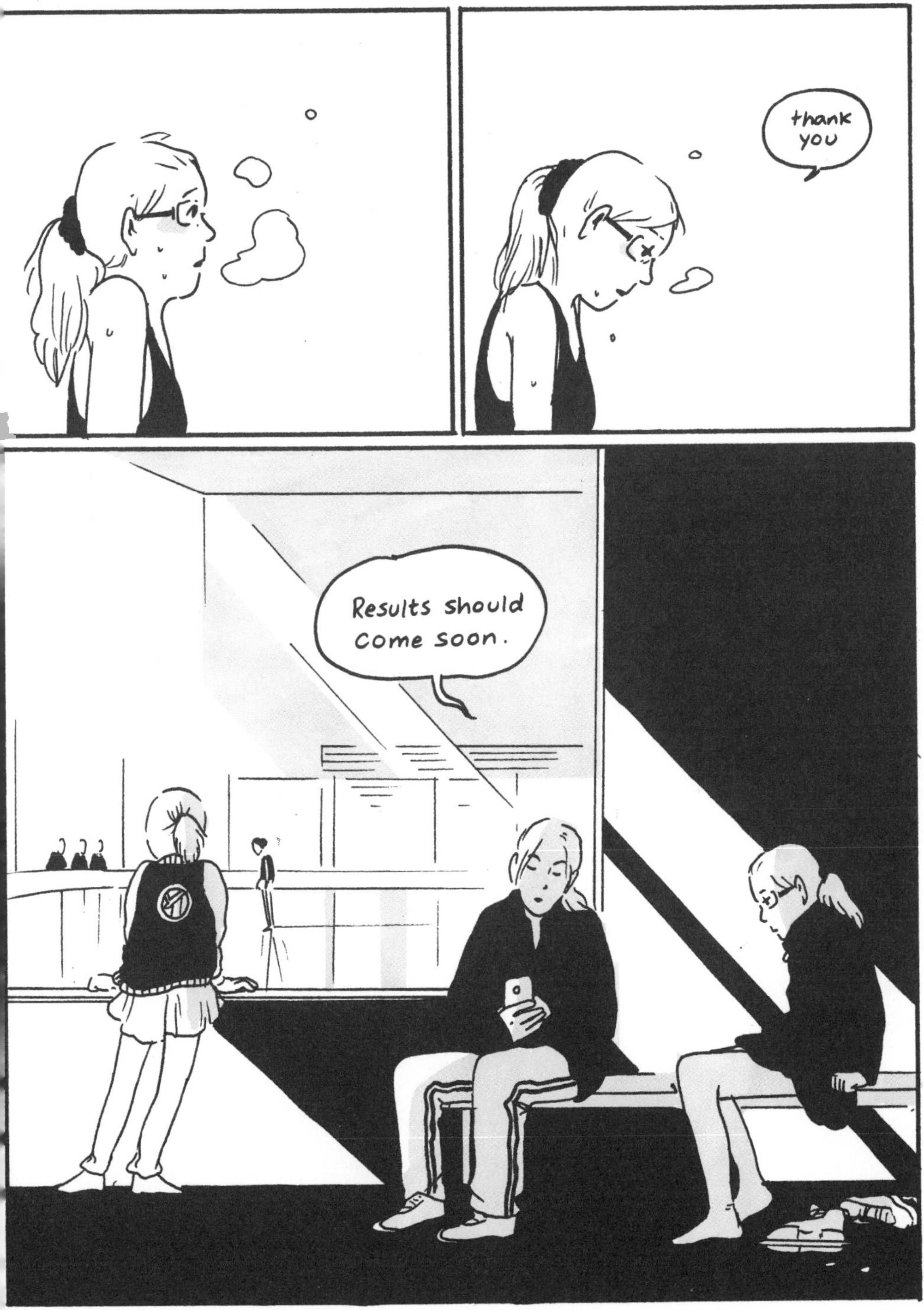
thank you
Results should come soon.

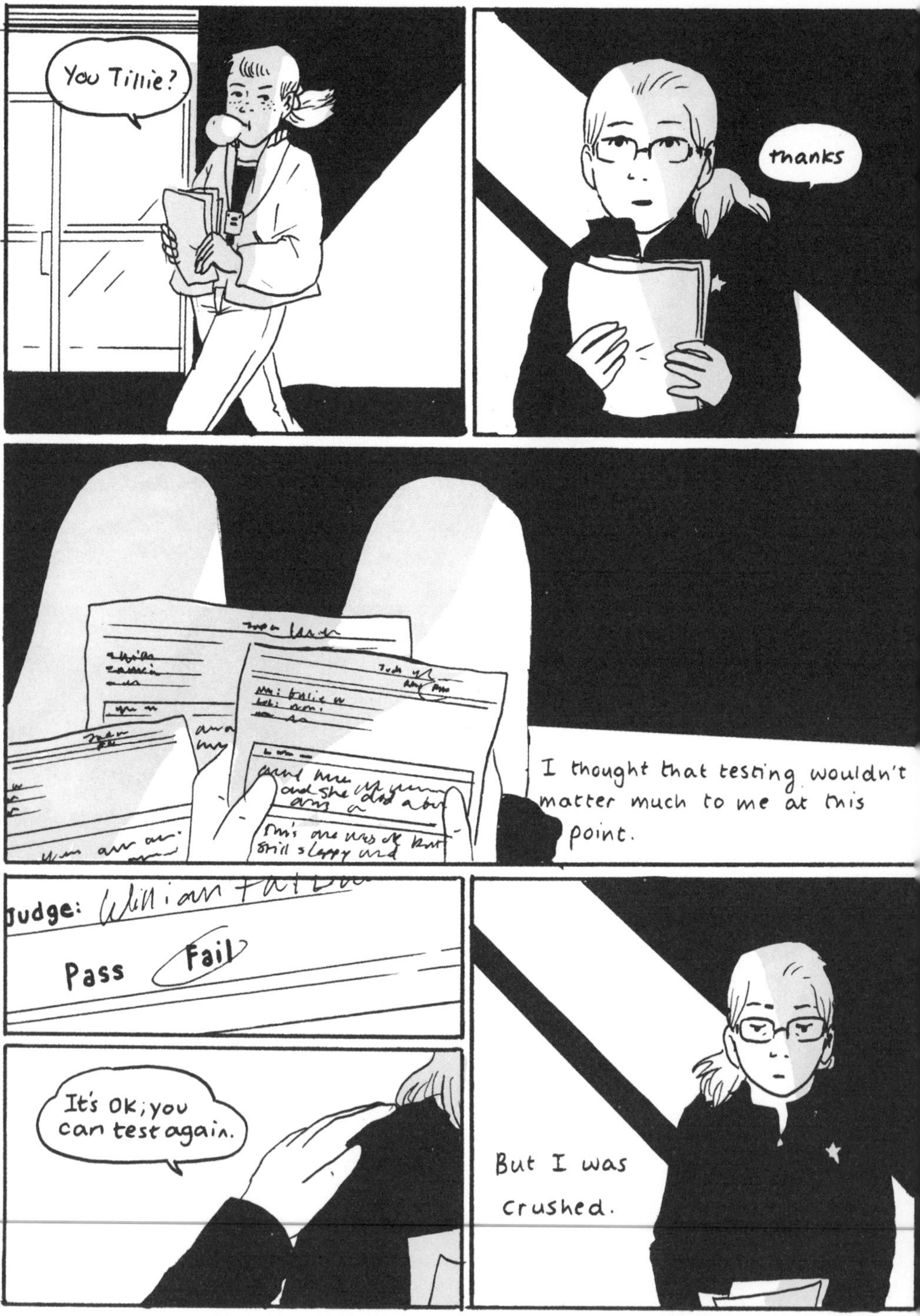
You Tillie?
thanks
I thought that testing wouldn't matter much to me at this point.
Judge:
Pass
Fail
It's OK; you can test again.
But I was crushed.

279

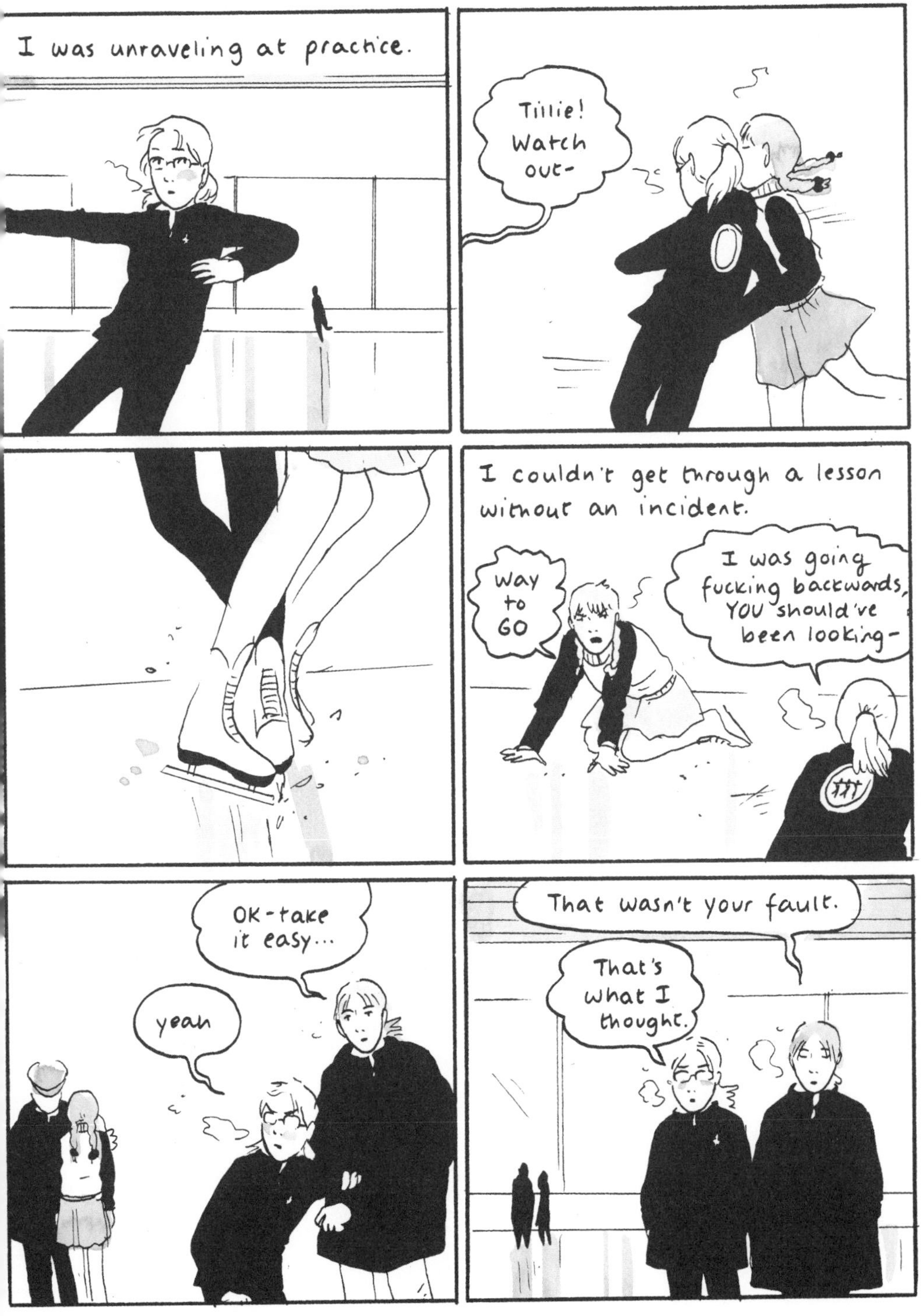
I was unraveling at practice.
Tillie! Watch out-
I couldn't get through a lesson without an incident.
way to GO
I was going fucking backwards, YOU should've been looking-
OK-take it easy...
yeah
That wasn't your fault.
That's what I thought.

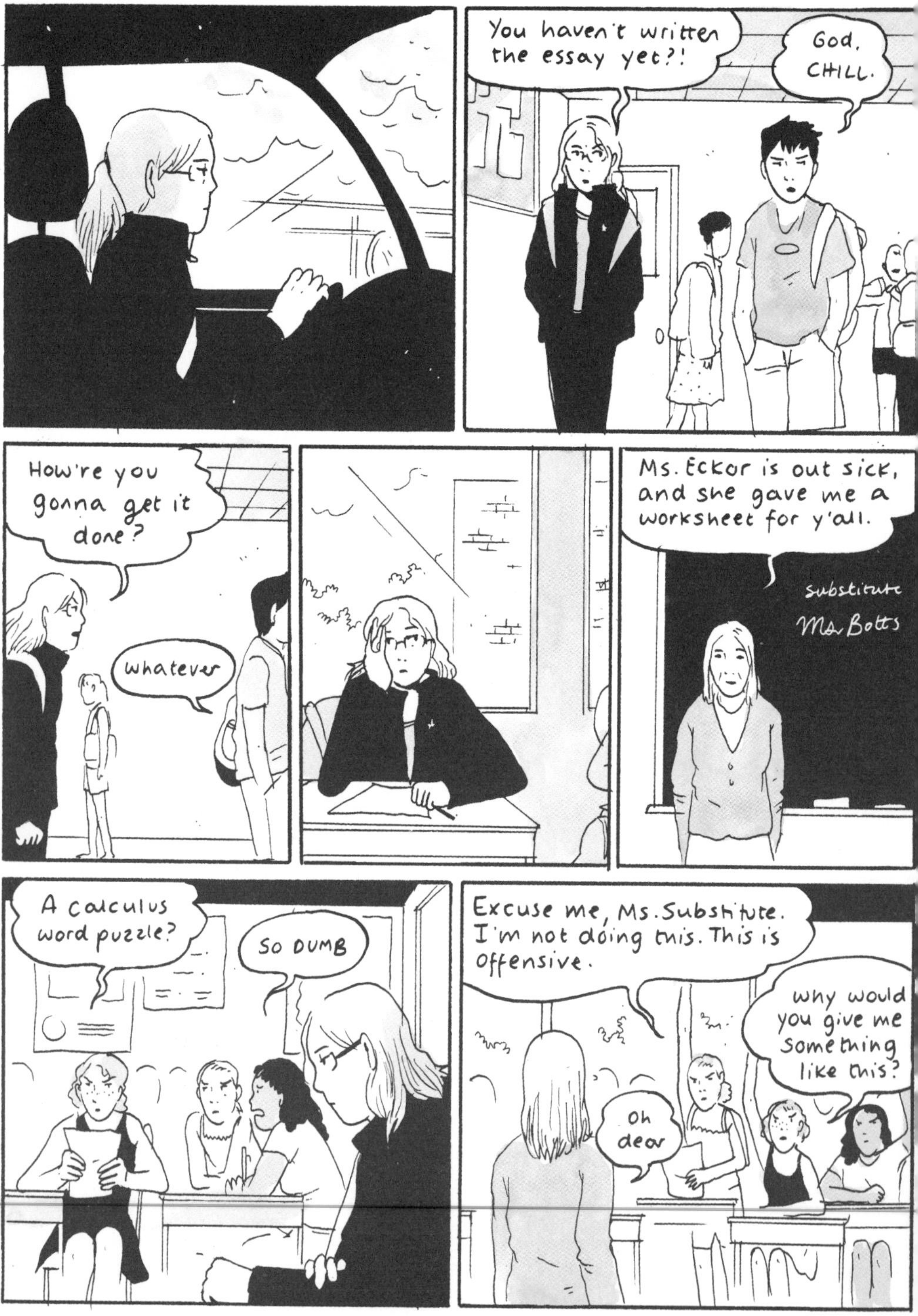
You haven't written the essay yet?!
God, CHILL.
How're you gonna get it done?
whatever
Ms. Eckor is out sick, and she gave me a worksheet for y'all.
substitute
Ms. Botts
A calculus word puzzle?
So DUMB
Excuse me, Ms. Substitute. I'm not doing this. This is offensive.
why would you give me something like this?
Oh dear

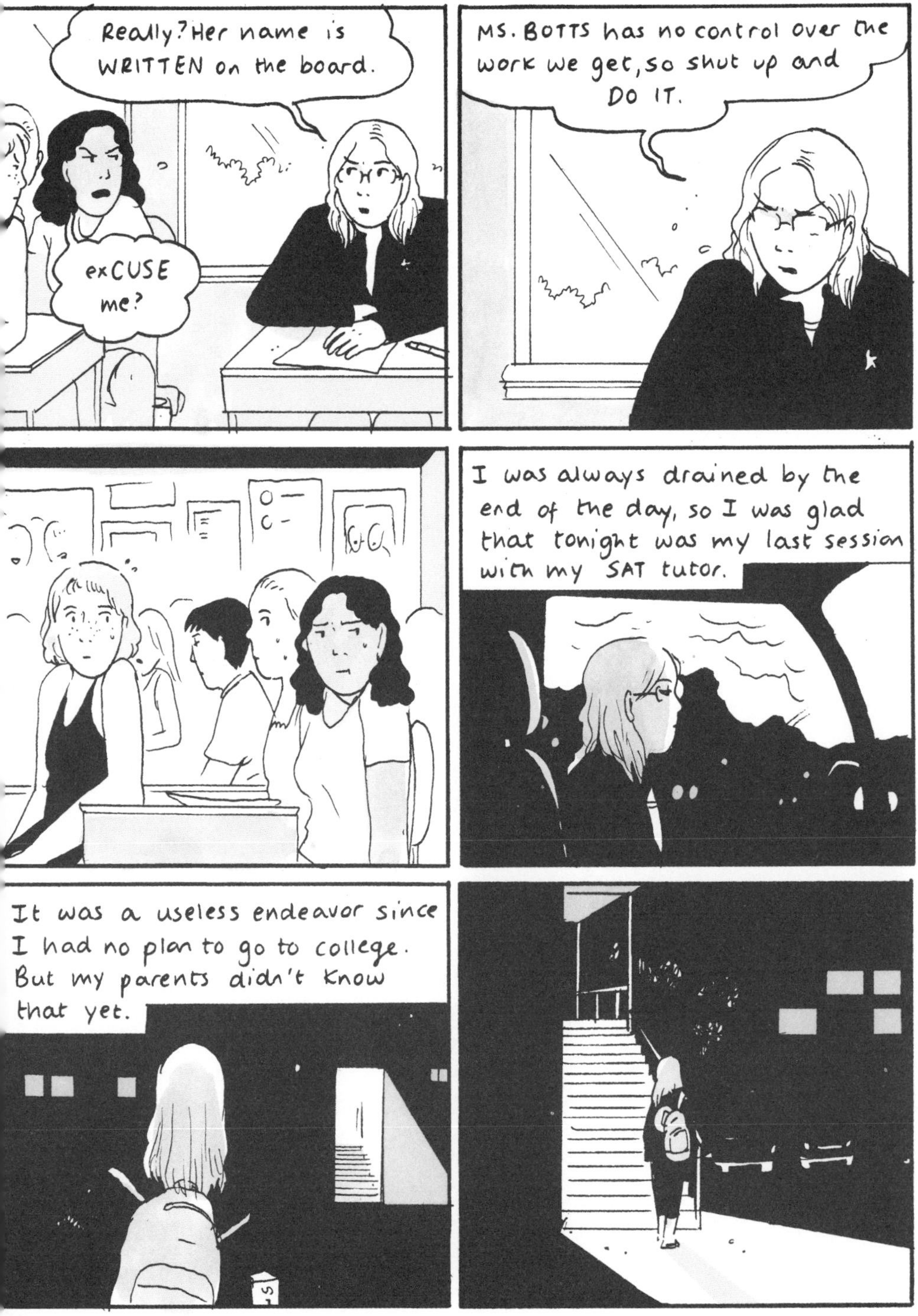
Really? Her name is WRITTEN on the board.
exCUSE me?
MS. BOTTS has no control over the work we get, so shut up and DO IT.
I was always drained by the end of the day, so I was glad that tonight was my last session with my SAT tutor.
It was a useless endeavor since I had no plan to go to college. But my parents didn't know that yet.

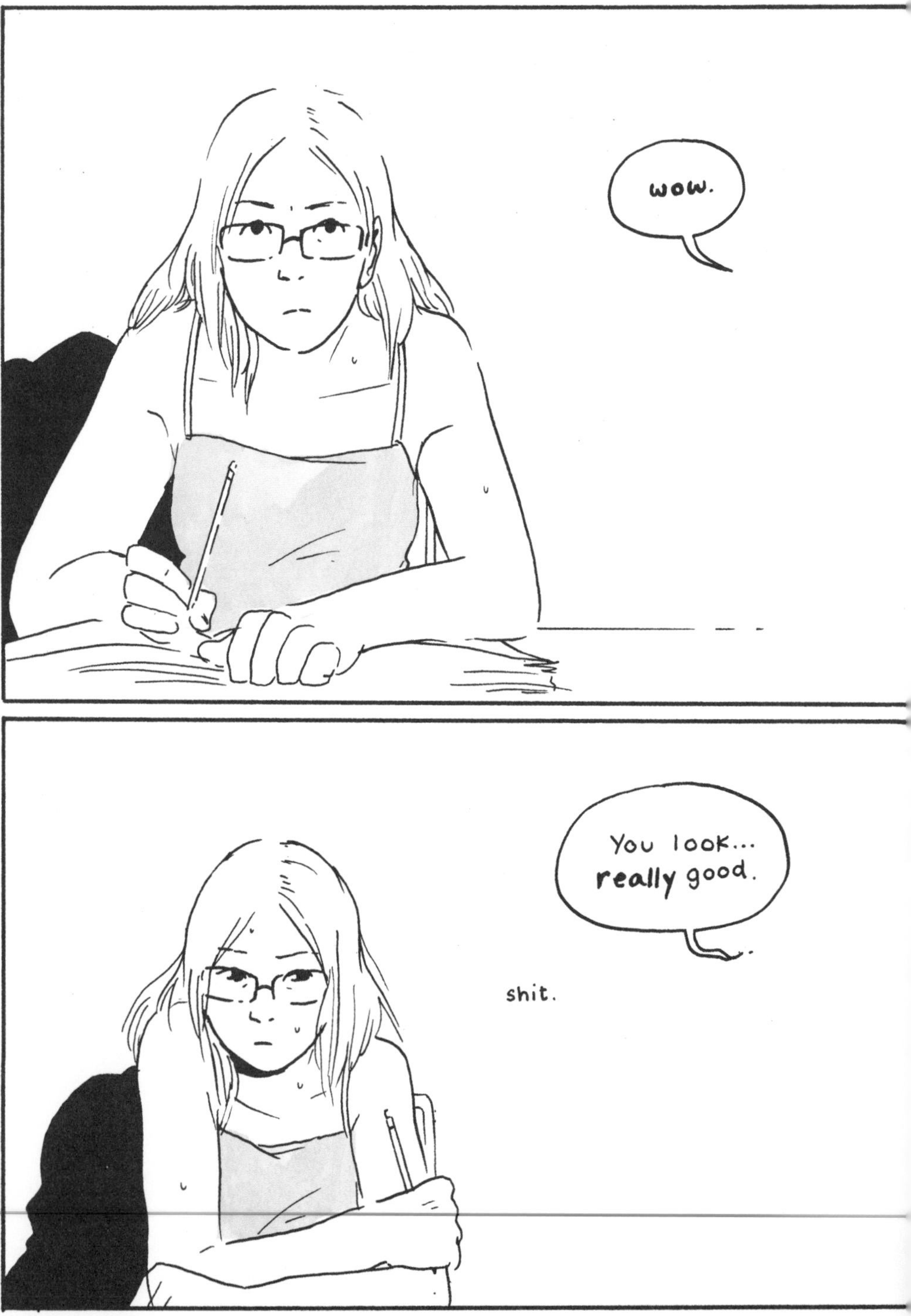
wow.
You look... really good.
shit.

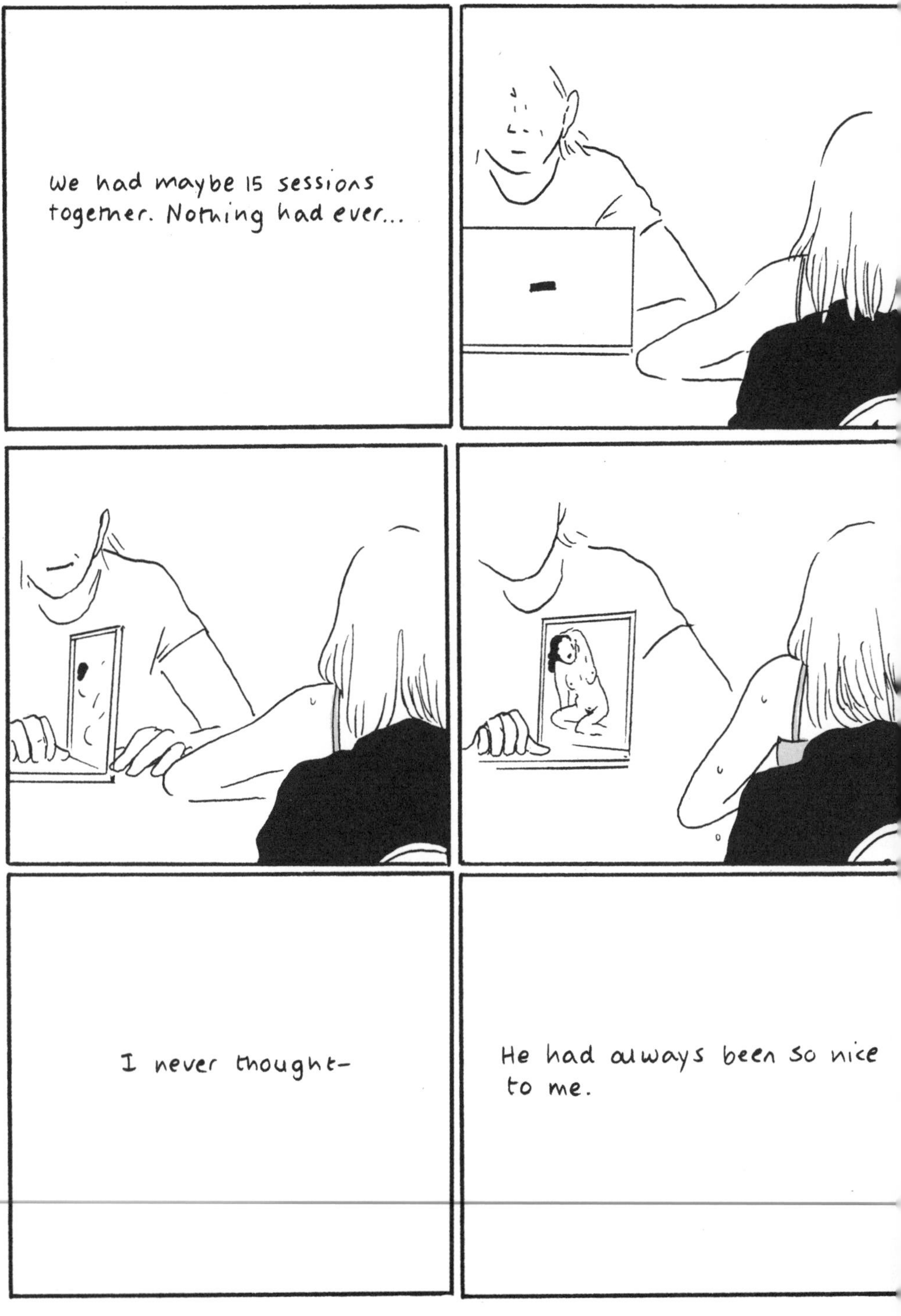
We had maybe 15 sessions togetner. Notning had ever...
I never thought-
He had always been so nice to me.

I felt more than just fear. I felt hurt. I thought we had actually been friends.

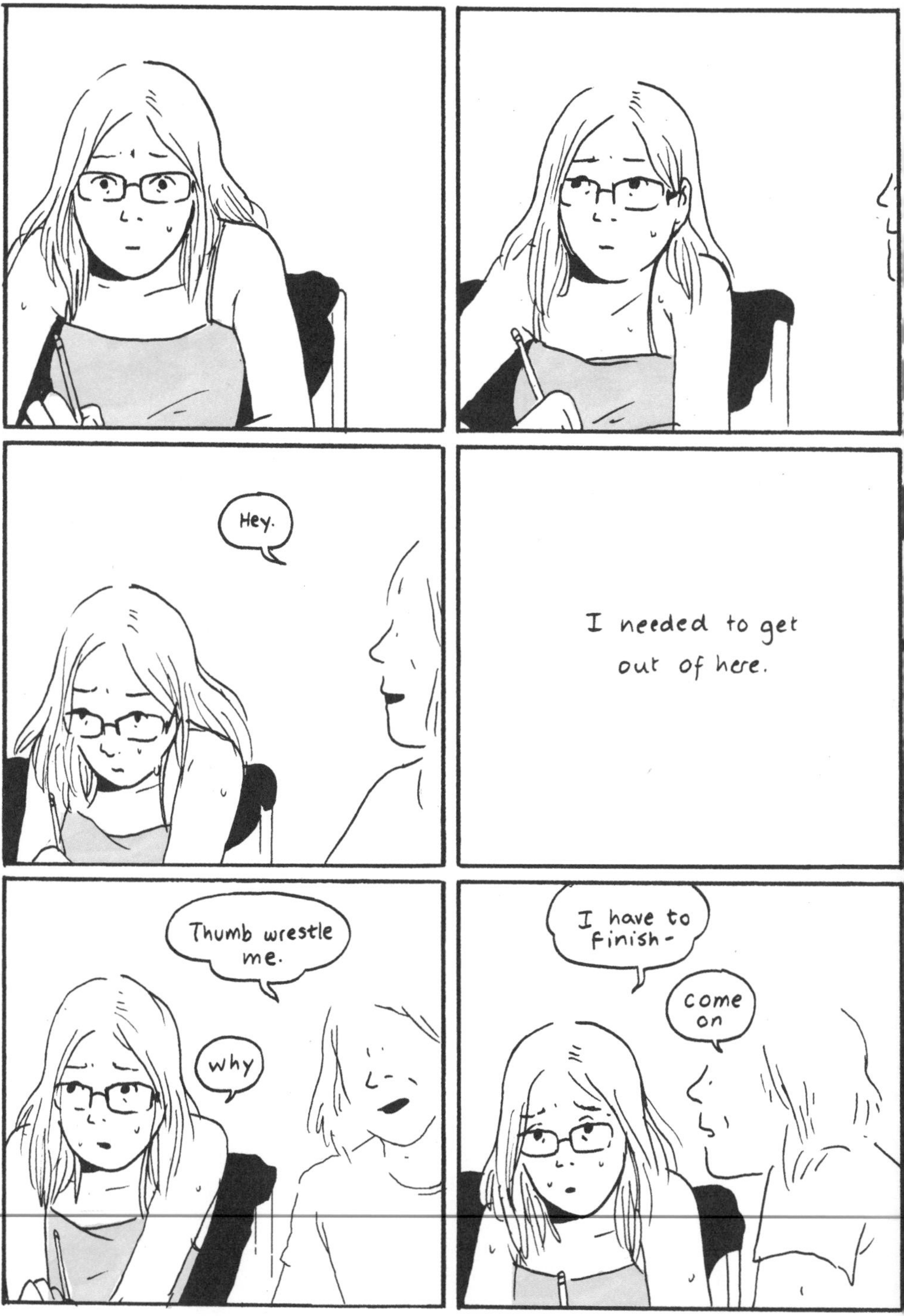
Hey.
I needed to get out of here.
Thumb wrestle me.
why
I have to finish-
come on

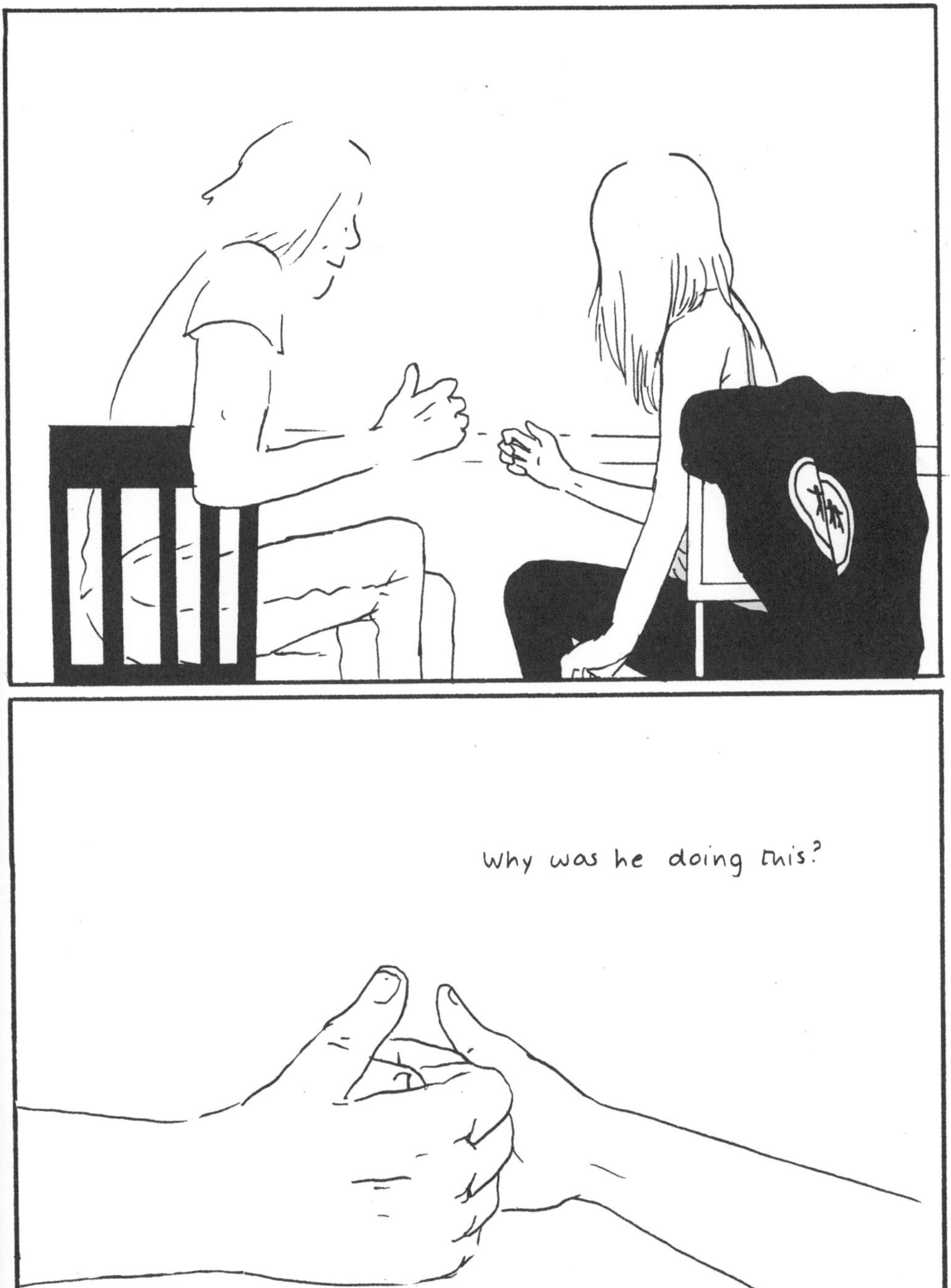
Why was he doing this?

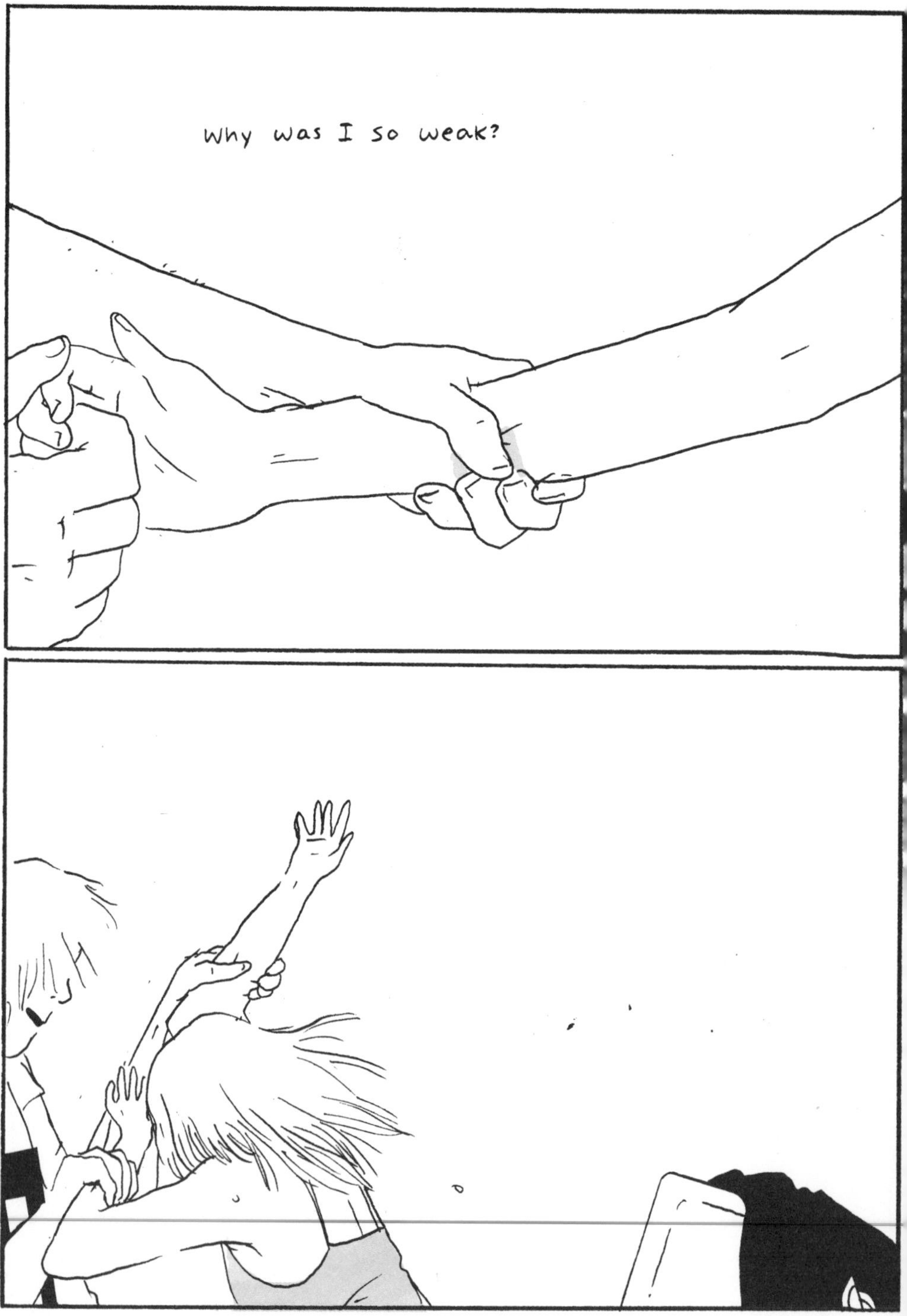
Why was I so weak?

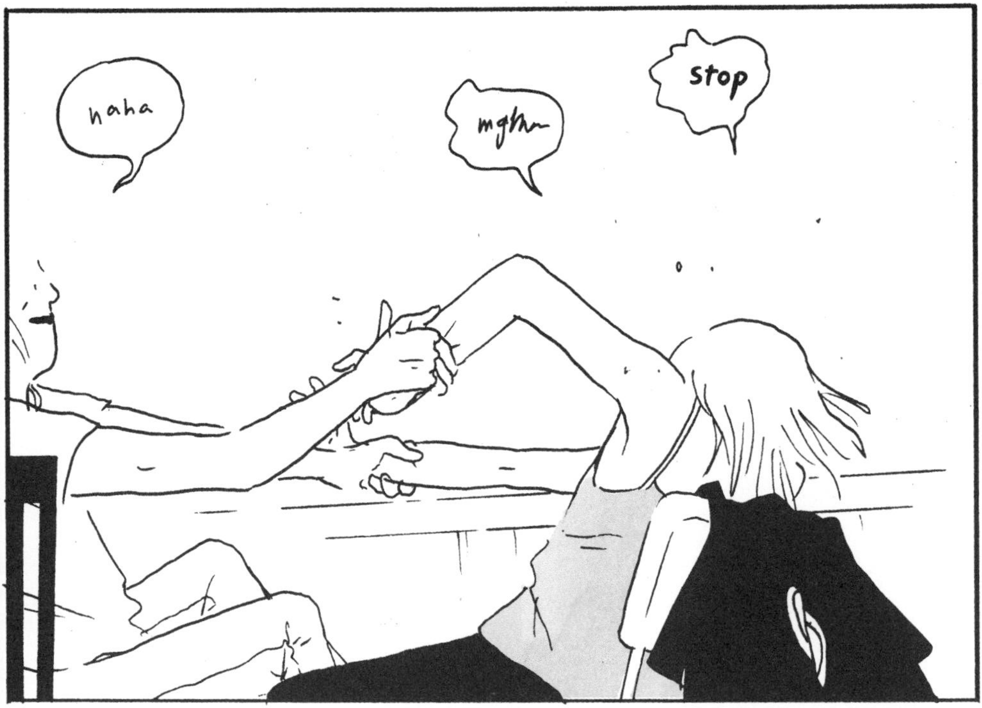
haha
mgthm
stop

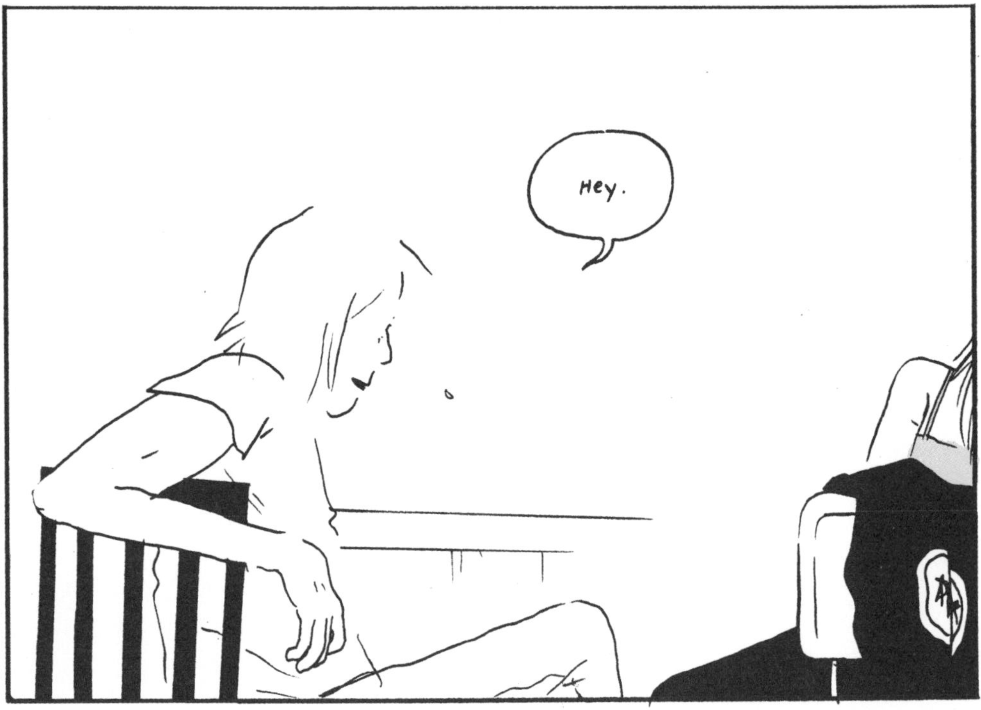
Hey.

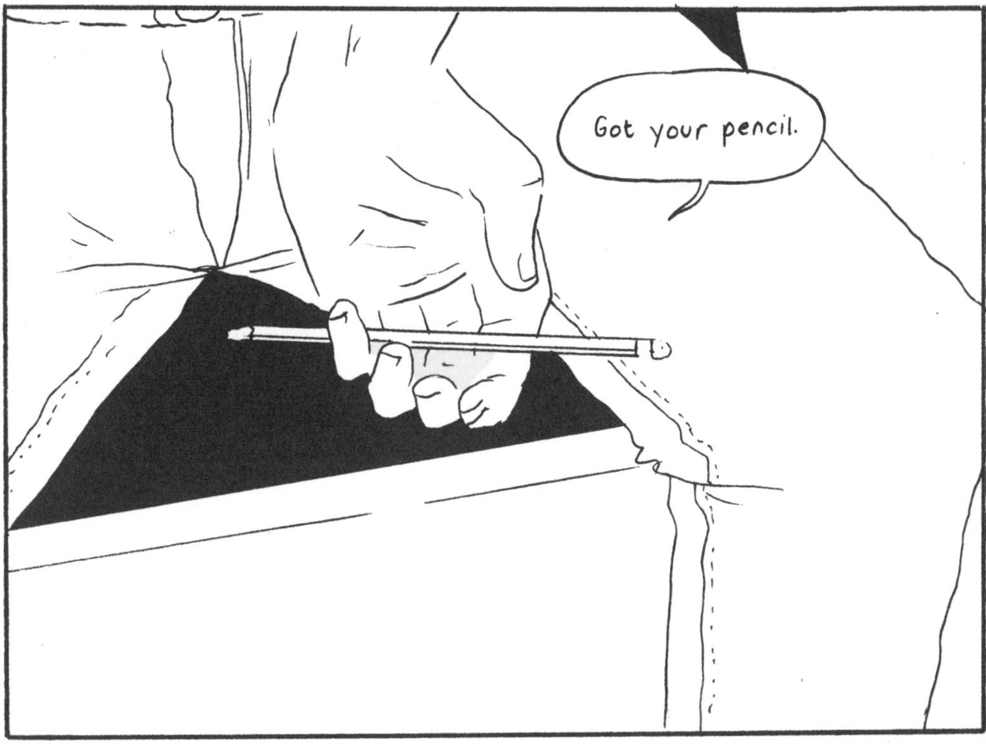
Got your pencil.

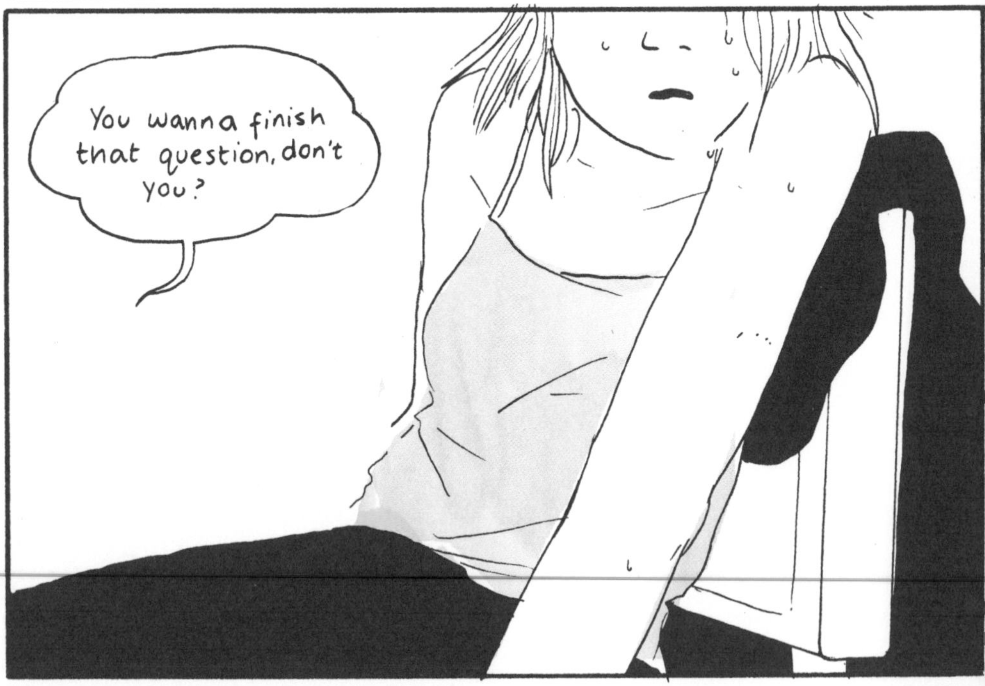
You wanna finish that question, don't you?

why did I take my jacket off
Give it back.
You gotta get it.
why did I take my fucking jacket off fuck

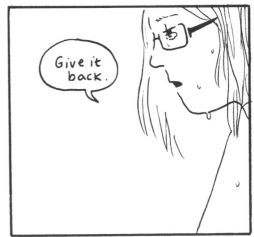

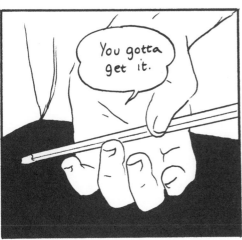

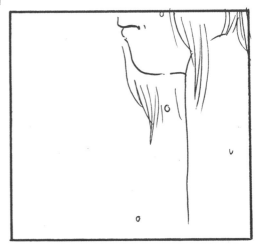

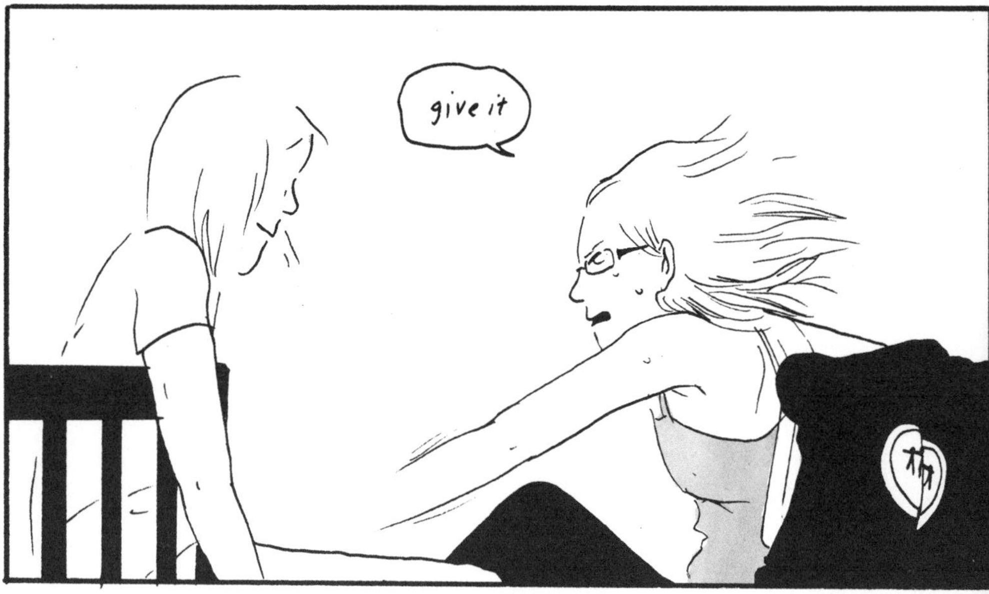
give it

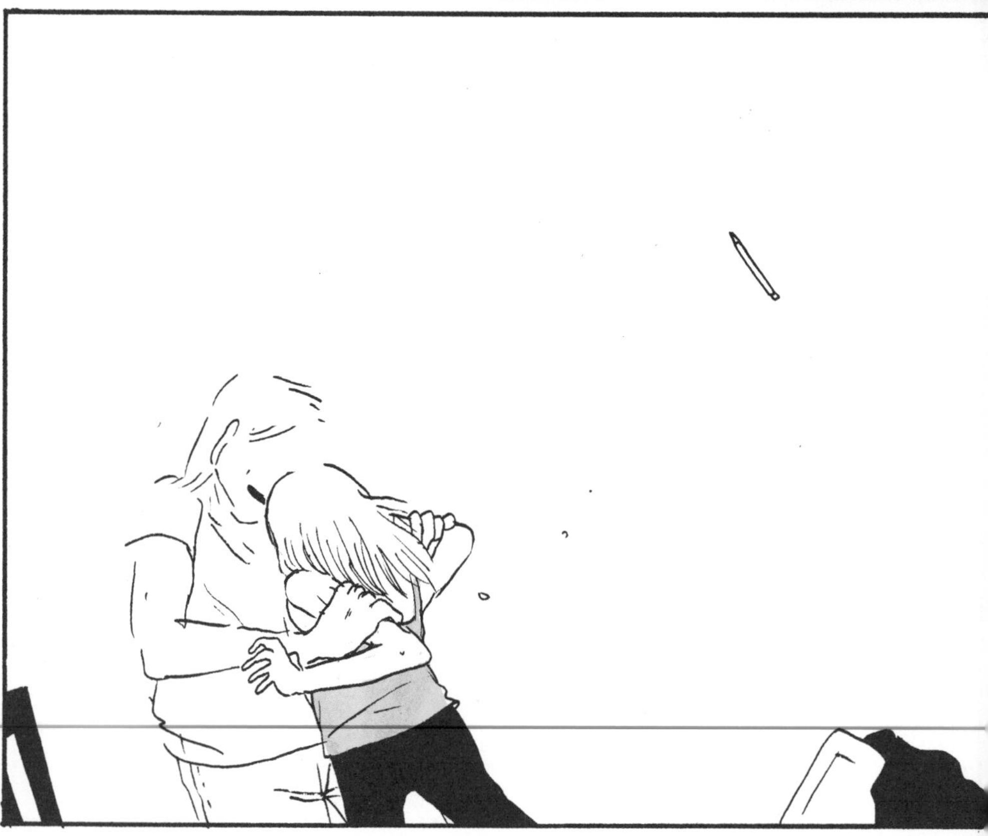

I know now that none of it was my fault. But I told myself for years it had happened because I wore a tank top.

And I did fight back. But I always felt like I didn't do enough.

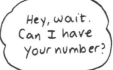
Hey, wait. Can I have your number?

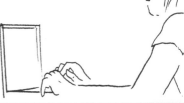

It was nothing. It had to be nothing.

He pushed me around and tried to...

973...
861...

But I was lucky, wasn't I? I fought him until he got tired and quit trying.

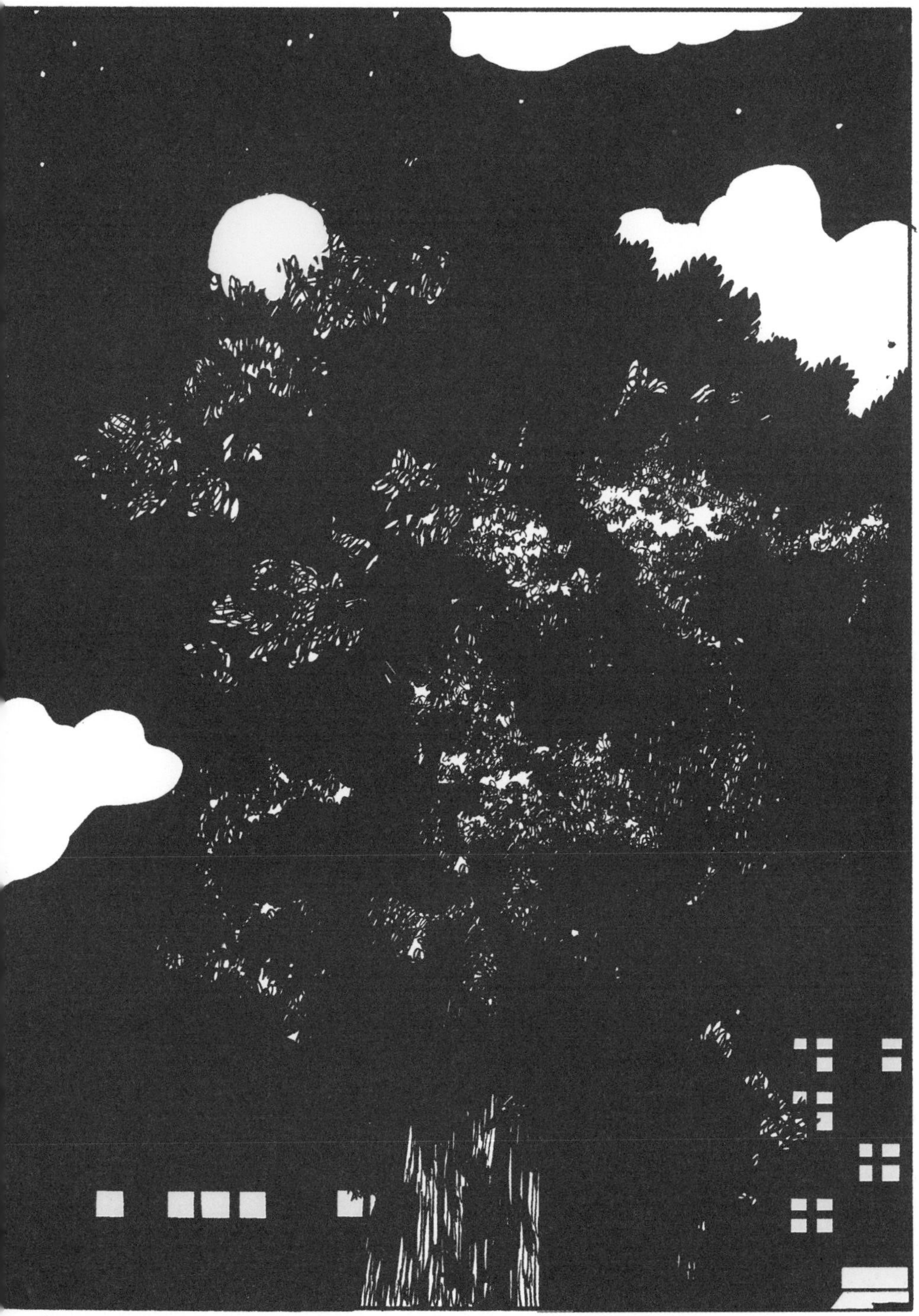

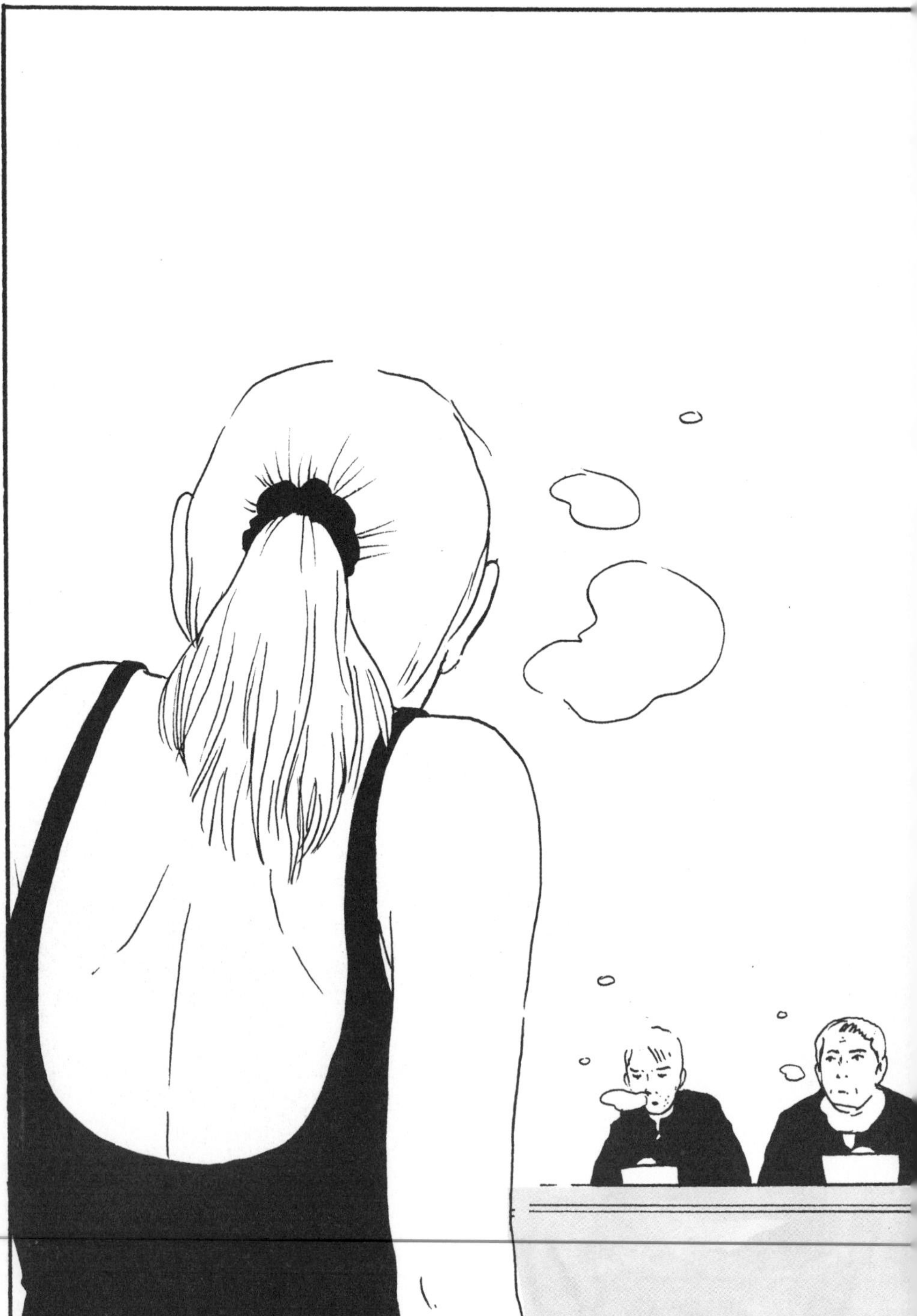

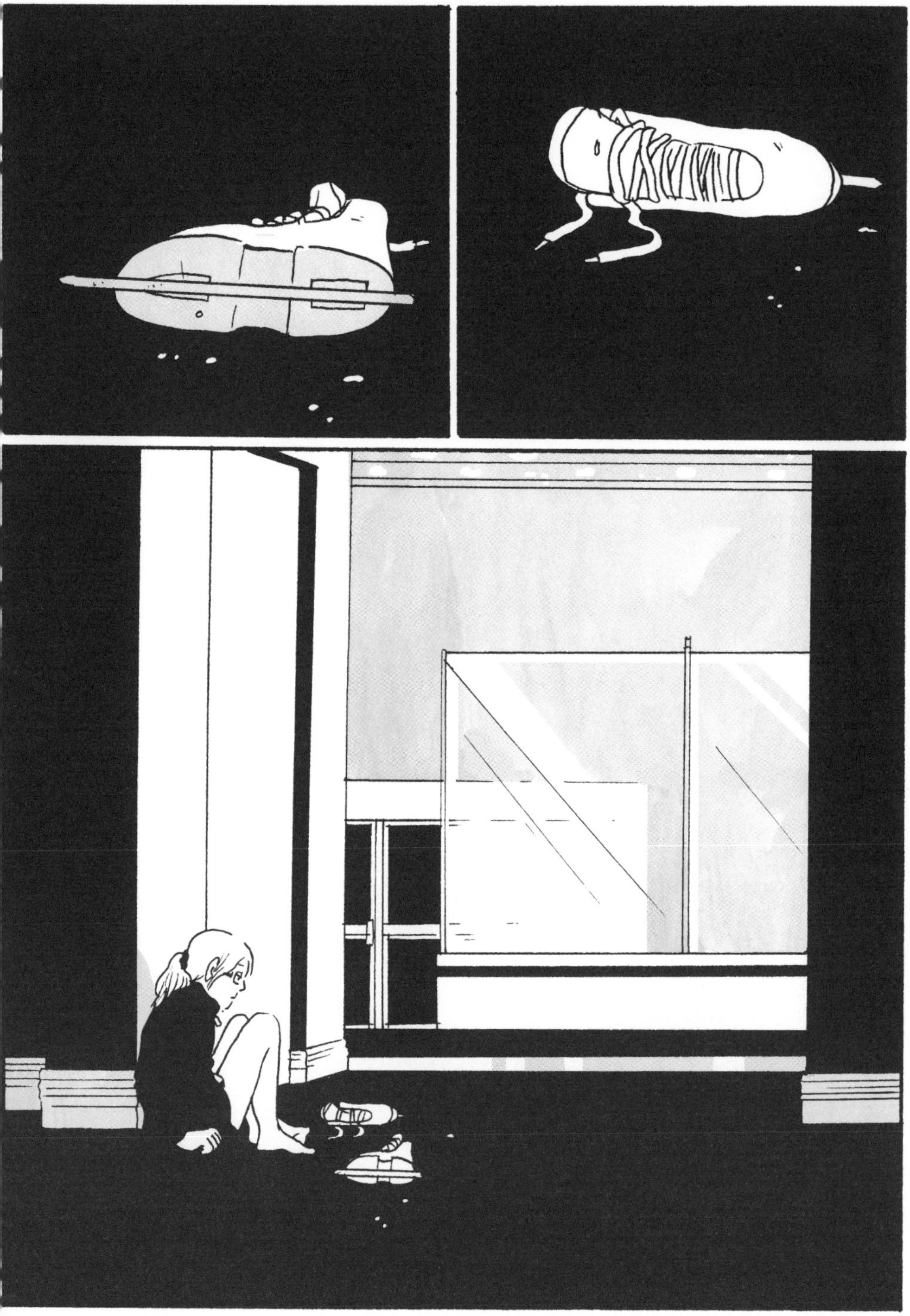

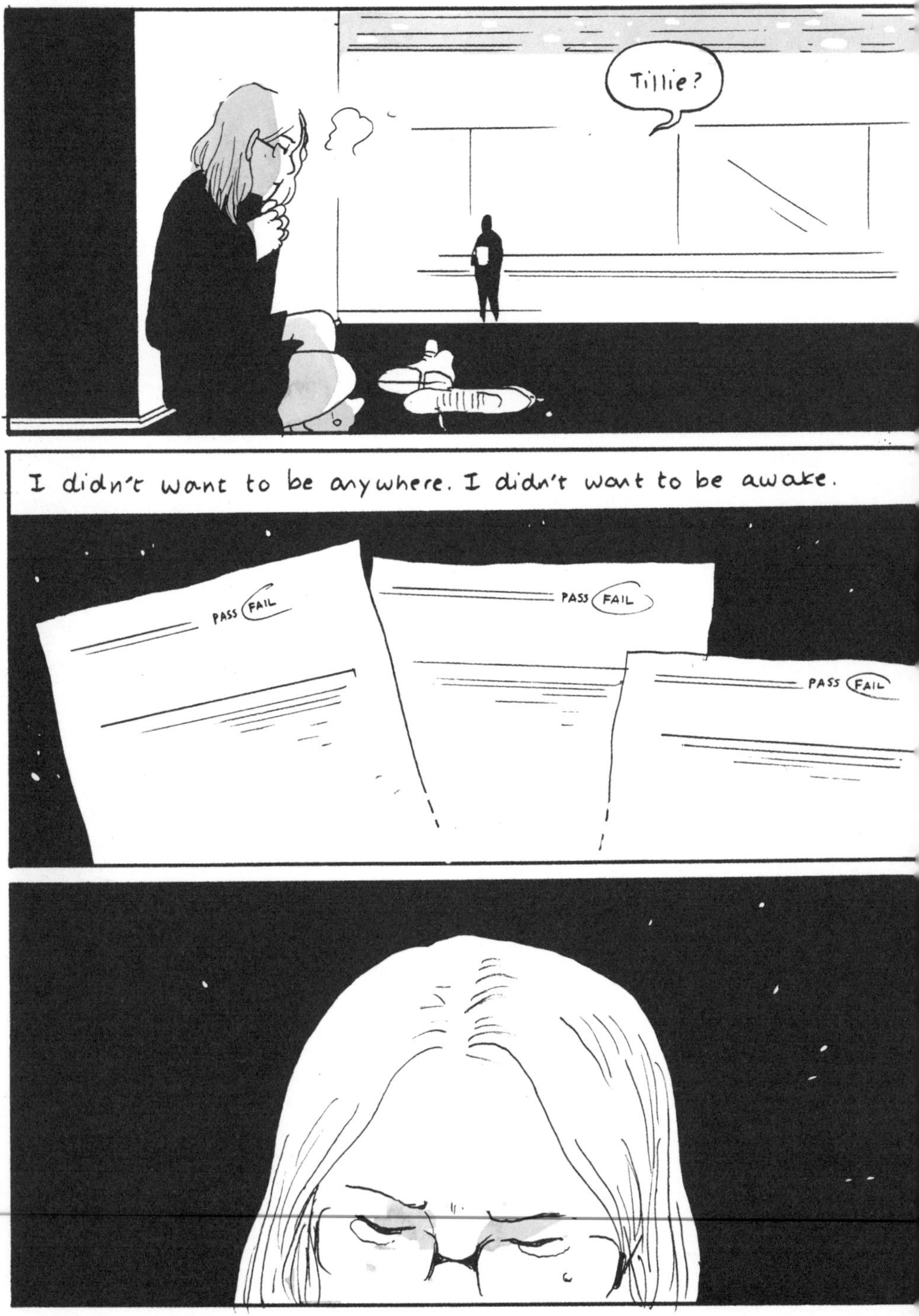
Tillie?
I didn't want to be anywhere. I didn't want to be awake.
PASS FAIL
PASS FAIL
PASS FAIL

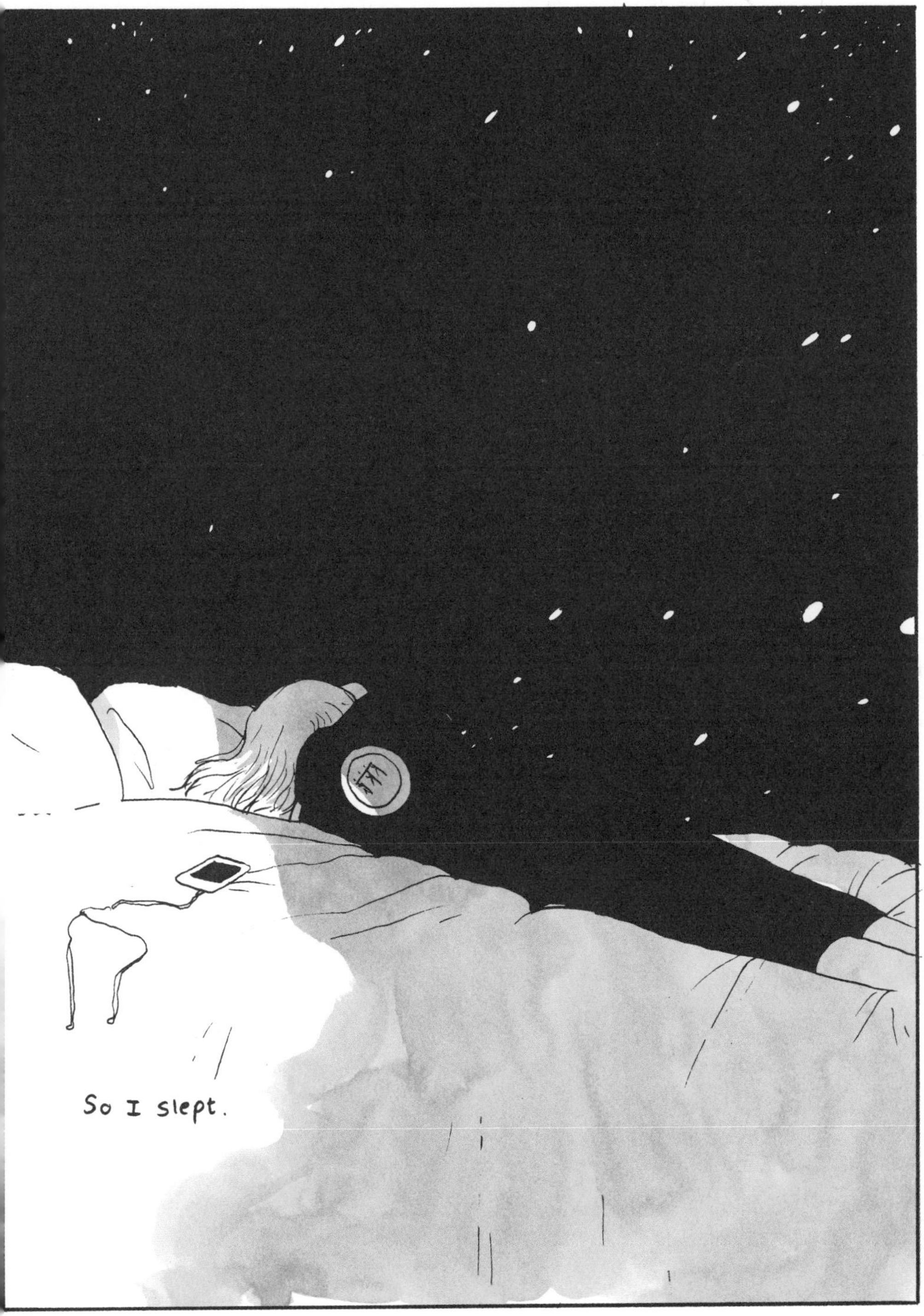
So I slept.

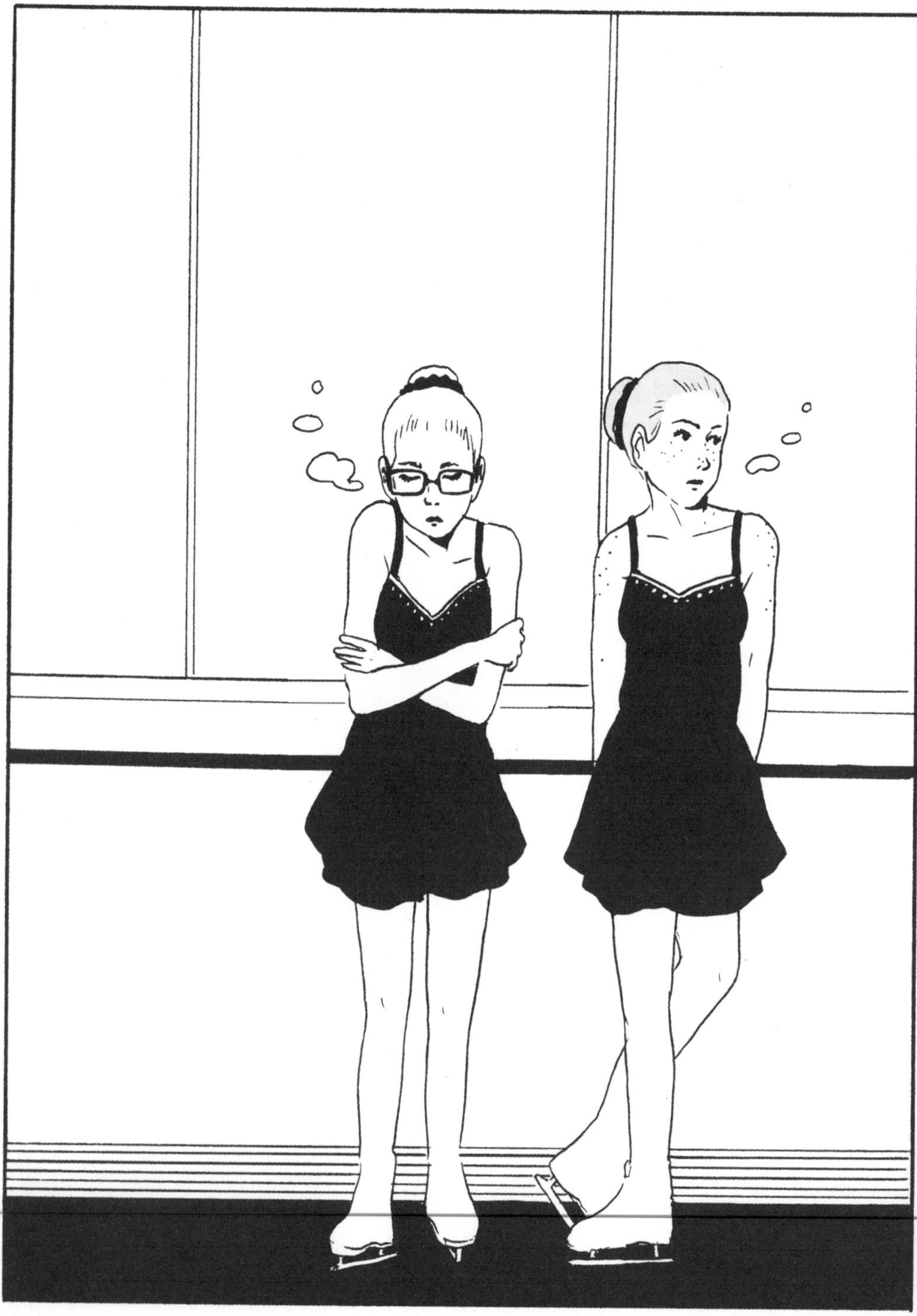

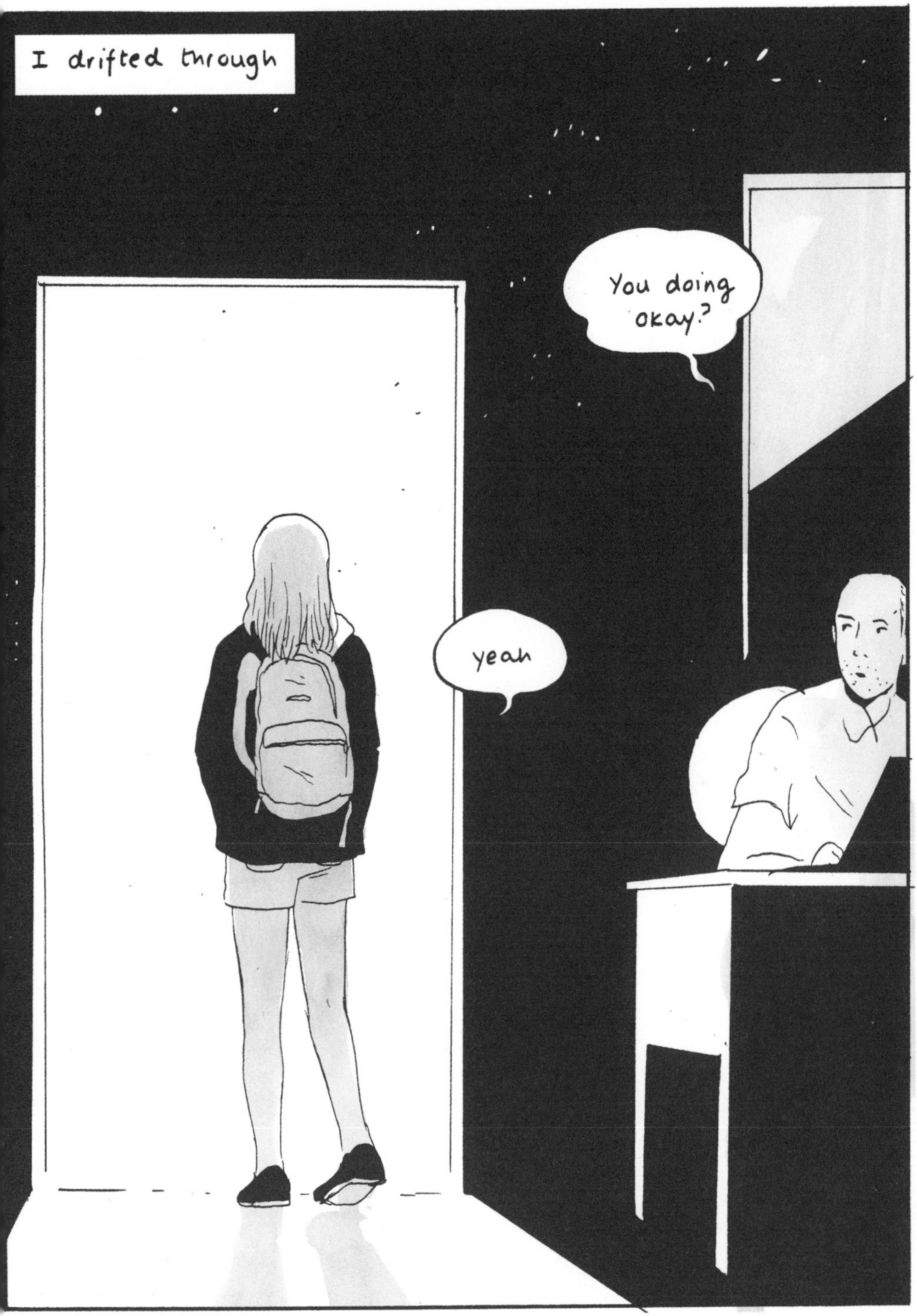
I drifted through
You doing okay?
yeah

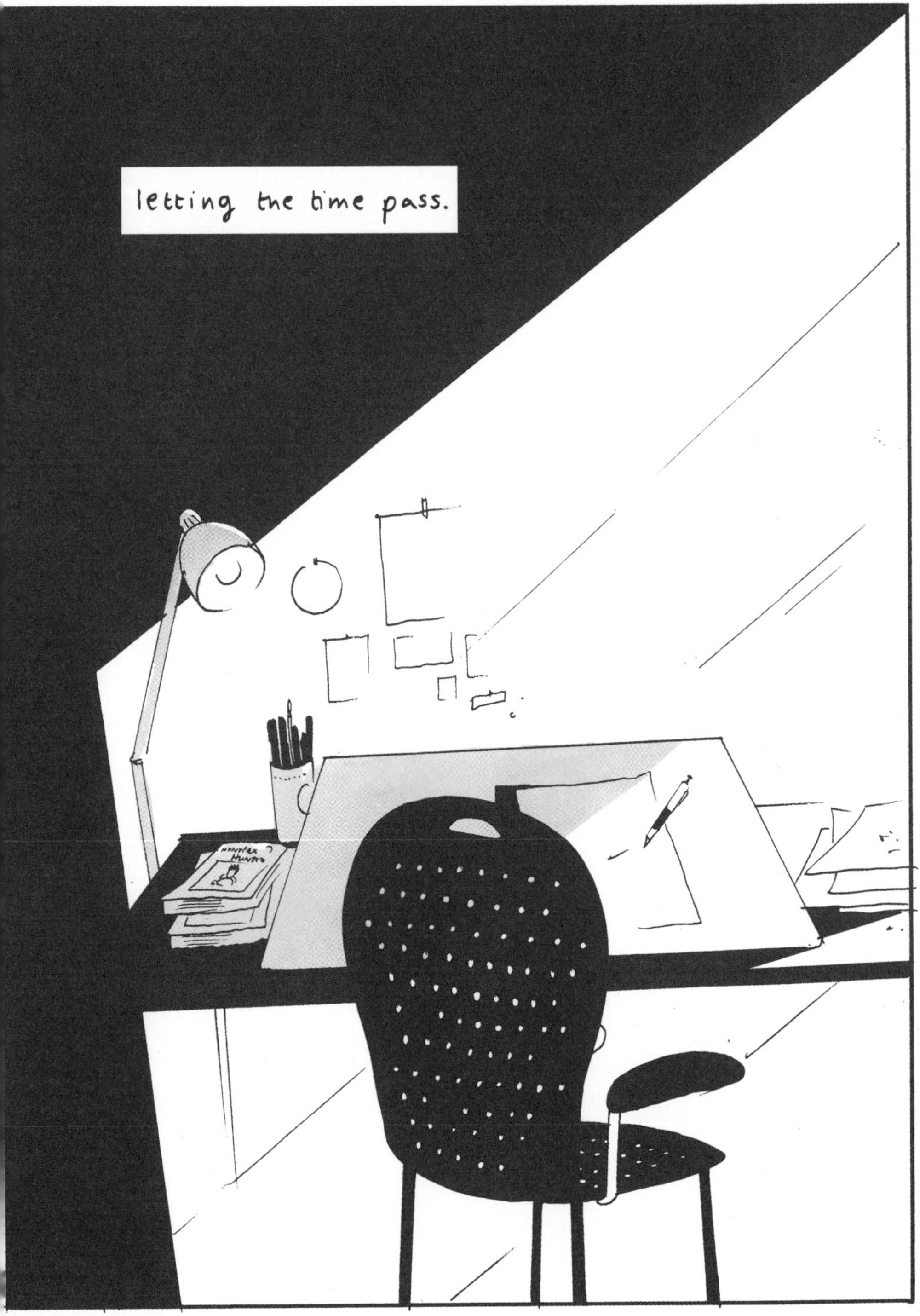
letting the time pass.

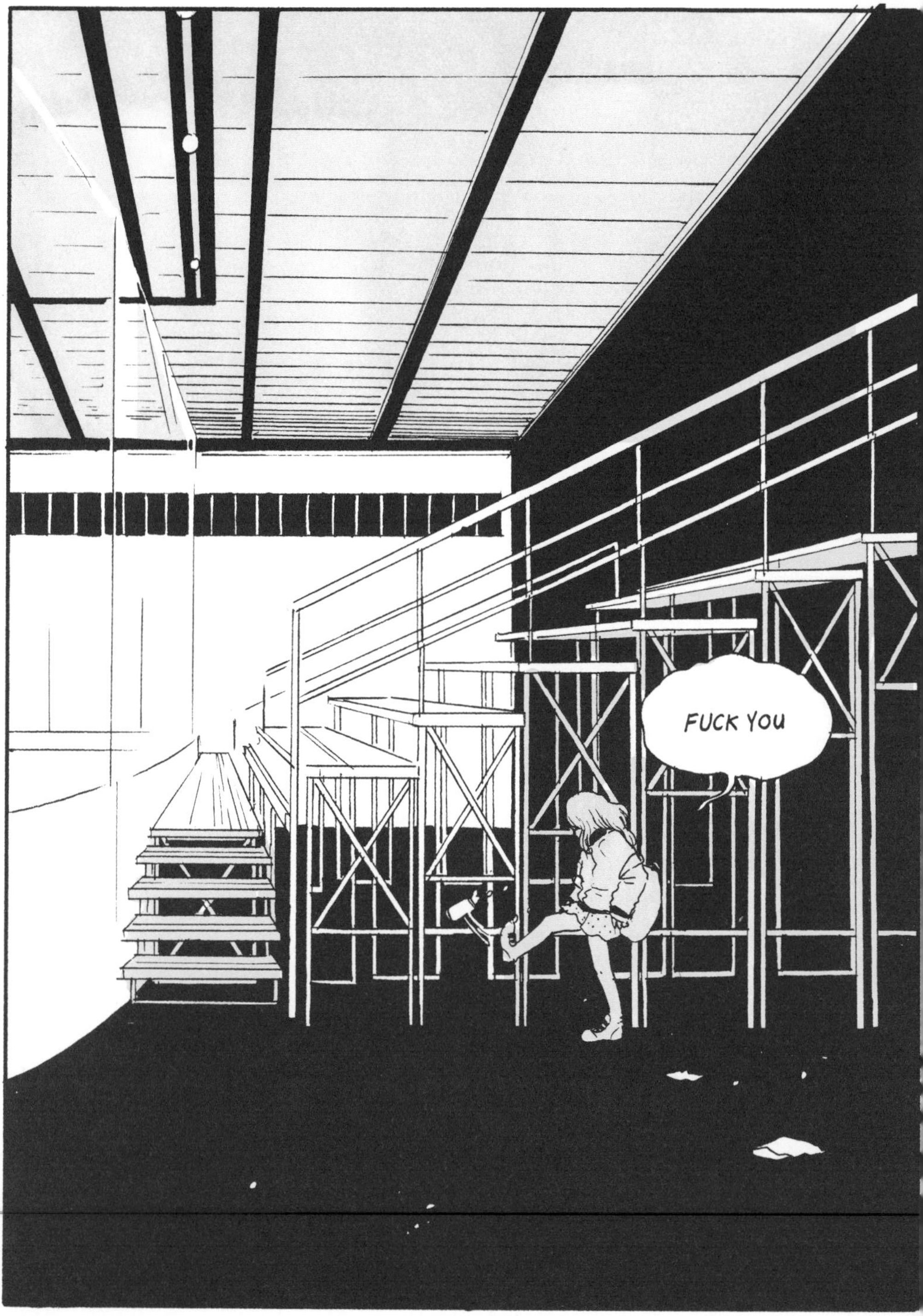
FUCK YOU

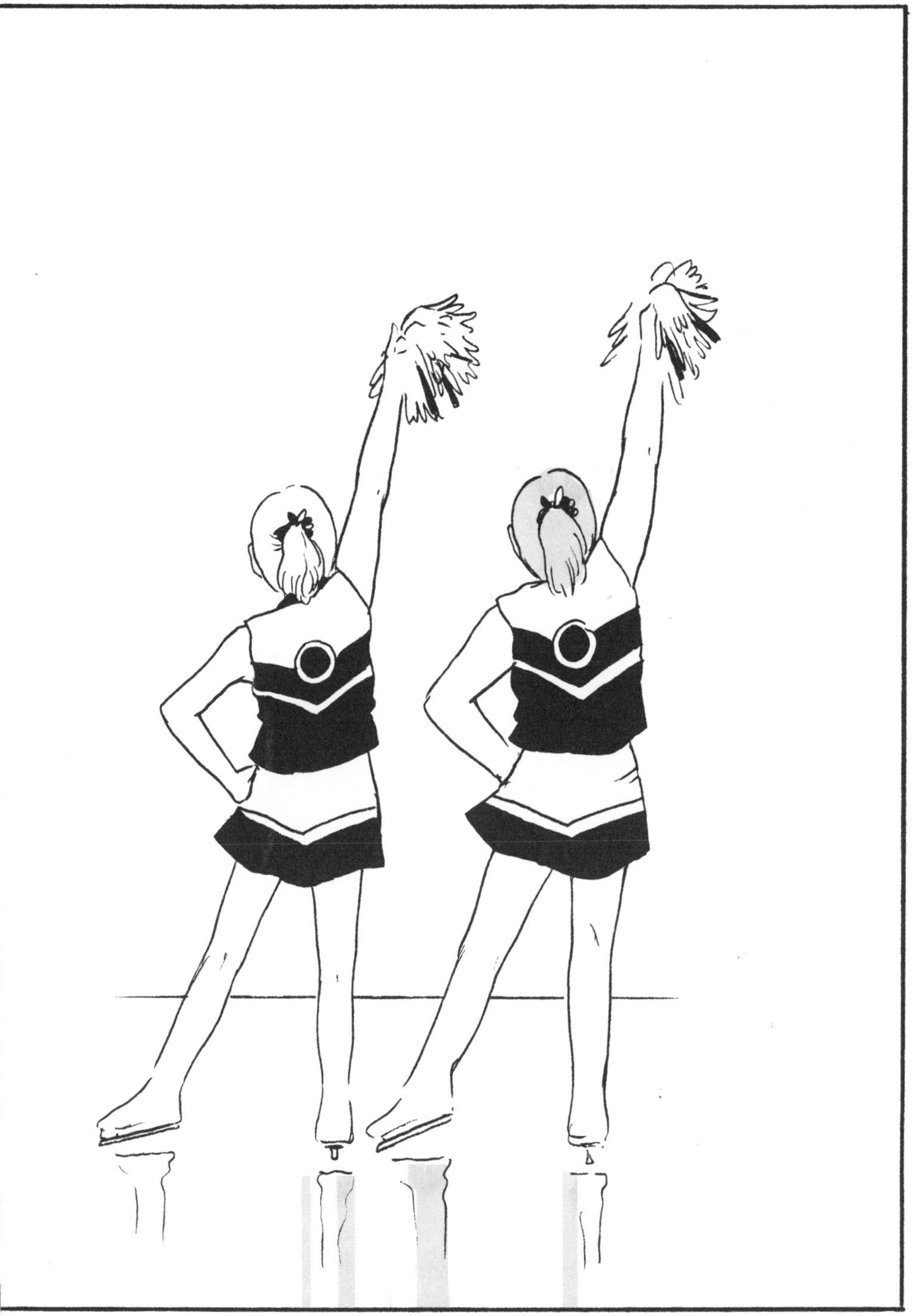

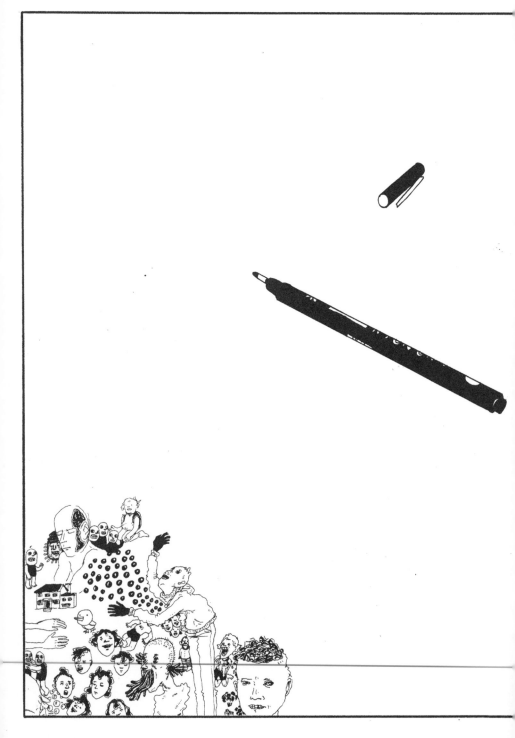

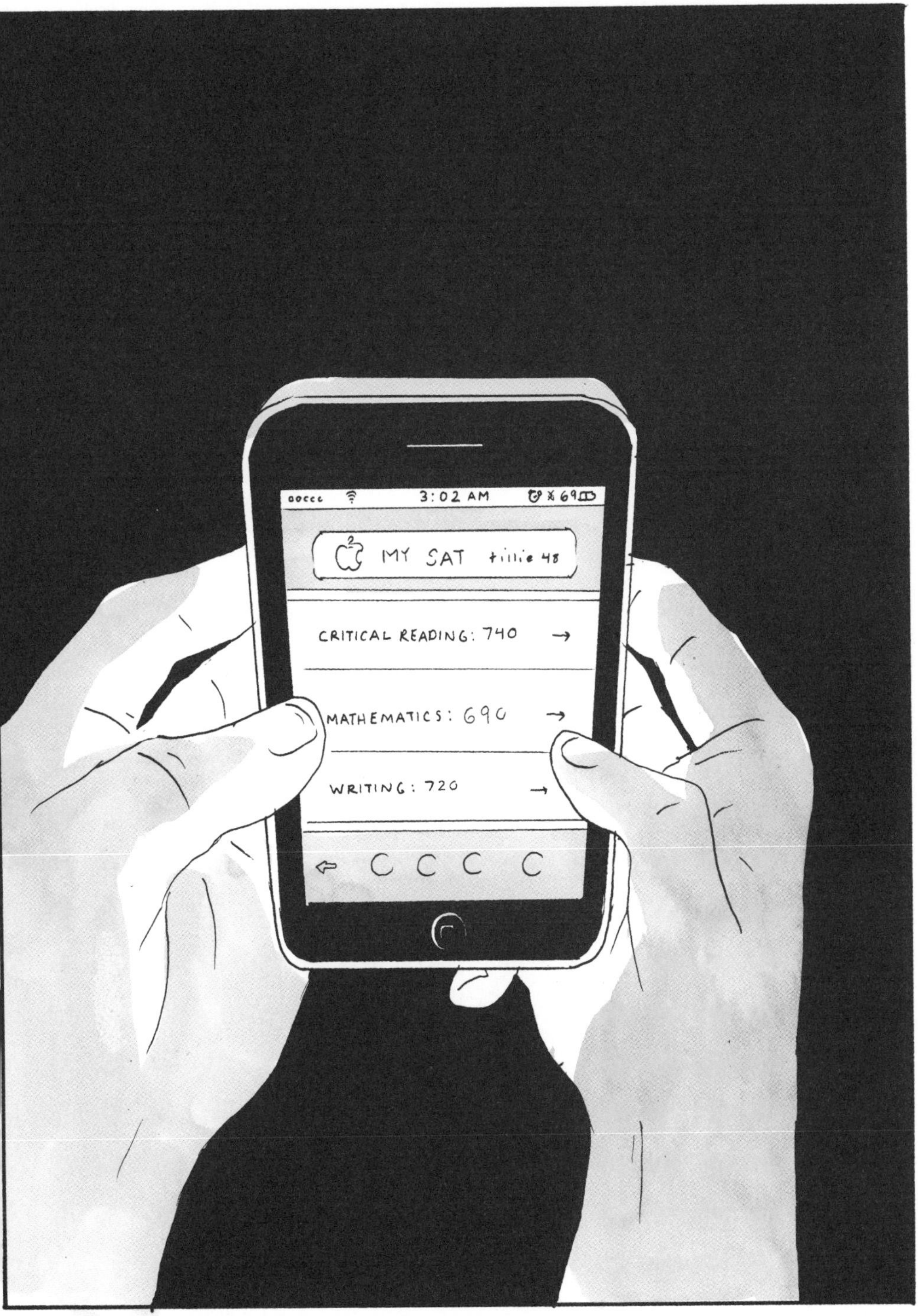
3:02 AM
69
MY SAT
tillie 48
CRITICAL READING: 740
MATHEMATICS: 690
WRITING: 720

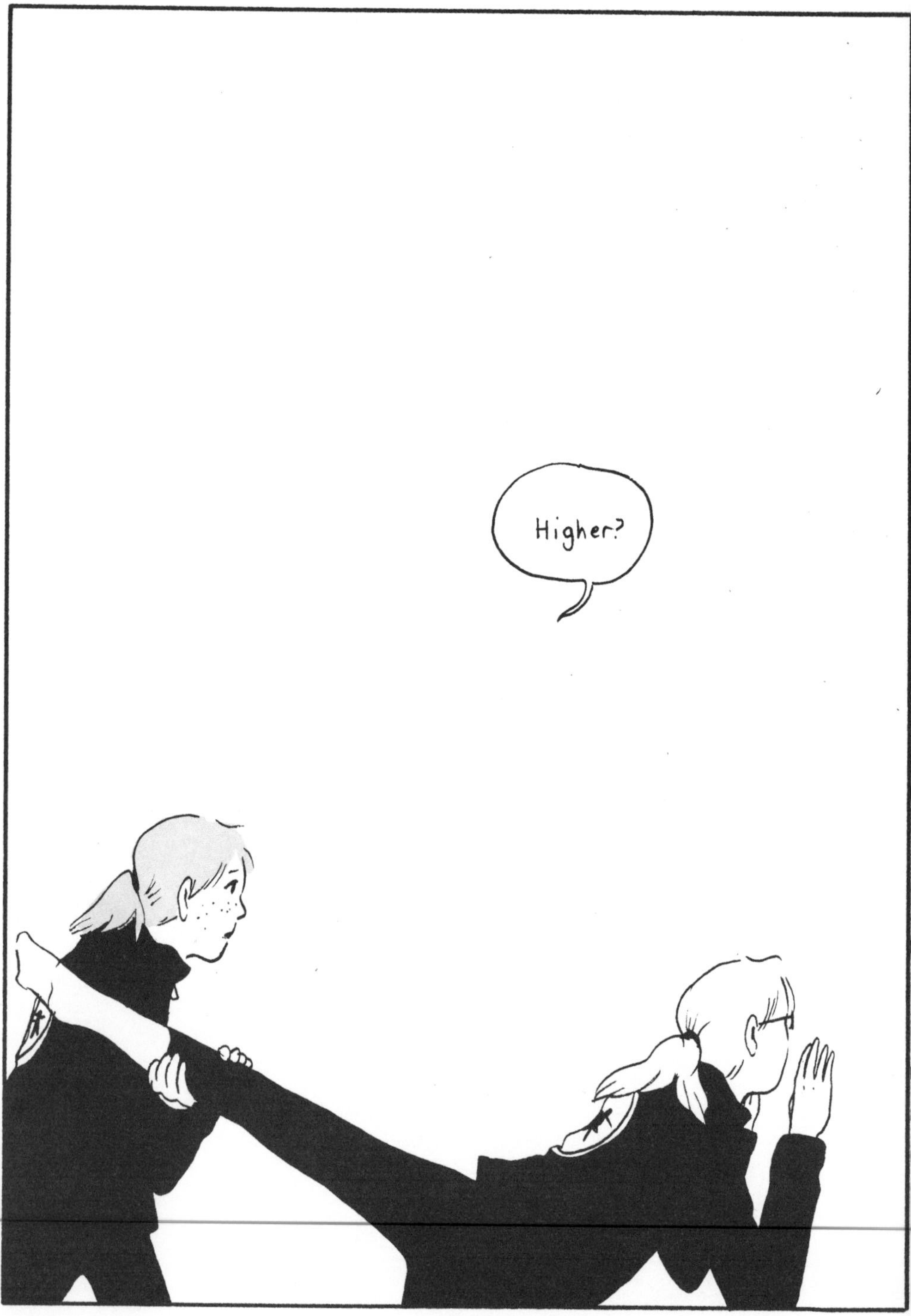
Higher?

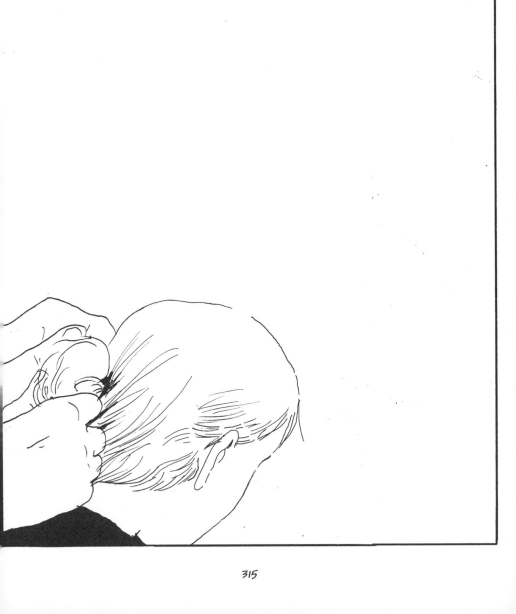

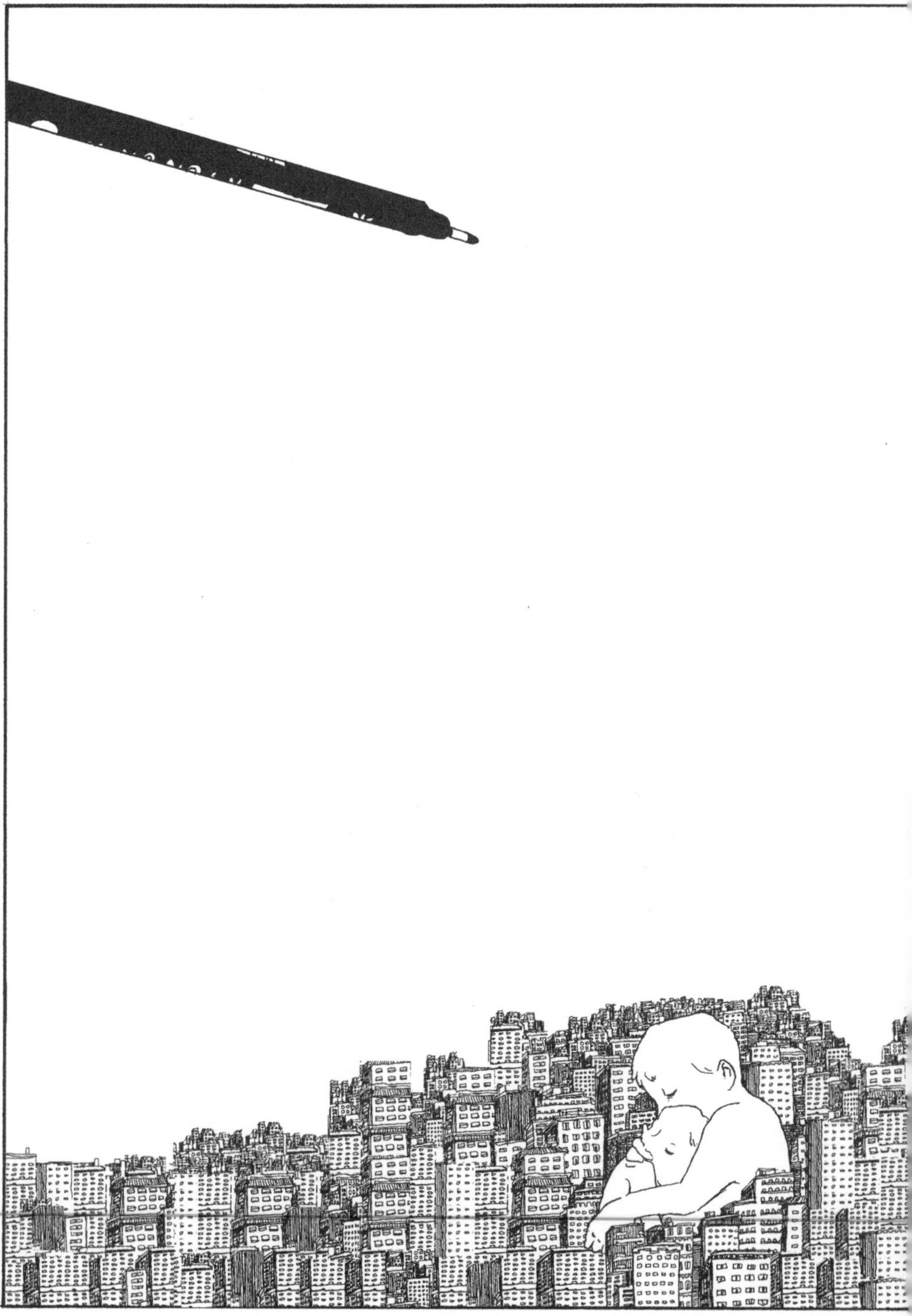

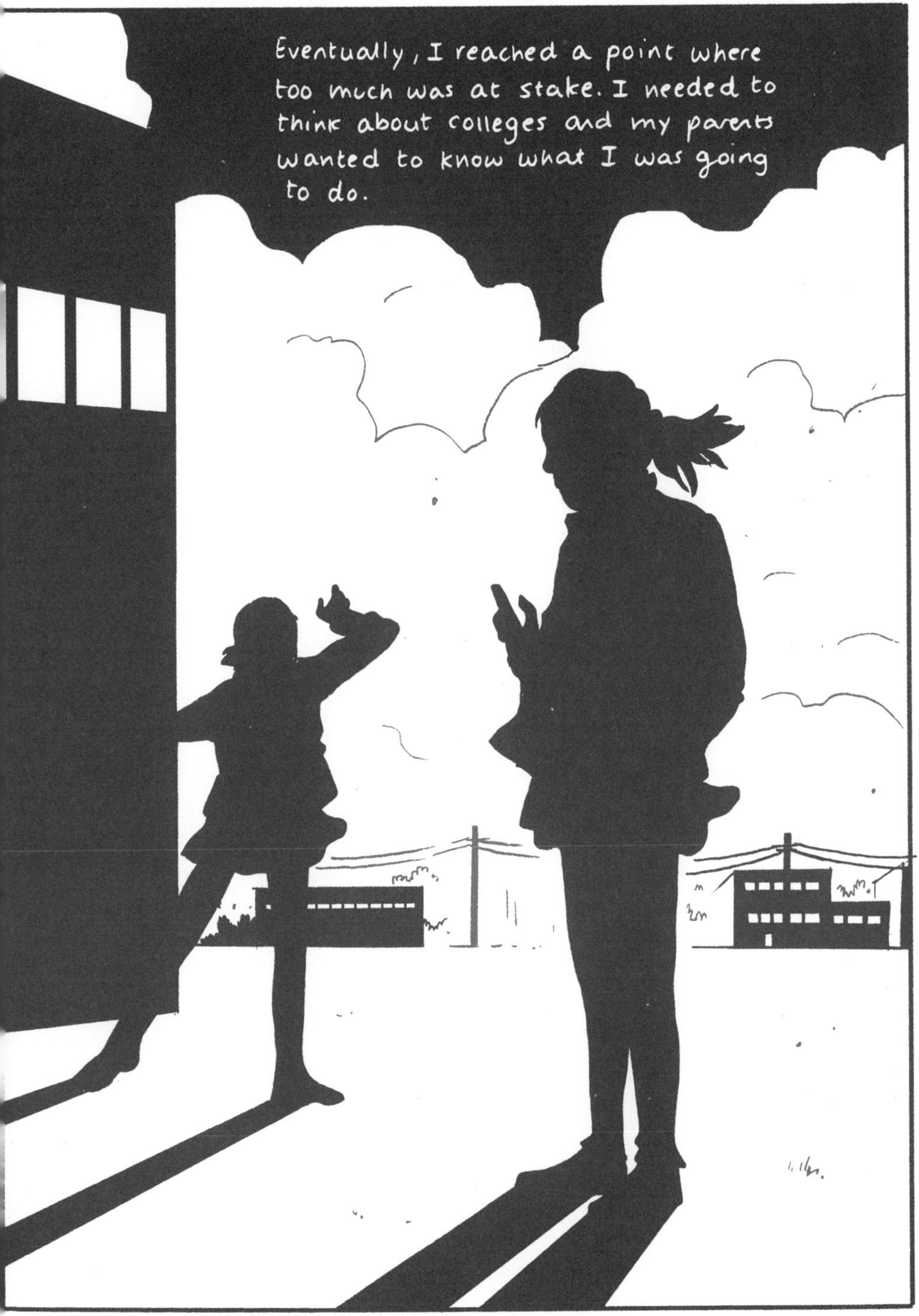
Eventually, I reached a point where too much was at stake. I needed to think about colleges and my parents wanted to know what I was going to do.

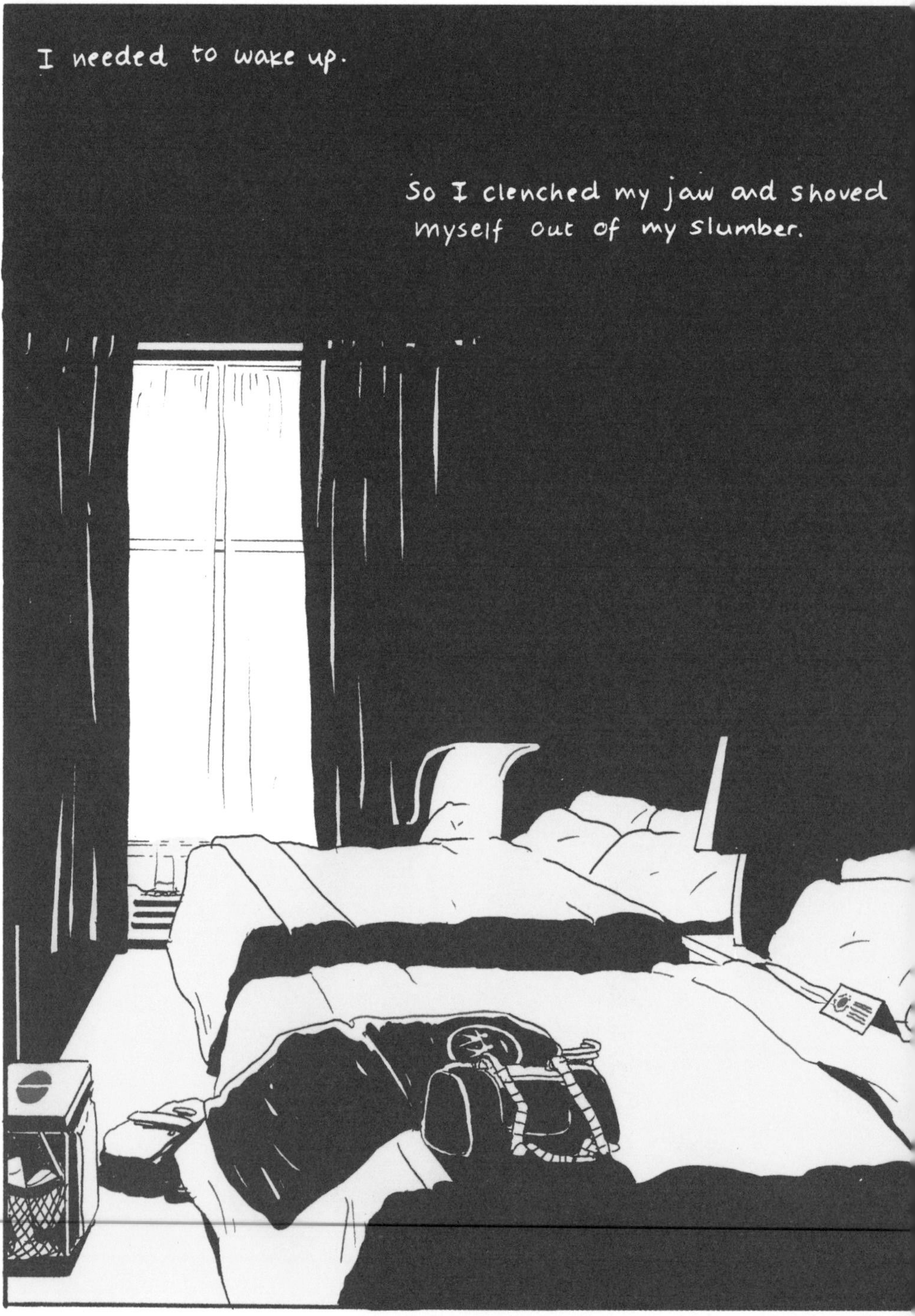
I needed to wake up.
So I clenched my jaw and shoved myself out of my slumber.

9

LUTZ

A Lutz was an awkward jump.
You went into it with your body
angled one direction, but to get
into the air you had to shove
yourself the other way.

Lutzes always made me tense.

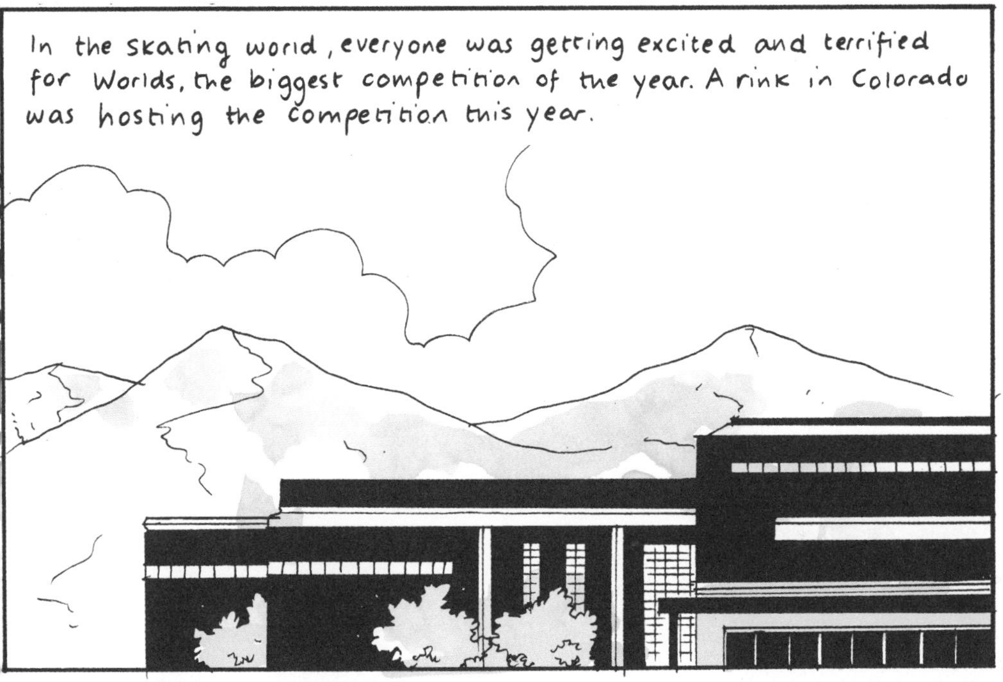
In the skating world, everyone was getting excited and terrified for Worlds, the biggest competition of the year. A rink in Colorado was hosting the competition this year.

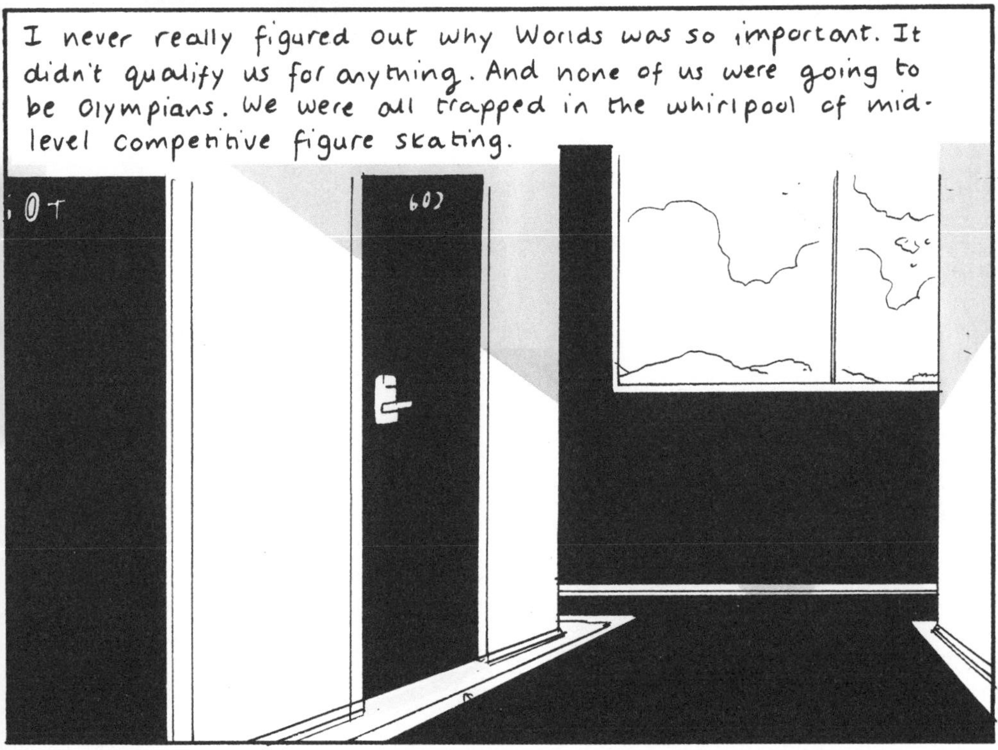
I never really figured out why Worlds was so important. It didn't qualify us for anything. And none of us were going to be Olympians. We were all trapped in the whirlpool of mid-level competitive figure skating.

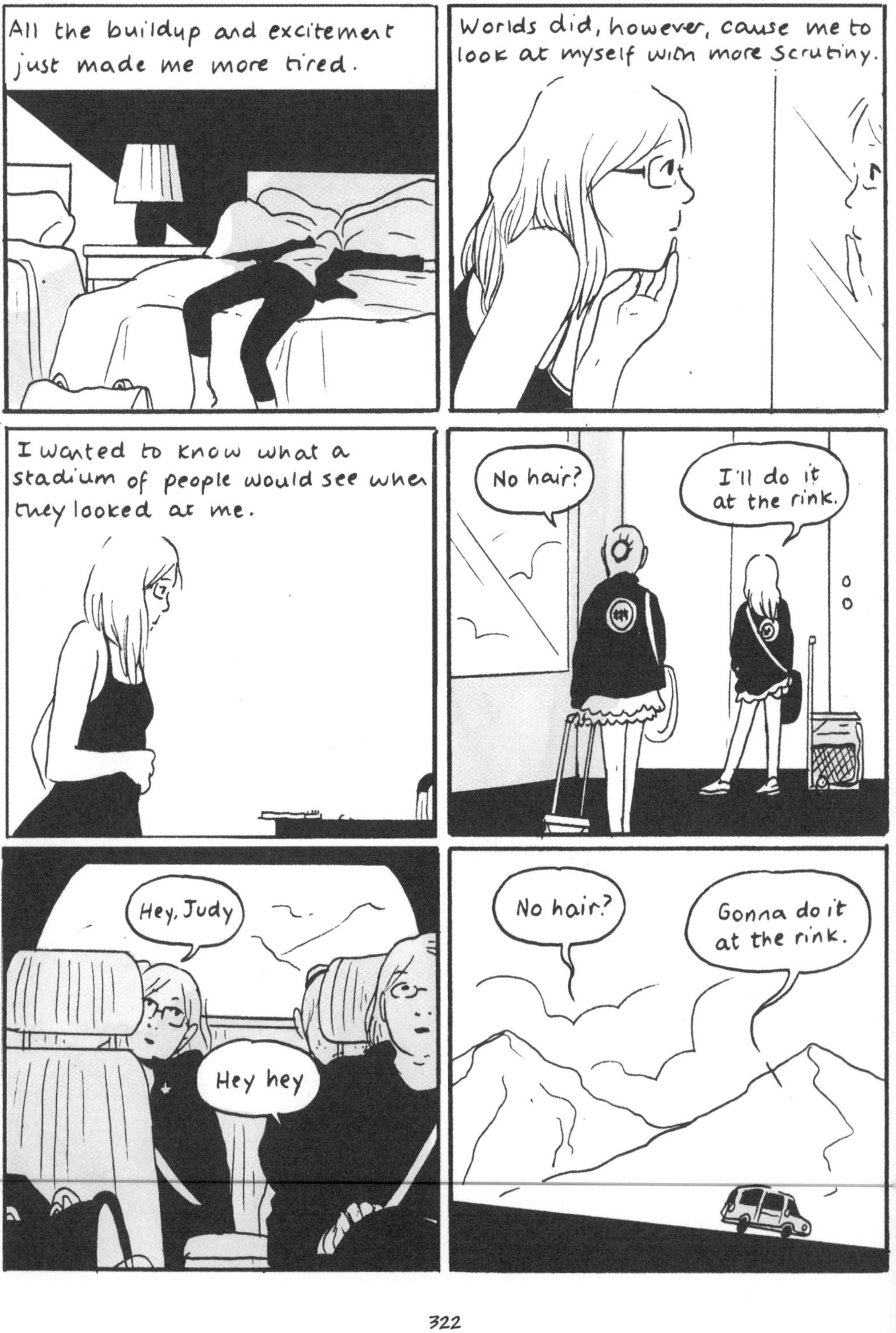
All the buildup and excitement just made me more tired.
Worlds did, however, cause me to look at myself with more scrutiny.
I wanted to know what a stadium of people would see when they looked at me.
No hair?
I'll do it at the rink.
Hey, Judy
Hey hey
No hair?
Gonna do it at the rink.

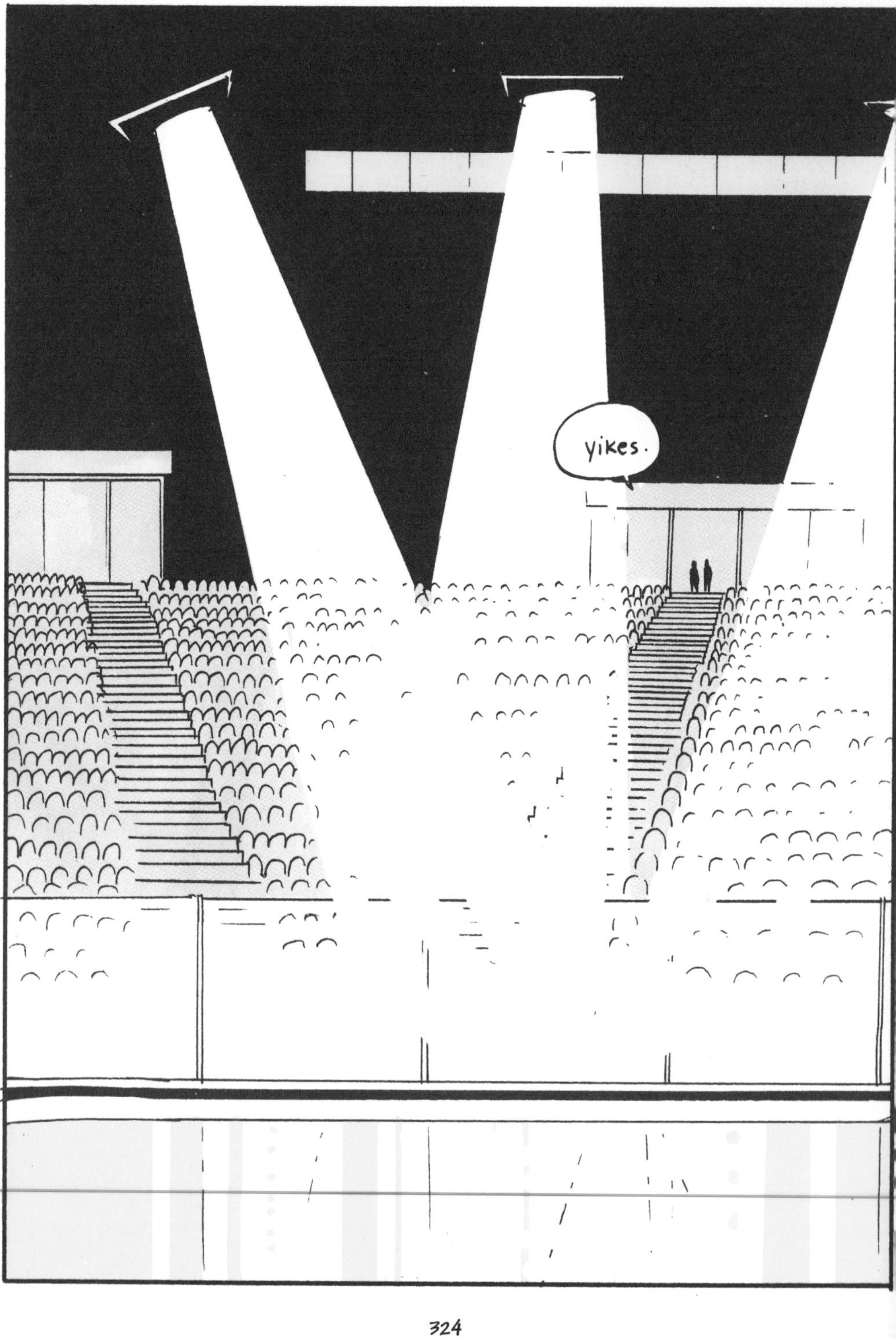
yikes.

326

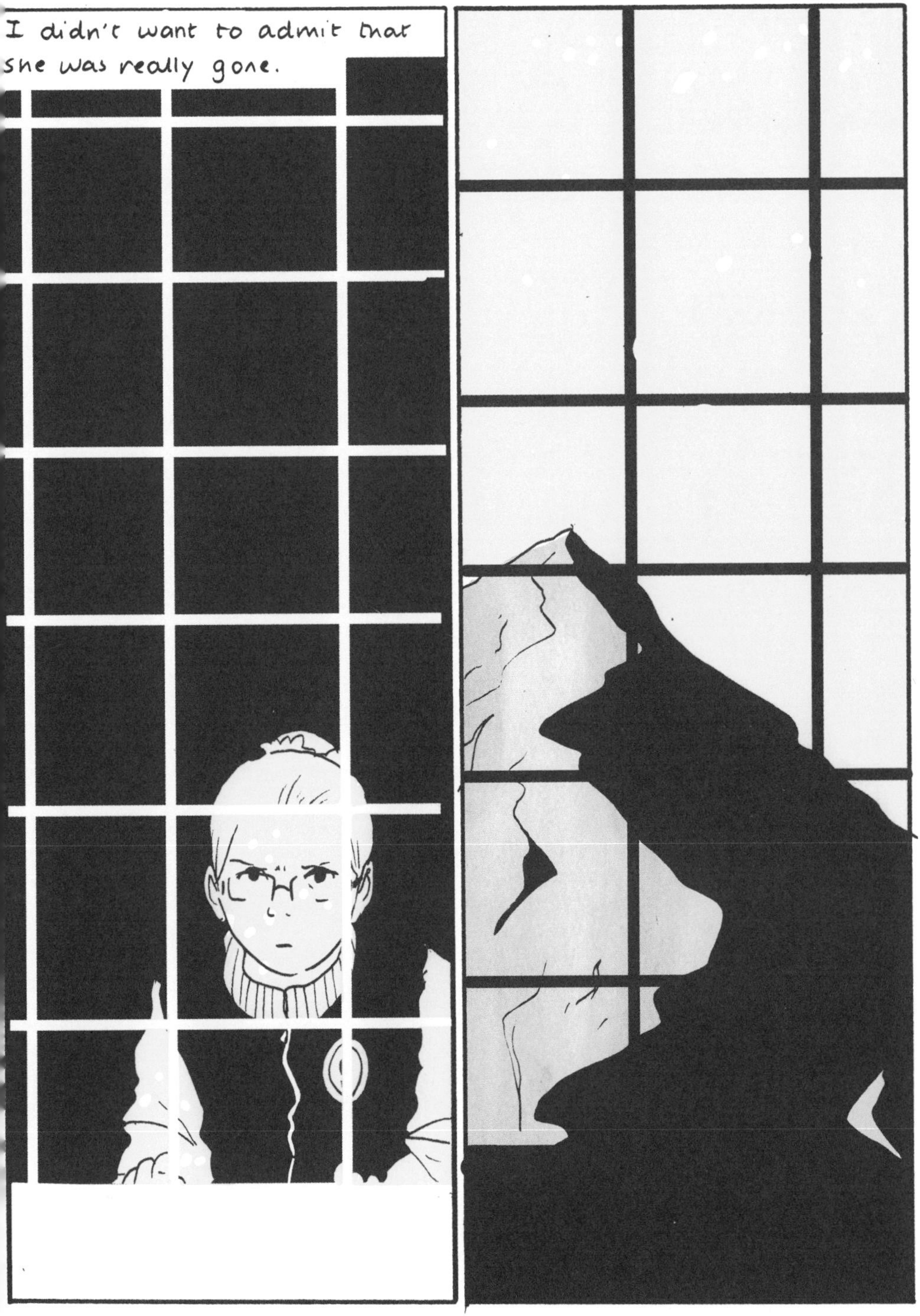
I didn't want to admit that she was really gone.

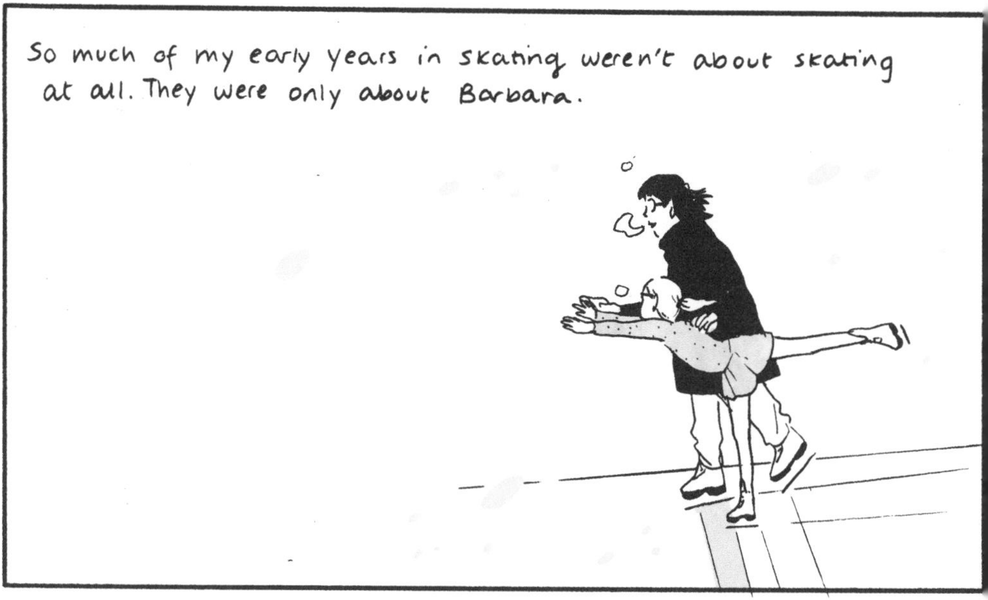
So much of my early years in skating weren't about skating at all. They were only about Barbara.

Sometimes I even think that I kept skating for so many years because I was searching for her replacement, thinking that the rink was where I would find someone to care about me.

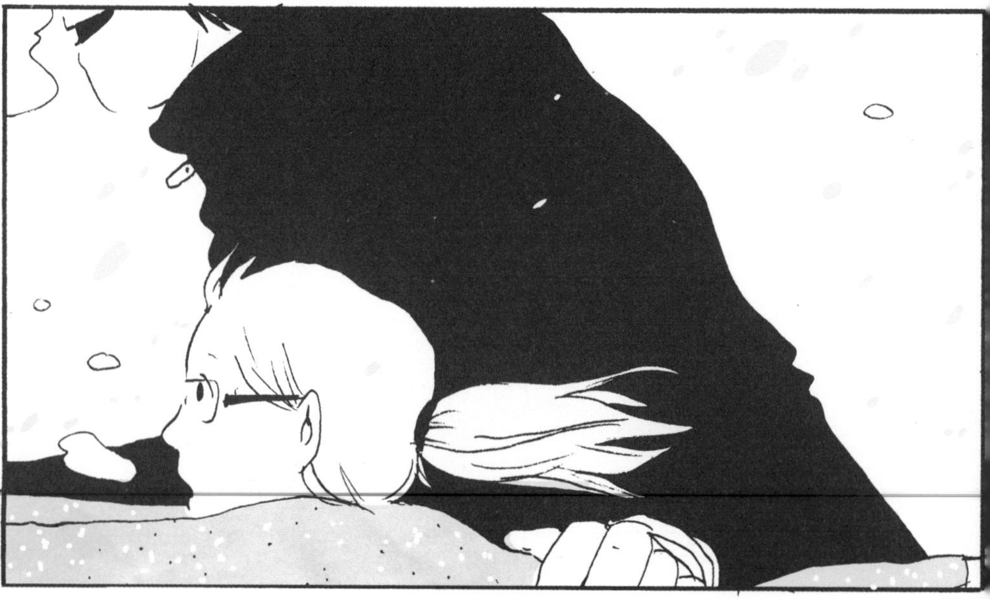

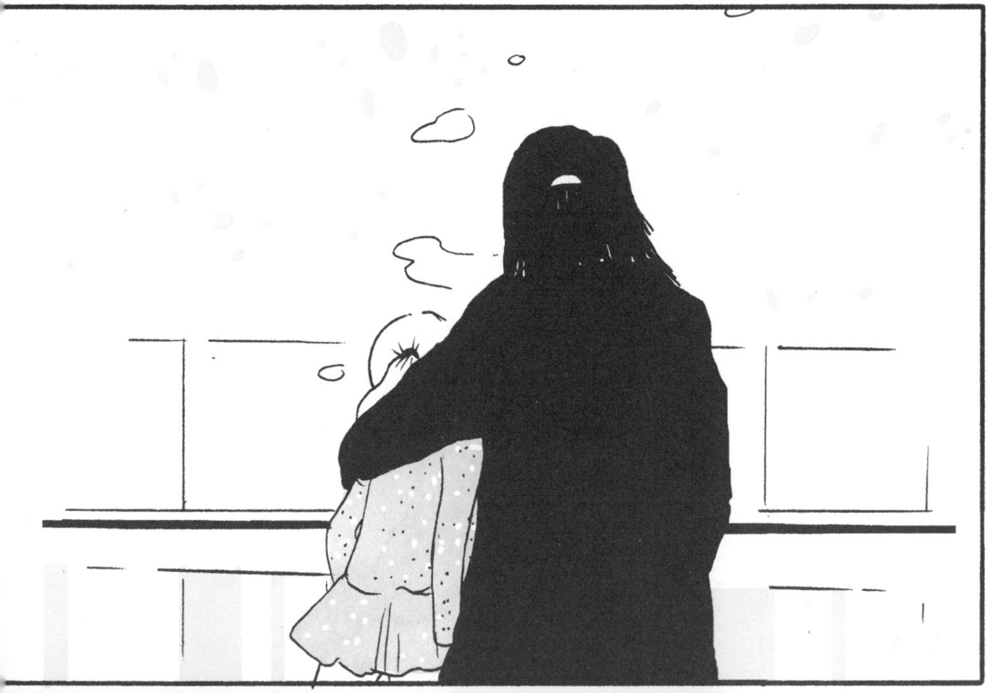

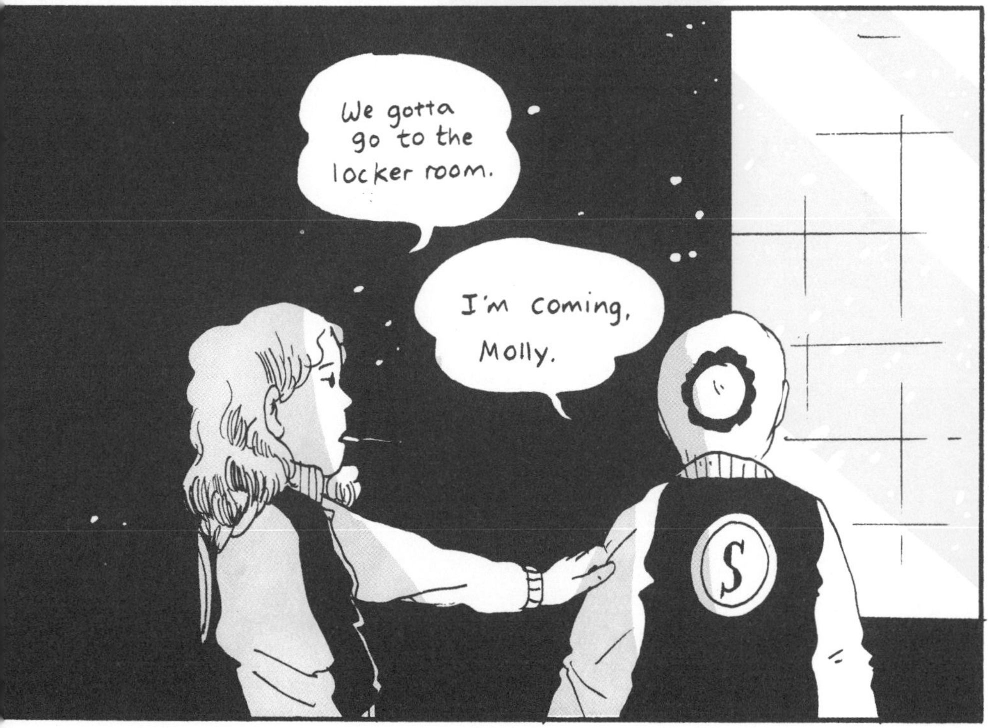
We gotta go to the locker room.
I'm coming, Molly.

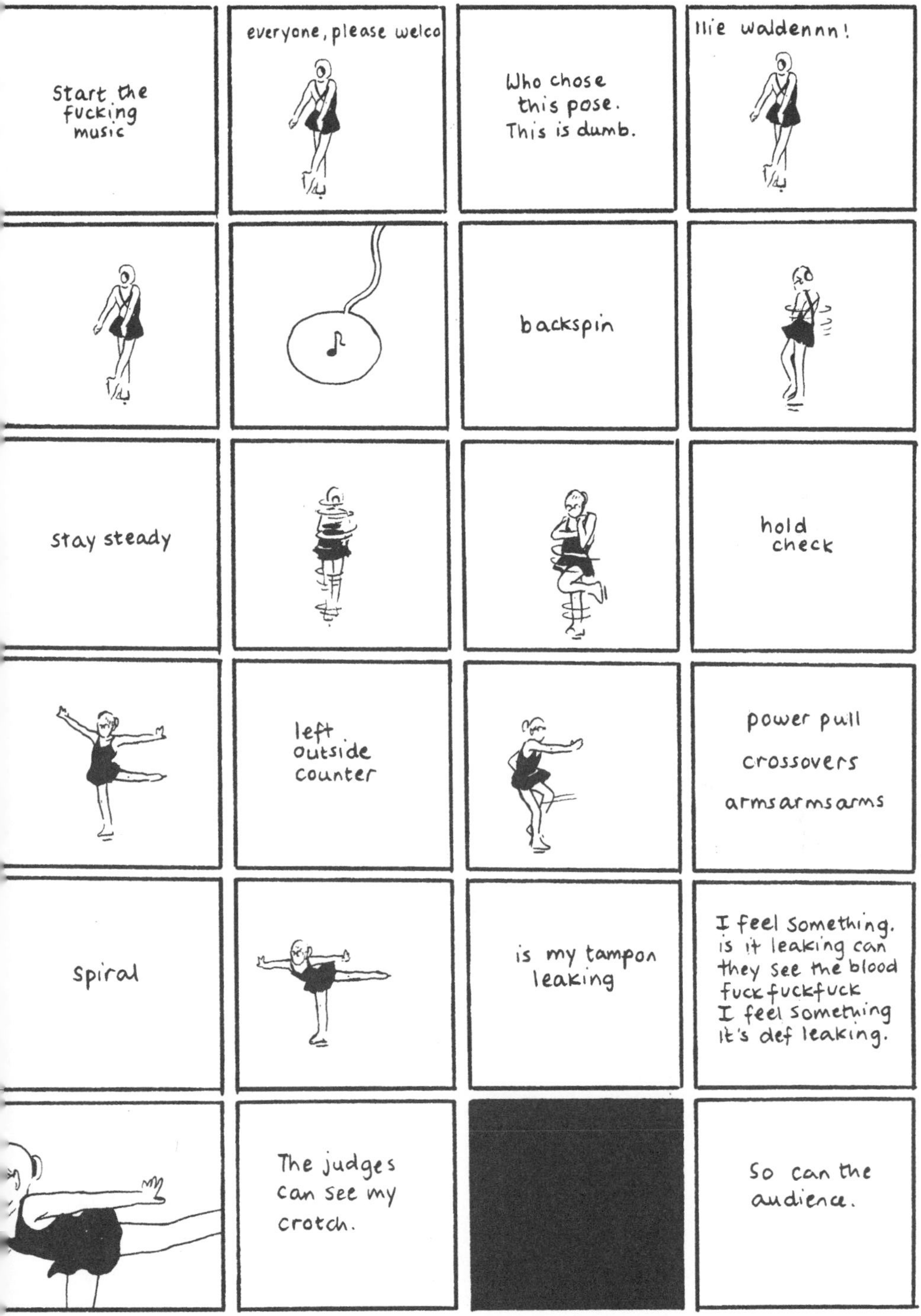

Start the fucking music

everyone, please welco

Who chose this pose. This is dumb.

Ilie waldennn!

backspin

stay steady

hold check

left outside counter

power pull
crossovers
armsarmsarms

Spiral

is my tampon leaking

I feel something. is it leaking can they see the blood fuck fuckfuck I feel something it's def leaking.

The judges can see my crotch.

So can the audience.

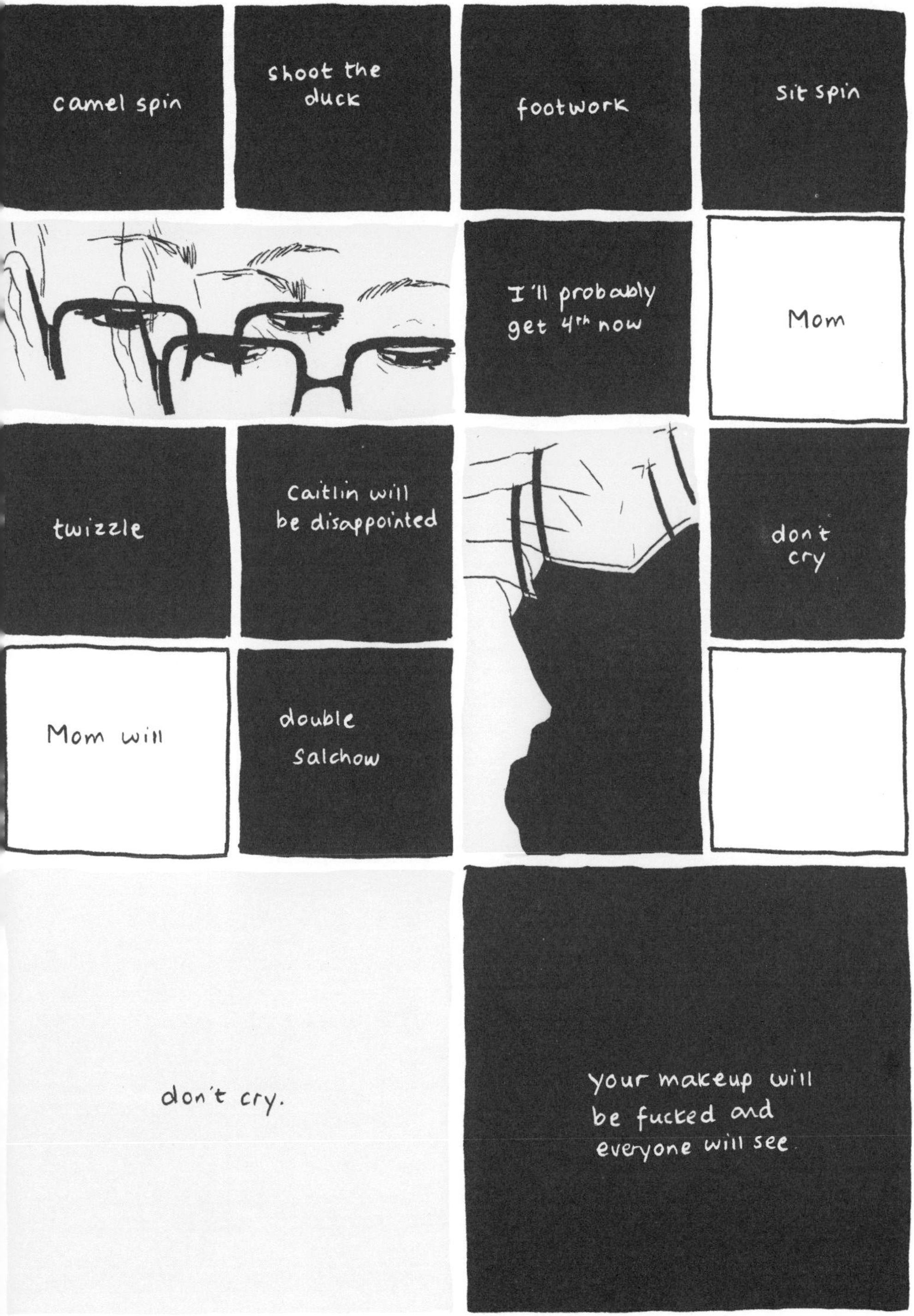
camel spin
shoot the duck
footwork
sit spin
I'll probably get 4th now
Mom
twizzle
Caitlin will be disappointed
don't cry
Mom will
double salchow
don't cry.
your makeup will be fucked and everyone will see.

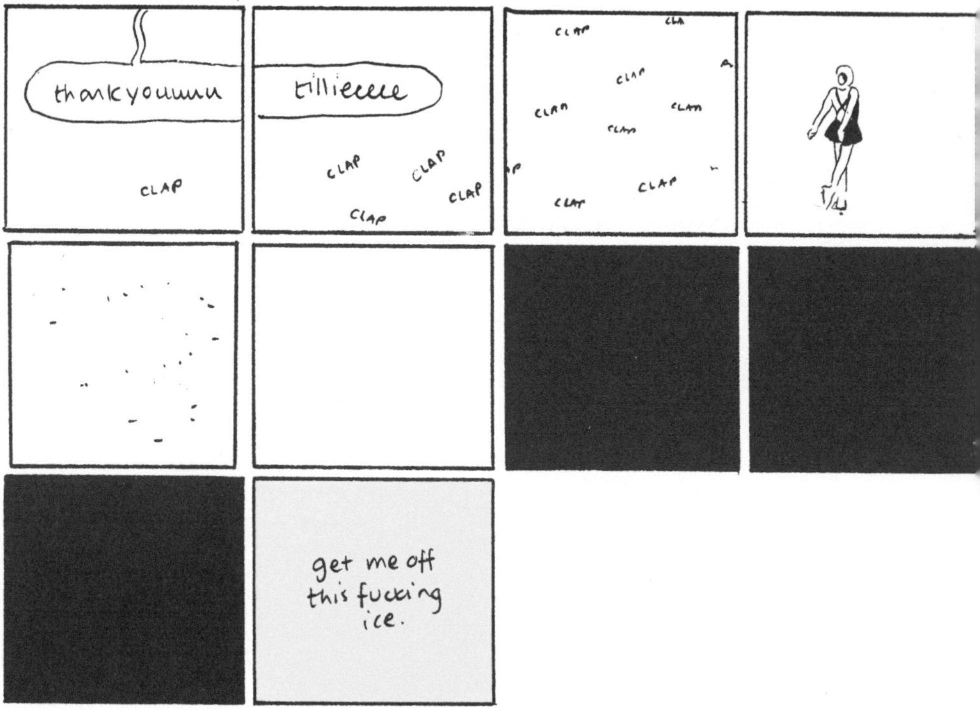
thankyouuuu
CLAP
tilllieeeee
CLAP
CLAP
CLAP
CLAP
CLAP
CLAP
CLAP
CLAP
CLAP
CLAP
get me off this fucking ice.

beep

I couldn't sleep.

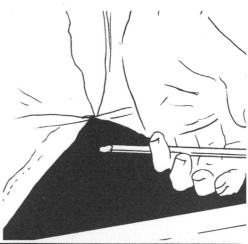

Every time I closed my eyes I saw everything that still hurt.

beep

prrp

beep

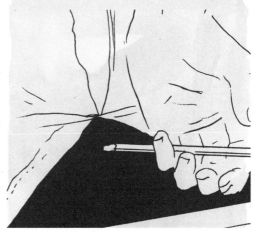

It had only been a few weeks since Worlds and I had barely slept since then.

All I could do to stay awake was grip the wheel.

4:07

My mind stretched far back.

I remembered that night when I had been lucky. That night where the car had missed.

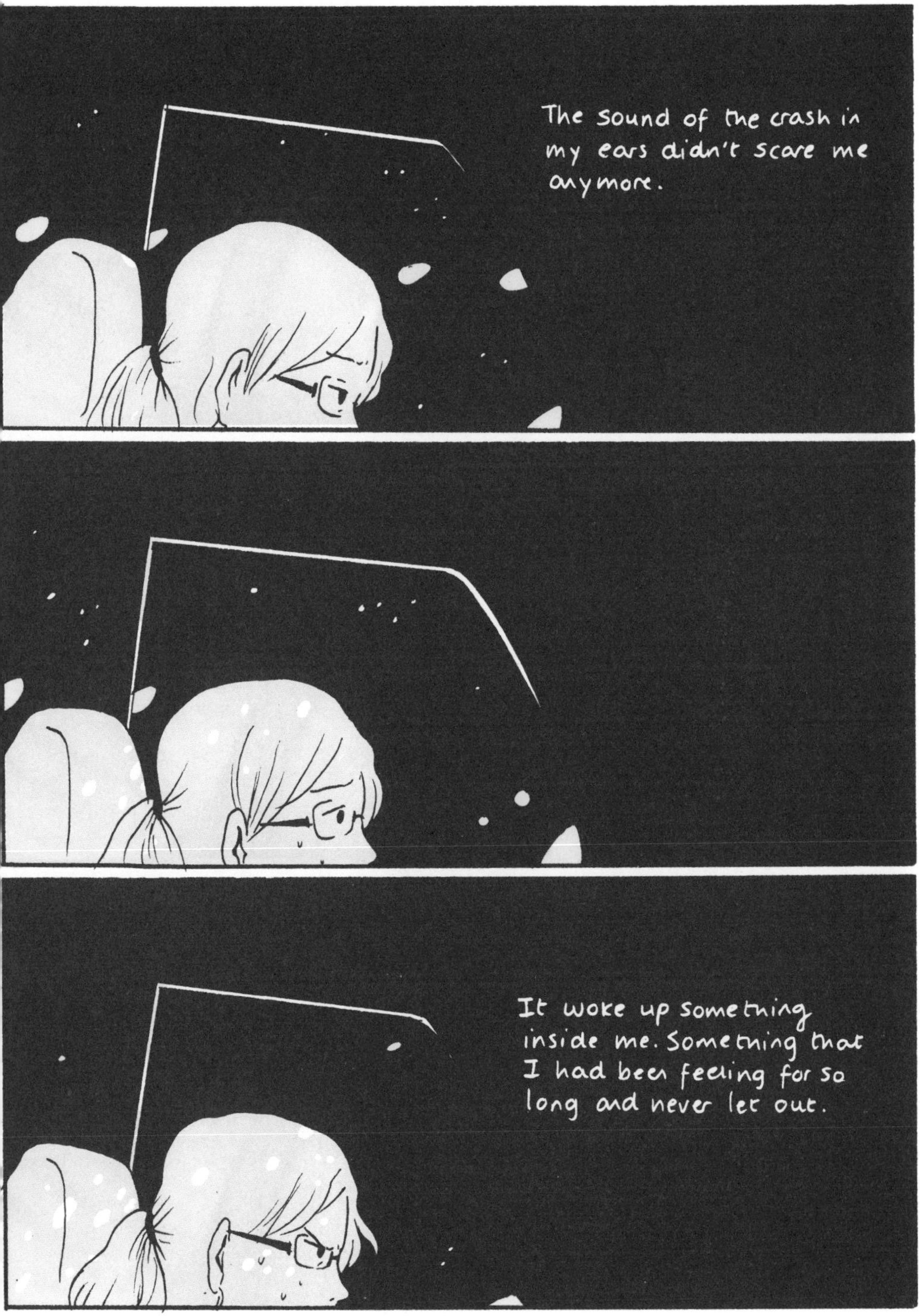
The sound of the crash in my ears didn't scare me anymore.
It woke up something inside me. Something that I had been feeling for so long and never let out.

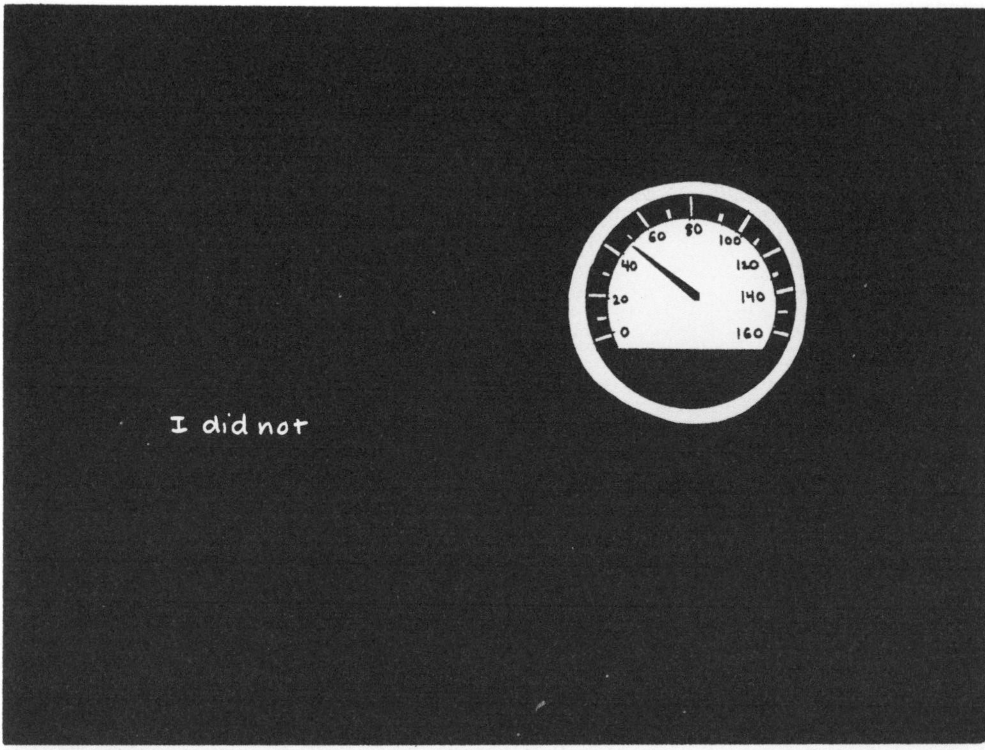
I did not

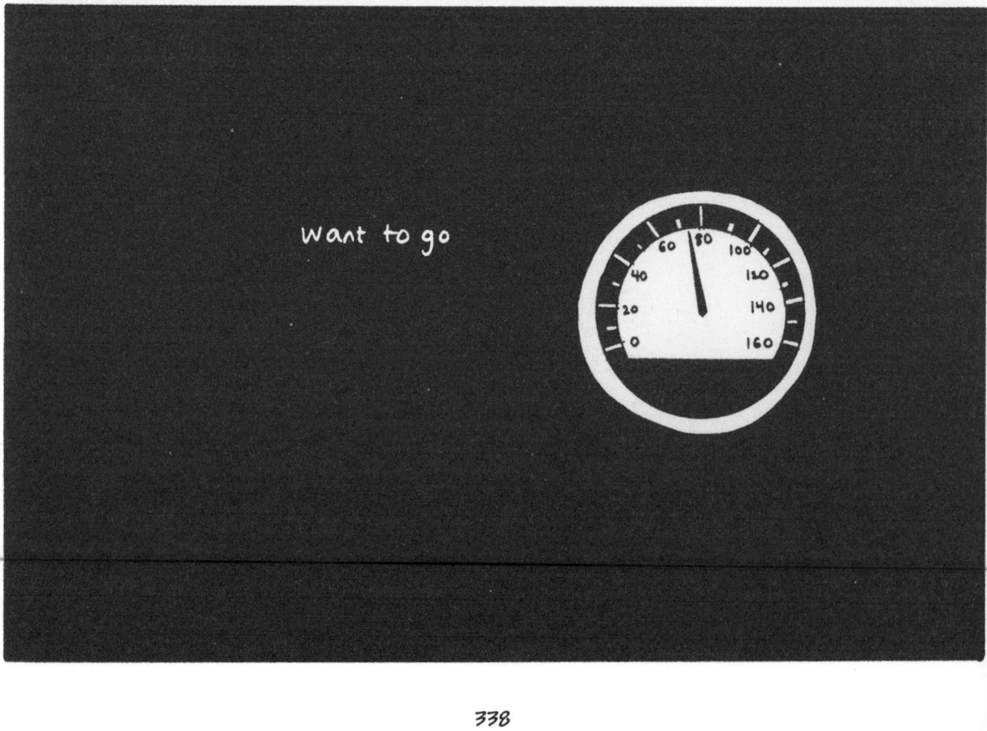
want to go

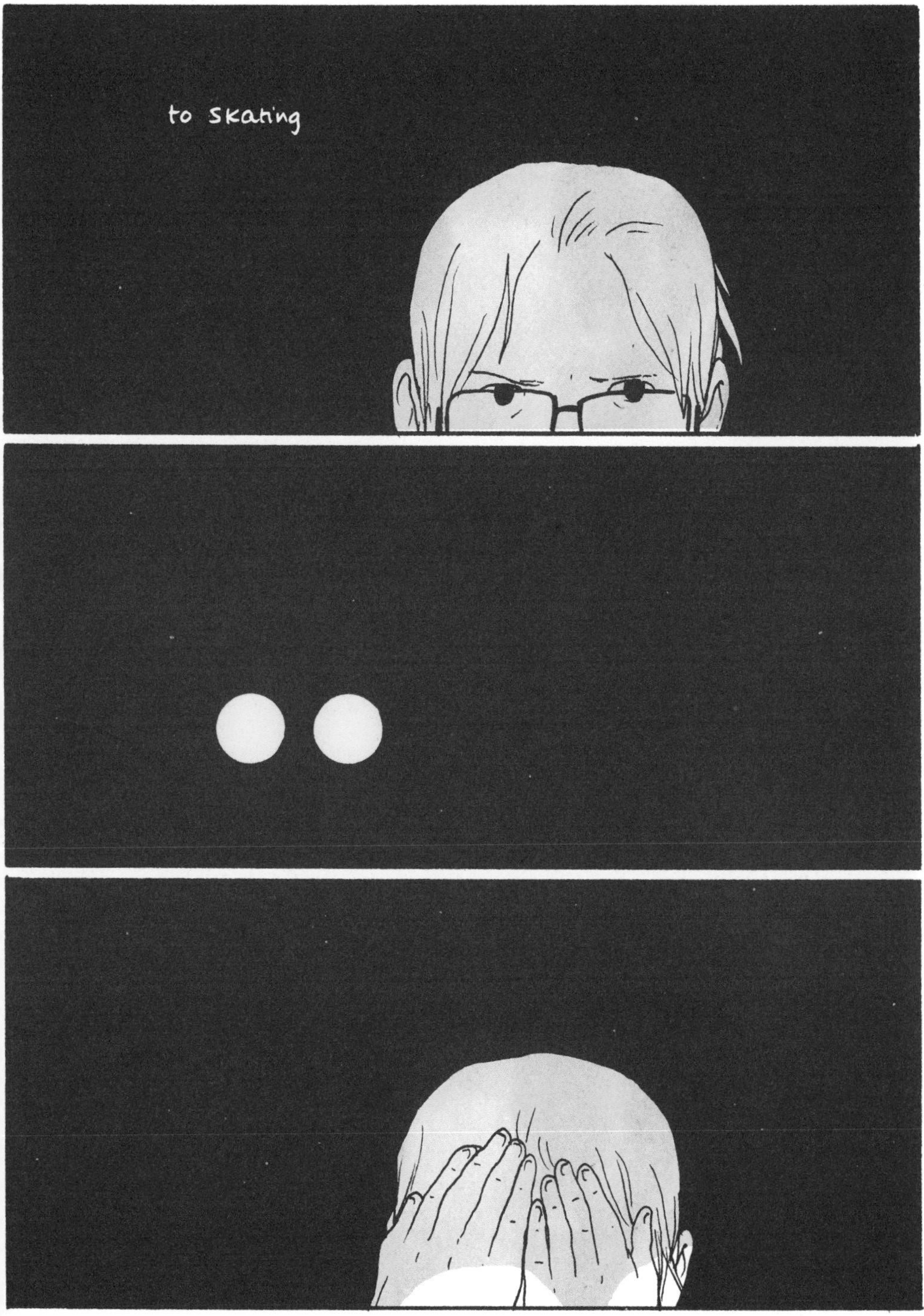
to skating

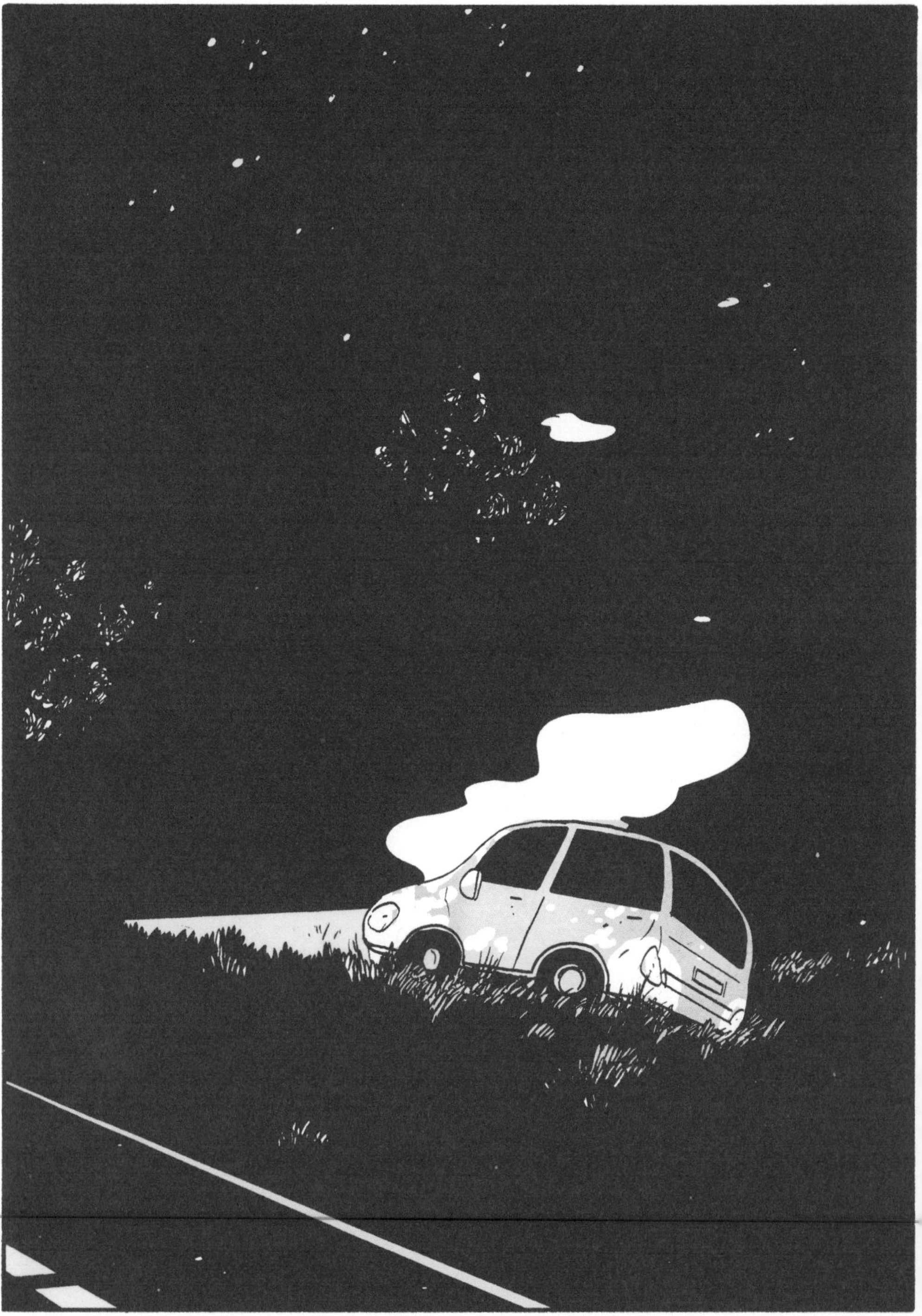

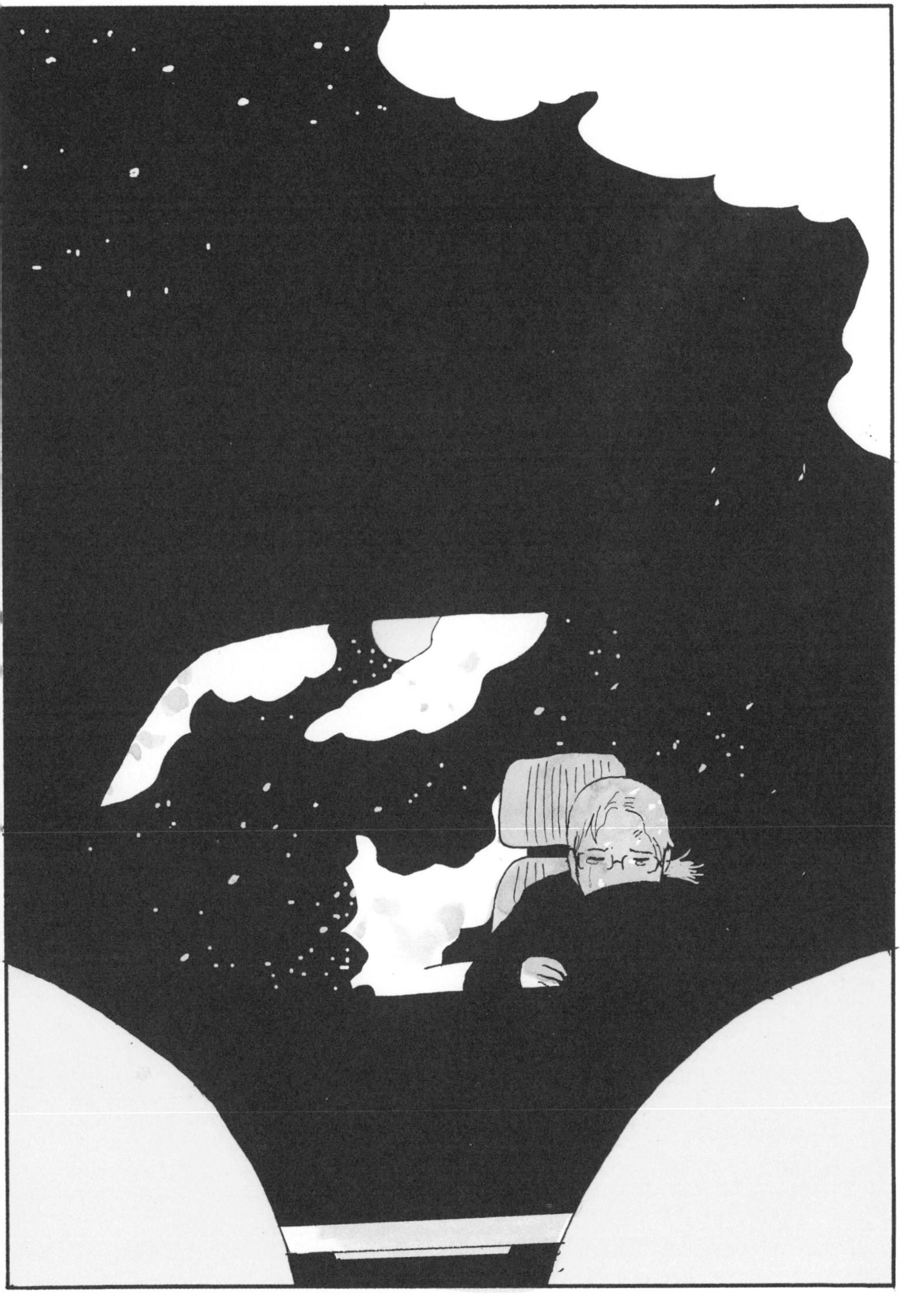

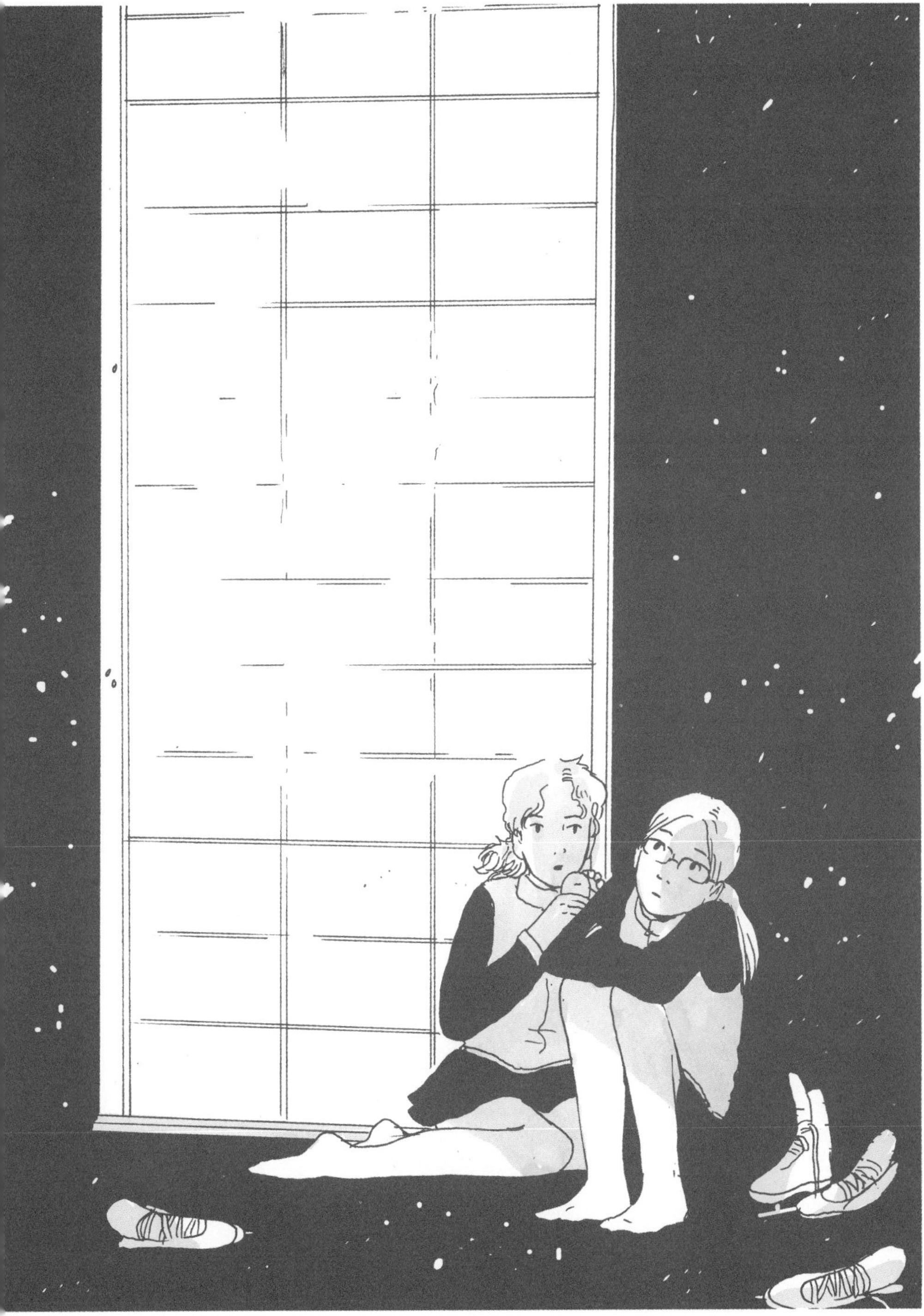

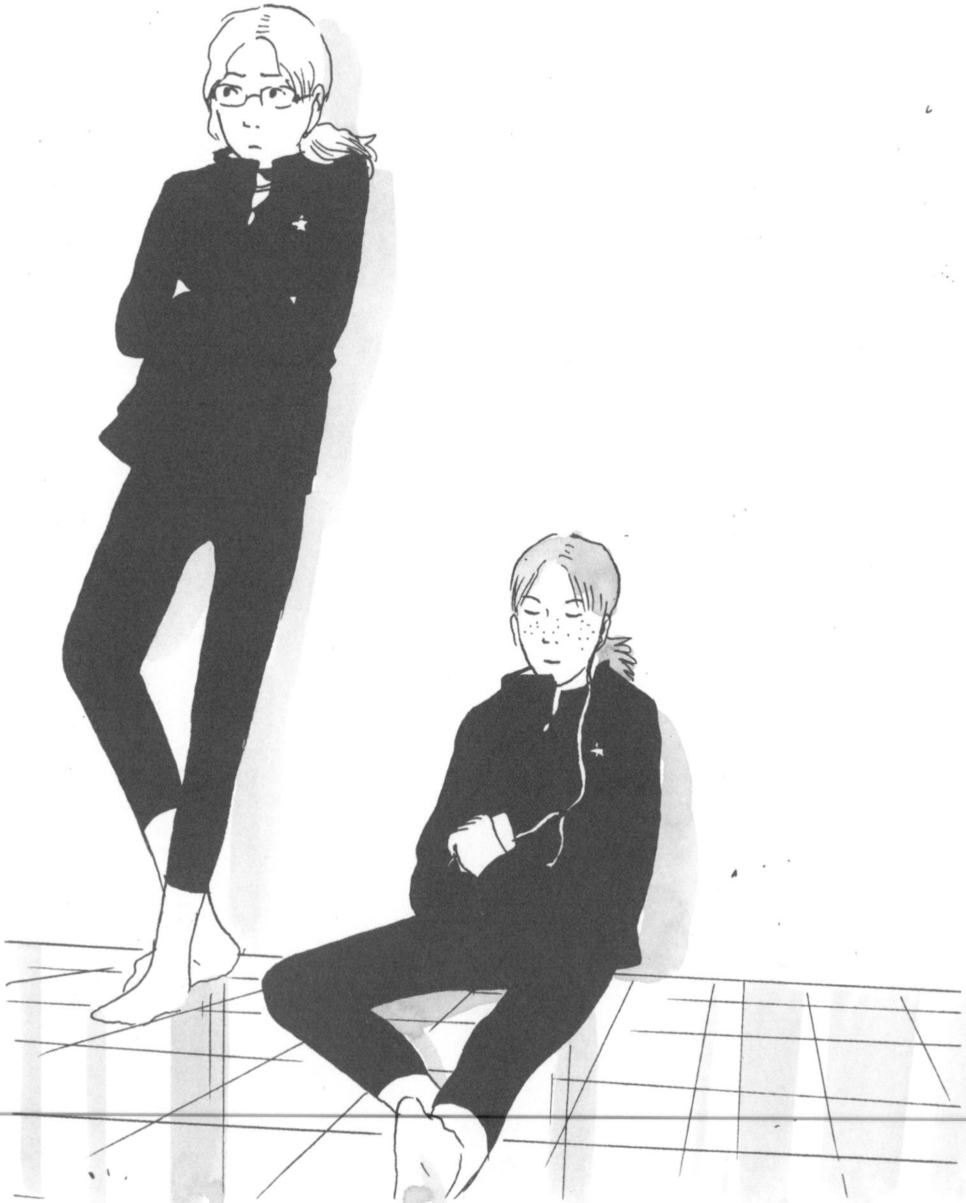

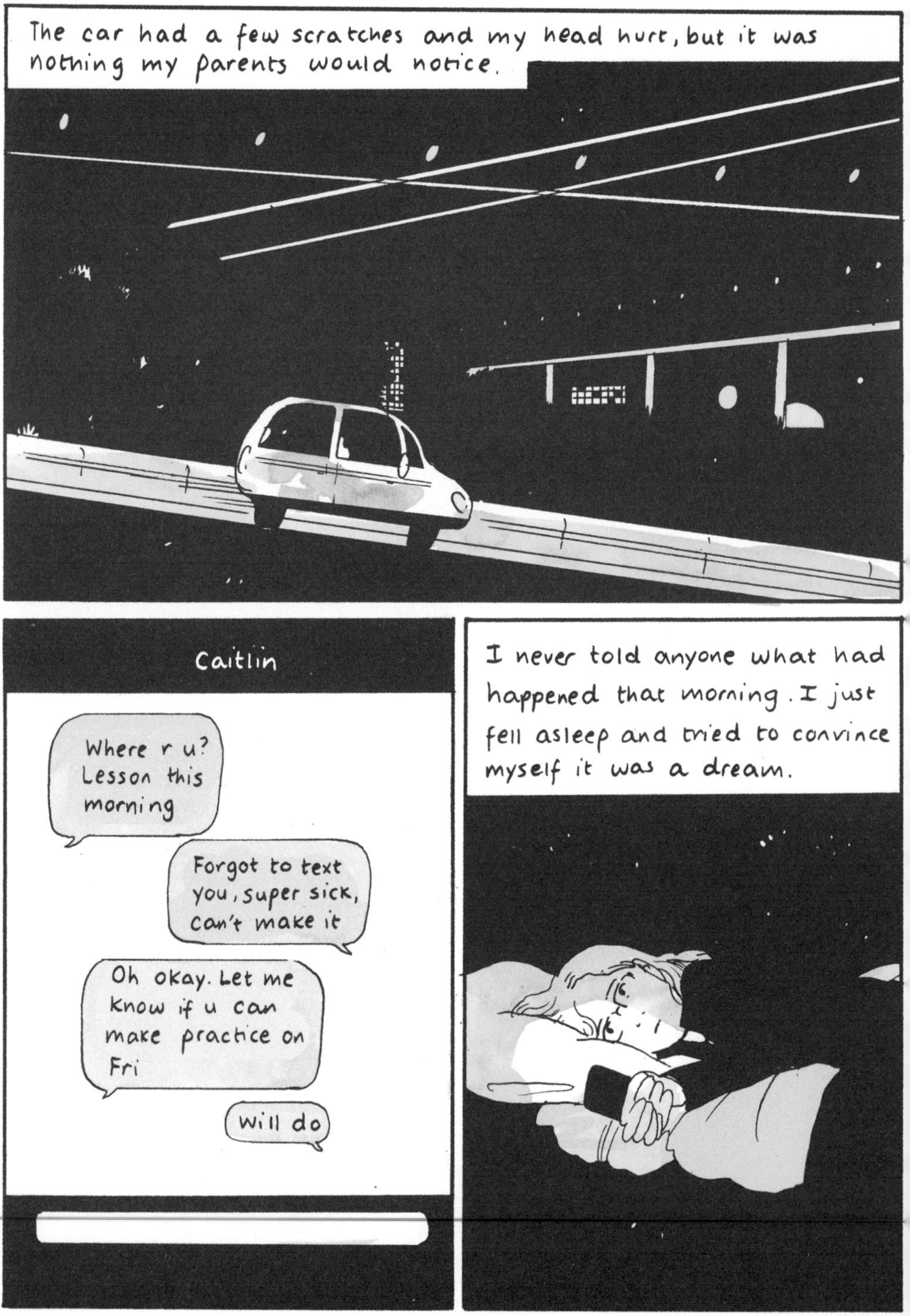
The car had a few scratches and my head hurt, but it was nothing my parents would notice.
Caitlin
Where r u? Lesson this morning
Forgot to text you, super sick, can't make it
Oh okay. Let me know if u can make practice on Fri
Will do
I never told anyone what had happened that morning. I just fell asleep and tried to convince myself it was a dream.

I had kept going to cello lessons with Victoria through high school.

Play the forte with more bow.

She made me feel relaxed. I could be myself so easily with her. She felt less and less like a teacher and more like a close friend.

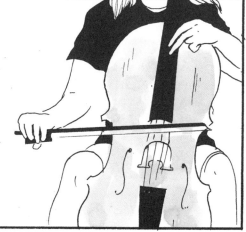

The night I had gone off the road faded into the past as I shoved it out of my mind. Just like before, I stayed quiet.

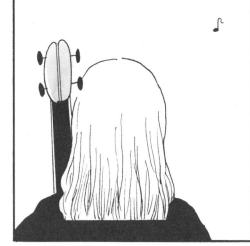

I felt like I was sick. I refused to process anything, so I just let it all sit inside me and rot.

But when I was with Victoria

That was beautiful, sweetie.

I felt a little bit better.

351

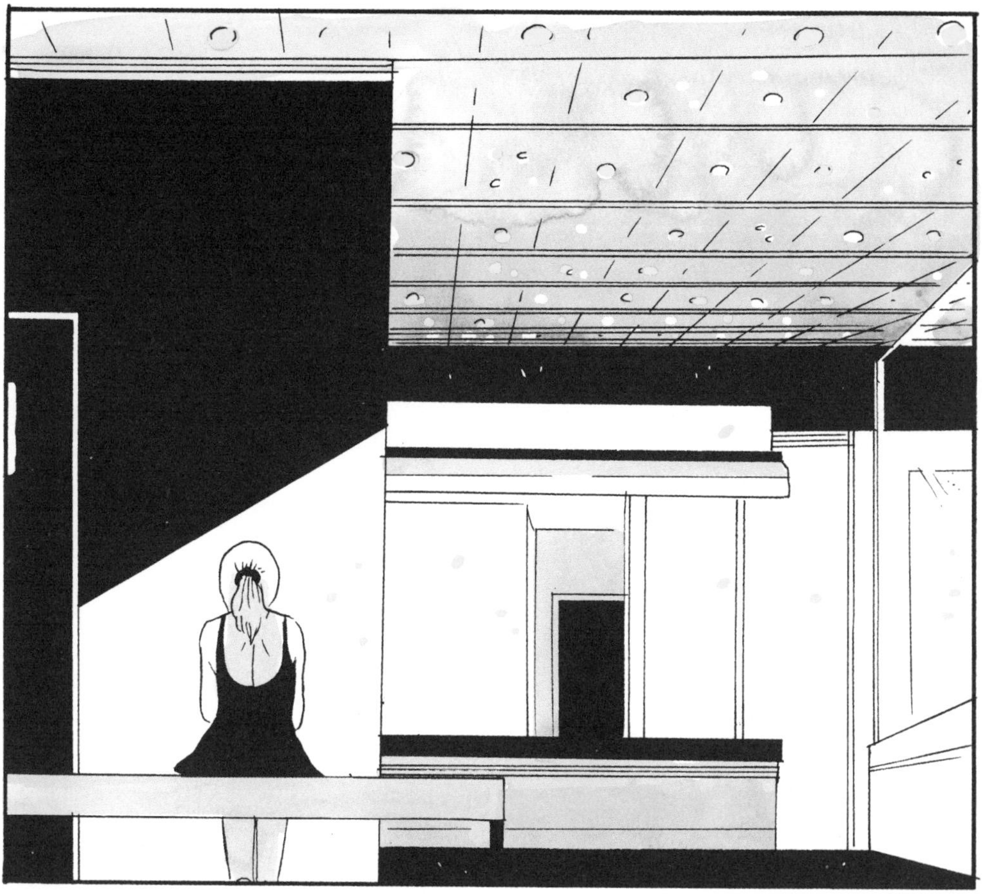
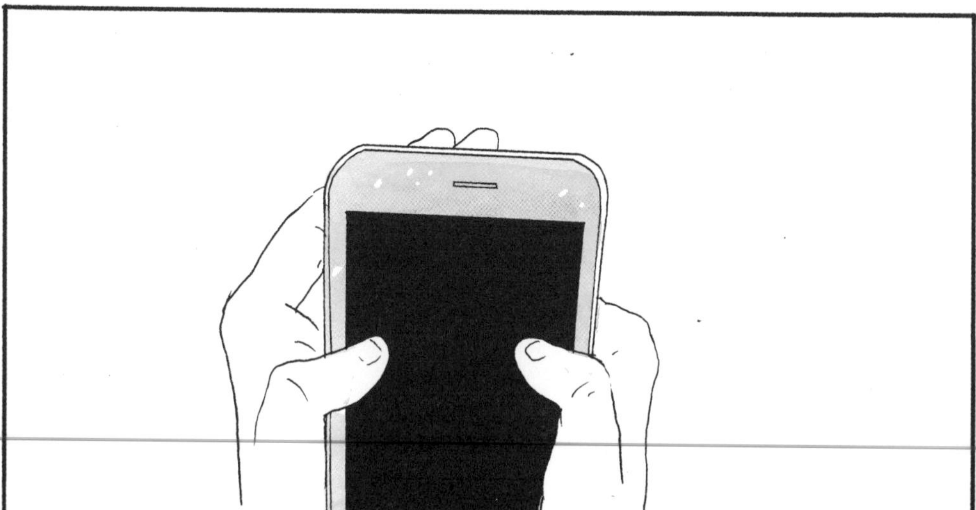

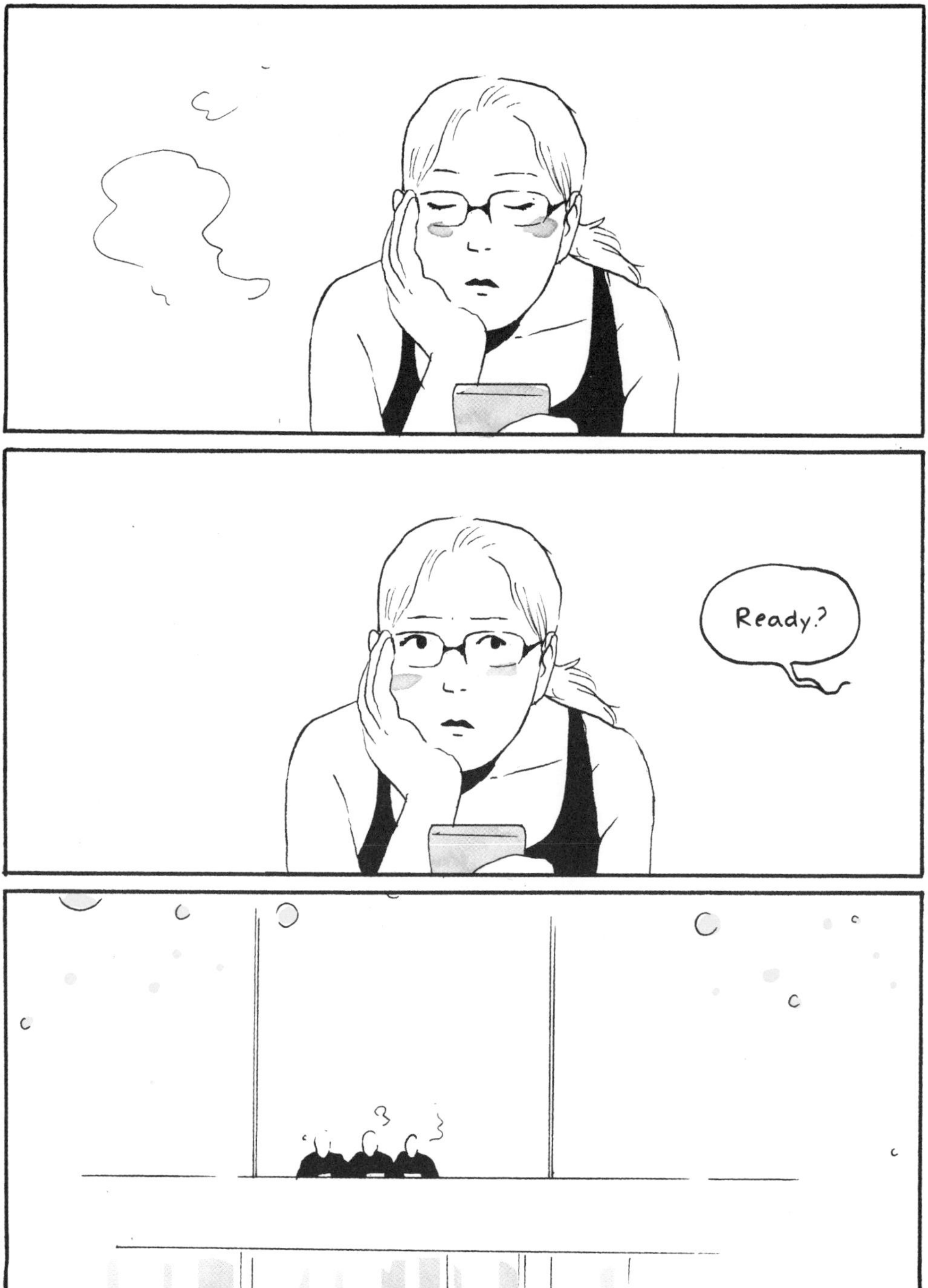
Ready?

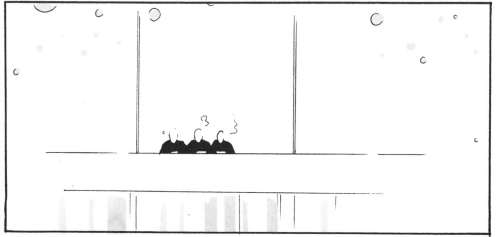

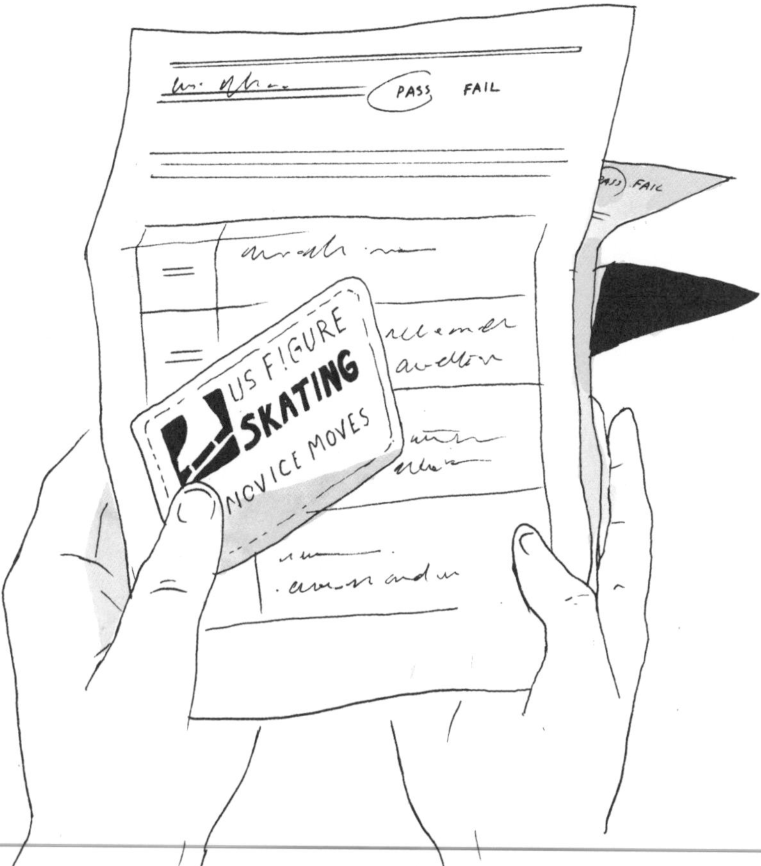
PASS
FAIL
PASS
FAIL
US FIGURE
SKATING
NOVICE MOVES

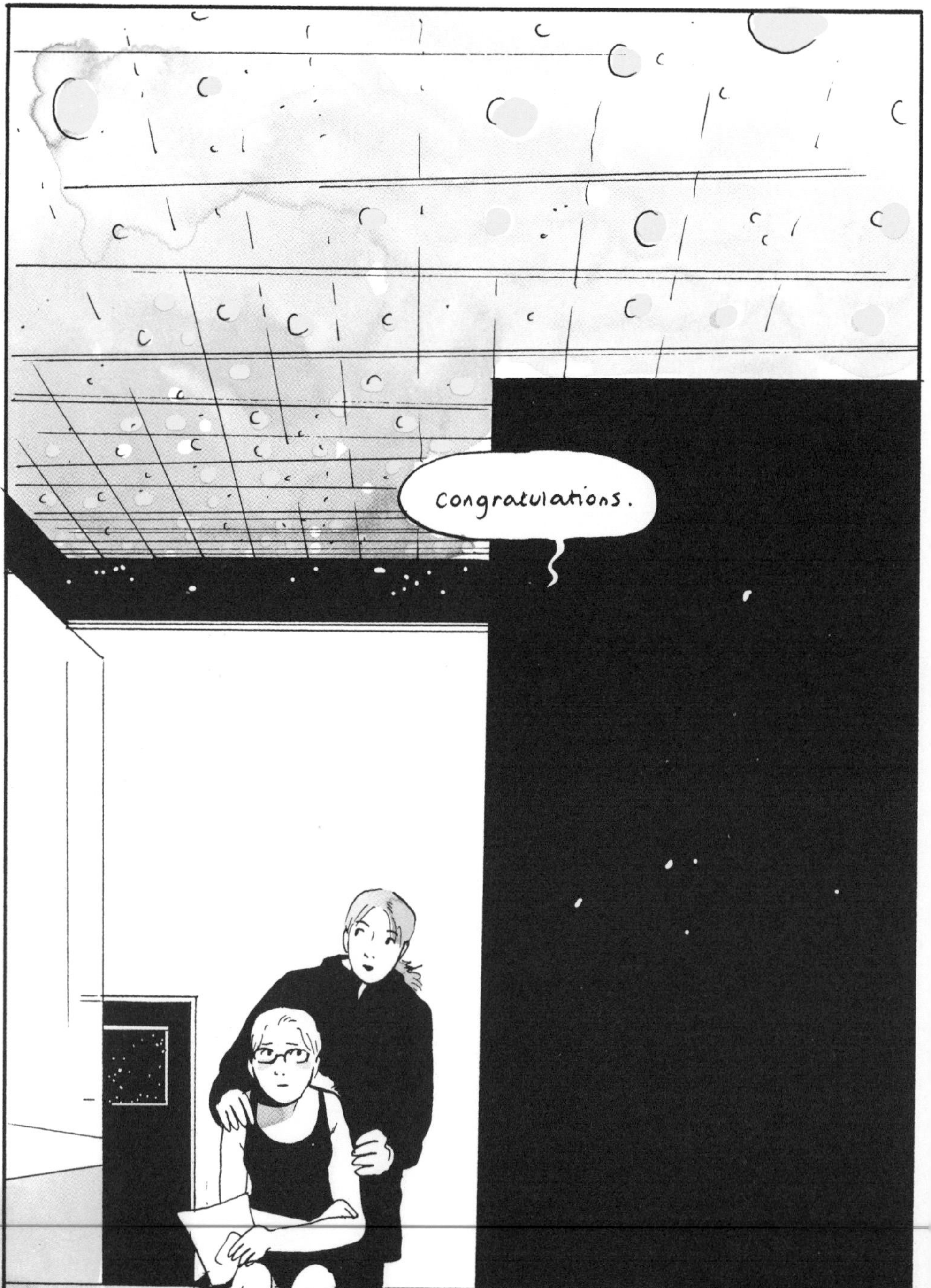
congratulations.

10

TWIZZLE

I learned to do a twizzle when I was about 6. It was simple. You push forward on one foot and rotate once.

That was it.

For some reason they always made me laugh. Something about the quick spinning motion made the blood rush to my head, making me usually burst out in giggles.

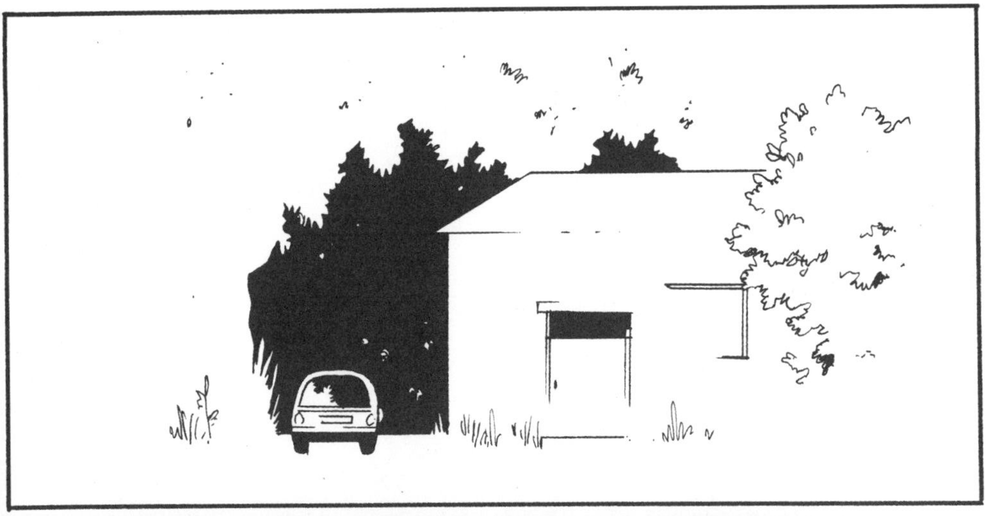

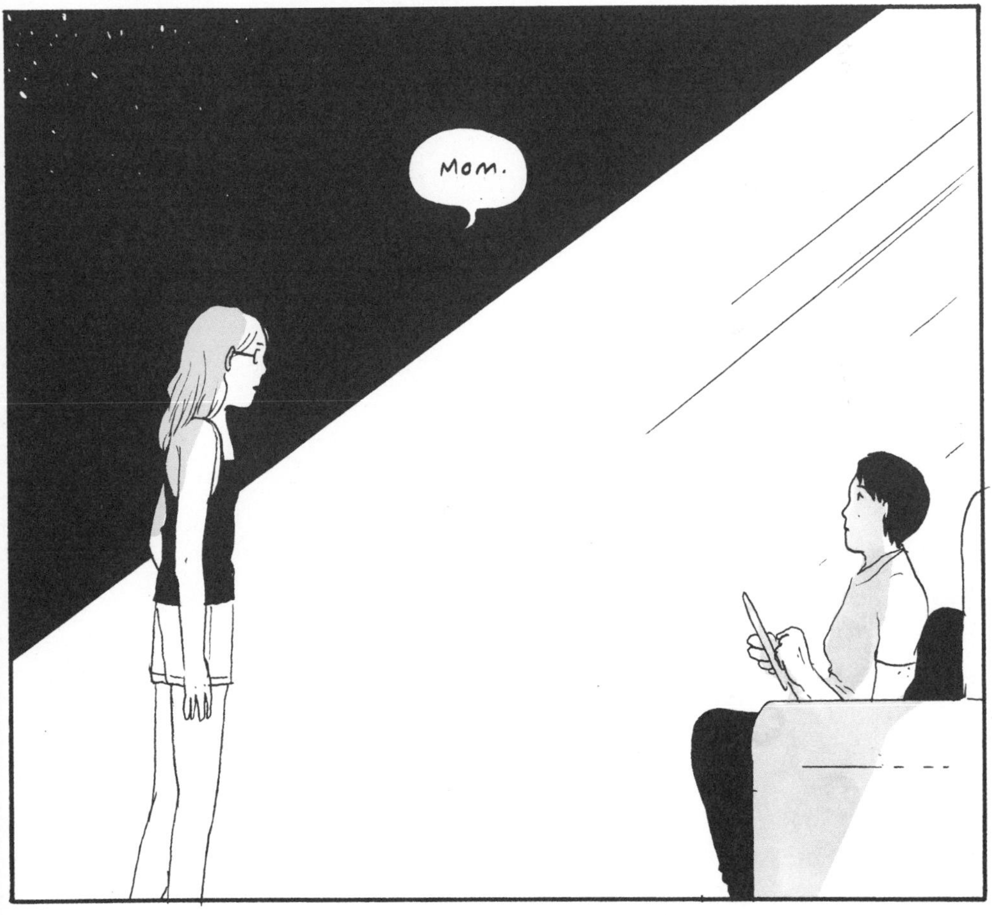
MOM.

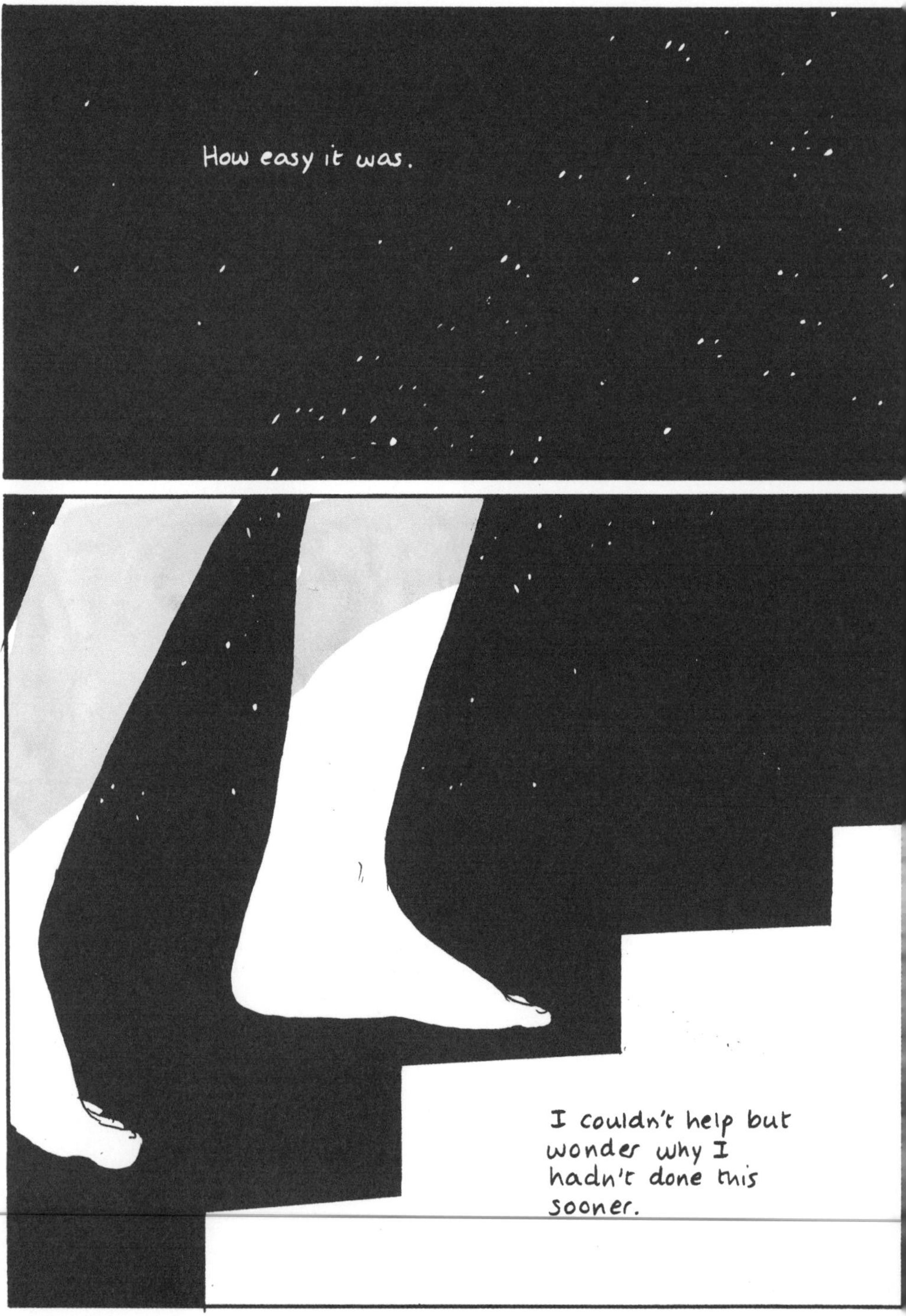
How easy it was.
I couldn't help but wonder why I hadn't done this sooner.

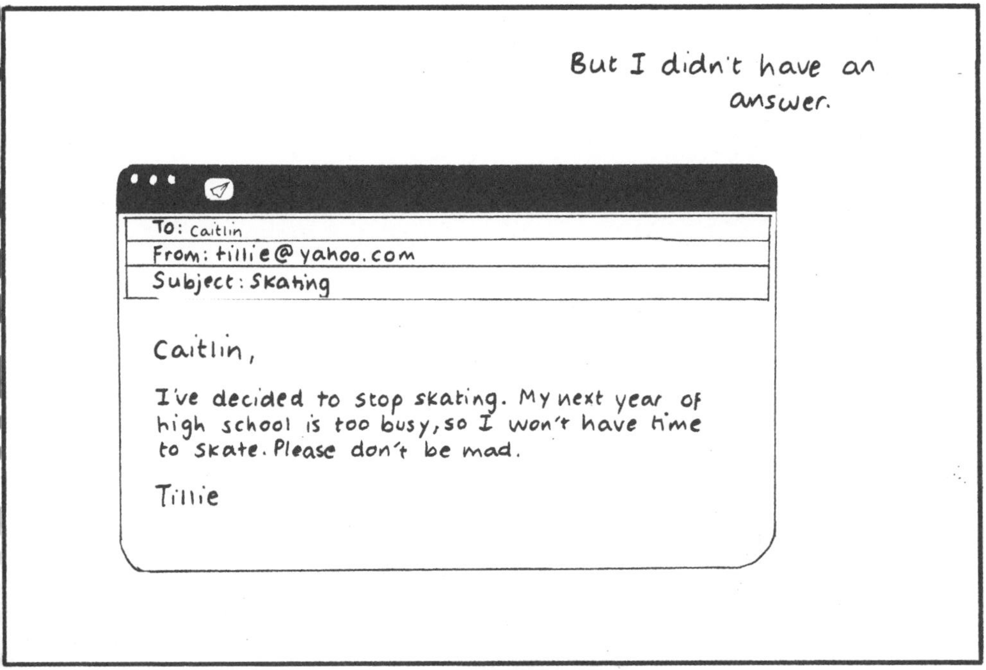
But I didn't have an answer.
To: Caitlin
From: tillie@yahoo.com
Subject: Skating
Caitlin,
I've decided to stop skating. My next year of high school is too busy, so I won't have time to skate. Please don't be mad.
Tillie

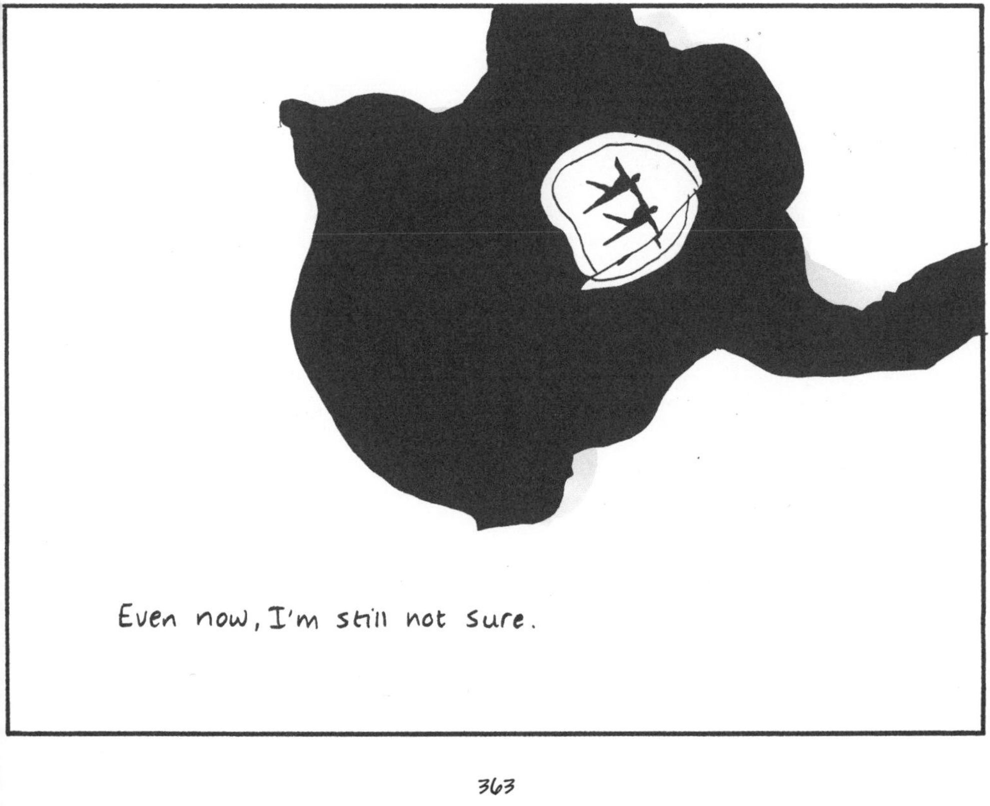
Even now, I'm still not sure.

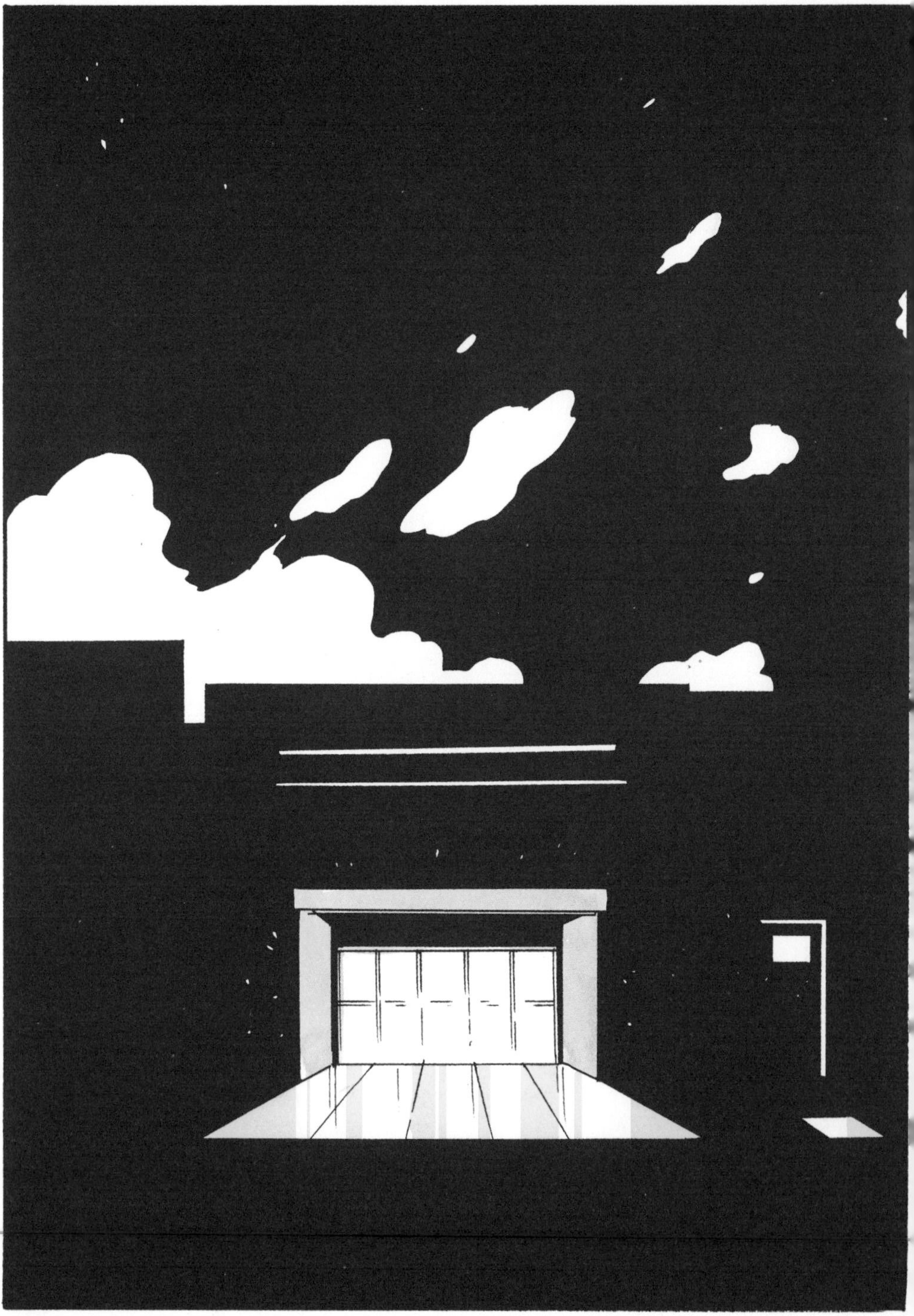

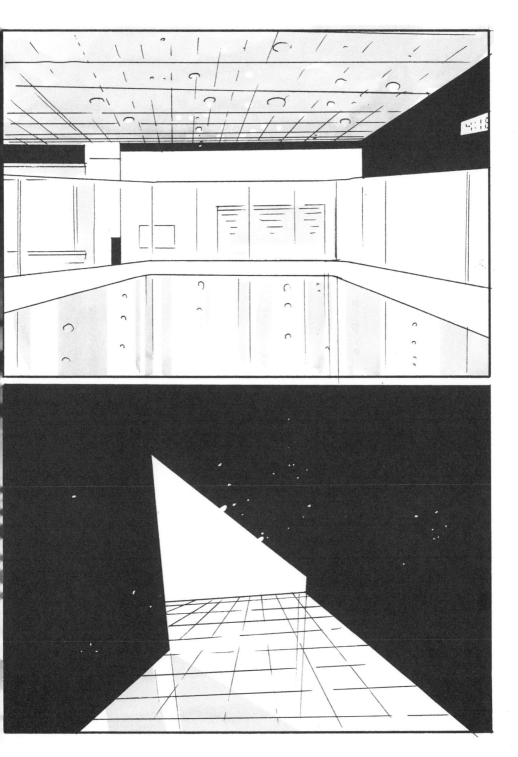

I didn't want to skate. But I couldn't say no to Caitlin. Not when she looked so sad.

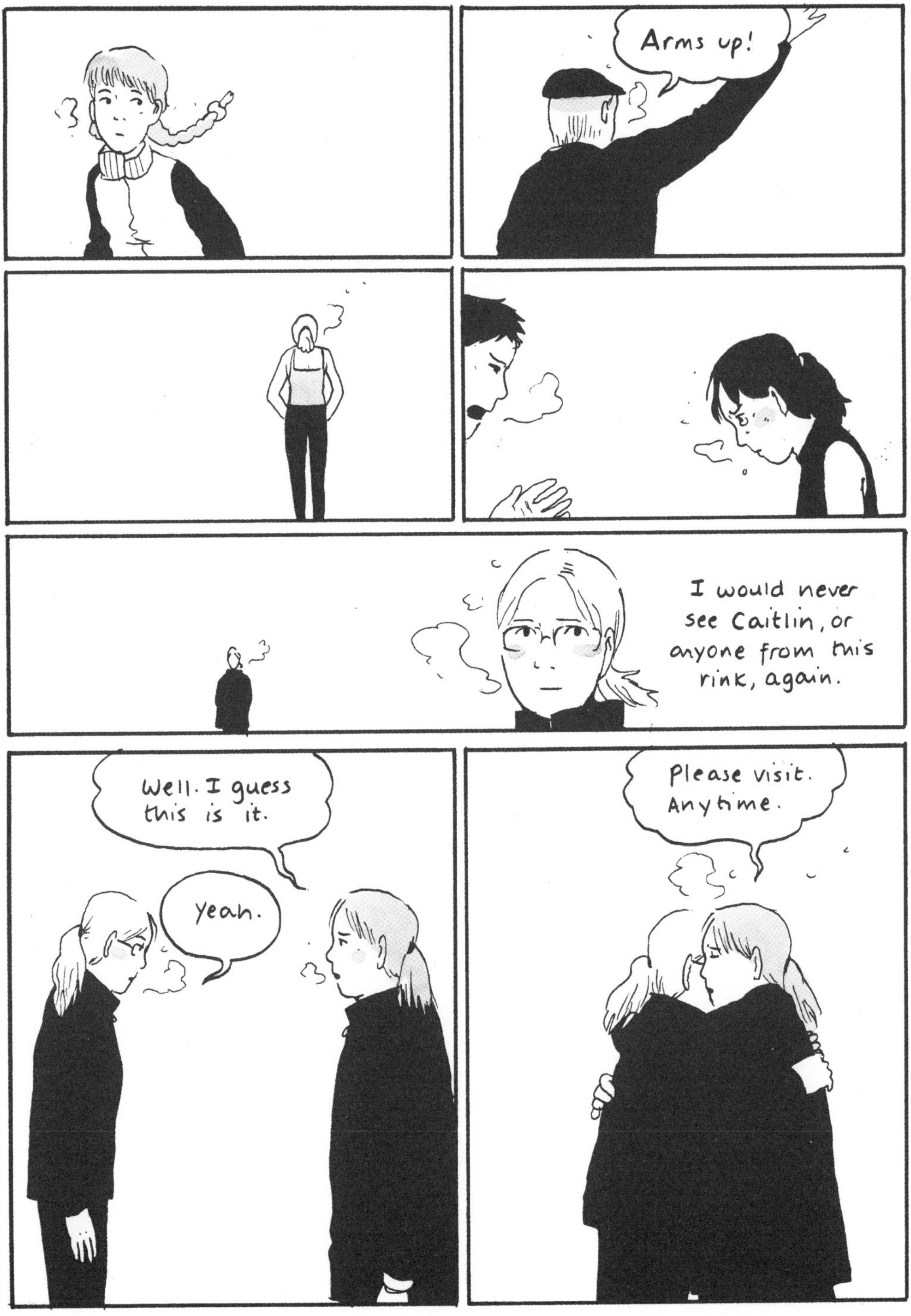
Arms up!
I would never see Caitlin, or anyone from this rink, again.
Well. I guess this is it.
yeah.
Please visit. Anytime.

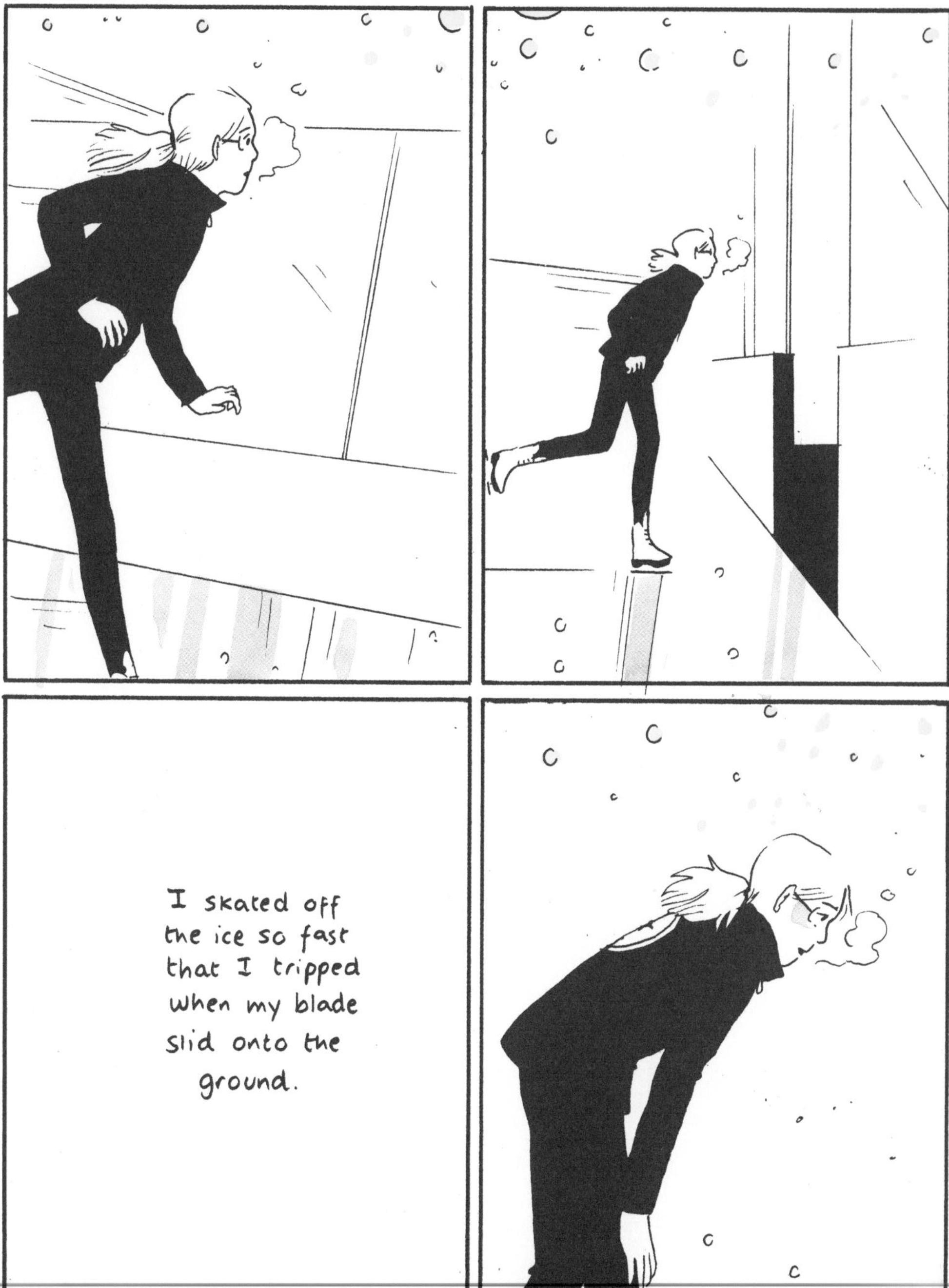
I skated off the ice so fast that I tripped when my blade slid onto the ground.

To top it all off, I made it out that morning without paying for the session. The mom table glared at me the whole way out.

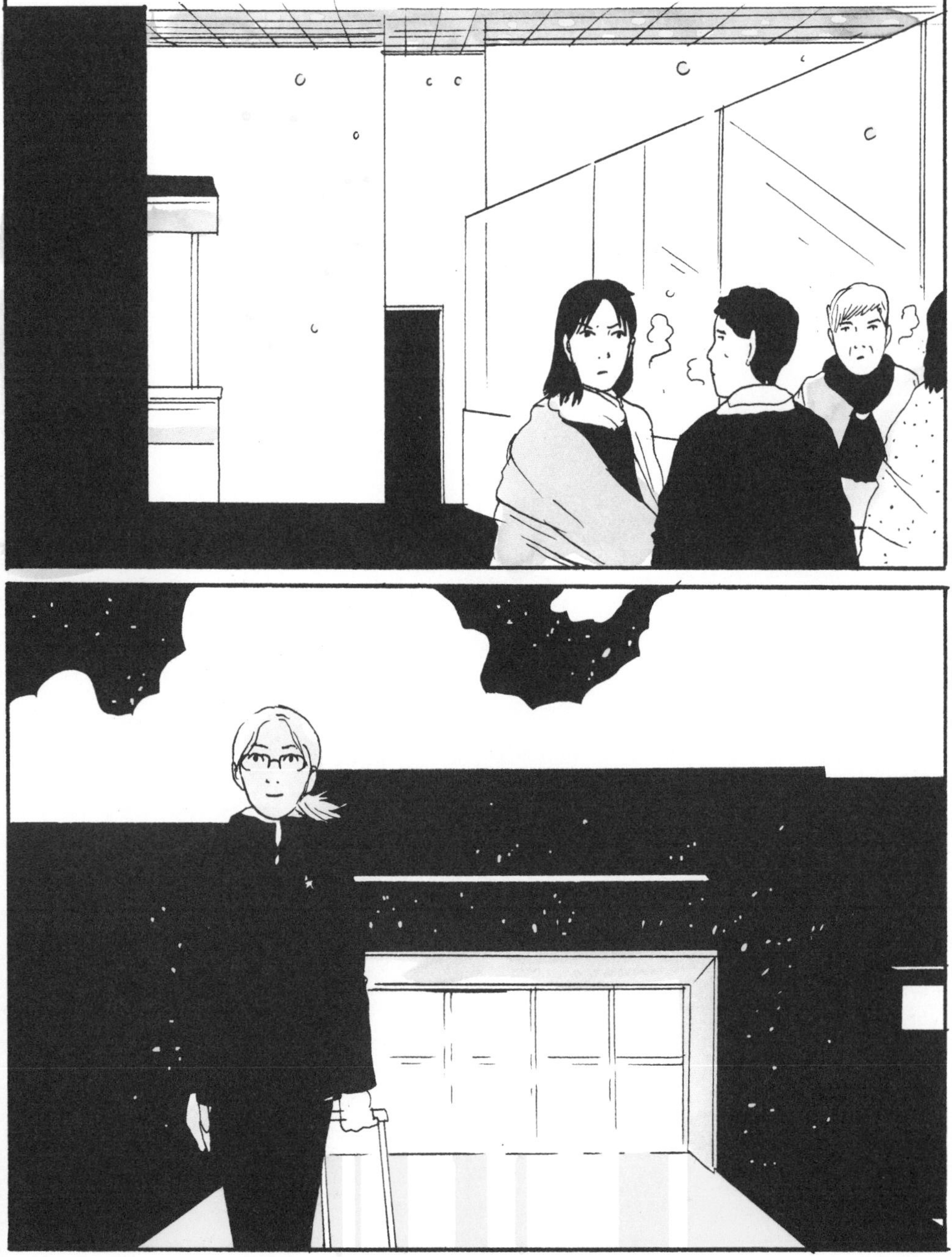

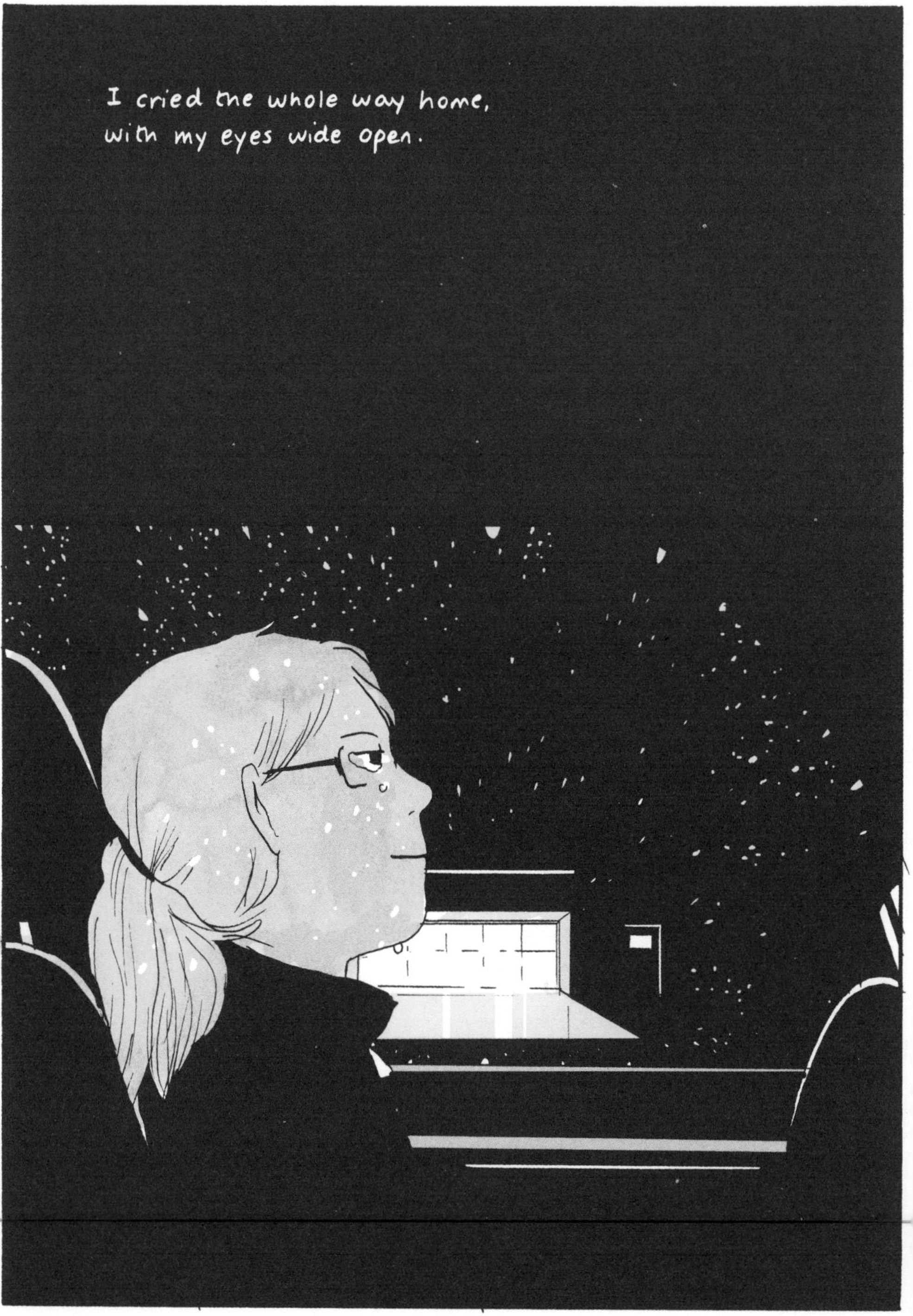
I cried the whole way home,
with my eyes wide open.

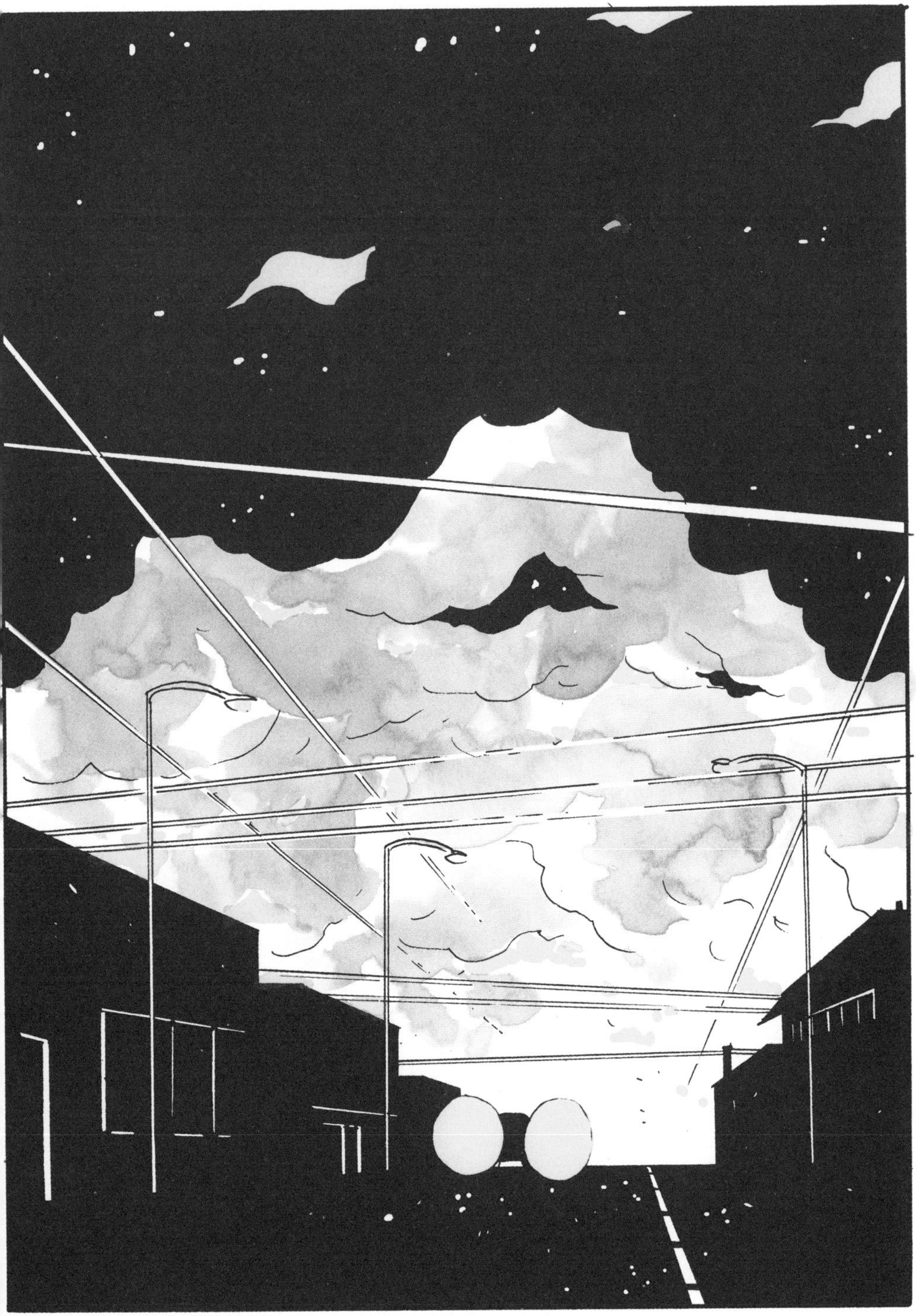

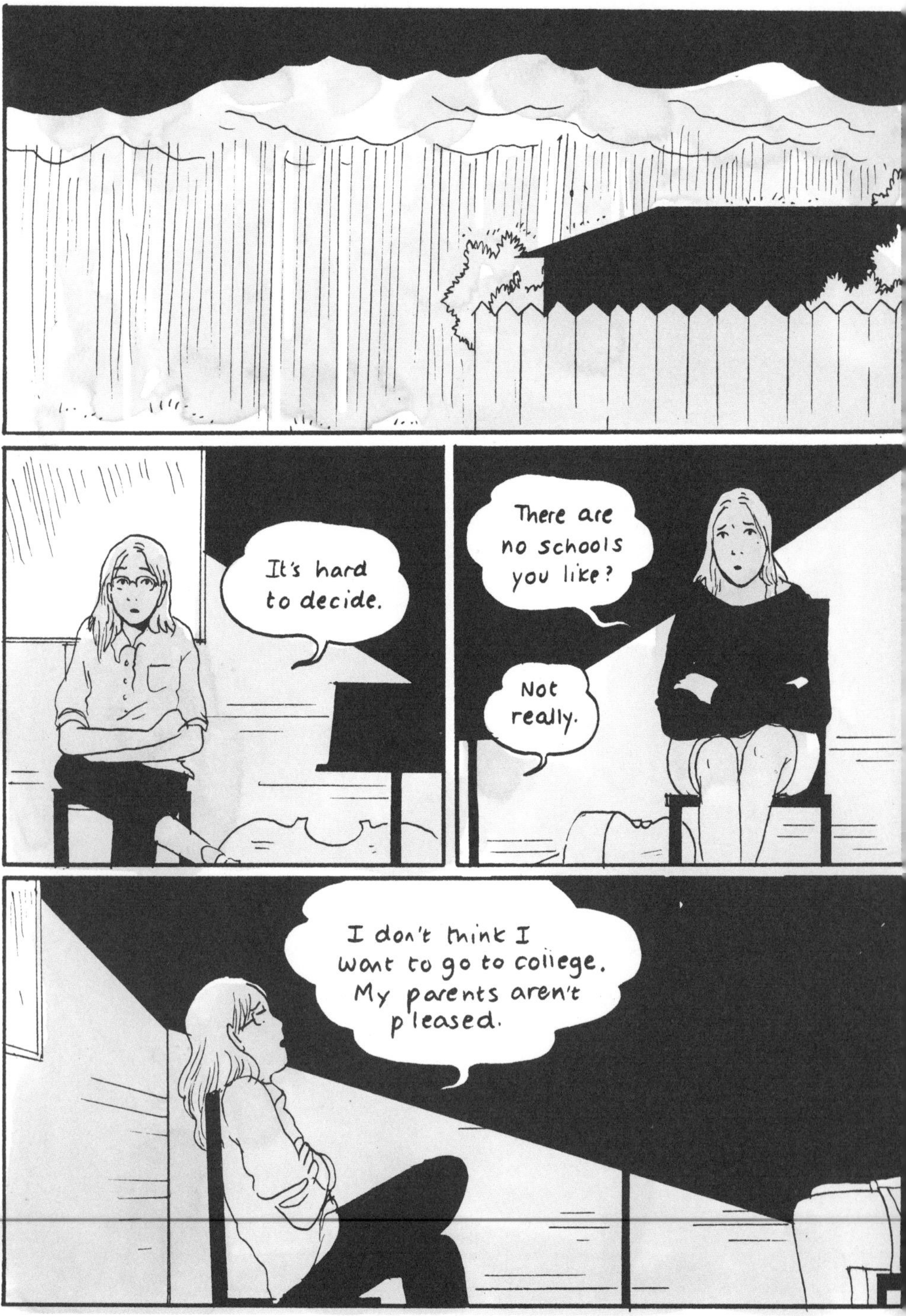
It's hard to decide.
There are no schools you like?
Not really.
I don't think I want to go to college. My parents aren't pleased.

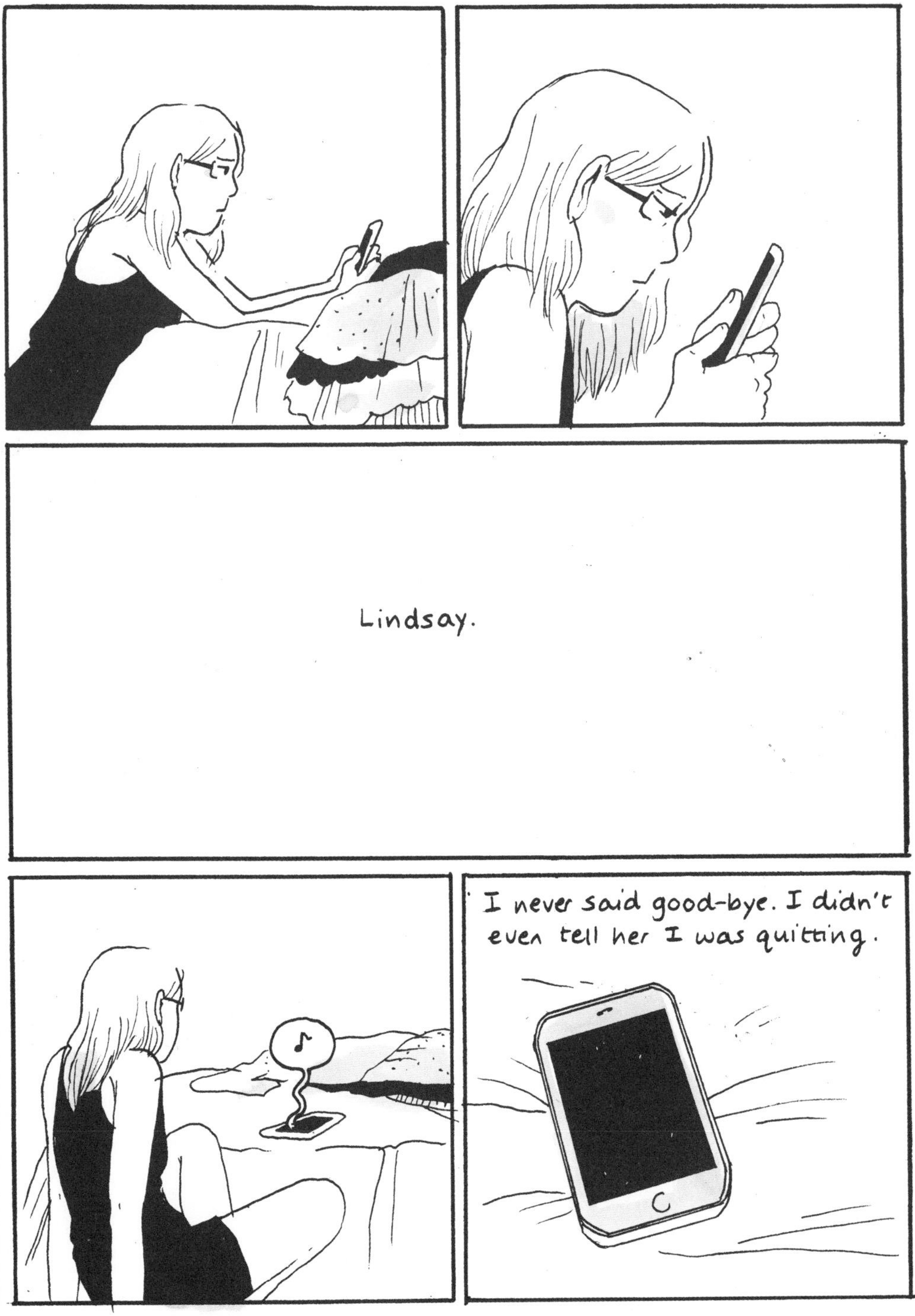
Lindsay.
I never said good-bye. I didn't even tell her I was quitting.

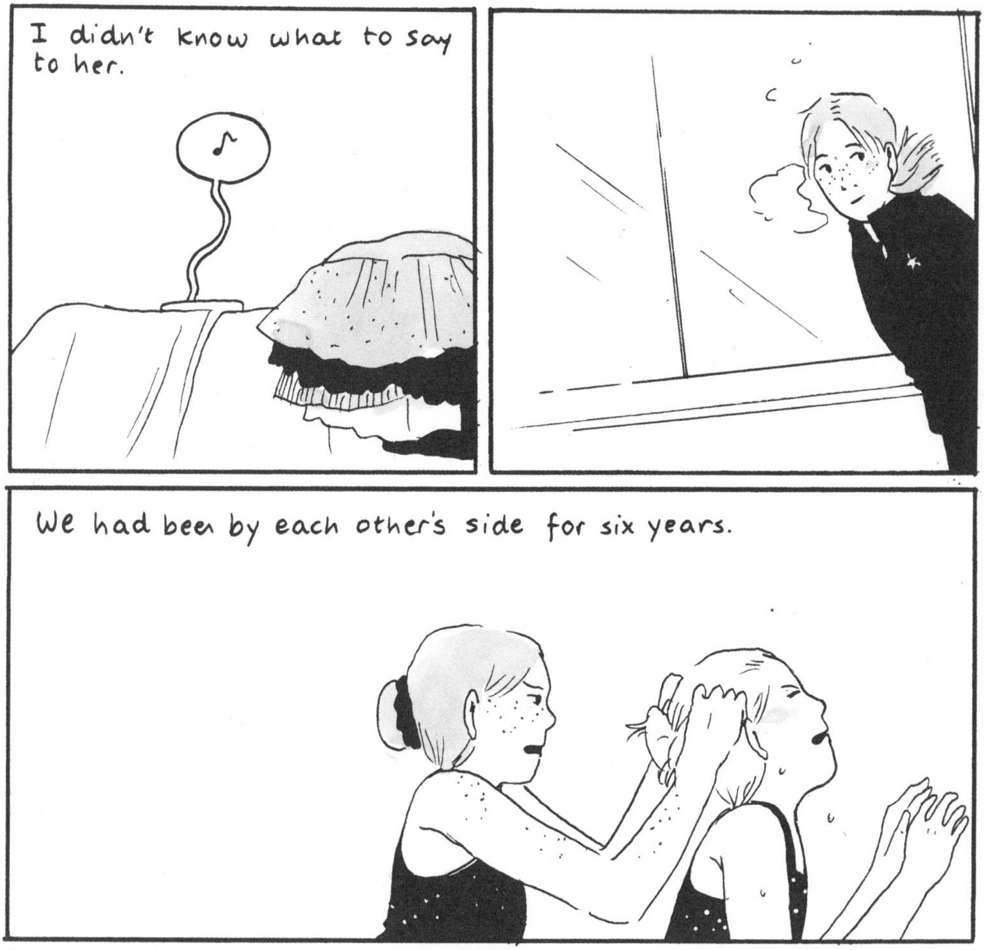
I didn't know what to say to her.
We had been by each other's side for six years.
And that whole time I had never been a good friend to her.
I never really got to know her, and I never let her get close to me.

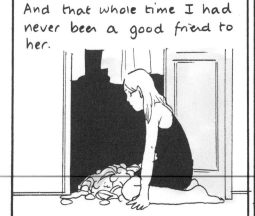

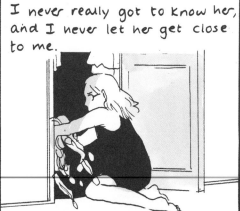

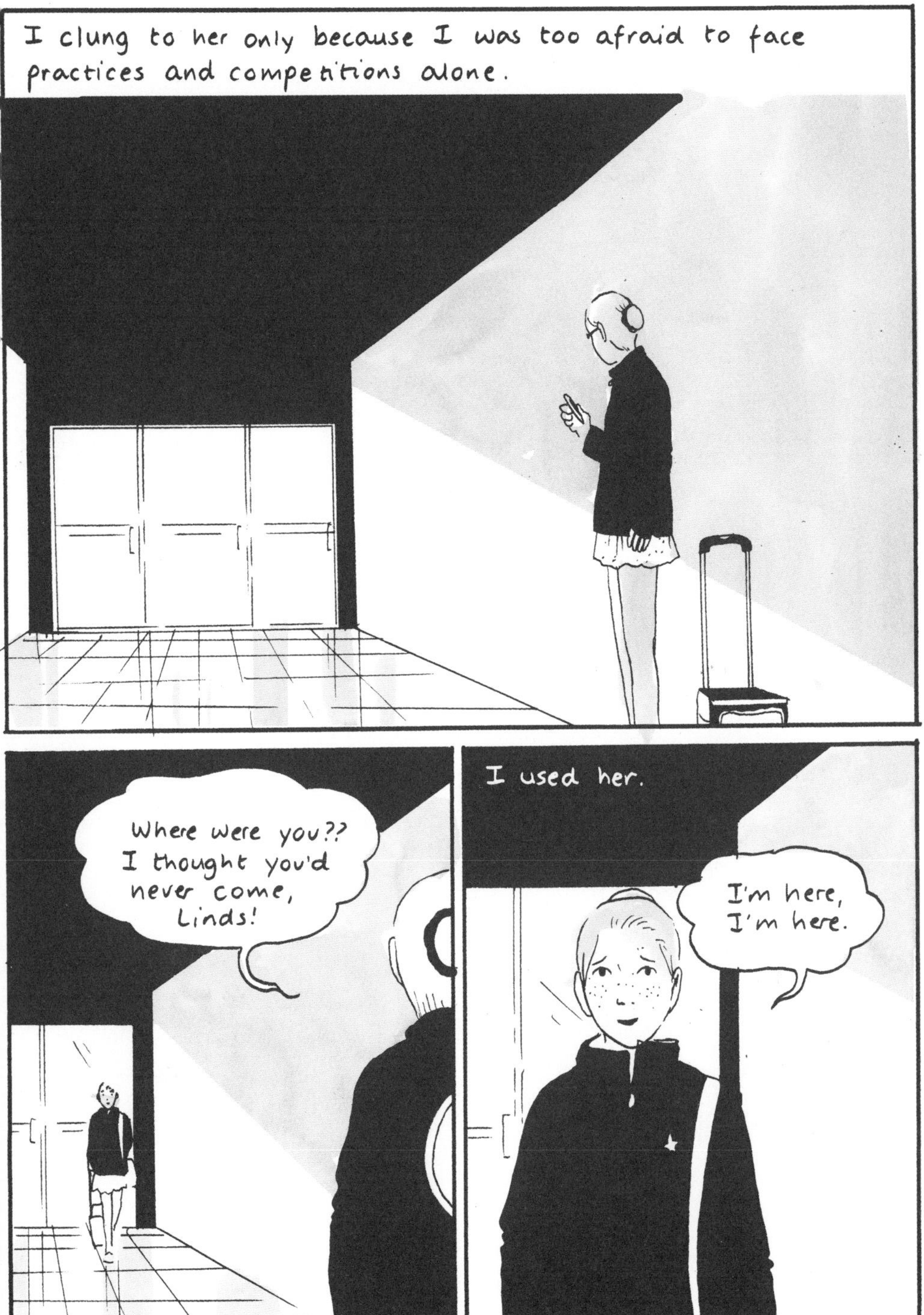
I clung to her only because I was too afraid to face practices and competitions alone.
Where were you?? I thought you'd never come, Linds!
I used her.
I'm here, I'm here.

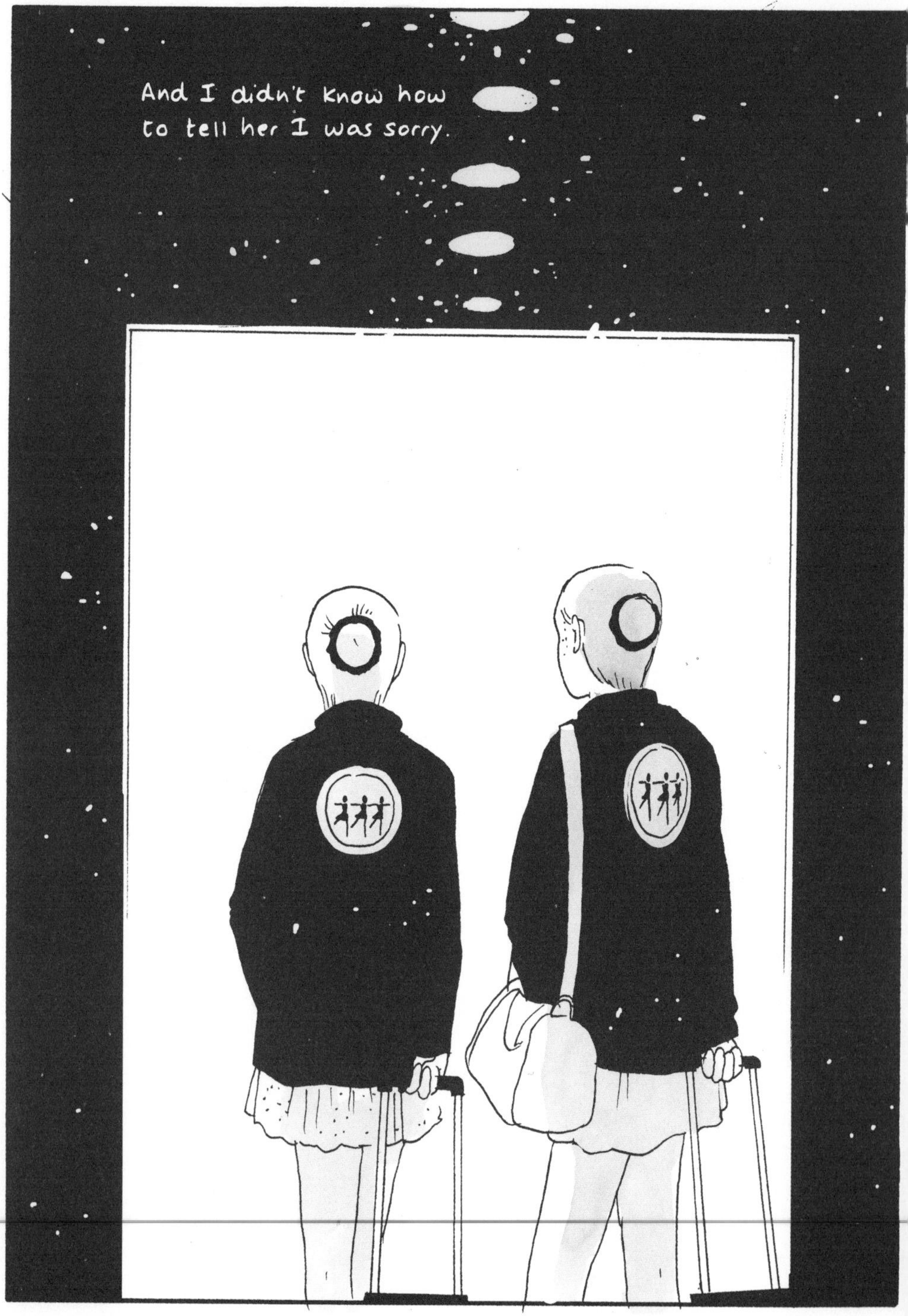
And I didn't know how
to tell her I was sorry.

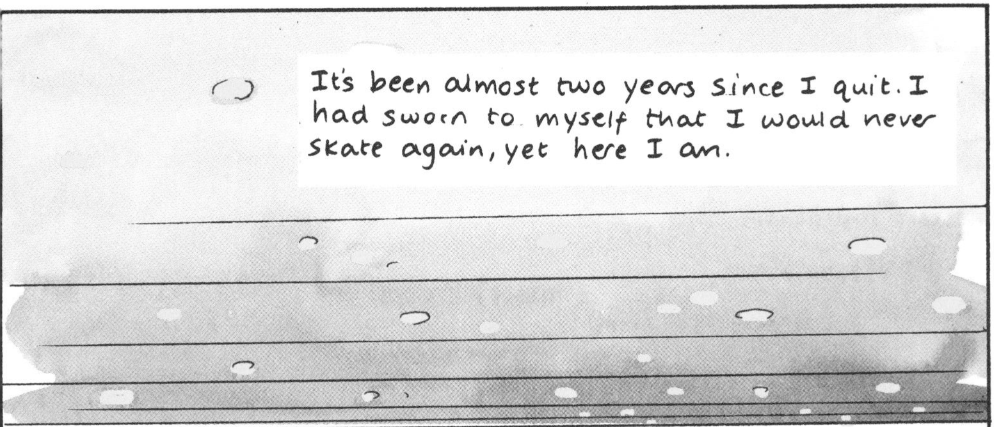
It's been almost two years since I quit. I had sworn to myself that I would never skate again, yet here I am.

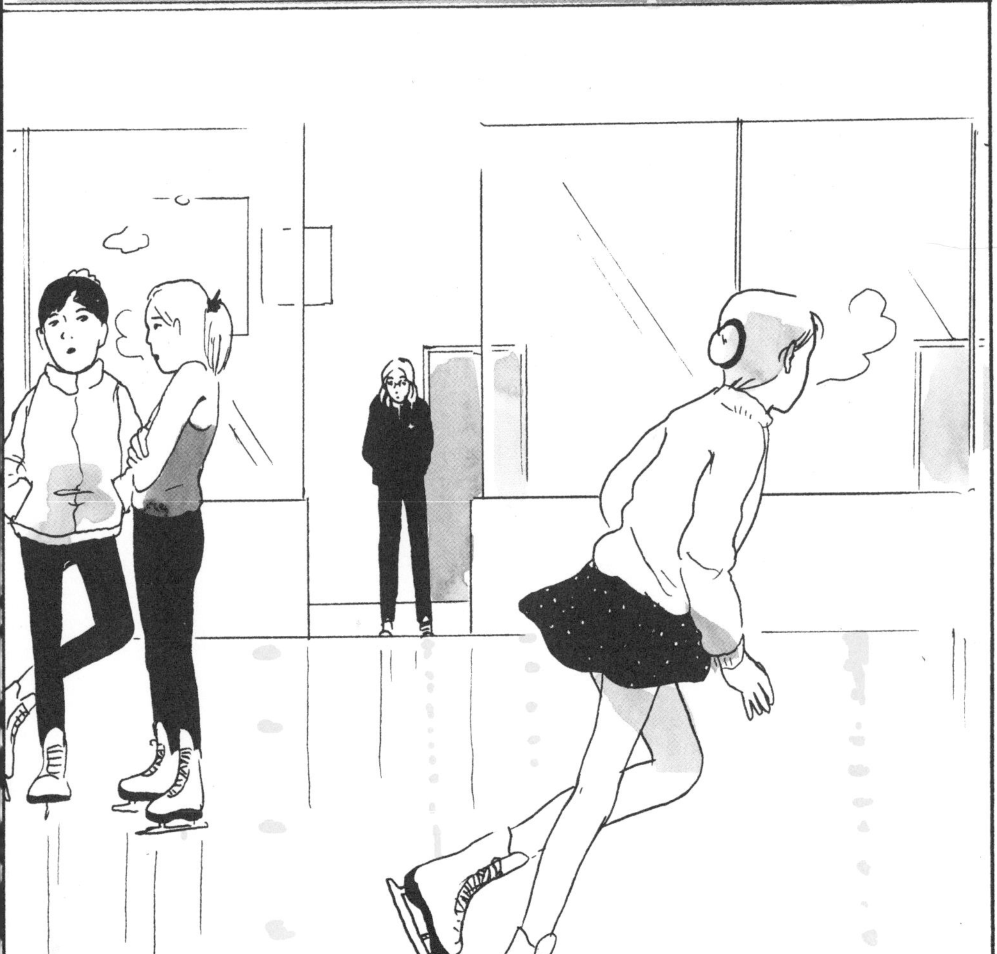

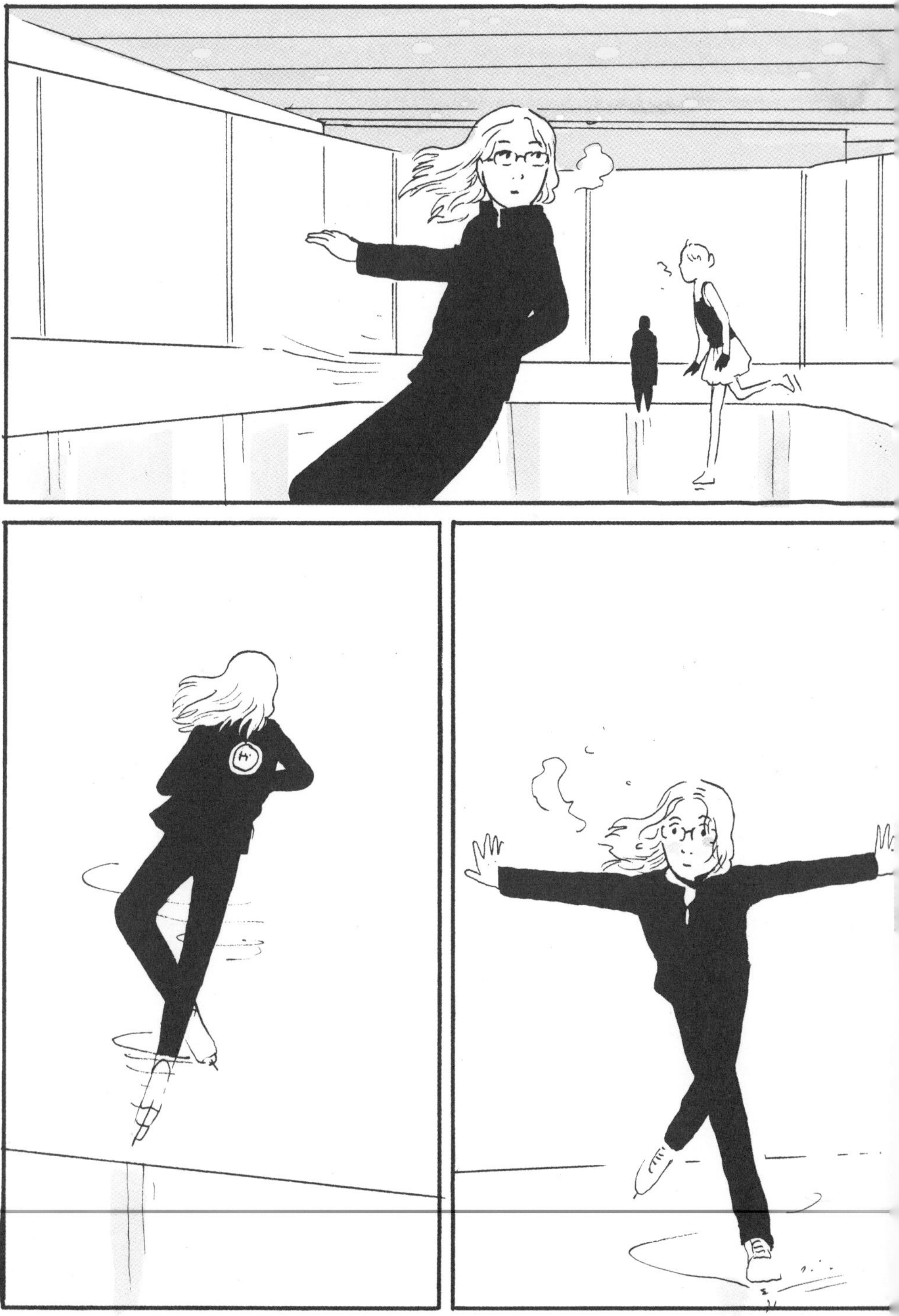

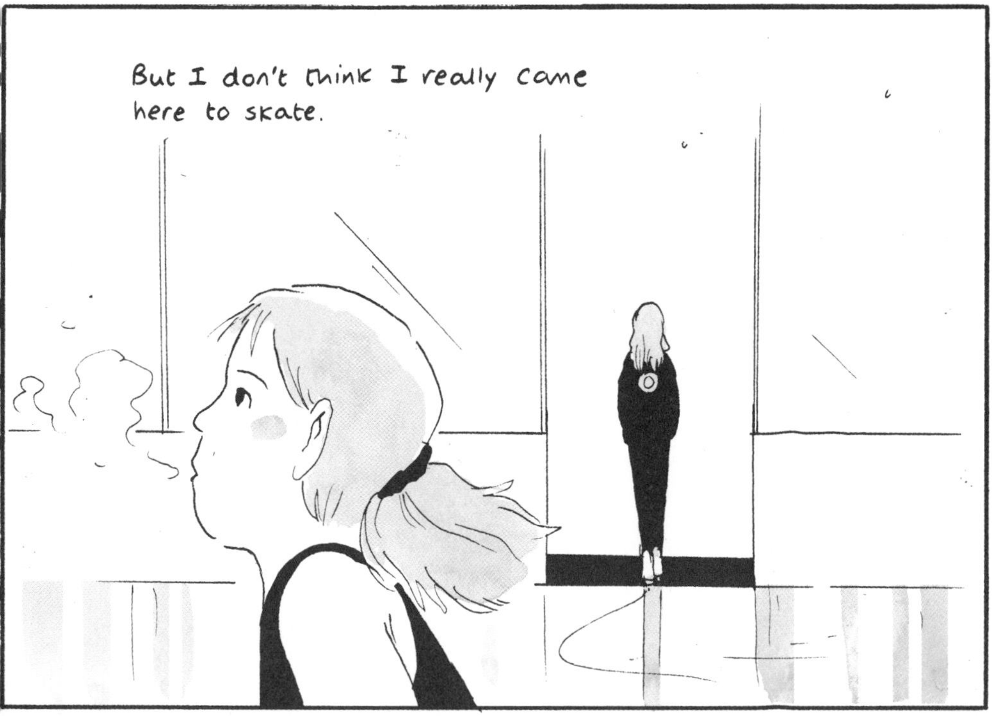
But I don't think I really came here to skate.

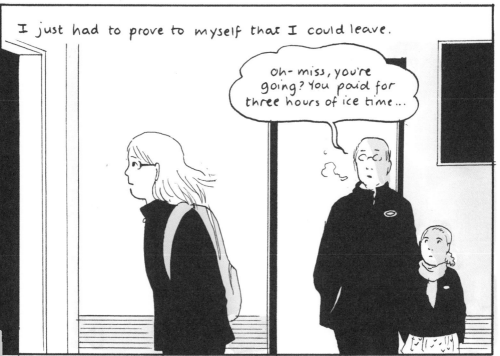

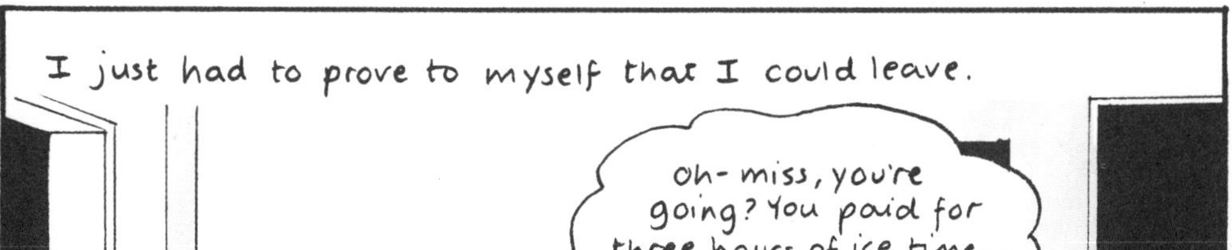
I just had to prove to myself that I could leave.
Oh- miss, you're going? You paid for three hours of ice time...

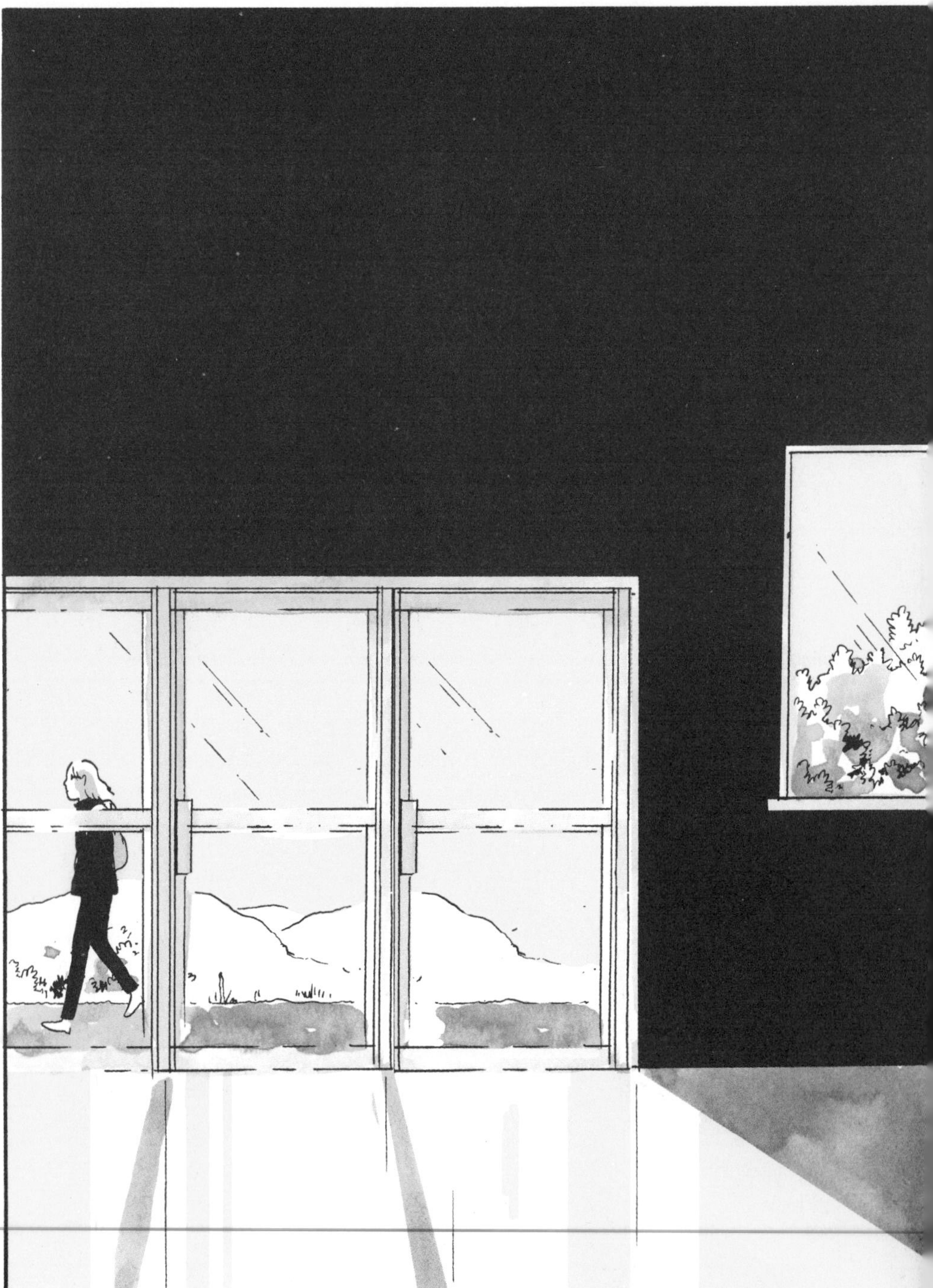

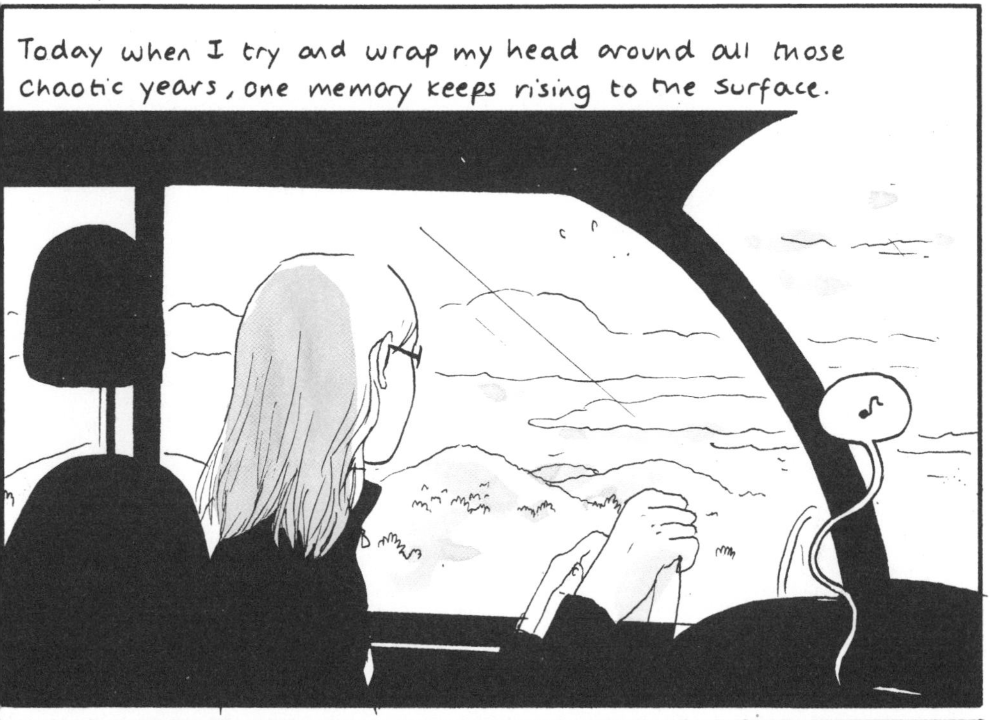
Today when I try and wrap my head around all those chaotic years, one memory keeps rising to the surface.

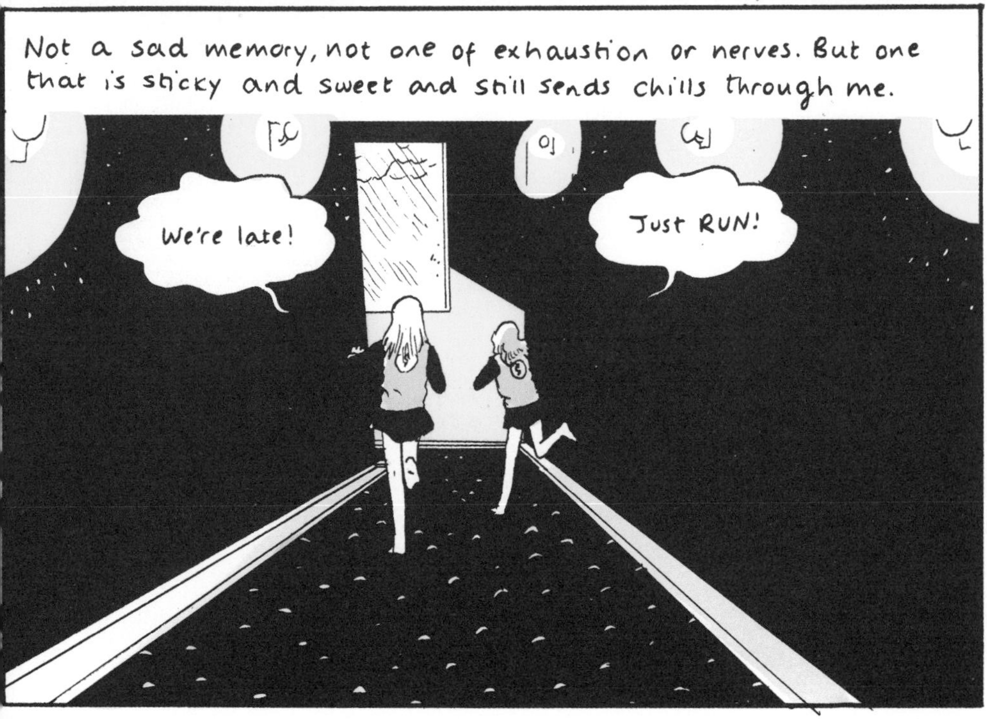
Not a sad memory, not one of exhaustion or nerves. But one that is sticky and sweet and still sends chills through me.
We're late!
Just RUN!

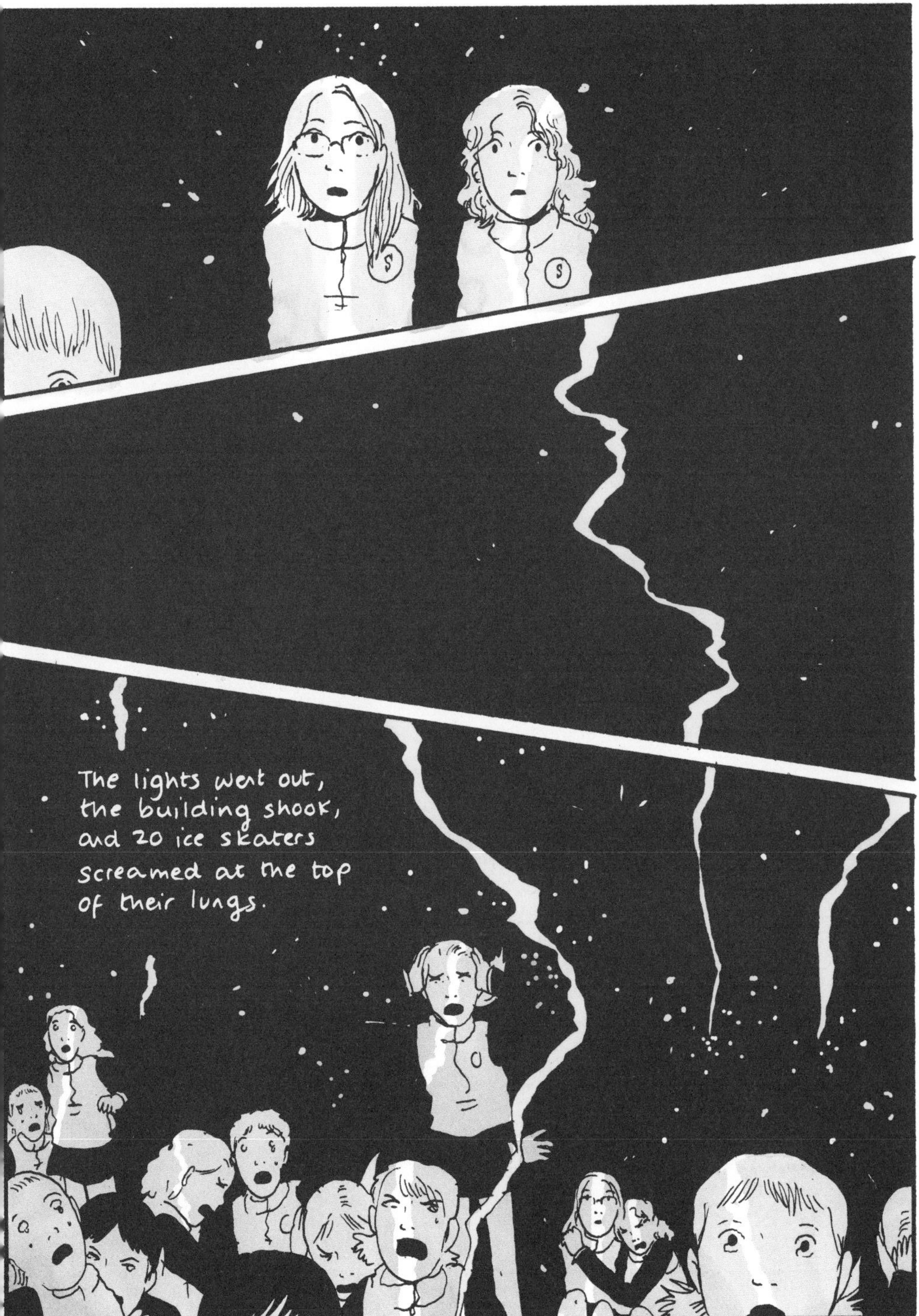
The lights went out, the building shook, and 20 ice skaters screamed at the top of their lungs.

A hurricane had landed right on top of us.

As soon as the shock wore off, excitement spread through us.

Let's go!

RUN AWAY!

THE HOTEL'S GONNA FALL OVER!

We all took off running through the dark, trembling hotel. It was the first time I remember our coach had no control over us.

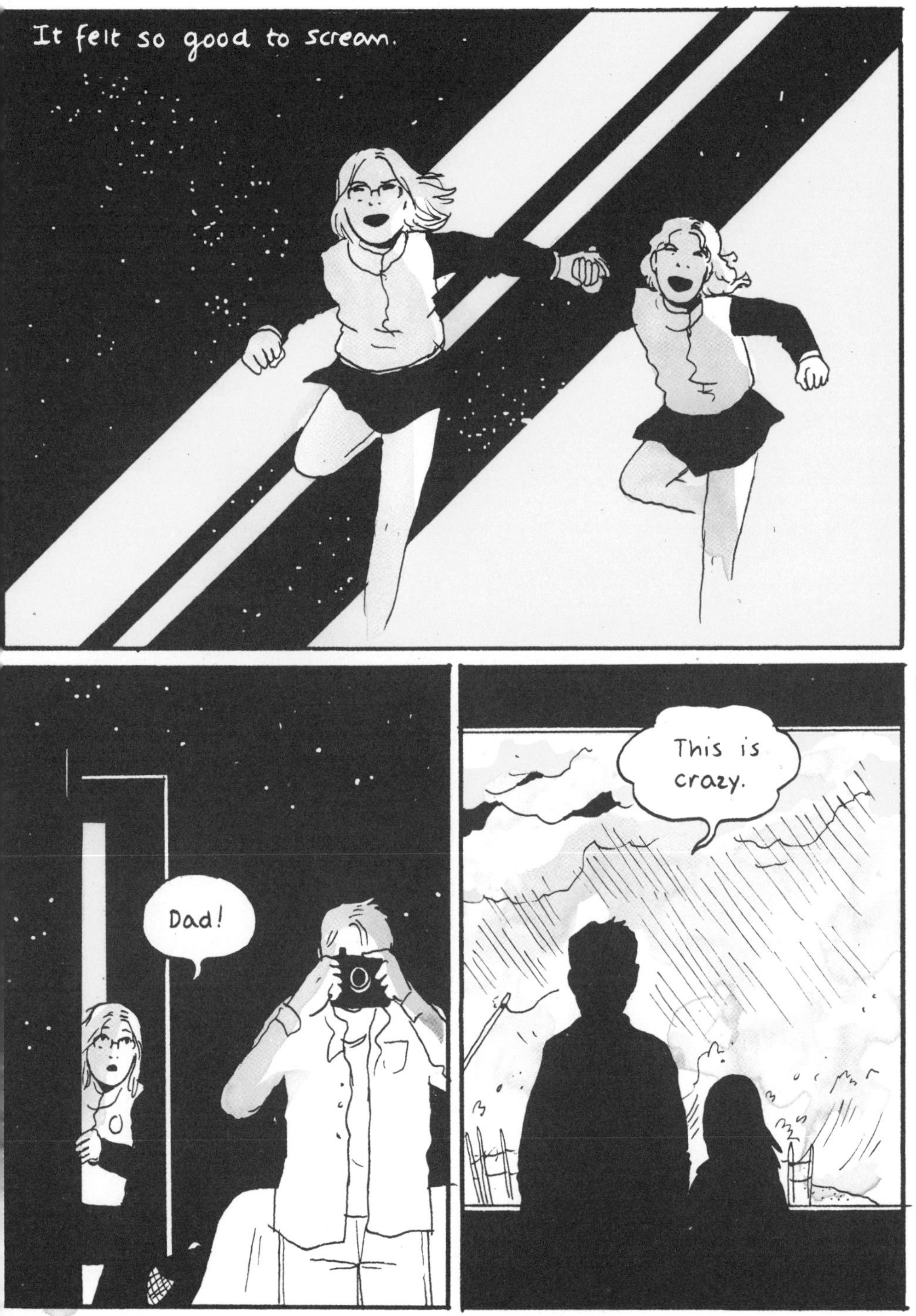
It felt so good to scream.
Dad!
This is crazy.

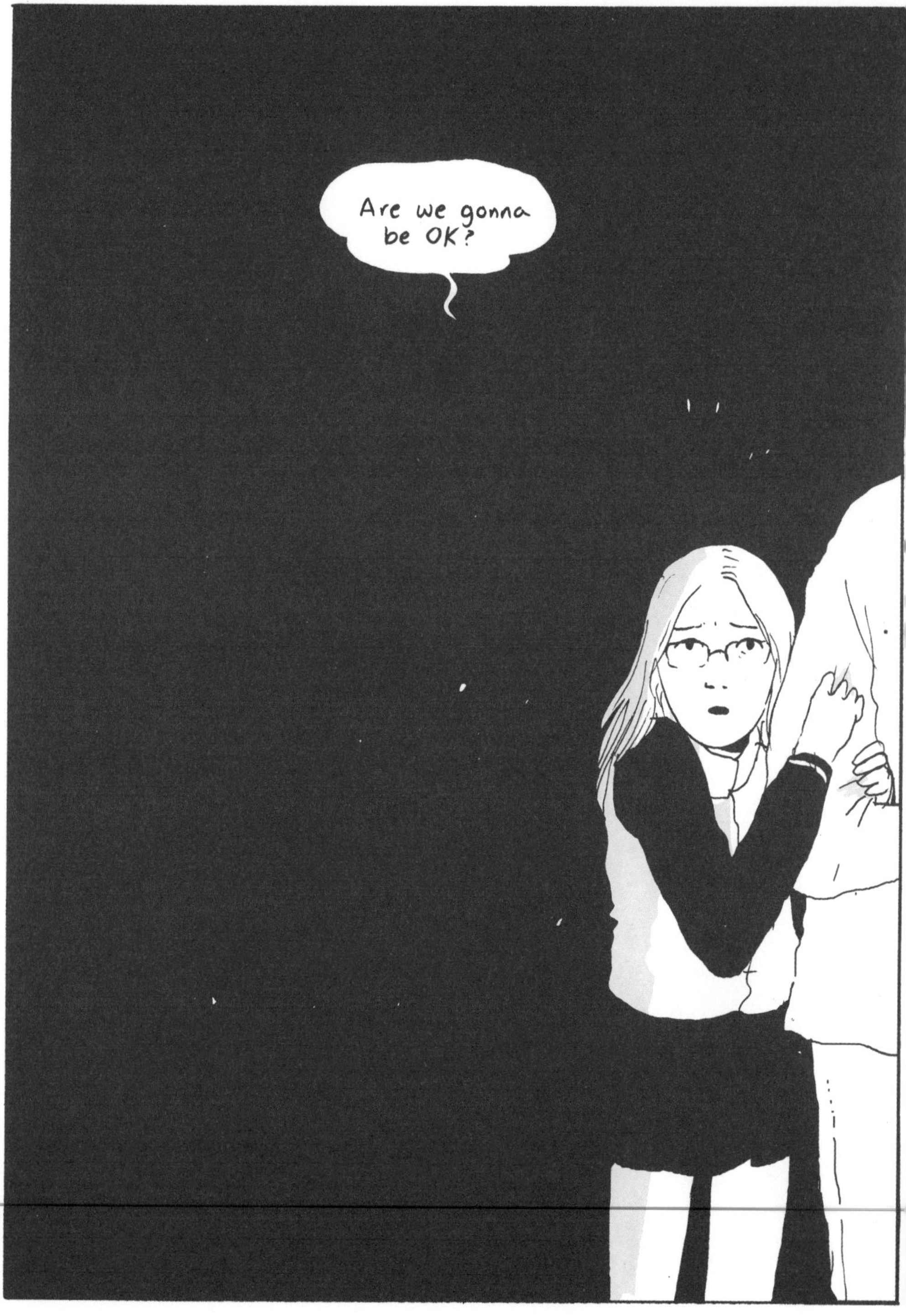
Are we gonna be OK?

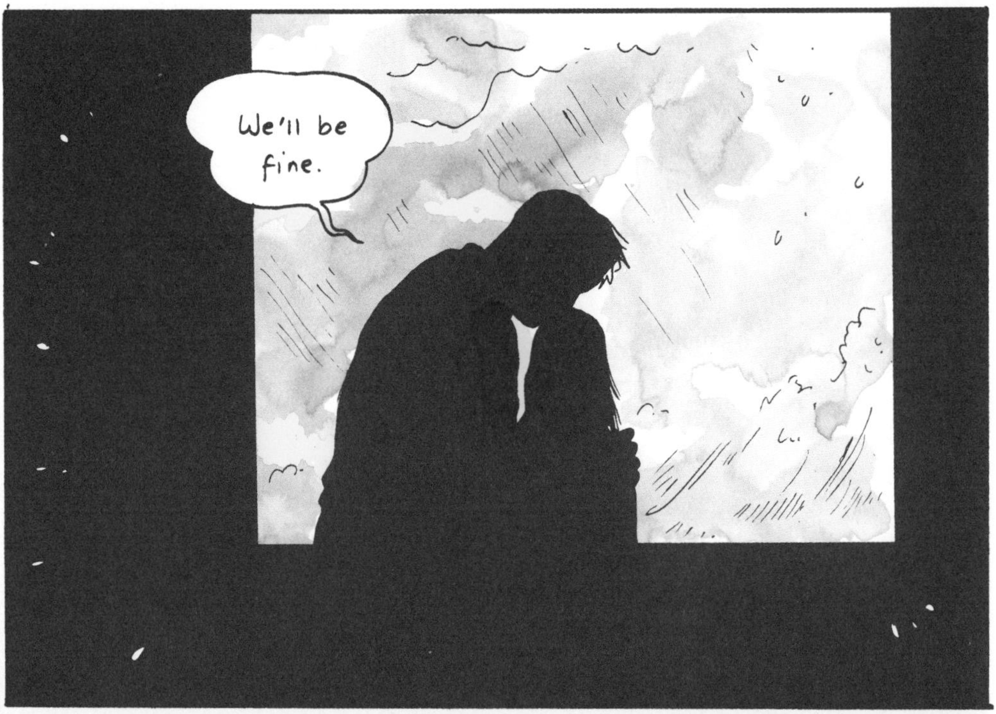
We'll be fine.

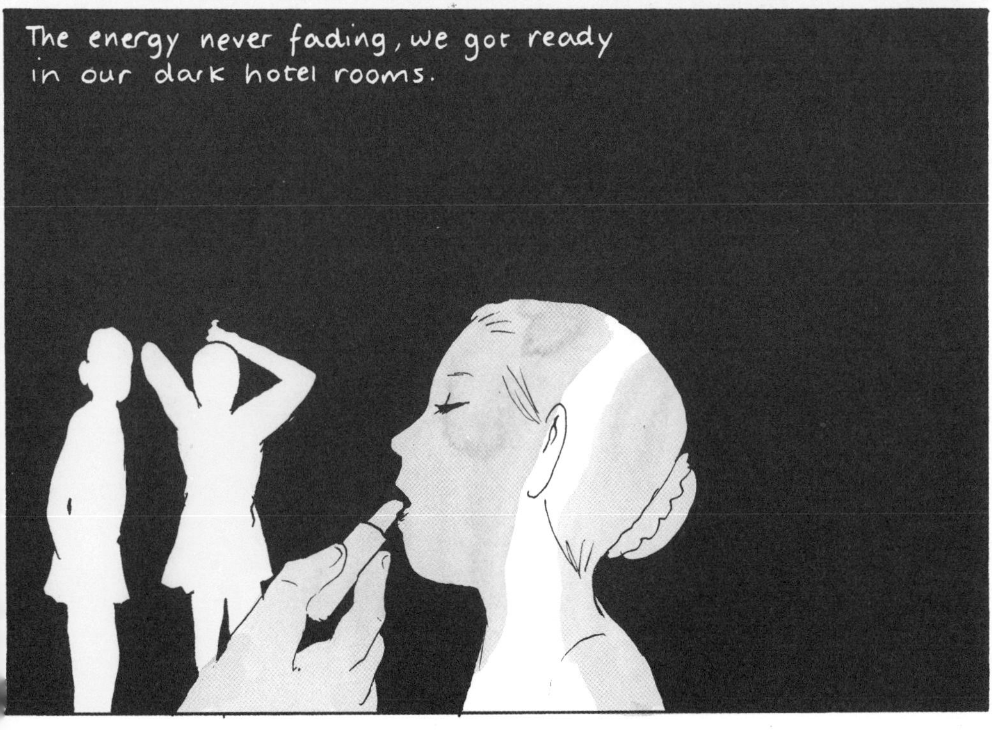
The energy never fading, we got ready in our dark hotel rooms.

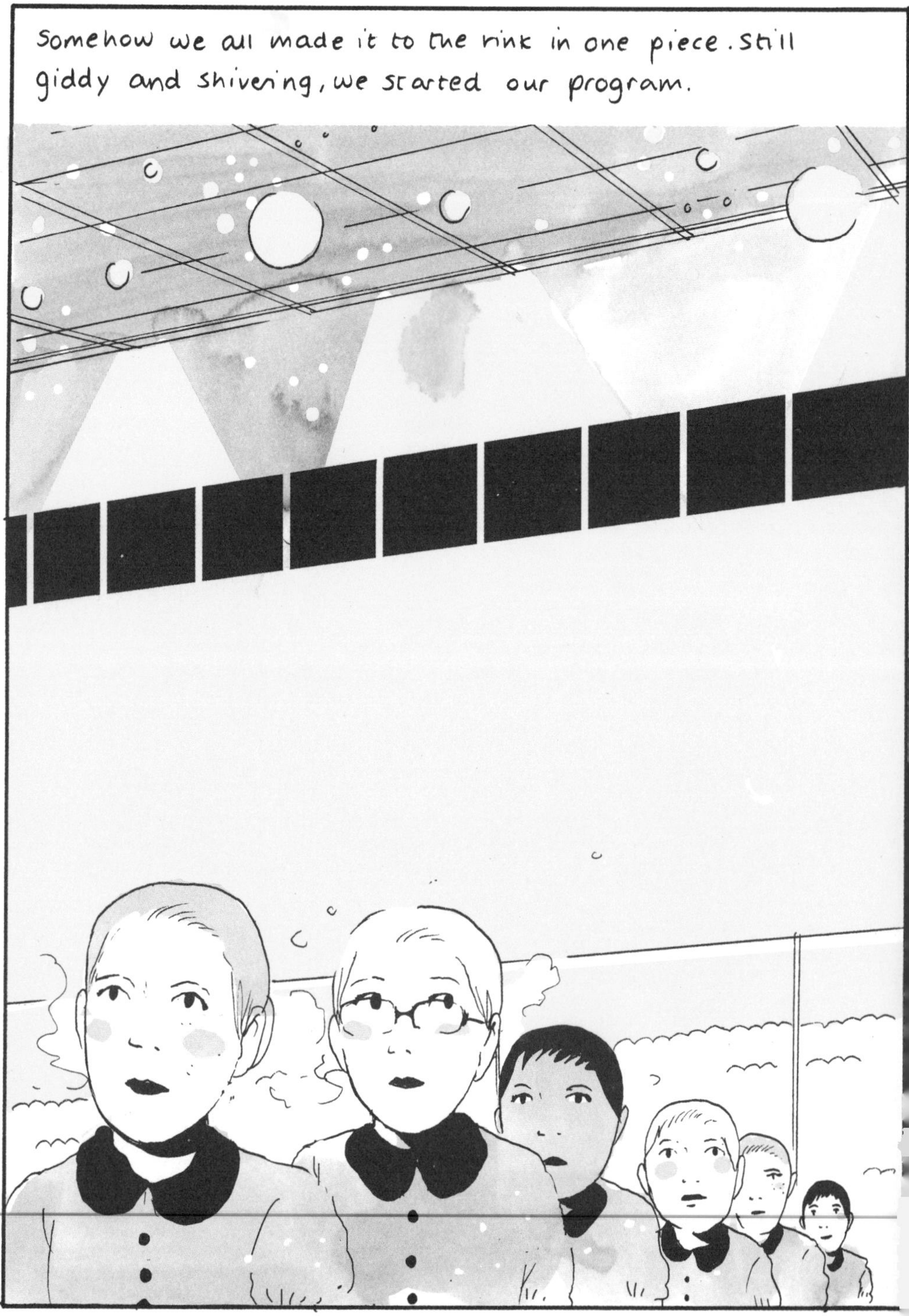
Somehow we all made it to the rink in one piece. Still giddy and shivering, we started our program.

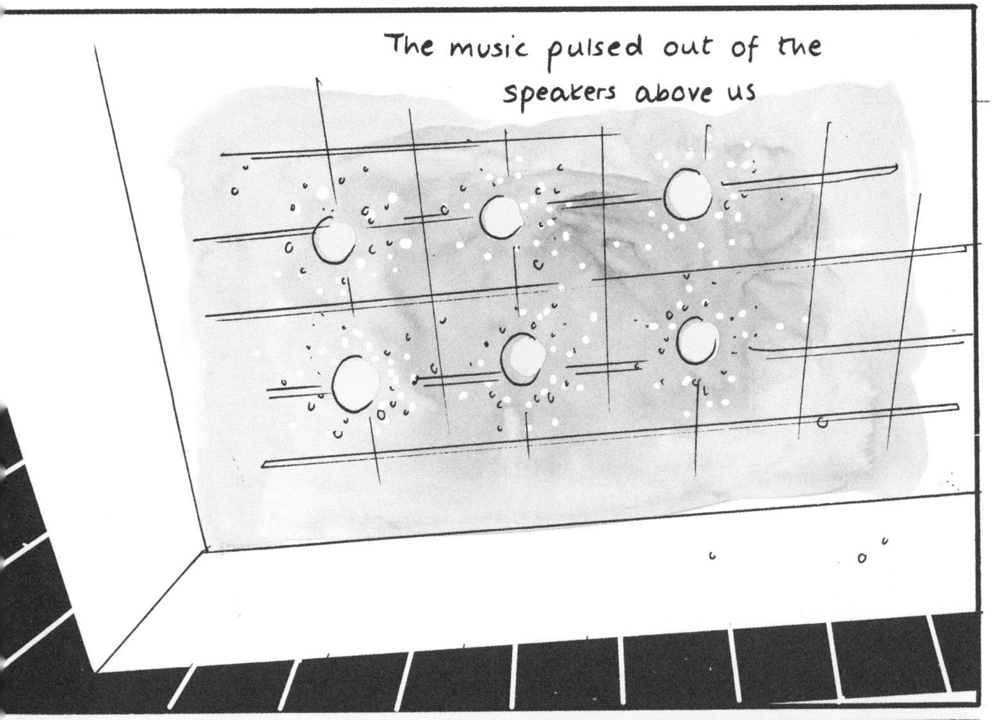
The music pulsed out of the speakers above us

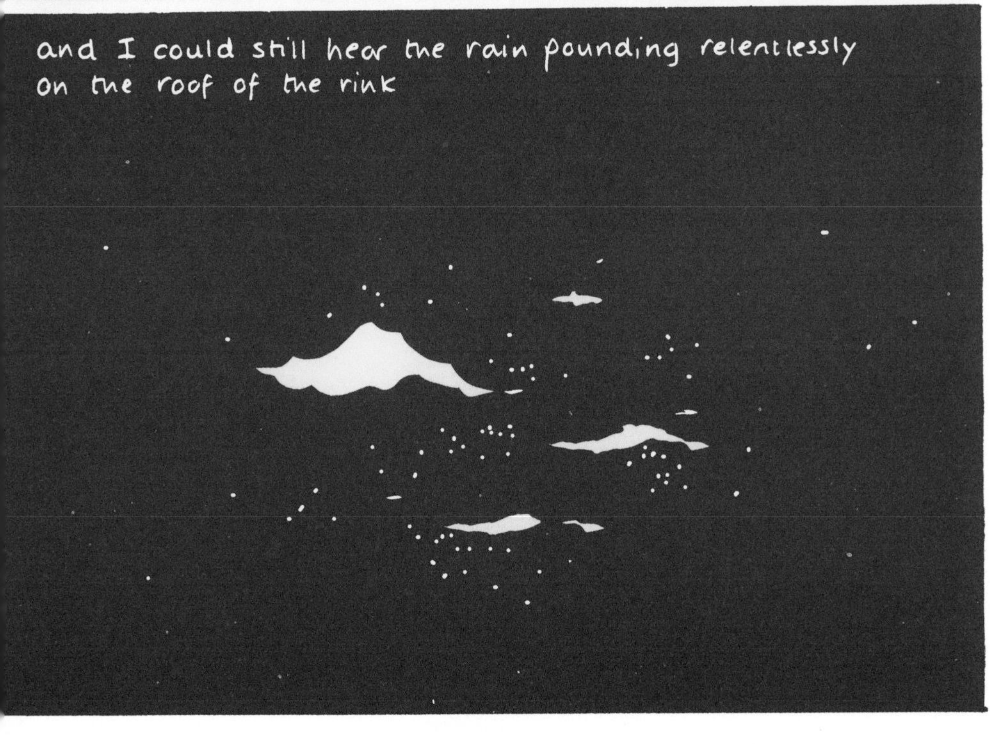
and I could still hear the rain pounding relentlessly on the roof of the rink

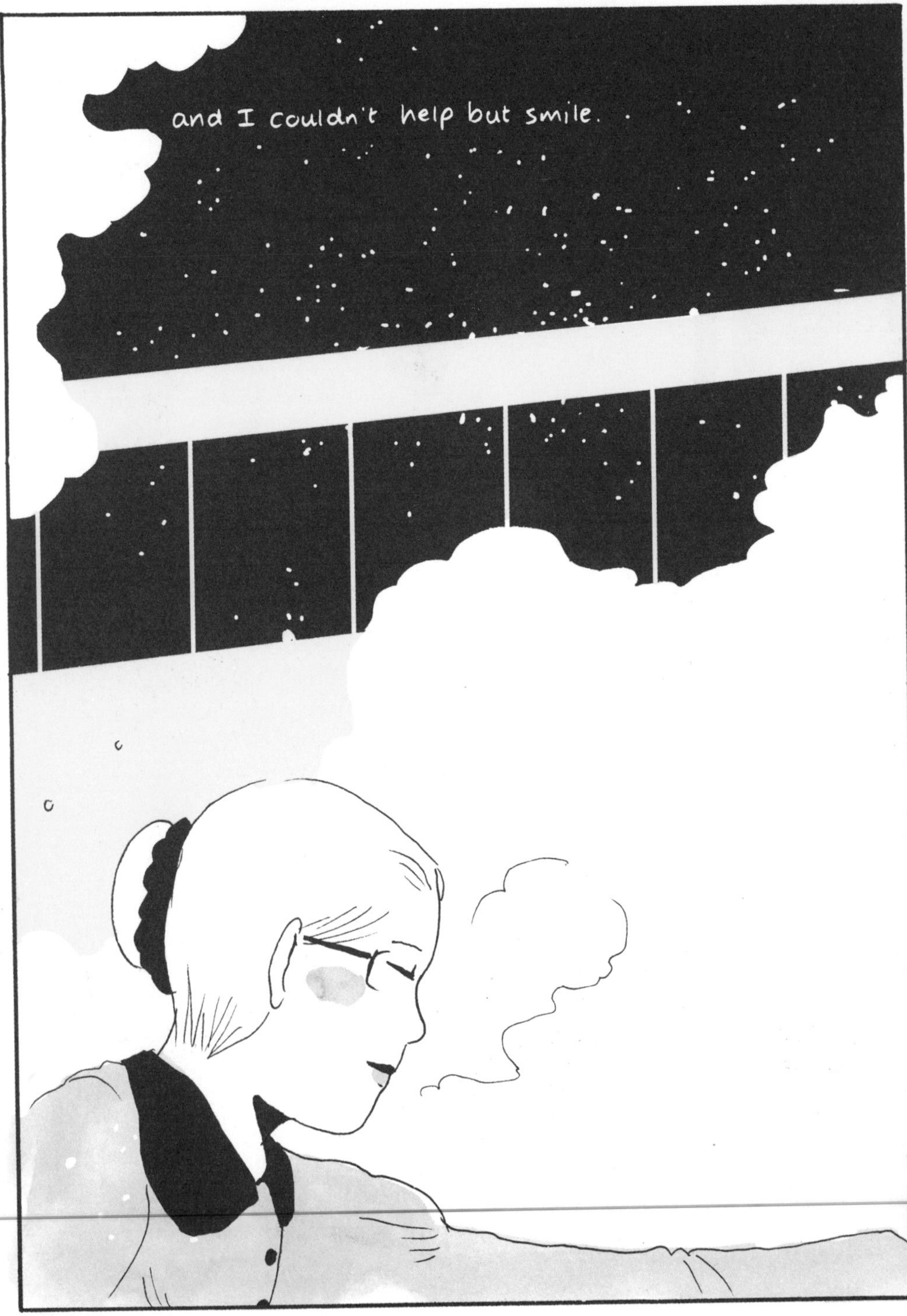
and I couldn't help but smile.